The Philosophy of Money and Finance

The Philosophy of
Money and Finance

Edited by
JOAKIM SANDBERG
and
LISA WARENSKI

OXFORD
UNIVERSITY PRESS

Great Clarendon Street, Oxford, OX2 6DP,
United Kingdom

Oxford University Press is a department of the University of Oxford.
It furthers the University's objective of excellence in research, scholarship,
and education by publishing worldwide. Oxford is a registered trade mark of
Oxford University Press in the UK and in certain other countries

© Oxford University Press 2024
Except Chapter 1 © Joakim Sandberg and Lisa Warenski

The moral rights of the authors have been asserted

Published in the United States of America by Oxford University Press
198 Madison Avenue, New York, NY 10016, United States of America

British Library Cataloguing in Publication Data
Data available

Library of Congress Control Number: 2023942266

ISBN 978–0–19–289880–7

DOI: 10.1093/oso/9780192898807.001.0001

Printed and bound by
CPI Group (UK) Ltd, Croydon, CR0 4YY

MIX
Paper | Supporting
responsible forestry
FSC
www.fsc.org   FSC® C013604

Contents

IV. POLITICAL PHILOSOPHY

List of Contributors

Boudewijn de Bruin is Professor of Financial Ethics at University of Groningen, the Netherlands, and Visiting Professor in the Financial Ethics Research Group at University of Gothenburg, Sweden. He is the author of *Ethics and the Global Financial Crisis: Why Incompetence Is Worse than Greed* (Cambridge University Press, 2015) and *The Business of Liberty: Freedom and Information in Ethics, Politics, and Law* (Oxford University Press, 2022).

François Claveau is Associate Professor of Applied Epistemology at University of Sherbrooke, Canada. He is a philosopher of the social sciences with a multidisciplinary background (philosophy, political science, economics, science and technology studies). He currently holds the Canada Research Chair in Practical Epistemology.

Christopher J. Cowton is Emeritus Professor at Huddersfield Business School, University of Huddersfield, UK, where he was previously Professor of Accounting (1996–2016) and Professor of Financial Ethics (2016–2019). He also has a part-time role as Associate Director at the Institute of Business Ethics, a registered charity that promotes high standards of ethical business behaviour. For over a decade, he was editor of the journal *Business Ethics: A European Review.*

David G. Dick was Associate Professor of Philosophy and Fellow in the Canadian Centre for Advanced Leadership in Business, Haskayne School of Business, at University of Calgary, Canada. His research interests were the philosophy of money, business ethics, and metaethics.

Peter Dietsch is Professor in the Department of Philosophy at University of Victoria, Canada. He is the author of *Catching Capital: The Ethics of Tax Competition* (Oxford University Press, 2015) and co-author of *Do Central Banks Serve the People?* (Polity Press, 2018).

Jérémie Dion is a PhD candidate in Science and Technology Studies at University of Quebec at Montreal, Canada. His research interests are social epistemology, philosophy of science, political philosophy, and computational humanities.

Richard Endörfer is Associate Researcher in Practical Philosophy and member of the Financial Ethics Research Group at University of Gothenburg, Sweden. He recently finished his PhD thesis entitled "Weapons of Mass Destruction: Financial Crises from a Philosophical Perspective" (2022).

Clément Fontan is Professor of European Economic Policies at Catholic University of Louvain, Belgium. He has published widely in philosophy, politics, and economics. His fields of specialization are political economy, European studies, central banks, and financial ethics.

Conrad Heilmann is Associate Professor of Philosophy and Co-Director of the Erasmus Institute for Philosophy and Economics at the Erasmus School of Philosophy, Erasmus University Rotterdam, the Netherlands. He recently co-edited the *Routledge Handbook of the Philosophy of Economics* (Routledge, 2021).

Lisa Herzog is Professor of Political Philosophy and Director of the Center for Philosophy, Politics and Economics at University of Groningen, the Netherlands. She was a Rhodes Scholar at University of Oxford (2007–2010). She has won several awards for her research, including the Sir Ernest Barker Prize in political theory (2011), the Deutscher Preis für Philosophie und Sozialethik (2019), and the Ammodo Science Award for fundamental research (2021).

Frank Hindriks is Professor of Ethics, Social and Political Philosophy at University of Groningen, the Netherlands. His research concerns social ontology and collective ethics. He is a member of the Royal Holland Society of Sciences and Humanities and a founding member of the International Social Ontology Society.

Aaron James is Professor of Philosophy at University of California, Irvine, USA. He is the author of *Fairness in Practice: A Social Contract for a Global Economy* (Oxford University Press, 2012) and co-author of *Money from Nothing: Why We Should Learn to Stop Worrying about Debt and Love the Federal Reserve* (Melville House Press, 2020).

Lars Lindblom is Senior Associate Professor in Applied Ethics at Linköping University, Sweden. He works with issues in the intersections between theories of justice, public policy, and science. He is executive editor of the journal *De Ethica—A Journal of Philosophical, Theological, and Applied Ethics.*

Marco Meyer is Research Group Lead in Philosophy at University of Hamburg, Germany. He holds a PhD in Philosophy from the University of Cambridge and a PhD in Economics from the University of Groningen. His research group investigates what organizations have a duty to know and what qualities help them to fulfill those duties.

Kate Padgett Walsh is Associate Professor of Philosophy at Iowa State University, USA. She is interested in points of intersection between Hegel's thought and contemporary ethical issues. Her recent work has examined the ethical dimensions of debt in light of recent social and political developments.

Asya Passinsky is Assistant Professor of Philosophy at Central European University in Vienna, Austria. She was a Rhodes Scholar at University of Oxford, where she completed her BPhil in philosophy. She is currently writing a book on the metaphysics of social objects.

Nolan Pithan recently graduated with a BA in Philosophy from Iowa State University, USA.

Joshua Preiss is Professor of Philosophy and Director of the Program in Philosophy, Politics, and Economics at Minnesota State University, Mankato, USA. He is the author of *Just Work for All: The American Dream in the 21st Century* (Routledge, 2021) as well as creator and host of the podcast series *Pandemic Ethics.*

Joakim Sandberg is Professor of Practical Philosophy and Director of the Financial Ethics Research Group at University of Gothenburg, Sweden. He is also Professor of Economics and Finance from a Humanist Perspective at University of Groningen, the Netherlands, and Vice Director of the Sustainable Finance Lab, a collaboration between several Swedish universities and companies.

Marta Szymanowska is Associate Professor of Finance in the Department of Finance at Rotterdam School of Management, Erasmus University Rotterdam, the Netherlands. She has published in leading academic journals such as *Journal of Finance* and *Journal of Financial Economics*.

Melissa Vergara-Fernández is Postdoctoral Researcher in Philosophy at the Erasmus Institute for Philosophy and Economics, Erasmus School of Philosophy, Erasmus University Rotterdam, the Netherlands. She works on the philosophy of science of financial economics, with a current focus on economic modeling and model failure.

Adrian Walsh is Professor of Philosophy and Political Theory at University of New England, Australia, and Visiting Professor in the Financial Ethics Research Group at University of Gothenburg, Sweden. He is the co-author of *The Morality of Money: An Exploration in Analytic Philosophy* (Palgrave Macmillan, 2008) and co-editor of *The Ethical Underpinnings of Climate Economics* (Routledge, 2016).

Lisa Warenski is Affiliated Associate Professor of Philosophy at the City University of New York Graduate Center, USA, and Research Associate at University of Connecticut, USA. She is a former corporate credit analyst and loan officer with over eight years' experience working in major money center banks in New York City.

Introduction

Joakim Sandberg and Lisa Warenski

Wouldn't it be strange if there were something that we used almost every day and which was so important to us that it determined our fate both as individuals and as societies, yet we seldom stopped to think about what it is, how it works, and how it ought to work? We believe that there is such a thing: money. Most people in contemporary society use money nearly every day, in the form of either cash or electronic transactions. Our fate as individuals is often connected to how much money we make, and whether we manage to save some of it in the bank or invest it in financial assets. And it is ultimately the flow of money in society that determines our common future. Yet, we rarely stop to consider the curious nature of this thing called money—if it is even a "thing" at all. How can those small pieces of paper in your wallet be such a big deal? How can something so abstract have such tangible consequences in society? And what is a plausible ethical stance to have toward money?

If money is strange, then the broader world of finance is even stranger. "Finance" is an umbrella term that encompasses various aspects of the management of money and the buying and selling of money-like assets. Typical such assets include stocks, bonds, credit contracts, insurance contracts, and derivatives (futures, options, swaps, etc.). "Finance" can also refer to the institutional infrastructure that we use to manage these assets, which includes organizations such as banks, investment funds, and central banks. How can these very abstract "assets" have such importance? How can so much power over our destiny be vested in the numbers that roll across bankers' computer screens? And what role should we give to financial assets and financial institutions in our society?

The philosophy of money and finance seeks to answer these types of questions, and takes a look "under the hood" of money and finance. Utilizing the tools of analytic philosophy, it seeks to elucidate and critically assess the nature of the financial realm and the norms that guide it. We might say that one of the goals of the discipline is to make the invisible, unapparent, or simply unnoticed structures of money and finance more visible to us. This is important so that we can better understand, interpret, and evaluate them. Another goal may be to propose important changes to those structures in the light of central ethical or political aims.

Joakim Sandberg and Lisa Warenski, *Introduction* In: *The Philosophy of Money and Finance*. Edited by: Joakim Sandberg and Lisa Warenski, Oxford University Press. © Oxford University Press 2024.
DOI: 10.1093/oso/9780192898807.003.0001

Philosophizing about money and finance is not entirely new, of course. Already in antiquity, Plato and Aristotle theorized about the true nature and purpose of money. In the Middle Ages, Augustine and Thomas Aquinas continued this tradition and, among other things, sought to reconcile the norms of the market with the demands of virtue. In the Early Modern period, philosophers such as Adam Smith and John Stuart Mill developed a more individualistic and utilitarian perspective on money and markets, which ultimately gave rise to the separate discipline of economics. Economics has evolved into a more empirically oriented study of productive activities and financial flows that is coupled with a more mathematical style of theorizing and making predictions. While economics, of course, has a lot to teach us about the practical side of money and finance, we would argue that it cannot answer some of the more fundamental and normative questions about them.

Fortunately, over the last half century or so, there has been a renewed and growing interest in philosophical treatments of money and finance. We suggest that there are several possible explanations for this. One is the transformation of Western society into what is sometimes called financial capitalism—that is, a form of market economy in which finance and investment plays an ever-increasing role. Another explanation is the growing awareness in society of the many substantial challenges that our economic system now faces—including financial, public health, and social crises, as well as the global climate crisis. Relatedly, there has perhaps been a growing awareness in academia of the important limitations of economics when it comes to addressing some of our more foundational and normative questions about financial assets and their distribution. These challenges seem to call for scholarship that goes beyond the readily observable and quantifiable.

It seems fair to say that academic writing on the philosophy of money and finance really has taken off during the last two decades. A significant event during this time was the Global Financial Crisis of 2008. According to many, the crisis exposed significant defects in the global financial system that need to be addressed in various ways. It also demonstrated how all-important that system has become to the broader economy and society. As is often the case, times of crisis spurred new ideas and an increased interest in alternative thinking about an important subject.

About This Volume

The purpose of this edited volume is to provide a comprehensive introduction to the emerging field of the philosophy of money and finance. We have gathered together some of the leading scholars in the field, as well as some emerging scholars, to contribute their thoughts on what we perceive to be some of the most significant topics. Each of the chapters is a new text, written exclusively for this volume. We have made a special effort to demonstrate the full breadth of the field—from very foundational questions to more applied ones, and from very theoretical questions to more normative ones.

The volume is divided into four main parts, corresponding to four major subdisciplines in analytic philosophy: Metaphysics, Epistemology (including Philosophy of Science), Ethics, and Political Philosophy. Each part contains four chapters on different but interrelated topics. The particular topics in the chapters reflect the interests of their authors, and there are no doubt additional topics that could be understood to be central and could have been included. But one has to start somewhere, and we hope that some of these other topics can be taken up in future work.

We hope that the reader will find this volume useful in several ways. First, we have aimed to keep the texts as accessible and non-technical as possible so that they can be read by a broad range of people, including scholars from adjacent disciplines, students, and the intellectually curious public. We thereby hope that it can serve as an introduction to this fascinating field of inquiry. Second, we have aimed to give a comprehensive overview of the types of questions and perspectives that are common in the burgeoning literature in the field. We thereby hope that the volume can be used as a roadmap that points the reader further toward more specific topics or discussions that are of particular interest. Finally, the chapters are not merely descriptive but contain original and sometimes controversial contributions to ongoing academic debates. We thereby invite the reader to engage in philosophical reflection and to join us in the continued philosophical discussion and debate about money and finance.

Part I: Metaphysics

Metaphysics is the philosophical study of the nature of reality, both the natural reality that we live in and the social reality that we help to create. As noted, money and finance are strange "things" indeed in the sense that there must be more to them than just the pieces of paper in our wallets and the numbers on certain computer screens. They are in some sense abstract entities that exist on the basis of social conventions or practices. But exactly how does that work? What is it that makes those pieces of paper into money, and what makes the numbers on the bankers' computer screens have financial value?

If the nature of money and finance was already strange in ancient times, it has become all the more so over roughly the last half century with the advent of electronic bank accounts, credit cards, and Bitcoin. These technological inventions have created a situation in which our finances can feel even more abstract and out of reach. Happily, however, it seems that these developments have rejuvenated the philosophical discussion about the nature of money and finance. Some argue that we need new theories to account for these new forms of money, while others argue that the developments help us to see the true nature of money that has been the same all along.

Part I of this volume contains four chapters: three that concern the nature of money and one that concerns truth in financial accounting, a domain that is central to finance. In Chapter 1, Frank Hindriks analyzes the nature of money on the basis of contemporary debates in the field of social ontology. More specifically, he investigates whether one can give a unified metaphysical account of both traditional money, for example paper notes, and modern money (electronic bank accounts). Whereas paper money is naturally regarded as a material or concrete object, the same does not seem to hold for electronic money. Even if we were to destroy the computers that store the electronic information about our money, we would not say that it is lost. Should we therefore say that money is always an abstract object (e.g. a credit relation), or is it perhaps better conceived of as a property of an agent (e.g. the property of having purchasing power)? Hindriks ultimately argues that no unified account can be given, and therefore we should say that money is sometimes a material object and sometimes the property of an agent.

In Chapter 2, Asya Passinsky analyzes the nature of cryptocurrencies like Bitcoin. Drawing on classical philosophical treatments of the nature of money, the main alternatives again seem to view it as either something concrete, a commodity, or something abstract, a credit relation. Looking closer at those two strands of the literature, they seem to present rather different stories about not only money's nature but also its origin and function. Passinsky proceeds to discuss the nature, origin, and function of cryptocurrencies in order to compare them with the theoretical alternatives. She argues that both of the classical accounts can capture some of the story of cryptocurrencies, but that neither of them seems perfect for the job; we therefore need to explore a hybrid account. Inspired by Aristotle, Passinsky calls her own account a "hylomorphic" one that sees crypto-currencies as both concrete and abstract at the same time.

In Chapter 3, David G. Dick gives a new twist to the discussion by asking how many people it would take to create a new currency. We typically take the longevity and widespread use of the dollar as a sign that it is more "real money" than, for example, Bitcoin and other cryptocurrencies. However, Dick argues that we must be careful to separate the metaphysical question, about what *is* money, from the normative question, about what is *better* money. Upon review of the metaphysical theories, it seems that what makes something into money is either its functionality or its social acceptance. Dick then goes on to argue that irrespective of what metaphysical position one adopts, it would take no more than two people to create a new currency because having two people is sufficient for something to be able to function as a medium of exchange, a unit of account, and a store of value.

In Chapter 4, Christopher J. Cowton takes up the metaphysical question of the nature of truth in the domain of financial accounting. Financial accounting is central to business and finance in that it is the system by which transactions are recorded, summarized, and presented. Cowton demonstrates several difficult decisions that accountants face when it comes to delineating, timing, and valuing various financial transactions. The question is then whether one of these options will give the *true* account of the transactions, and in what sense of "true." He considers three prominent philosophical accounts of truth: correspondence (with some external reality), coherence (with established propositions), and usefulness (for some broader human purposes). Cowton ultimately argues that all three of these notions of truth have some resonance with what accountants are trying to do, even if it seems difficult to give an exact theory of truth for financial accounts. Thus, it is not the case that "anything goes" in this realm.

Part II: Epistemology

Epistemology is the philosophical study of cognitive successes, such as knowledge, understanding, and justified belief, and the processes and methods that realize them. Correlatively, epistemology studies cognitive failures. Given the elusive and partially abstract nature of money and finance, it is not difficult to see how there are many questions about how we can and should go about forming judgments within and about the financial realm. Financial agents, both individually and collectively, engage in judgments about various financial assets and how to manage them. In so doing, they must, among other things, make judgments about financial risk. The Global Financial Crisis demonstrated with excruciating clarity what can happen when bankers fail to understand what risks they are taking and, consequently, what risks they are imposing on society.

Connected to epistemology is the discipline of philosophy of science, which encompasses the philosophical study of scientific methods of understanding— including their foundations, reliability, and implications. Economics, including its subdiscipline financial economics, is the science that studies the financial realm. Financial economics is a fairly young science, but it has quickly become well respected (as demonstrated, e.g., by several Nobel Memorial Prizes), and it is held in high regard by the financial industry. Truth be told, however, even most financial economists came rather unprepared for the Global Financial Crisis and the severe defects that it exposed in the global financial system. There is therefore an increasing and important debate among both philosophers and economists about the reliability of some of the central methods and assumptions of financial economics.

Part II contains four chapters: two address epistemic issues pertaining to financial economics, and two consider applications of epistemology in financial practice. In Chapter 5, Lisa Herzog considers the conditions under which financial markets can be expected to give us undistorted and useful information about the real economy. According to mainstream financial economics, asset price developments tell us something about economic fundamentals because they contain information about current and future profits, where these profits are adjusted by estimations about risk. But can we really trust the financial markets to accurately represent economic fundamentals? Herzog argues that what we want here is "epistemic efficiency," which is to say that we want the markets to represent information that is relevant to our central needs without systematic distortions. However, financial markets cannot be assumed to be epistemically efficient since they are rife with distortions. She argues that epistemic efficiency should therefore be understood as a guiding principle for future regulation of financial markets as opposed to an automatic feature of them. Furthermore, in order for the information that these markets represent to be socially worthwhile, reforms in other parts of the economic system would be needed.

Chapter 6, authored by Conrad Heilmann, Marta Szymanowska, and Melissa Vergara-Fernández, provides a roadmap for how philosophers of science could engage more with the science of financial economics. The chapter begins by giving an abridged account of the emergence of financial economics, identifying its historical origins and tracing its evolution into a distinct branch of economics. The authors then go on to argue that financial economics is best characterized by its *use of models* and its *performative* nature. This argument is made through consideration of the Capital Asset Pricing Model (CAPM), a model that played and continues to play a central role in analyzing asset prices. The centrality of the CAPM to asset prices poses philosophical questions about its role in explanation, the content of claims made in asset-pricing research, and the evaluation of its theoretical implications and the evidence for these implications. Finally, the authors briefly consider the question of non-epistemic values insofar as they may be reflected in or adopted by financial economics.

In Chapter 7, Lisa Warenski turns our attention to epistemic practices in financial institutions. She considers a rather spectacular case of epistemic failings in a major money center bank: JPMorgan Chase & Co.'s so-called London Whale trading losses in 2012, in which the bank lost over US$6.2 billion. The London Whale losses were so large that they roiled the world's credit markets, and they raised concerns that derivative contracts once again posed a systemic risk to the US banking system. Warenski relays the story of the losses and, as the drama unfolds, it becomes clear that a number of the missteps in the events leading to the losses were epistemic in character. She considers whether some of these missteps were instances of ways in which we, as reasoners, are generally prone to error. She suggests that the deliberate adoption of what she calls "good epistemic practices" could help guard against errors of reasoning, and she identifies some specific such practices that might have helped to prevent some of errors that were implicated in the London Whale losses.

In Chapter 8, Boudewijn de Bruin investigates how insights from epistemology and social science could be utilized to bolster the European Union's recent Sustainable Finance Action Plan, which aims to direct more private finance to environmentally friendly and socially responsible economic activities. De Bruin argues that the Action Plan is an example of reflexive law, an approach to law that conceives of it as offering guidance to actors by means of processes and procedures. He identifies some challenges for reflexive law, and then goes on to argue for an emendation that he calls "epistemic law." Epistemic law encourages individuals and organizations to engage in epistemic activities such as acquiring, processing, and communicating information, and it sets standards for the acceptability of investigative methods and what should count as evidence. De Bruin illustrates how an epistemic approach to law could address and overcome some of the challenges to the successful implementation of the Action Plan.

Part III: Ethics

Ethics is the philosophical study of how the world *ought* to be, and especially how we ought to treat each other—that is, the appropriateness of character traits, actions, and norms that affect other people. Given that money and finance have such a strong social dimension, it should be obvious that they raise an array of important moral and ethical questions. Interestingly, however, many people seem to think that money and ethics are somehow at opposite poles and, therefore, that the term "financial ethics" is a bit of an oxymoron. In many of the early philosophical and religious treatments of money and finance, the whole field was condemned as immoral. Think, for example, of the biblical sayings that "the love of money is the root of all evil" (1 Timothy 6:10) and that "it is easier for a camel to go through the eye of a needle than for a rich man to enter the kingdom of God" (Matthew 19:24). In more recent times, it seems safe to say that we accept most practices involving money and finance as either socially necessary or even beneficial. However, this does not mean that we have an easy time understanding the relationship between our financial reality and our moral ideals.

The field of financial ethics has grown rather rapidly in recent years. Philosophers have come to see that mainstream ethical theories, such as virtue ethics, utilitarianism, and contractualism, have a lot to say about the appropriateness of various monetary and financial practices. For instance, the theories can be used to partially explain what went wrong in the Global Financial Crisis and to chart a path for more responsible banking practices in the future. The theories can also give input into what role the financial industry ought to play in addressing some of contemporary society's most pressing challenges such as rising inequalities and climate change.

The four chapters in Part III address different but interrelated questions in financial ethics. In Chapter 9, Adrian Walsh considers the historical condemnations of "the love of money," i.e. the profit motive as a *motive*. It seems that many classical philosophers understood both money and ethics in very stark ways in this debate: equating the profit motive with pure egoism and virtue with pure altruism. This gave rise to the idea that the profit motive is wholly incompatible with ethics. However, Walsh develops a broader taxonomy of the various ways in which pecuniary motives can be combined with ethical goals or constraints. He thereby argues that it is perfectly possible to combine the pursuit of money with considerations of virtue, and that this is probably how most people behave. This holds true even if we accept the view that the pursuit of money has no moral content or merit on its own.

In Chapter 10, Kate Padgett Walsh and Nolan Pithan dive deeper into virtue ethics and seek to find the version of this theory that is most useful for analyzing contemporary financial practices. A classical version of virtue ethics focuses only on the motivations and character traits of individuals, emphasizing virtuous traits such as honesty, moderation, and empathy. While such a focus can be useful for moral education in finance, the authors argue that it fails to recognize the structural or collective challenges of the contemporary financial system. An alternative version of virtue theory, the "capabilities approach," instead looks at how the various practices of finance contribute to or impede human flourishing more broadly. In the end, the authors argue that the most fruitful approach probably is an integrated one which takes input from both of these versions in order to analyze the interplay between individual characters and societal structures.

In Chapter 11, Richard Endörfer discusses which ethical theory best captures the immorality of banks' contributions to financial crises. One can understand the build-up of financial crises as a situation in which banks impose severe risks on society by, for example, extending too many or too risky loans. Virtue ethics suggests that the morality of an action depends on the motivation or character of the agent in question, but Endörfer argues that the relevant banks need not have callous motivations or vicious characters. Utilitarianism suggests that the morality of an action depends on its consequences for everyone affected, but Endörfer argues that a credit expansion may well provide economic advantages for rich financiers that in this sense outweigh the economic disadvantages of the eventual crises. The theory that gives the best explanation in the context is instead contractualism, which suggests that the morality of an action depends on the strength of the complaints that various affected people may have against it—and where those that stand to lose the most also have the strongest complaints.

In Chapter 12, Aaron James analyzes the contractualist nature of money itself. Starting from the metaphysical theory that money consists in an abstract credit relation, one can start to think about what ethical norms pertain to that relation. James argues that, at the very least, an inherent norm is the following: anyone (person A) who owes a debt to someone else (person B) must be able to settle (cancel or offset) this debt by presenting some product, service, or debt of comparable value. This norm is inherent in the notion of money itself and therefore is binding across all possible organizations of the monetary system. The most interesting upshot of this norm is that the state cannot organize its national currency in just any way it pleases; instead, it is bound by an ethical obligation to provide a type of money that exists in sufficient quantities, that all citizens have access to, and that is reasonably stable in value. This upshot is a good segue to the final part of the volume.

Part IV: Political Philosophy

Political philosophy is the philosophical study of how we ought to organize society on the collective level, including various types of social and political institutions. As noted, we currently live in a society in which money and finance have become so important that they determine our fate both as individuals and as a collective. It therefore seems pertinent to critically evaluate the monetary and financial system from the standpoint of core political values such as democracy, freedom, equality, and sustainability. The "system" that here pertains to finance has several parts, including private financial organizations such as banks and investment funds, financial exchanges or markets such as stock markets and bond markets (on both national and global levels), and various layers of regulatory institutions such as central banks and financial supervisory authorities.

The dominant trend in financial regulation over the last half century or so has been one of liberalization and deregulation, as in many other policy areas. This has probably contributed to creating a truly global financial system in which money flows with lightning speed throughout the industrialized world. However, many suggest that regulatory priorities now have to change in light of the major challenges facing our society, including financial, public health, and social crises, as well as the global climate crisis. The financial system stands at the apex of these developments and can potentially be mobilized to change the world, but the debate is still on about which direction the changes should take.

Part IV contains four chapters that highlight somewhat different political focal points. In Chapter 13, Marco Meyer evaluates the financial system with reference to distributive justice, for which a central concern is the relative situation of society's worst-off citizens. More specifically, he asks whether access to credit tends to improve the situation of the worst-off and therefore makes society more equal, or whether it tends to worsen their situation and makes society less equal. It turns out that much depends on what type of credit we analyze. Secured forms of credit, for example mortgage loans, tend to be long-term and have low interest rates. But unsecured credit is short-term and expensive. Since poor people have limited access to secured credit, the direct effect of the credit market tends to be negative for the worst-off. However, to the extent that the credit is used for productive investments that stimulate the economy for all, the overall effect of the credit system may well be positive for them.

In Chapter 14, Joshua Preiss evaluates the financial system with reference to freedom. Given the political trend of liberalization and deregulation over recent decades, one would expect that people's financial freedoms should have increased considerably. However, Preiss argues that much depends on what we mean by "freedom." The politically dominant view holds that more freedom simply means less interference from the state (and hopefully more wealth). But the removal of regulations has created a situation in which a small number of too-big-to-fail banks have enormous control, and the assets they sell are typically too abstract or complex for the general public to comprehend. An alternative view on freedom is that it is better understood as the absence of domination—and on this dimension it seems that people's financial freedoms have actually decreased over the last few decades.

In Chapter 15, Peter Dietsch, Clément Fontan, Jérémie Dion, and François Claveau discuss how central banks can and should deal with the topic of environmental sustainability. Given the enormous challenge of climate change, it is understandable that many central banks around the world seek to promote sustainability by, for example, increasing awareness about climate risks among private banks and increasing financial flows to green industries. The crucial normative question in this context is whether they have the political legitimacy to do so in their role as delegated but independent authorities. The authors argue that this is a complicated issue that puts central banks between a rock and a hard place. On the one hand, they may not have "input legitimacy" to care about sustainability (in the sense of a direct mandate from policymakers) while, on the other hand, doing so may strengthen their "output legitimacy" (in the sense of delivering what citizens want). The best way of adjudicating this conflict between input and output legitimacy may be to rethink the institutional set-up of central banks.

Finally, in Chapter 16, Joakim Sandberg and Lars Lindblom wrap things up by analyzing the political arguments for embracing cryptocurrencies such as Bitcoin. Should this be viewed as a right-wing or a left-wing political project, and do the arguments hold up to philosophical scrutiny? It seems that many proponents of Bitcoin appeal to libertarianism and the idea that each individual has a right to choose his or her own currency. However, the authors argue that Bitcoin could undermine the state's ability to safeguard people's autonomy and safety—which are the very values that libertarians hold dear. An alternative is to appeal to egalitarianism and see Bitcoin as a way of "democratizing" money and finance.

The authors contend that this argument seems more persuasive in relation to certain developing countries that currently struggle with corrupt officials and/or corrupt bankers, but it seems less persuasive for the rest of the world.

Acknowledgments

This volume took about five years to put together, from the first idea to the finished product. We are very grateful to everyone who helped us out during this journey. First and foremost, we thank the outstanding authors who contributed with chapters. They were at times asked to revise their texts on relatively short notice, but at other times asked to wait during a long production process. We are both honored and humbled by their participation in this project as well as their encouragement along the way.

We also thank the broader group of researchers who participated in the peer-review process. (We list them below to give appropriate credit.) They provided excellent and constructive feedback to the authors and helped us to ensure the highest level of quality throughout the volume—all of this during the Covid pandemic. We are very grateful for their assistance.

Finally, we wish to thank the people behind the scenes who helped bring this project to fruition. Our editor, Peter Momtchiloff, and our production editor, Henry Clarke, at Oxford University Press, were incredibly professional, and provided strategic guidance and support. We also thank our proofreader and copyeditor extraordinaire, Angie Joachim.

Lisa dedicates this volume to her former undergraduate mentor and friend, the late Ingrid Hess Stadler.

List of Peer Reviewers

Lennart B. Ackermans
Erasmus University Rotterdam, NL

Paul Bloomfield
University of Connecticut, USA

Eyja M. J. Brynjarsdóttir
University of Iceland, Iceland

Emanuele Campiglio
University of Bologna, Italy

Rutger Claassen
Utrecht University, NL

François Claveau
University of Sherbrooke, Canada

Thomas Delcey
University of Burgundy, France

Alexander Douglas
University of St Andrews, UK

Josep Ferret Mas
University of Reading, UK

Francesco Guala
University of Milan, Italy

Tobias Hansson Wahlberg
Lund University, Sweden

Conrad Heilmann
Erasmus University Rotterdam, NL

Frank Hindriks
University of Groningen, NL

Graham Hubbs
University of Idaho, USA

Emilio Marti
Erasmus University Rotterdam, NL

Marco Meyer
University of Hamburg, Germany

Jeffrey Moriarty
Bentley University, USA

Andrew Newton
Birkbeck, University of London, UK

Tadhg Ó Laoghaire
University of Gothenburg, Sweden

Martin O'Neill
University of York, UK

Kate Padgett Walsh
Iowa State University, USA

Steven Ross
City University of New York, USA

Tobey K. Scharding
Rutgers University, USA

Georg Schmerzeck
University of Gothenburg, Sweden

J. P. Smit
University of Stellenbosch, South Africa

Johanna Thoma
London School of Economics, UK

J. D. Trout
Illinois Institute of Technology, USA

Juri Viehoff
University of Manchester, UK

Christian Walter
Fondation Maison des Sciences de l'Homme, France

Gabriel Wollner
University of Bayreuth, Germany

Chase Wrenn
University of Alabama, USA

PART I
METAPHYSICS

1

The Social Ontology of Money

Frank Hindriks

Many things have been used as money. Pieces of metal and paper have turned out to be rather convenient in this respect. More exotic examples are squirrel pelts (in medieval Finland) and large limestones with holes in them (on the isle of Yap until the late nineteenth century). For a long time, it has been natural to assume that money is a concrete object (or, more precisely, that it is always realized in the form of concrete objects). However, nowadays there is ample reason to doubt this. In particular, electronic money and cryptocurrencies are not plausibly regarded as concrete objects. For instance, they are not things that people can see or touch. But if money is not a concrete object, what is it?

Although electronic money has been around for some time now, philosophers have still not come to terms with it. In his otherwise penetrating reflections on the ontology of money, Uskali Mäki (2021) does not mention it. John Searle (1995) has struggled with the issue. Initially, he argued that money is an institutional status that is imposed on concrete objects. As a consequence, the relevant objects can be said to be money. However, Barry Smith (2003) pointed out that this idea makes little sense when it comes to electronic money. After all, in that case, there is nothing on which the status is imposed. In response, Searle (2003, 2010) has conceded that, in the case of electronic money, there is no concrete object that has this status. But this leaves open what exactly its ontological standing is.

To shed light on this, I consider the function of institutions, which is to generate cooperative benefits (Hindriks & Guala, 2021; Schotter, 1981; Tuomela, 2002). The institution of money generates such benefits by coordinating behaviors between people in a way that reduces transaction costs. This coordinating role of money plays a central role in two recent social ontologies of money, that of Francesco Guala (2016, 2021) and that of J. P. Smit, Filip Buekens, and Stan Du Plessis (2016). Guala's point of departure is the idea that concrete objects feature in coordination institutions as signaling devices, which facilitate their participants to converge on a mutually beneficial course of action (Guala & Hindriks, 2015; Hindriks & Guala, 2015). However, he claims that mere representations can also serve this purpose. In light of this, Guala (2021) proposes that money is a concrete object in some cases, and an abstract object in others. Smit, Buekens, and Du Plessis (2016) argue that money is always an abstract object. Concrete objects can

Frank Hindriks, *The Social Ontology of Money* In: *The Philosophy of Money and Finance.* Edited by: Joakim Sandberg and Lisa Warenski, Oxford University Press. © Oxford University Press 2024.
DOI: 10.1093/oso/9780192898807.003.0002

be used to represent it, but they are not money. In this chapter, I critically assess these views.

The main problem with views that take money to be an abstract object in some or all cases is that abstract objects cannot enter into causal relations, whereas money can. In light of this, I consider a third possibility: instead of an object, money is a property, a property of an agent. In other words, no thing can be money; but agents can have money. Furthermore, having money is a matter of having social power, including purchasing power (Cohen, 2011). A fourth alternative is that money is a concrete object in some cases, and a property of an agent in others (Hindriks, 2012, 2013). To shed light on the plausibility of these different views, I start by briefly introducing the commodity and credit theories of money (section 1). I then go on to discuss Searle's social ontology of money (section 2), and the nature and function of institutions (section 3). In section 4, I bring all this to bear on the ontological standing of money. I argue specifically that it should never be regarded as an abstract object. And I conclude that, at least in some cases, money is not an object at all.

1. Money and Its Functions

Economists define money as a generally accepted means of exchange, a store of value and a unit of account. These three characteristics of money are its functions. The term "function" is used here in its ordinary sense, as the purpose for which something is used. According to the Commodity Theory of money, money is itself a commodity, just as the things you buy with it. It is a concrete object to which people attribute value independently of its use as a means of exchange. As a generic means of exchange, money solves the problem of the double coincidence of wants. In a barter economy, I can buy something from you only if you want what I have to offer. With money, people can buy things irrespective of what others want. Thus, money reduces transaction costs relative to a barter economy.

According to the Credit Theory, money was introduced by the state to facilitate paying taxes. The idea is that the state issues pieces of paper that people can use for paying taxes. Using such pieces of paper commits them to offering goods at a later point in time. Thus, money comes with an obligation to repay a debt. In this respect, it is similar to the credit someone might have in a store. The Credit Theory is particularly suitable for explaining the existence of fiat money. As repaying a debt takes time, store of value is the primary function of money from the perspective of the Credit Theory. Furthermore, the state plays a central role in stabilizing the value of money, as people will always be able to use it to pay taxes.[1]

---

[1] For more on the Commodity Theory and the Credit Theory, see Guala (2016). Marx is often regarded as a proponent of the Commodity Theory, and Keynes of the Credit Theory.

Money can be realized in the form of concrete objects, such as shells, furs, and stones. However, banks often have more money on their balance sheets than in their vaults. For centuries, they have been able to create money at the stroke of a pen. This reveals that concrete objects are not essential to money. The invention of electronic money has made this even more obvious. Instead, electronic money requires a device for electronically storing currency, such as a computer system or a chip card. Even so, it cannot plausibly be identified with bits. Electronic records merely represent money. This is why electronic money presents a puzzle for the ontology of money. In light of this, I ask whether money is ever a concrete object. Furthermore, if or when it is not, what is it?

2. Status Function and Deontic Powers

According to John Searle (1995, 2010, 2015, 2017), institutions are systems of constitutive rules that enable the creation and maintenance of status functions. To explain what he means by this, I first discuss the notion of a status function and then that of a constitutive rule. Status functions consist of deontic powers, or rights and obligations. Examples of status functions are police officer, property, and marriage. A police officer ought to prevent and solve crimes. If something is your property, then other people are not permitted to take it without your permission. And being married entitles you to certain tax reductions. Money is also a status function (Searle, 2017, p. 1460). It consists of the "deontic power to buy, pay and close debts" (Searle, 2017, p. 1463). And it provides people with "the ability to buy and sell and the ability to incur and pay debts" (Searle, 2017, p. 1466). This in turn implies that money is a store and measure of value. Thus, institutional entities have status functions that confer deontic powers on people.

Institutional statuses are sometimes attributed on an ad hoc basis, as when someone is made the leader of the group without there being a procedure for this. In other cases, they presuppose a constitutive rule, which is a rule that has the following structure: X counts as Y in C. For instance, Barack Obama counts as the 44th president of the United States. He has this status because he meets the conditions under which people count as presidents. And he had the deontic powers that come with the office. Similarly, money presupposes constitutive rules, one for each currency. Searle gives the following example: "Bills issued by the Bureau of Engraving and Printing (X) count as money (Y) in the United States (C)" (1995, p. 28).[2] For a constitutive rule to be in force, it has to be collectively accepted.

---

[2] Although the Bureau of Engraving and Printing prints it, US American money is issued by the Federal Reserve.

As Searle conceives of them, constitutive rules specify the conditions something has to meet in order to have a status function. But it does not mention deontic powers. To see how they are connected, I distinguish between two kinds of rules (Hindriks, 2012, 2013, 2021). The first, which I call "a base rule," concerns the context-specific features of money, such as the kind of paper it is made from and what is printed on it. The second, to which I refer as "a status rule," specifies its deontic powers, such as the power to fulfill debts. This "dual conception of constitutive rules," as I call it, solves another problem. Searle has been criticized for offering a theory of currencies rather than of money as such. The charge is that Searle is concerned with the contingent features of particular kinds of money, but has little to say about its necessary features (Mäki, 2021, pp. 251–5). As I see it, base rules pertain to particular currencies, while the status rule explicates what money is as such. In particular, the deontic powers that feature in it are the essential features of money.

Searle initially claimed: "money must come in some physical form or other" (1995, p. 35). In the case of electronic money, this status is imposed on "a blip on a computer disk" (Searle, 1995, p. 56). Smith (2003, p. 287) criticized Searle in this respect, arguing that what is stored on an electronic device is not money itself, but a representation or record thereof. Searle (2003, p. 307) has actually accepted this criticism. He now claims that, insofar as electronic money is concerned, the status function is not imposed on anything (Searle, 2006, 2010). But this is a somewhat mysterious claim in the context of an ontology of status imposition. It gives rise to more questions than it answers. In particular, if the status function is not imposed on anything, then how are its deontic powers realized? And how can money play a causal role in social interactions if it has no physical reality?

In this last respect, it is instructive to contrast Searle's theory to that of Mäki's. Searle explicates the functions of money in terms of deontic powers. In contrast, Mäki claims that "money is a bundle of causal powers" (2021, p. 247). He goes on to argue that those causal powers are "sustained by an institutional structure" (Mäki, 2021, p. 247). The underlying idea is that, for money to exist in a contemporary society, an extensive institutional structure has to be in place, including property rights and a state that enforces them along with markets and a banking system. So, the question remains what money is, if or when it is not a concrete object. The challenge is to provide an answer that accounts for the causal dimension of money.

3. Institutions and Their Function

To make progress regarding this issue, it is important to cast the net wider and consider other theories of institutions. The two most influential kinds of theories regard them as rules that guide or structure human interaction (rule theories) or as stable regularities in behavior (equilibrium theories). Rule theories typically focus on how rules define the options people have and structure their interactions (Hodgson, 2006; North, 1990; Rawls, 1955; Searle, 1995). Rules about inheritance, property, and taxation have substantial consequences for what people do, as do legal rules that define what is criminal behavior and what is not. For rules to be in force, they have to be accepted within a certain population. Furthermore, they capture the normative dimension of institutions. They feature rights and obligations, in Searle's terms: deontic powers. Such rules are enforced by means of formal and informal sanctions. And they can be regarded as legitimate or taken to have authority within the relevant group of people (Bicchieri, 2006; Hart, 1961; Hindriks, 2019).

According to equilibrium theories, institutions are stable behavioral regularities that can be explained in terms of the preferences and expectations of their participants (Binmore, 2010; Schotter, 1981; Sugden, 1986). The preferences of the participants are interdependent: each prefers to behave in a certain way because others do so as well (Bicchieri, 2006; Lewis, 1969). Think, for instance, of traffic participants who drive on the same side of the road, or of farmers who help each other with the harvest. The former is an example of an institution that facilitates coordination, the latter of an institution that enables cooperation. In both cases, all participants benefit (at least relative to the worst possible outcome). In a broad sense, these are benefits from cooperation. In light of this, generating such benefits is often regarded as the etiological function of institutions (Schotter, 1981; Tuomela, 2002). This is the property that explains why they exist and persist (Hindriks & Guala, 2021; Wright, 1973).[3]

The main problem is that each of these two kinds of theories seems to be incomplete. Equilibrium theories capture the behavioral dimension of institutions. In contrast, rule theories address their normative and symbolic dimensions. But neither does justice to all three of the dimensions of institutions. To resolve this problem, a number of hybrid theories have been proposed (Aoki, 2001; Crawford & Ostrom, 1995; Greif & Kingston, 2011). According to one such theory, the Rules-in-Equilibrium Theory, institutions are rules that specify strategies that form an equilibrium (Guala & Hindriks, 2015; Hindriks & Guala, 2015). In this sense, coordination institutions are rules in equilibrium. The second core claim of this theory is that signaling devices play a central role in creating and maintaining equilibria. Think, for instance, of smoke signals and traffic lights, of police uniforms and wedding rings. These objects function as signaling devices in that they enable people to converge on similar responses to a certain situation such that they behave in a mutually beneficial manner.

---

[3] The claim that institutions have a function faces some well-known challenges (Brennan et al., 2013; Elster, 2015; Eriksson, 2019). Pettit (1996, 2000) and Hindriks and Guala (2021) defend the claim and address the challenges.

How do these ideas transpose to money? First, money solves a coordination problem, the double coincidence of wants. Second, the overarching function of money is to generate cooperative benefits. These consist of the reduction in transaction costs that it achieves relative to a barter economy. Things that are money fulfill this function by being used for particular purposes—as a means of exchange, a store of value, and a unit of account. Third, in order for something to be used for these purposes, it has to be sustained as money by interdependent preferences and mutually sustaining expectations. This means that people must prefer to use a particular object as a means of exchange on the condition that others do; they must actually expect each other to do so. As this will motivate them to do so, their expectations are self-reinforcing.

As mentioned in the introduction, the coordinating role of money is central to two recent social ontologies of money, that of Guala (2016, 2021) and that of Smit, Buekens, and Du Plessis (2011, 2014, 2016). Guala argues that people can solve the problem of the double coincidence of wants by converging on a particular commodity. Relying on the hybrid or unified social ontology that he and I have presented elsewhere (Guala & Hindriks, 2015; Hindriks & Guala, 2015), he proposes that commodity functions as a signaling device and thereby serves to reduce transaction costs (Guala, 2016, p. 172). To explain the stability of fiat money, Guala (2016, p. 40) invokes the state as a central authority and he proposes that it is itself a signaling device: it declares the rule and thereby the strategies due to which a particular currency is money. And its declaration makes it salient what is money in the context at issue. Furthermore, Guala (2021) argues that, although it can be, money need not be a concrete object. In particular, electronic money is an abstract object.

According to Guala (2016, p. 32), institutions are rules that people are motivated to follow. Thus, for something to be money, people must be motivated to use it as such. However, some of the things people would ordinarily think of as money do not meet this condition. Consider a currency that is subject to hyperinflation. Because of this, it has become worthless and people start using something else as money. As it is still the official currency, ordinary people will regard it as money. However, Guala (2016, p. 170) maintains that it ceases to be money because it malfunctions.[4] Thus, he believes that bills and coins are artifacts that can but need not be money. What ultimately matters for being money is not whether an entity is accepted as such, but whether it performs its functions. And, depending on circumstances, an abstract object can do so just as well as a concrete object.[5]

---

[4] Malfunctioning artifacts play a prominent role in critical discussions of Searle's theory more generally (Almäng, 2016; Hindriks, 2020; Miller, 2001; Rust, 2017; Smith, 2003).

[5] In line with this, and against Searle, Guala (2016, p. 169) argues that a declaration is neither necessary nor sufficient for something to be money.

Smit, Buekens, and Du Plessis (2011, 2014, 2016) offer a reductive account of institutional objects. To this end, they invoke the core insight of equilibrium theories, namely that stable patterns of behavior can be explained in terms of preferences and expectations. They propose that institutional objects can be reduced to ordinary objects toward which people are incentivized to act in certain ways.[6] Thus, money is an object that people are incentivized to acquire for exchange or transfer of ownership.[7] One might think that, when people are incentivized, there must be someone who incentivizes them. However, this does not follow on their use of the term: "When we say that someone is incentivized to perform an action we merely mean that there is, for that person, some reason for action, whatever this may be" (Smit et al., 2014, p. 1818).

Against this background, Smit et al. (2011, 2014, 2016) defend two striking claims. First, all money is backed up by preferences. It follows that there is no substantial difference between commodity money and fiat money. Second, concrete objects that appear to be money are merely records thereof (Smit et al., 2011, p. 17). Hence, money is an abstract object. They support this conclusion by means of their "elimination argument." If people had perfect memories, they could perform market transactions without concrete objects, in fact without any record-keeping devices at all. To illustrate how this would work, they draw an analogy with chess: "We can think of physical notes and coins as being like chess played on a board and think of electronic records as being like chess notation" (Smit et al., 2016, p. 11). This is meant to establish that the objects do not really matter in the end, except for practical or epistemic purposes. Thus, notes and coins are more like electronic records then they appear: "the states achieved by updating a financial ledger or exchanging notes and coins can both be interpreted as being records of some abstract fact" (Smit et al., 2016, p. 9). They conclude that money is a position "on an abstract mathematical object, namely a relative ratio scale" (Smit et al., 2016, p. 1).

In sum, Smit, Buekens, and Du Plessis take money to be an abstract object. If concrete objects play a role at all, they are merely records of money. In contrast, Guala argues that money can but need not be an abstract object. It can also be a concrete object. This entails that money can have one of two ontological standings. I refer to theories of this kind as "hybrid" or "dualist." In the next section, I discuss the plausibility of various theories of the ontology of money. I start with three pure or monist views, according to which money always has one and the same ontological standing.

---

[6] One might think that, when people are incentivized, there must be someone who incentivizes them. However, this does not follow on their use of the term: "When we say that someone is incentivized to perform an action, we merely mean that there is, for that person, some reason for action, whatever this may be" (Smit et al., 2014, p. 1818). For this and other reasons, I interpret them as offering an equilibrium theory.

[7] It follows that they reduce rights and obligations to what people are disposed to do. This interpretation is confirmed by the fact that Smit et al. (2014) also explicate property in terms of incentivization.

4. The Ontological Standing of Money

4.1 Monism

Before the invention of electronic money, it was rather intuitive to regard money as a concrete object. Money seemed to be a social artifact, a material object that is meant to serve a particular purpose. It was a thing that you could put in your wallet. Some of us still use wallets to carry money around. If wallets are for holding money, then it must be a concrete object, at least some of the time. However, electronic money is not a concrete object. You cannot carry it around in your pocket or even touch it. Electronic money exists due to electronic records. Yet, it is far from obvious that electronic records are money. Instead, they are most plausibly seen as representations of money (Searle, 2003; Smith, 2003). Furthermore, those records do not represent concrete objects (what would they be?). Thus, it is implausible to take all instances of money to be concrete objects. It follows that anyone who wants to defend a pure or monist conception of money has to reject the idea that money is a concrete object. The problem with this is that, intuitively, money seems to be a concrete object at least some of the time. The monist has to bite the bullet and reject this intuition.

The salient alternative is to regard money as an abstract object. On this view, electronic records represent abstract objects. In this respect, they resemble characters that represent numbers. For instance, "7" represents the number 7. According to the monist version of this view, money is always an abstract object. This implies that pieces of metal and pieces of paper are not money. Instead, they represent it, just as electronic records do. The main virtue of the abstract-object view is that it can account for electronic money. However, money has temporal, spatial, and causal properties. It comes in existence at a certain point in time in a particular region. And monetary transactions can, for instance, cause a recession, a bank run, or a war. The problem with this is that abstract objects do not seem to have such properties. It is particularly difficult to see how the abstract-object view can account for the fact that money can enter into causal relations.

A third alternative is to regard money as a property of an agent. For an agent to have money is for her to have a certain amount of purchasing power. During a market exchange, this property is transferred from the buying agent to the selling agent. When this happens, the first agent loses purchasing power, while the second acquires more of it. The property of having purchasing power is the agential equivalent of being a means of exchange. It can be represented by means of concrete objects or electronic records. Such representations also serve as a store of value. And the units that feature in those representations can be used as a measure of value. Thus, the property of having money captures all three functions of money. As I take the first to imply the other two, I refer to this third proposal as "the money-as-power view." It could be called "the money-as-property view," but this would be confusing because of the intimate relation between money and the institution of property, which plays a central role in what follows.

Jerry Cohen (2011, p. 185) embraces this third view when he argues that money is social power. He points out that someone who owns something has the right to exclude or prevent others from using it. When someone actually does so, she interferes with someone else's action. Money is the power to remove this kind of constraint. As such, it functions as an entry ticket to goods and services (Cohen, 2011, p. 181). This is particularly clear in situations where you actually need to buy a ticket. If you board a train without one, you will be removed from it. But it also holds in other situations. If you take a sweater from a department store, you will be physically stopped by a security guard. But if you use money, you do not face this constraint. In light of this, Cohen proposes that "the whole point of money is to extinguish interference," to wit to remove the constraints the agent would other-wise face (2011, p. 178).[8] Now, as Cohen conceives of it, social power is a property of an agent. He emphatically argues that "money is *not*, in fact, a thing" and that "money is no object" (Cohen, 2011, pp. 174 and 177).[9]

Thus, the money-as-power view can account for the way in which money functions in practice and how it affects the ways in which agents interact. In this context, two things are particularly important. First, the money-as-power view can solve the puzzle of electronic money. Instead of being money, the electronic records represent money. More specifically, they represent the amount of purchasing power that a particular agent has expressed in terms of a particular currency. Second, this view is well placed to account for the causal dimension of money. Causes are property exemplifications. This implies that, if money is a property, its instantiations can be causes. A problem that this view faces is that causal relata are commonly taken to be exemplifications of intrinsic properties. And social properties are extrinsic. In response, one can deny that there are causal relations in the social domain (Wahlberg, 2020). The other option is to allow for the possibility that exemplifications of extrinsic properties can be causes (Baker, 2009).

It follows that, in these respects, the money-as-power view performs better than its two rivals. The concrete-object view cannot account for the existence of electronic money. The abstract-object view cannot account for the fact that money can enter into causal relations. In contrast, the money-as-power view can account for both. Thus, the idea that money is a property of an agent deserves to be taken seriously.

---

[8] Cohen qualifies this view in two respects. First, money provides access to goods and services only in certain circumstances, including for instance that the other is willing to sell (2011, p. 177). Second, when it does not yet exist, money can induce the creation of a good or the provision of a service. Even so, it still functions as an entry ticket in such cases (Cohen, 2011, pp. 197–9).

[9] Lawson (2016) argues that money is a social position, such as that of a referee. I take this to imply that he also regards money as a property of an agent.

4.2 Dualism

Intuitively, money seems to be a concrete object at least some of the time. As just discussed, the monist has to bite the bullet and reject this intuition. But there is an alternative: to give up monism. According to dualism, money can have one of two ontological standings. If it is to capture the intuition, one of them must be that of a concrete object. This means that there are two hybrid views to consider, to which I refer as "abstract–concrete dualism" and "object–property dualism." Abstract–concrete dualism assumes that money is always an object, but that it is either an abstract or a concrete object. Object–property dualism is the view that money is either a concrete object or a property of an agent. As discussed in section 3, Guala (2016) defends abstract–concrete dualism. Elsewhere, I have defended object–property dualism (Hindriks, 2012, 2013).

Below I ask which of these two kinds of dualism is most attractive. Here I ask the prior question whether dualism is to be preferred to monism. Philosophers tend to prefer unified accounts over disunified accounts. It is unclear, however, how much weight this consideration should carry. Perhaps it is nothing more than a tie-breaker. This would mean that: if two accounts are equally good at accommodating the phenomena, then monism wins. If this is the situation, a preference for monism does not justify rejecting the intuition. Instead, the intuition supports rejecting monism. However, it would be too quick to conclude that dualism has the upper hand. The thing to realize is that the elimination argument, which I presented in section 3, can be seen as an argument against dualism.

Smit et al. (2011, 2014, 2016) claim that, if people had perfect memories, they could do without record-keeping devices altogether. They take this to imply that concrete objects are not money, but merely representations thereof. And they conclude that money is always an abstract object. But how strong is this argument really? Beings with perfect memories do not need a checkerboard to play chess. Even so, this does not imply that, say, a wooden checkerboard is not a concrete object. And it does not follow either that, in spite of appearances, the wooden object is not a checkerboard. It is a social artifact and as such a concrete object with a function. Presumably, Smit et al. (2011, 2014, 2016) will not deny this. However, it sheds doubt on their argument. The fact that people could do without certain entities does not establish that the ones that are actually in use are not real. People can of course achieve certain purposes without objects. But this is perfectly consistent with the claim that, when they do use objects for those purposes, those objects are social artifacts.

To support the elimination argument, Smit et al. (2016) present a thought-experiment concerning exchange in a prison:

> Consider a prison with unusually honest inmates, all with prodigious memories, that have a cigarette economy. Suppose a guard wishes to punish some inmate by

stealing five cigarettes from him. The prisoners are in uproar at such blatant injustice and decide to treat the inmate as if the cigarettes have never been stolen.

(p. 16)

They maintain that the prisoner does not lose any money in this scenario. And they conclude from this that money must be an abstract object. However, things could easily have gone the other way, in particular with less honest and more forgetful prisoners. Then the prisoner would have lost money. So, this example does not unambiguously support the view that money is an abstract object. Thus, the elimination argument does not support monism.

Strikingly, Guala invokes similar considerations in support of the opposite conclusion. He considers a pure credit system in which people buy things by coming to owe the other something, for instance eggs in the future in exchange for fish now. But he also observes that, in practice, credit is often combined with money. Although credit can work in small communities, it is likely to fail in larger ones, in particular because not everybody can be expected to honor their debts. This "problem of imperfect commitment" can to some extent be solved, but doing so requires costly policing institutions, including legal codes and fine collectors. Because of the costs involved, a trusted currency is likely to work better than pure credit.

Guala points out that "as the number of people grows large, the points should better be recorded in a ledger supervised by a trusted authority" (2021, p. 271). But this ledger system is redundant when people use concrete objects as money, as the points are then simply attributed to whomever carries the objects. Thus, concrete objects can be money. In support of this point, Guala points out, "it would certainly be strange to say that the money that I have in my pocket is an abstract entity" (2021, p. 275). This counts in favor of regarding some instances of money as concrete objects. Even so, material money is just one device among others for keeping track of who has how many points. The balance on your bank account is another one. Hence, money can also be an abstract object. In effect, Guala turns the elimination argument on its head. He grants that we could do without concrete objects as money. However, he also explains why in some cases we do not. In this way, the fact that we have not eliminated the use of concrete objects supports dualism.

To account for the various manifestations of money, Guala distinguishes between money as an institution and money as an object. As an institution, money consists of rules that are in equilibrium. Those rules explain which objects are money, irrespective of whether they are abstract or concrete. Thus, rules are prior to objects. Guala claims that "institutions cognitively unburden our minds by providing easy and standardized solutions" (2021, p. 268). This claim should caution us against taking the elimination argument and the prison thought-experiment too seriously. Although there might be agents who can do without concrete objects and even without ledgers, they are not us. And our limitations as human beings explain why we have institutions and why concrete objects often play a role in them.

Thus, we learn little about institutions if we abstract from our limitations. By way of analogy, Guala considers traffic lights. He points out that a middle-sized material object is not needed to avoid traffic accidents. An alternative is to rely on the following rule:

> Take the rule: on even days, cars coming from Rue Danton give way to cars coming from Boulevard Saint-Germain; on odd days, it's the other way around.
>
> (Guala, 2021, p. 275)

This rule presupposes a calendar that functions as a record, just like money in bank accounts. If it were in force, even and odd days would then play the same role as traffic lights. In this situation, there would be no such lights. But this does not mean that, as things are, there are no traffic lights or that they are not material objects. Similarly, money can but need not be realized by means of concrete objects. Thus, the elimination argument fails to establish that money is always an abstract object, and Guala uses this result to defend abstract–concrete dualism.

Strikingly, Cohen uses it to argue that money is always a property of an agent. He imagines that "people all had wonderful memories and were all law-abiding, and [that] information flowed rapidly from person to person" and he concludes that, under such circumstances, "money could take the form of nothing more than common knowledge of people's entitlements" (2011, p. 185).[10] Entitlements or rights are properties of agents. This suggests that the elimination argument supports the money-as-power view as a monist account of money.

However, this view faces a significant problem: it cannot account for unowned money. Suppose you decide to become a hermit. On the central square in the city where you lived until now, you throw all your money in the air while saying that it no longer belongs to you and that it will belong to whomever gets their hands on it first. It seems that the pieces of paper you give away remain money even after you throw them in the air and before someone catches them. But during this period, they or the power they provide do not belong to a particular agent. This suggests that purchasing power inheres in objects that are used as money. Electronic money is agent-specific. It has, so to speak, its bearer written into it. In contrast, money in the form of a concrete object provides purchasing power to whomever

---

[10] The term "entitlement" suggests that someone is obligated to satisfy it, as is the case with claim rights. But no one is obligated to trade with someone just because she has money. In light of this, money should be explicated in terms of normative power instead, to wit the power to change property rights conditional on the other agent's willingness to sell.

happens to possess it. This explains why, when it is a concrete object, money need not be owned. It follows that money can but need not be a concrete object. And this implies that monist views are inadequate.

4.3 Abstract–Concrete versus Object–Property Dualism

But how to choose between abstract–concrete dualism and object–property dualism? Recall Mäki's claim that "money is a bundle of causal powers sustained by an institutional structure" (2021, p. 247). Money presupposes other institutions such as banks, contracts, markets, property, and the state. Such institutions need to be in place in order for money to function properly. As such, they enable monetary exchanges. Mäki argues that being a means of exchange is a causal power of money. It follows that the institutions mentioned sustain the causal processes that are involved in market transactions. Now, just as objects, agents can bear the appropriate relations to institutions. Furthermore, they can also play a causal role in monetary exchanges. This suggests that the money-as-power view has no problems accommodating the causal dimension of money. And this counts in favor of object–property dualism.

What about abstract objects? Smit et al. (2016, p. 1) take money to be a position on a relative ratio scale. Such a scale is an abstract object. In light of this, they conclude that money is an abstract object too. However, a position on a scale is not as such an institutional object. Furthermore, it is not clear what, if any relations it bears to the institutions mentioned. Finally, it is difficult to see how, even if it bore some relation to them, an abstract object could acquire causal powers. Note that these problems are due to the strong claim that money *is* an abstract object. The weaker claim that money *involves* abstract objects is significantly more plausible. To support this claim, consider rosaries, which are concrete objects. How many beads there are on a rosary can be expressed in terms of a number, which is an abstract object. But this does not mean that rosaries are abstract objects. Similarly, the claim that money involves a relative ratio scale makes perfect sense. However, for the reasons discussed, it is problematic to equate the two. And the rosary example reveals that there is no need to do so. Thus, I propose that instances of money involve positions on relative ratio scales without being identical to them. The fact that their value is expressed in numbers in no way entails that they are abstract objects.

This line of argument extends to properties of agents. Consider the height of a human being or the amount of taxes she has to pay. Both are properties of an agent, and both can be quantified and expressed in numbers. As numbers are abstract objects, these properties involve such objects. However, they are not identical to them. Similarly, the position on the scale settles how much purchasing power an agent has without being identical to it. In light of this, I conclude that, although money always involves abstract objects, it can never be equated with them. And this implies that abstract–concrete dualism is mistaken. The alternative that remains is that money is either a concrete object or a property of an agent (Hindriks, 2012, 2013). The upshot is that object–property dualism is more plausible than abstract–concrete dualism.

5. Conclusion

Money is a rather common and ordinary phenomenon. At the same time, it has been claimed to be a somewhat "mysterious entity" (Mäki, 2021, p. 246). This chapter provides ample support for this claim. It reveals that several very different views about its ontological standing have at least some initial plausibility. A rather intuitive view is that money is a concrete object. In part because of technological innovations, this can no longer be regarded as the whole truth about the onto-logical standing of money. Two salient monist alternatives are that it is an abstract object or a property of an agent.

Although they are somewhat unusual, I have argued that dualist positions deserve to be taken seriously as well. It is, after all, quite intuitive that people can carry around money in their wallets, which would mean that it is a concrete object some of the time. But what about money that is stored on a computer system? One option is to regard it as an abstract object. However, this view has great difficulty accounting for the causal properties of money. In light of this, I have argued that electronic money is best regarded as a property of an agent.

Thus, the alternative that remains is object–property dualism: Money is either a concrete object or a property of an agent.

Acknowledgments

I thank Francesco Guala, J. P. Smit, Lisa Warenski, and an anonymous referee for their helpful comments.

References

Almäng, J. (2016). Legal Facts and Dependence on Representations. *Journal of Social Ontology*, 2(1), 1–15. https://doi.org/10.1515/jso-2014-0027

Aoki, M. (2001). *Toward a Comparative Institutional Analysis*. MIT Press.

Baker, L. R. (2009). *Non-Reductive Materialism* (A. Beckermann, Brian P. McLaughlin, & S. Walter, Eds.; pp. 109–27). Oxford University Press. https://doi.org/10.1093/oxfordhb/9780199262618.003.0007

Bicchieri, C. (2006). *The Grammar of Society*. Cambridge University Press.

Binmore, K. (2010). Game Theory and Institutions. *Journal of Comparative Economics*, *38*, 245–52.

Brennan, G., Eriksson, L., Goodin, R. E., & Southwood, N. (2013). *Explaining Norms*. Oxford University Press.

Cohen, G. A. (2011). *Freedom and Money* (M. Otsuka, Ed.; pp. 166–99). Princeton University Press.

Crawford, S. E. S., & Ostrom, E. (1995). A Grammar of Institutions. *American Political Science Review*, *89*(3), 582–600. https://doi.org/10.2307/2082975

Elster, J. (2015). *Explaining Social Behavior*. Cambridge University Press.

Eriksson, L. (2019). Varieties and Functions of Institutions. *Analyse & Kritik*, *41*(2), 383–90. https://doi.org/10.1515/auk-2019-0024

Greif, A., & Kingston, C. (2011). Institutions: Rules or Equilibria? In N. Schofield & G. Caballero (Eds.), *Political Economy of Institutions, Democracy and Voting* (pp. 13–43). Springer. https://doi.org/10.1007/978-3-642-19519-8_2

Guala, F. (2016). *Understanding Institutions*. Princeton University Press.

Guala, F. (2021). Money as an Institution and Money as an Object. *Journal of Social Ontology*, *6*(2), 265–79. https://doi.org/10.1515/jso-2020-0028

Guala, F., & Hindriks, F. (2015). A Unified Social Ontology. *Philosophical Quarterly*, *65*(259), 177–201.

Hart, H. L. A. (1961). *The Concept of Law*. Clarendon Press.

Hindriks, F. (2012). But Where Is the University? *Dialectica*, *66*(1), 93–113.

Hindriks, F. (2013). The Location Problem in Social Ontology. *Synthese*, *190*(3), 413–37. https://doi.org/10.1007/s11229-011-0036-0

Hindriks, F. (2019). Norms that Make a Difference: Social Practices and Institutions. *Analyse & Kritik*, *41*(1), 125–46.

Hindriks, F. (2020). How Social Objects (Fail to) Function. *Journal of Social Philosophy*, *51*(3), 483–99. https://doi.org/10.1111/josp.12334

Hindriks, F. (2021). Can Constitutive Rules Bridge the Gap between Is and Ought Statements? In P. D. Lucia & E. Fittipaldi (Eds.), *Revisiting Searle on Deriving "Ought" from "Is"* (pp. 211–38). Palgrave MacMillan.

Hindriks, F., & Guala, F. (2015). Institutions, Rules, and Equilibria: A Unified Theory. *Journal of Institutional Economics*, *11*(3), 459–80. https://doi.org/10.1017/s1744137414000496

Hindriks, F., & Guala, F. (2021). The Functions of Institutions: Etiology and Teleology. *Synthese*, *198*, 2027–43.

Hodgson, G. M. (2006). What Are Institutions? *Journal of Economic Issues*, *40*(1), 1–25.

Lawson, T. (2016). Social Positioning and the Nature of Money. *Cambridge Journal of Economics*, *40*, 961–96.

Lewis, D. K. (1969). *Convention: A Philosophical Study*. Harvard University Press.

Mäki, U. (2021). Reflections on the Ontology of Money. *Journal of Social Ontology*, 6(2), 245–63. https://doi.org/10.1515/jso-2020-0063

Miller, S. (2001). *Social Action: A Teleological Account*. Cambridge University Press.

North, D. (1990). *Institutions, Institutional Change and Economic Performance*. Cambridge University Press.

Pettit, P. (1996). Functional Explanation and Virtual Selection. *The British Journal for the Philosophy of Science*, 47(2), 291–302.

Pettit, P. (2000). Rational Choice, Functional Selection and Empty Black Boxes. *Journal of Economic Methodology*, 7(1), 33–57. https://doi.org/10.1080/135017800362239

Rawls, J. (1955). Two Concepts of Rules. *The Philosophical Review*, 64(1), 3–32.

Rust, J. (2017). On the Relation between Institutional Statuses and Technical Artifacts: A Proposed Taxonomy of Social Kinds. *International Journal of Philosophical Studies*, 25(5), 704–22. https://doi.org/10.1080/09672559.2017.1381139

Schotter, A. (1981). *The Economic Theory of Social Institutions*. Oxford University Press.

Searle, J. R. (1995). *The Construction of Social Reality*. The Free Press.

Searle, J. R. (2003). Reply to Barry Smith. *American Journal of Economics and Sociology*, 62(1), 299–309.

Searle, J. R. (2006). Social Ontology: Some Basic Principles. *Anthropological Theory*, 6(1), 12–29. https://doi.org/10.1177/1463499606061731

Searle, J. R. (2010). *Making the Social World: The Structure of Human Civilization*. Oxford University Press.

Searle, J. R. (2015). Status Functions and Institutional Facts: Reply to Hindriks and Guala. *Journal of Institutional Economics*, 11(3), 507–14. https://doi.org/10.1017/s1744137414000629

Searle, J. R. (2017). Money: Ontology and Deception. *Cambridge Journal of Economics*, 41(5), 1453–70. https://doi.org/10.1093/cje/bex034

Smit, J. P., Buekens, F., & Plessis, S. du. (2011). What Is Money? An Alternative to Searle's Institutional Facts. *Economics and Philosophy*, 27(01), 1–22. https://doi.org/10.1017/s0266267110000441

Smit, J. P., Buekens, F., & Plessis, S. du. (2014). Developing the Incentivized Action View of Institutional Reality. *Synthese*, 191(8), 1813–30. https://doi.org/10.1007/s11229-013-0370-5

Smit, J. P., Buekens, F., & Plessis, S. du. (2016). Cigarettes, Dollars and Bitcoins—An Essay on the Ontology of Money. *Journal of Institutional Economics*, 12(2), 327–47. https://doi.org/10.1017/s1744137415000405

Smith, B. (2003). The Ontology of Social Reality. *American Journal of Economics and Sociology*, 62(1), 285–99.

Sugden, R. (1986). *The Economics of Rights, Co-operation and Welfare.* Blackwell.

Tuomela, R. (2002). *The Philosophy of Social Practices.* Cambridge University Press.

Wahlberg, T. H. (2020). Causal Powers and Social Ontology. *Synthese, 197*(3), 1357–77. https://doi.org/10.1007/s11229-018-1763-2

Wright, L. (1973). Functions. *The Philosophical Review, 82*(2), 139–68.

2

Cryptocurrency

Commodity or Credit?

Asya Passinsky

1. Introduction

Joseph Schumpeter wrote in 1917, "There are only two theories of money which deserve the name: the commodity theory and the claim theory" (1917: 649). The commodity theory, which is typically associated with Aristotle, John Locke, Adam Smith, Karl Marx, and Karl Menger, holds that commodities are central to understanding the nature of money. The claim or credit theory, which is associated with Georg Friedrich Knapp, Alfred Mitchell Innes, and John Maynard Keynes, holds instead that money is to be understood in terms of credit and debt. To this day, the commodity theory and the credit theory are regarded by many theorists as the two main rival accounts of the nature of money.

Yet in recent years, the institution of money has been revolutionized in ways that most commodity and credit theorists could hardly have anticipated. The revolution is the advent of cryptocurrency. The first cryptocurrency, bitcoin, was invented in the late 2000s. The central ideas behind this new form of money were described in a 2008 paper entitled "Bitcoin: A Peer-to-Peer Electronic Cash System," authored by a person or group of people under the pseudonym Satoshi Nakamoto. In early 2009, bitcoins officially came into existence. Since then, countless alternative cryptocurrencies have been developed. According to *Coinmarketcap*, a cryptocurrency market research website, there are more than 22,000 cryptocurrencies in existence as of March 2023, and the total value of all the crypto coins in circulation exceeds $1 trillion. It is undeniable that cryptocurrency plays an important role in today's world of business and finance.

Supposing that cryptocurrency is a new form of money, the question arises whether the commodity and credit theories can adequately account for it. This is the central question that I address in this chapter. The question is interesting and important for two reasons. On the one hand, we currently lack a good understanding of the nature of cryptocurrency. Examining cryptocurrency through the lens of the two traditional accounts of money may help us to acquire a better understanding of this new phenomenon. On the other hand, cryptocurrency can serve as an important new test case for the commodity and credit theories. Any

Asya Passinsky, *Cryptocurrency: Commodity or Credit?* In: *The Philosophy of Money and Finance.* Edited by: Joakim Sandberg and Lisa Warenski, Oxford University Press. © Oxford University Press 2024.
DOI: 10.1093/oso/9780192898807.003.0003

theory of the nature of money that hopes to be adequate for the twenty-first century must be able to account for all existing forms of money, including cryptocurrency. Thus, examining the commodity and credit theories from the vantage point of cryptocurrency may help us to adjudicate between these two theories, which in turn may help us to move beyond the current stalemate in the literature.

I shall argue that neither the commodity theory nor the credit theory on its own can adequately account for cryptocurrency, but that a hybrid of the two theories can adequately do so. Here is a roadmap of the chapter: In section 2, I provide an overview of what cryptocurrency is and how it differs from standard forms of money. The next four sections examine the commodity and credit theories in light of the advent of cryptocurrency. Section 3 expounds and interprets the commodity theory, and section 4 considers whether and to what extent this theory can accommodate cryptocurrency. Sections 5 and 6 do the same for the credit theory. Finally, in section 7, I propose a hybrid hylomorphic account of money which draws on aspects of both the commodity and credit theories, and I argue that this hybrid account avoids the main problems faced by both theories.

2. Cryptocurrency

Cryptocurrency is regarded by many experts and laypersons alike as a new form of money.[1] The central feature that it shares with more familiar forms of money, such as US dollars or euros, is that it is designed to be a medium of exchange. Moreover, the more established cryptocurrencies, such as bitcoin and ethereum, fulfill this function of being a medium of exchange to some extent. Bitcoin, for instance, is routinely used as a medium of exchange in some corners of the internet (Hazlett and Luther 2020: 148). Of course, the number of merchants who accept bitcoin in exchange for goods and services is still relatively small, especially in comparison with the number of merchants who accept mainstream currencies such as US dollars or euros. But in this regard, bitcoin is not so different from standard currencies which are not widely traded.

Furthermore, given that cryptocurrency is designed to be an alternative to standard forms of money, it is plausible to suppose that it is designed to serve the other characteristic functions of money, namely being a unit of account and a store of value. And again, the more established cryptocurrencies do seem to fulfill these functions to at least some degree—though there is significant disagreement among experts over just how well these cryptocurrencies perform these functions. For instance, the economist David Yermack has argued that bitcoin functions poorly as a store of value due to its high price volatility (2015: 40–1), whereas the

---

[1] There are some experts who disagree. For example, Yermack (2015) maintains that bitcoin is more similar to a speculative investment than a bona fide currency.

cryptocurrency expert David Zeiler maintains that bitcoin has become a store of value like gold (Ashford 2023). However, even if the skeptics are right and cryptocurrencies function poorly as a unit of account and a store of value, cryptocurrencies would not be so different in this regard from standard currencies which are functioning poorly, such as the Argentine peso or the Zimbabwean dollar.

A final point of similarity between cryptocurrency and standard currencies is that the most established cryptocurrency—namely, bitcoin—is legal tender in certain jurisdictions, which means that it is "recognized by law as a means to settle a public or private debt or meet a financial obligation, including tax payments, contracts, and legal fines or damages."[2] At present, there are two countries which recognize bitcoin as legal tender. El Salvador was the first to do so, adopting bitcoin as legal tender in 2021. The Central African Republic followed suit in 2022. Thus, until quite recently, a significant difference between cryptocurrency and standard currencies was that cryptocurrencies were not legal tender in any jurisdiction. But that has since changed.

Still, there are several important differences between cryptocurrency and standard currencies. The first is that standard currencies have physical tokens. For example, there are physical US dollar bills and physical quarters and dimes which trade hands in market transactions. Many standard currencies also have electronic tokens. Thus, there are electronic US dollars which never trade hands but nevertheless exist in someone's bank account. However, there is no standard currency that has only electronic tokens. All standard currencies have at least some physical manifestations. In contrast, cryptocurrencies are entirely virtual or digital. There are no physical crypto coins which would serve as the analogue of US dollar bills or quarters. A crypto coin is, by its very nature, a virtual or digital thing.

Another key difference between cryptocurrencies and standard currencies is that standard currencies are largely issued, controlled, and maintained by a government, central bank, or other public authority. For example, US dollars are largely issued, controlled, and maintained by the US government and the Federal Reserve.[3] In contrast, cryptocurrencies are issued, controlled, and maintained entirely by private individuals. Many cryptocurrencies, including bitcoin and ethereum, are also decentralized. This means that there is no central authority at all—public or private—which is charged with issuing, controlling, and maintaining the currency. Instead, the currency is issued, controlled, and maintained by a diffuse network of individuals. For example, any bitcoin transaction is validated by another participant in the bitcoin system who is mining for bitcoins.

---

[2] This definition of "legal tender" is from *Investopedia* (2021: para. 1).

[3] It should be noted that private commercial banks also play a role in the issuance of standard currencies such as the US dollar, as these banks effectively create new money when they extend loans to customers. Thanks to Joakim Sandberg for this point.

In exchange for successfully validating a transaction, the bitcoin miner is rewarded with new units of the currency.[4]

A final distinctive feature of cryptocurrency is its reliance on cryptography—hence the "crypto" in cryptocurrency. In the case of standard currencies, people use the currency largely because they have trust in the public authority that is responsible for issuing and controlling the currency. For example, people use US dollars because they have sufficient trust in the US government and the Federal Reserve. But in the case of cryptocurrencies, there is no public authority that issues or backs the currency, and so the currency cannot rely on trust in the same way that standard currencies do. Instead, cryptocurrencies rely on cryptographic proof, as Nakamoto (2008) explains in his paper outlining the idea of bitcoin. Specifically, cryptography is used to control the creation of new bitcoins at a rate that was determined when the system was created. This ensures that the supply of bitcoins remains low enough that bitcoins retain their value. Cryptography is also used to validate and record all bitcoin transactions. This ensures that an individual who transfers bitcoins to another party is in fact the owner of these coins and is transferring them only once. Other cryptocurrencies employ cryptography in a similar fashion to muster confidence among would-be users.[5]

To summarize, cryptocurrencies resemble standard currencies insofar as they are designed to be a medium of exchange, unit of account, and store of value. And like standard currencies, they tend to fulfill these functions to at least some extent. Moreover, like standard currencies, the most established cryptocurrency is legal tender in certain jurisdictions. However, unlike standard currencies, cryptocurrencies are entirely virtual; they are issued and controlled by private individuals and not by a government or central bank; and their ability to function as money essentially relies on cryptography rather than trust in a public authority.

3. The Commodity Theory

Let us now proceed to examine the two main rival theories of money to see how well they are able to accommodate cryptocurrency. I begin with the commodity

---

[4] Some have argued that bitcoin is in fact more centralized than it appears to be. For example, Stefan Eich points out that bitcoin's mining algorithm favors large conglomerates of miners and that as a result, the creation of new bitcoins and the validation of bitcoin transactions is mostly in the hands of a small number of large conglomerates (2019: 94). But even if Eich is right that bitcoin is more centralized than its proponents claim, it remains the case that bitcoin is still less centralized than standard currencies. Furthermore, it is a contingent feature of bitcoin that its mining algorithm favors large conglomerates of miners. It is not essential to cryptocurrency as such that it employ such a mining algorithm.

[5] As Eich notes, cryptocurrencies still rely on trust to some extent (2019: 94). For example, there must be mutual trust among the users of the cryptocurrency, trust in the underlying code, and trust in any authority that is charged with adjudicating exceptional cases. So, cryptography does not altogether obviate the need for trust. Still, trust plays a much more limited role in the case of cryptocurrencies than in the case of standard currencies.

theory. This theory has a long and illustrious history, having been endorsed in one form or another by many preeminent philosophers and economists, including Aristotle (*Politics* I.8–10), Locke (*Second Treatise* V.36–51), Smith (1776/1981: ch. 4), Marx (1867/1906: ch. 3), and Menger (1892). Unsurprisingly, there are many different versions and interpretations of this theory, and so our first task is to identify the central commitments of the theory. Following Geoffrey Ingham (2004: ch. 1), I shall construe the commodity theory as being committed to three central claims: a claim about the origin of money, a claim about the ontology of money, and a claim about the function of money. Let me elaborate on each of these claims in turn.

Commodity theorists tell a familiar story about how money emerged out of the exchange of commodities. One of the best-known versions of this story may be found in chapter 4 of Adam Smith's *An Inquiry into the Nature and Causes of the Wealth of Nations* (1776/1981).[6] Smith argues that once there is division of labor in a society, a barter economy will naturally emerge. Every industrious person will specialize in producing one good and will thus end up with a surplus of this good, which they will then seek to exchange for other goods (1776/1981: ch. 4, para. 1). However, such a system of barter is inconvenient and inefficient because it requires a "double coincidence of wants." That is, each party must concurrently want what the other has. But this condition is oftentimes not met. Smith contends that a solution to this problem emerges spontaneously out of the self-interested actions of individuals:

> In order to avoid the inconvenience of such situations, every prudent man in every period of society, after the first establishment of the division of labour, must naturally have endeavored to manage his affairs in such a manner, as to have at all times by him, besides the peculiar produce of his own industry, a certain quantity of some one commodity or other, such as he imagined few people would be likely to refuse in exchange for the produce of their industry.
>
> (Smith 1776/1981: ch. 4, para. 2)

Gradually, the actions of individuals become coordinated so that everyone is stocking up on the same commodity, and everyone is accepting this commodity in exchange for their own produce. This one commodity thereby becomes a medium of exchange.

Smith notes that different commodities played the role of medium of exchange in different societies throughout history, for example, cattle in antiquity, shells in some parts of India, dried cod in Newfoundland, tobacco in Virginia, and sugar in some of the West India colonies (1776/1981: ch. 4, para. 3). But he suggests that all

---

[6] For another influential account, see Menger (1892: §§6–9).

societies eventually settle on some precious metal as their preferred medium of exchange. The reason is that metal is durable, easily divisible, and easily re-combinable, which makes it especially well-suited for being a medium of exchange (1776/1981: ch. 4, para. 4). Still, there is a problem with using precious metals in the form of "rude bars, without any stamp or coinage" as a medium of exchange; namely, they need to be weighed and their purity needs to be ascertained, and both of these tasks can be tedious and difficult. The solution to this problem which naturally emerges is regulation of the money supply by a public authority (1776/1981: ch. 4, para. 7). Thus, we have the emergence of money in one of its most familiar forms, namely metal coins issued and guaranteed by the government.

It is important to note that this story about the origin of money may be interpreted in several different ways. First, it is not entirely clear whether the story is meant to account for only the first forms of money or all forms of money. On the former interpretation, the story is only meant to explain how barter money and coined money came into being, whereas on the latter interpretation it is also meant to explain how paper money, electronic money, and other forms of money came into being. Second, it is unclear whether the story is providing a historical account of how money happened to originate or a philosophical account of how money must have originated. On the former interpretation, the story is giving an account of the actual contingent origin of money, whereas on the latter inter-pretation it is giving an account of the necessary origin of money.[7] I shall remain neutral on both of these interpretive issues. On my construal, then, the com-modity theorist is committed to some version of the following claim about the origin of money:

COMMODITY ORIGIN: The first (or, all) forms of money actually (or, necessarily) originated spontaneously out of the market exchange of commodities, as a solution to the inconveniences of barter.

Commodity theorists also typically subscribe to a certain ontology of money. According to this ontology, a token of money just is a commodity. Thus, Aristotle conceives of money as "something that [is] a useful thing in its own right and that [is] convenient for acquiring the necessities of life: iron or silver or anything else of that sort" (*Politics* I.9 1257a37–9). How exactly we construe the commodity ontology will of course depend on how exactly we construe commodities. According to one standard definition, a commodity is a raw material or a primary

---

[7] Some of Smith's remarks suggest that he takes himself to be giving an account of the necessary origin of money. For example, he says that "every prudent man in every period of society...must naturally have endeavored" to stockpile one commodity (1776/1981: ch. 4, para. 2). Furthermore, he claims that "it has been found necessary, in all countries that have made any considerable advances towards improvement, to affix a publick stamp" on certain quantities of metals (1776/1981: ch. 4, para. 7).

(i.e. basic) agricultural product that can be bought and sold.[8] Given this definition, the commodity ontology has it that a token of money just is a raw material or a basic agricultural product. This view would accommodate nearly all of Smith's examples of money, including cattle, shells, dried cod, tobacco, sugar, and precious metals.[9] However, the view cannot account for coined money or paper money, as metal coins and printed pieces of paper are neither raw materials nor basic agricultural products.

This problem can be dealt with by adopting a broader definition of commodities.[10] In particular, we may take a commodity to be a material thing that has some utility or value for us independently of its value in exchange.[11] Metal coins and printed pieces of paper are commodities in this broader sense because they do have some limited use value independently of their exchange value. Thus, for example, printed pieces of paper can be used as scratch paper, as material for a paper airplane, or as wallpaper.[12] I will interpret the commodity theorist's ontological claim in terms of this broader notion of a commodity, as the resulting claim is more plausible since it can accommodate coined money and paper money. Thus, I construe the commodity theorist's claim about the ontology of money as follows:

COMMODITY ONTOLOGY: A token of money is a commodity, in the sense of being a material thing that has some use value independently of its exchange value.

Finally, some interpreters construe the commodity theory as being committed to the view that the central or primary function of money is being a medium of exchange.[13] The other characteristic functions of money (viz., being a unit of

---

[8] This definition of "commodity" is from Oxford Languages.

[9] The view also accommodates Locke's main examples of money, which include gold, silver, diamonds, shells, and pebbles (*Second Treatise* V.46). However, Locke also writes that money is "some lasting thing that men might keep without spoiling" (*Second Treatise* V.47), which precludes many primary agricultural products from being money.

[10] Ingham offers another solution on behalf of the commodity theorist, which is to construe a token of money as "itself a tradable commodity, or the direct representative of a commodity or commodities" (2004: 33). Cf. also Menger, who writes of "certain commodities (these being in advanced civilizations coined pieces of gold and silver, together subsequently with documents representing those coins) becoming universally acceptable media of exchange" (1892: 239). However, to say that a token of money represents a commodity or commodities is not yet to say what this token of money *is*, any more than to say that Michelangelo's *David* represents David is to say what *David* is. In neither case have we specified the ontological nature or identity of the relevant entity (e.g. whether it is a material thing identical to its matter, a material thing distinct from its matter, or some other kind of thing). Thus, the view in question does not really provide an ontological account of money. Thanks to Olivier Massin for helpful discussion of this point.

[11] Marx construes commodities along these lines, writing that "a commodity is, in the first place, an object outside us, a thing that by its properties satisfies human wants of some sort or another" (1867/ 1906: 41).

[12] German banknotes were famously used as wallpaper during the period of hyperinflation following World War I.

[13] See Ingham (2004: 24) and Hubbs's unpublished manuscript "Only Two Theories Deserving of the Name: Explanations of the Ontology of Money."

account and a store of value) are taken to be secondary to, or derivative of, the function of being a medium of exchange. It is not entirely clear what this claim of centrality or primacy amounts to, and there are various ways in which one might try to spell it out. I propose to formulate the claim in essentialist terms, drawing on a neo-Aristotelian conception of essence.[14] According to this conception, a claim about the essence of a given item specifies what it is to be that item. The claim provides a partial or complete "real definition" of the item, which is a definition of the item itself as opposed to a definition of our word for it or our concept of it. Thus, for example, the claim that water is a substance composed of H_2O molecules is plausibly construed as a claim about the essence of water, as it specifies what it is to be water and provides a real definition of water. Likewise, a claim about the essence of money specifies what it is to be money and provides a real definition of money. My proposal, then, is to construe the commodity theorist's claim about the function of money as follows:

COMMODITY FUNCTION: It is essential to something's being money that it function as a medium of exchange, but it is not essential to something's being money that it function as a unit of account or a store of value.

In other words, the medium of exchange function specifies what it is to be money, whereas the unit of account and store of value functions do not specify what it is to be money. These latter functions are either necessary accidents (i.e. necessary but inessential features) or contingent features of money tokens, which are causally or constitutively explained by the medium of exchange function of money tokens.

4. Cryptocurrency as Commodity

Having articulated the commodity theory's central claims about money's origin, ontology, and function, we are now ready to consider whether and to what extent the theory can accommodate cryptocurrency. Let us begin with the claim about money's function, as it is the most conducive to cryptocurrency. As noted earlier, at least the more established cryptocurrencies, such as bitcoin and ethereum, fulfill the function of being a medium of exchange to some extent. Thus, if we restrict our attention to these cryptocurrencies, we do not find an obvious counterexample to the commodity theorist's claim that it is essential to something's being money that it function as a medium of exchange. The more established cryptocurrencies also fulfill the functions of being a unit of account and a store of value to some extent. But this is consistent with the view that money functions as a unit

---

[14] This conception of essence is prominent in contemporary analytic metaphysics. See, e.g. Fine (1994), Correia (2006), and Koslicki (2012).

of account and a store of value necessarily but accidentally, or contingently. So again, we do not find an obvious counterexample to the commodity theorist's claim that it is not essential to something's being money that it function as a unit of account or a store of value. It follows that the commodity theorist's claim about money's function can accommodate at least the more established cryptocurrencies.

Consider now the commodity theorist's claim about money's origin. Versions of this claim which pertain only to the first forms of money can accommodate cryptocurrency. For cryptocurrency is not one of the first forms of money; and it could not have been one of the first forms of money, as it requires advanced and sophisticated technology. However, versions of the claim which pertain to all forms of money cannot accommodate cryptocurrency. For cryptocurrency did not emerge spontaneously out of the market exchange of commodities as a solution to the inconveniences of barter. Instead, it was intentionally designed and created by individuals as a solution to the perceived problem of poorly managed government-issued currencies. The upshot is that some versions of the commodity theorist's claim about money's origin can accommodate cryptocurrency, whereas other versions of the claim cannot.

Finally, let us consider the commodity theorist's claim about money's ontology. Crypto coins do seem to belong to the ontological category of thing or object. Like physical coins, which are paradigmatic things, crypto coins can exist or fail to exist; they are located in time and persist through time; and they are capable of undergoing change over time. For example, a particular bitcoin can exist or fail to exist. If it exists, then it came into existence at a particular point in time and is therefore located in time. Furthermore, the bitcoin persists through time as it is transferred from one owner to another. And it can undergo change over time, such as fluctuations in its value. However, as noted earlier, crypto coins are not material things. They are entirely digital or virtual entities. As such, they are counterexamples to the commodity theorist's ontological claim.

It may be thought that the commodity theorist can deal with this problem by adopting an even broader definition of commodities. Specifically, the commodity theorist may simply drop the requirement that a commodity be a material thing. This move would accord with some recent usages of the term "commodity," which count cell phone minutes, bandwidth, and other such immaterial entities as commodities.[15] The resulting notion of a commodity would be that of a thing which has some utility or value for us independently of its value in exchange. A crypto coin, it may be argued, is a commodity in this very broad sense.

However, once the notion of a commodity has been broadened to this extent, it is unclear whether the resulting ontology is properly construed as a commodity

---

[15] See, e.g. Lioudis (2023).

ontology. After all, most commodity theorists take money to be material.[16] This indicates that materiality is a central aspect of the commodity theorist's ontology. But even setting this issue aside, the proposed modification is unsuccessful. For crypto coins are not commodities in the proposed sense of commodity: a crypto coin has absolutely no utility or value for us independently of its value in exchange. Unlike shells, cod, tobacco, sugar, pieces of metal, and even printed pieces of paper, crypto coins cannot be used for anything other than exchange. Thus, the ontology in question still cannot accommodate crypto coins. I conclude that cryptocurrency does pose a problem for the commodity theorist's ontology of money.

5. The Credit Theory

Let us now consider the credit theory. The credit theory has historically been the main alternative to the commodity theory. Versions of this theory were put forward by Knapp (1905/1924), Mitchell Innes (1913, 1914), and Keynes (1930/2013). More recently, the credit theory has been espoused by David Graeber (2011) and Stephanie Kelton (2020). I will argue that the credit theory also cannot accommodate cryptocurrency. I begin by expounding what I take to be the three central claims of the credit theory. These claims concern money's origin, ontology, and function, respectively.

Credit theorists offer a very different story of money's origin than commodity theorists. Here is Graeber's version of it:

> Say, for example, that Joshua were to give his shoes to Henry, and, rather than Henry owing him a favor, Henry promises him something of equivalent value. Henry gives Joshua an IOU. Joshua could wait for Henry to have something useful, and then redeem it. In that case Henry would rip up the IOU and the story would be over. But say Joshua were to pass the IOU on to a third party—Sheila— to whom he owes something else. He could tick it off against his debt to a fourth party, Lola—now Henry will owe that amount to her. Hence is money born.
>
> (Graeber 2011: 46)

In this story, money does not emerge as a medium of exchange that solves the problem of the double coincidence of wants. Rather, it emerges as an accounting tool that enables people to keep track of who owes whom what.

---

[16] See Aristotle (*Politics* I.9 1257a37–9), Locke (*Second Treatise* V.46–7), Smith (1776/1981: ch. 4), and Menger (1892: §1). It is less clear whether Marx construes money as something material, but it is also more controversial whether Marx is best construed as a commodity theorist.

However, as Graeber notes, "systems like these cannot create a full-blown currency system, and there's no evidence that they ever have" (2011: 47). The problem is one of trust. Why should someone trust that an IOU with Henry's signature is legitimate? After all, the signature might be forged, Henry may not be a man of his word, or Henry might not have the resources to make good on his promise. While it may be possible to ascertain all of this in a small village, it is practically impossible to do so in a larger society. State or chartalist credit theorists such as Knapp (1905/1924) and Keynes (1930/2013) came up with a solution to this problem—in a full-blown currency system, the IOUs are issued by the state rather than by private individuals. These IOUs are denominated in the state's own unit of account, and they are officially accepted as payment for taxes. People trust the IOUs insofar as they trust the state and have confidence that they will be able to use the IOUs to pay their taxes. Full-blown currency—that is to say, money in its modern form—is therefore a creation of the state.

As in the case of the commodity theory, it is important to note that this story about the origin of money may be interpreted in several different ways. First, it may be taken to concern either the first forms of money or all forms of money. Second, it may be construed as providing an account of either the actual contingent origin of money or the necessary origin of money. As before, I shall remain neutral on both of these interpretive issues. On my construal, then, the credit theorist is committed to some version of the following claim about the origin of money:

CREDIT ORIGIN: The first (or, all) forms of money actually (or, necessarily) originated as an accounting tool to keep track of who owes whom what.

Furthermore, I construe the chartalist credit theorist as being committed to some version of the following further claim:

CHARTALIST CREDIT ORIGIN: Money in its modern form actually (or, necessarily) originated through state decree.

Credit theorists typically also subscribe to a substantially different ontology of money than commodity theorists. According to credit theorists, money is not a material thing. "The eye has never seen, nor the hand touched a dollar," Mitchell Innes famously proclaimed (1914: 155). Instead, credit theorists construe money as an abstract relation, namely a credit/debt relation. Thus, Mitchell Innes says that "credit and credit alone is money" (1913: 392). More precisely, the credit theorist may be construed as maintaining that money is the abstract relation *having a claim or credit on*. An individual or entity x stands in the money relation to y just in case x has a claim or credit on y or y has a claim or credit on x. Credit theorists typically also hold that a unit of money or currency, such as the dollar or the euro, is an abstract entity. Specifically, it is taken to be an abstract unit of measurement like the centimeter or the pound, and what it measures is the size of a credit or debt.[17] Thus, according to the credit theorist's ontology of money, both money itself and units of money are abstract entities rather than material things. Here, then, is how I construe the credit theorist's claim about the ontology of money:

CREDIT ONTOLOGY: Money itself is an abstract credit/debt relation, and a unit of money is an abstract unit of measurement which measures the size of a credit/debt.

Finally, credit theorists tend to uphold the view that the central or primary function of money is being a unit of account. Thus, for example, Keynes writes that "money of account, namely that in which debts and prices and general purchasing power are *expressed*, is the primary concept of a theory of money" (1930/2013: 3, emphasis in original).[18] The other characteristic functions of money (viz., being a medium of exchange and a store of value) are taken to be secondary to, or derivative of, the function of being a unit of account. As in the case of the commodity theory, I propose to formulate this functionalist claim in essentialist terms. Specifically, I will construe the credit theorist's claim about the function of money as follows:

CREDIT FUNCTION: It is essential to something's being money that it function as a unit of account, but it is not essential to something's being money that it function as a medium of exchange or a store of value.

In other words, the unit of account function specifies what it is to be money, whereas the medium of exchange and store of value functions do not specify what it is to be money. These latter functions are either necessary accidents or contingent features of money tokens, and they are causally or constitutively explained by the unit of account function of money tokens.

6. Cryptocurrency as Credit

Having articulated the credit theory's central claims about money's origin, ontology, and function, let us now consider whether and to what extent the theory can accommodate cryptocurrency. I begin with the claim about money's function. As noted earlier, at least the more established cryptocurrencies fulfill the function of being a unit of account to some extent. So, if we restrict our attention to these

---

[17] See, e.g. Graeber (2011: 46).   [18] See also Ingham (2004: 56).

cryptocurrencies, we do not find an obvious counterexample to the credit theorist's claim that it is essential to something's being money that it function as a unit of account. The more established cryptocurrencies also fulfill the functions of being a medium of exchange and a store of value to some extent. But this is consistent with the view that money functions as a medium of exchange and a store of value necessarily but accidentally, or contingently. So again, we do not find an obvious counterexample to the credit theorist's claim that it is not essential to something's being money that it function as a medium of exchange or a store of value.

It may be objected that functioning as a medium of exchange is essential to cryptocurrencies because cryptocurrencies are primarily designed to serve the function of being a medium of exchange.[19] This objection presupposes that if Ks are primarily designed to serve function F, then it is essential to something's being K that it fulfill function F. While this principle has some intuitive plausibility, there are counterexamples to it. For example, chopsticks are primarily designed to serve the function of being eating instruments. Yet it is not essential to something's being a chopstick that it fulfill this function. Just consider a chopstick that is only used as a hair decoration. This is still a chopstick despite the fact that it never functions as an eating instrument.[20] Examples like this give us good reason to reject the principle underlying the present objection. The upshot, then, is that the credit theorist's claim about money's function can accommodate at least the more established cryptocurrencies.

Consider now the claims concerning money's origin which are put forward by the credit theorist and the chartalist theorist. Versions of the credit theorist's claim which pertain only to the first forms of money can accommodate cryptocurrency because cryptocurrency is not, and could not have been, one of the first forms of money. However, versions of this claim which pertain to all forms of money are more problematic because it is unclear whether cryptocurrency originated primarily as an accounting tool. As for the chartalist's claim, which pertains to money in its modern form, either version of this claim is problematic given that cryptocurrency is a modern form of money. For cryptocurrency originated out of the individual actions of private individuals and not through state decree. Thus, the chartalist's claim concerning money's origin cannot accommodate cryptocurrency. And while some versions of the credit theorist's claim can accommodate cryptocurrency, it is less clear whether other versions can.

Finally, let us consider the claim about money's ontology. Crypto coins are virtual or digital as opposed to material, and this accords well with the credit theorist's claim that money is abstract as opposed to concrete. However, as I argued earlier, a crypto coin is plausibly taken to be a thing or object rather

---

[19] Thanks to Graham Hubbs for raising this objection.
[20] This example is adapted from Thomasson (2014: 53–4). Cf. Koslicki (2018: §8.4.1) on how user intentions may sometimes override original author intentions.

than a relation or unit of measurement. For crypto coins possess many of the most characteristic features of things, including existing or failing to exist, being located in time, persisting through time, and being capable of undergoing change over time. In construing money as a relation and units of money as units of measurement, the credit theorist cannot account for the thing-like nature of crypto coins.

It may be objected that there is another important characteristic feature of things which crypto coins lack, namely having a single and relatively determinate location whenever they exist. My response to this objection is twofold. On the one hand, if the relevant notion of location includes location in digital space, then it may be argued that crypto coins do have a single and relatively determinate location in digital space. For example, any given bitcoin is located within the bitcoin blockchain. On the other hand, if the relevant notion of location is that of location in physical space, then I agree that crypto coins do not have a single and relatively determinate spatial location. In fact, I would argue that crypto coins do not have any spatial location whatsoever, as they are immaterial things.[21] However, it is not a characteristic feature of things in general that they have a single and relatively determinate spatial location whenever they exist. In particular, immaterial or abstract things, such as fictional characters, musical works, or novels, are not spatially located. Nevertheless, they are things or objects. Likewise, I suggest, crypto coins are things or objects despite not being spatially located. I conclude that cryptocurrency does pose a problem for the credit theorist's ontology of money.

7. A Hybrid Account

We have seen that the most problematic claim in the case of both the commodity theory and the credit theory is the claim concerning money's ontology. Neither the commodity ontology nor the credit ontology can adequately account for crypto coins: the former accounts for their thing-like nature but not their immateriality, whereas the latter accounts for their immateriality but not their thing-like nature. A natural thought is that a hybrid of the two ontologies—one that construes tokens of money as things but allows for these things to be immaterial or abstract—may be able to account for crypto coins. I shall now endeavor to develop such a hybrid ontology, drawing upon the resources of contemporary hylomorphism.[22]

---

[21] Crypto coins do bear a close relation to spatially located things. For example, bitcoins are stored on the bitcoin blockchain, and this blockchain is itself stored on a vast network of computers. But crypto coins are not spatially located where these computers are located, any more than the *Moonlight Sonata* is located where the computers on which it is stored are located. Thanks to an anonymous referee for pressing this point.

[22] For some prominent contemporary hylomorphic accounts of ordinary objects, see Fine (1982, 1999), Johnston (2006), and Koslicki (2008, 2018).

The basic idea of hylomorphism is that objects are compounds of matter and form. Consider, for example, an H_2O molecule. According to hylomorphism, this object has both matter and form. We may take the matter to be the two hydrogen atoms and the oxygen atom, and we may take the form to be a certain chemical arrangement that is exhibited by the atoms (viz., being chemically bonded in the appropriate way). The H_2O molecule, then, is a compound of these atoms and this chemical arrangement. Applying this basic idea to the case of money, we have it that tokens of money, such as dollar bills, metal coins, and bitcoins, are likewise compounds of matter and form.

Let me now develop the details of this hylomorphic conception of money.[23] I begin by addressing the following question: what serves as the matter of money tokens? In the case of physical money tokens such as quarters or dollars, the answer is straightforward: it is ordinary material objects that serve as matter. Thus, the matter of a quarter is a piece of metal, and the matter of a dollar bill is a piece of paper. But in the case of immaterial money tokens such as abstract "points," electronic dollars, or bitcoins, there are no ordinary material objects which may plausibly serve as matter. I suggest that in these cases, it is immaterial or abstract objects which play the role of matter. Thus, numbers may serve as the matter of abstract "points," and bits or blocks of data may serve as the matter of electronic dollars and bitcoins. One might worry that immaterial or abstract matter is a contradiction in terms because matter is, by definition, physical. But hylomorphists do not construe matter as physical by definition. In their view, an object's matter is just the substance or substances from which that object is made. Given this conception of matter, there is nothing inherently contradictory in the idea of immaterial or abstract matter. For there is nothing inherently contradictory in the idea of immaterial or abstract substance.[24] Indeed, many hylomorphists explicitly countenance hylomorphic compounds with immaterial or abstract matter.[25]

The next question that must be addressed is this: what plays the role of form for money tokens? Following Kit Fine (1982, 1999) and Mark Johnston (2006), I adopt the view that properties and relations may play the role of form. Thus, for example, the form of an H_2O molecule may be taken to be the relation *being chemically bonded in such-and-such way*. Given this general account of form, our task then is to specify the relevant properties or relations in the case of money tokens. My proposal is that the form of any given money token is a relational normative property, specifically a property involving a claim on or credit with some other individuals or entities. One important issue is whether this claim or

---

[23] Here I draw on the hylomorphic theory of social objects developed in Passinsky (2021).

[24] Thus, Descartes famously held that the mind is a nonphysical substance.

[25] See Aristotle (*Metaphysics* Z.10 1036a9–12), Fine (1999: 72), Johnston (2006: 654–5), and Evnine (2016: §4.4).

credit is moral, legal, or merely social in character. My view is that the nature of the relevant claim or credit may vary depending on the kind of money token at issue. Consider, for example, Henry's IOU. Its form is plausibly taken to be the relational normative property *being such that the bearer has a credit of such-and-such size with Henry*, where the relevant claim or credit is a moral one. In contrast, in the case of a US $1 bill, the form is plausibly taken to be the relational normative property *being such that the bearer has a credit of $1 with the US government*, where the relevant claim or credit is a legal one.[26] In still other cases, the relevant claim or credit may be purely social, having its basis in a prescribed or practiced social norm or rule. For example, consider a community in which there is a social practice of using seashells as money. The form of the seashell money tokens may be taken to be the relational normative property *being such that the bearer has a credit of such-and-such size with other members of the seashell money community*, where the relevant claim or credit is a purely social one that has its basis in the relevant social practice.

Having provided an account of the matter and form of money tokens, we must now clarify the sense in which these tokens are "compounds" of matter and form. I think that there are two viable approaches for the hylomorphist here, and I will mention both of them. The first approach holds that both the matter and the form of a given money token are literally proper parts of that token.[27] For example, the proper parts of Henry's IOU would include a particular piece of paper as well as the relational normative property *being such that the bearer has a credit of such-and-such size with Henry*. The second approach denies that a money token's form is a proper part of it. Instead, it holds that the real definition of any given money token makes reference to both the matter and the form of that token.[28] Thus, the real definition of Henry's IOU would make reference to both the particular piece of paper and the relevant relational normative property. According to the first approach, it is the money token itself which is made up of both matter and form, whereas according to the second approach, it is the real definition of the money token that has both a material and a formal aspect to it.

Finally, let us state the existence conditions for tokens of money. I take it that any money kind K is essentially associated with a range of suitable matter and a form. To illustrate, consider the money kind *US $1 bill*. This kind is essentially associated with a range of suitable matter, namely pieces of paper of a particular size and shape which bear a certain inscription and were printed by the US Bureau of Engraving and Printing.[29] The kind is also essentially associated with a form, namely the relational normative property *being such that the bearer has a credit of*

---

[26] Proponents of legal anti-positivism may argue that this legal claim entails a moral claim, as legal facts are necessarily partially grounded in moral facts in their view.

[27] See Fine (1999), Koslicki (2008: ch. 7), and Passinsky (2021) for hylomorphic views on which an object's form is a proper part of it.

[28] See Johnston (2006) for a hylomorphic view along these lines. [29] Cf. Searle (1995: 45–6).

$1 with the US government. The following principle, then, tells us when an object x constitutes a US $1 bill:

EXISTENCE $1 BILL: An object x constitutes a US $1 bill at a time t if and only if (*i*) x is a piece of paper of the right size and shape which bears the right inscription and was printed by the US Bureau of Engraving and Printing; and (*ii*) the bearer of x, qua bearer, has a credit of $1 with the US government at t.

Note that this principle entails that a counterfeit dollar bill is not a dollar bill. That is because the piece of paper which constitutes a counterfeit dollar bill was not printed by the US Bureau of Engraving and Printing, and so condition (*i*) is not met.[30] I take this to be a virtue of the account, as there is an intuitive difference between counterfeit dollars and real dollars.[31]

More generally, the following principle tells us when some objects $x_1, \ldots, x_n$ constitute an object of money kind K:

EXISTENCE: Some objects $x_1, \ldots, x_n$ constitute an object of money kind K at a time t if and only if (*i*) $x_1, \ldots, x_n$ are suitable matter for a K; and (*ii*) $x_1, \ldots, x_n$ instantiate the form associated with K at t.

Whenever some objects $x_1, \ldots, x_n$ constitute an object of money kind K at a time t, the resulting money token is a compound of matter and form. The matter of this compound consists of $x_1, \ldots, x_n$ and the form is the relevant relational normative property.

Let me now explain why I construe my hylomorphic account of money as a hybrid of the commodity and credit ontologies. On the one hand, my account takes tokens of money to be things, as per the commodity ontology. Furthermore, it makes room for money tokens that have ordinary material objects—including commodities—as their matter. On the other hand, my account holds that a credit or claim is involved in the very nature or identity of money, as per the credit theory. Moreover, it makes room for money tokens that have immaterial or abstract objects as their matter. Thus, my hylomorphic account incorporates central aspects of both the commodity and credit ontologies.

This hybrid ontology can accommodate cryptocurrency better than the commodity and credit ontologies. Unlike the commodity ontology, it can accommodate the virtual or digital nature of crypto coins because it allows for the matter of money tokens to be immaterial or abstract (and entirely useless in its own right).

---

[30] Since having been printed by the US Bureau of Engraving and Printing is a historical property, the kind *US $1 bill* is a historical kind (i.e. a kind whose conditions of membership include historical properties).

[31] Thanks to Graham Hubbs for discussion of this point.

Unlike the credit ontology, it can accommodate the thing-like nature of crypto coins because it treats them as things as opposed to relations or units. To illustrate, consider bitcoins. According to our hybrid ontology, a given bitcoin is a compound of matter and form. Its matter is plausibly taken to consist of immaterial or abstracts objects, such as blocks of data. And its form is plausibly taken to be the relational normative property *being such that the bearer has a credit of one bitcoin with other members of the bitcoin community*, where the relevant claim or credit is a purely social one that has its basis in the relevant social practice. The bitcoin is a compound of this matter and form either in the sense that the blocks of data and the relevant property are both parts of the bitcoin, or in the sense that the real definition of the bitcoin makes reference to both the blocks of data and the property. Finally, the existence conditions for bitcoins are given by the following principle:

EXISTENCE BITCOIN: Some objects $x_1, \ldots, x_n$ constitute a bitcoin at a time t if and only if (*i*) $x_1, \ldots, x_n$ are blocks of data that were generated through the process of mining; and (*ii*) the bearer of $x_1, \ldots, x_n$, qua bearer, has a credit of one bitcoin with other members of the bitcoin community at t.

As in the case of US $1 bills, this principle entails that a counterfeit bitcoin would not be a bitcoin. A counterfeit bitcoin, like a counterfeit dollar, would be something that resembles a real bitcoin but is not constituted by objects with the right sort of history. Specifically, a counterfeit bitcoin would not be constituted by blocks of data that were generated through the process of mining. Whether such counterfeit bitcoins are a practical possibility—as opposed to a mere theoretical possibility—is a question that I leave for the cryptography experts.

To conclude, let me briefly contrast my hylomorphic account of money with several existing views in the literature which may also be regarded as hybrid accounts. Francesco Guala (2020) maintains that money can take the form of either a material object (e.g. a bill or coin) or an abstract object (e.g. a "point" in a bank account). Guala's view is similar to my own in that we both hold that money tokens may be either material or immaterial. However, unlike Guala, I hold that any given money token is a compound of pre-existing material or immaterial objects and a relational normative property. An advantage of my view is that it preserves a deep ontological unity among the diverse array of money tokens: dollar bills, coins, "points" in a bank account, bitcoins, and so on are all ontologically unified in virtue of having a formal component which is a relational normative property involving a claim or credit.[32]

---

[32] Another virtue of my view is that it can explain why a given money token is not identical to its matter. The explanation is that the money token has a formal component which the matter lacks. For example, a dollar bill is not identical to the piece of paper which constitutes it because the relational normative property *being such that the bearer has a credit of $1 with the US government* is a component

Frank Hindriks defends a different disjunctive account according to which money is either a concrete object or a property of an agent, namely purchasing power.[33] For example, a dollar bill is a concrete object, whereas electronic money is a property of an agent. My view, like Hindriks's, appeals to properties to account for the nature of money. However, whereas Hindriks appeals to properties only in the case of electronic money, I appeal to properties in the case of all forms of money, including both concrete and electronic money. Again, I think that one advantage of my view is that it is more ontologically unified. It is hard to see what, if anything, ontologically unifies dollar bills and electronic money in Hindriks's view. On my view, it is clear what unifies these different forms of money: it is their formal component, which is a relational normative property involving a claim or credit. A further advantage of my view is that it can adequately account for cryptocurrency, whereas Hindriks's view cannot. For crypto coins are neither concrete objects (since they are immaterial) nor properties of an agent (since they are things).

Finally, Tony Lawson proposes a hybrid account according to which money is a "positioned thing or stuff, the latter being thereby incorporated as a component of a wider system, whereupon certain of its capacities (that are already possessed prior to its being positioned) are effectively harnessed to serve one or more system doings or functions that have come to be associated with money" (2016: 965–6). The property that any thing or stuff must possess prior to being positioned as money is being a reliable form of value (2016: 967). It is this property that grounds the capacities of the thing or stuff which are then harnessed to serve the system functions of money. While I agree with Lawson that certain pre-existing entities are "positioned" as money through our social practices, I disagree that these pre-existing entities must be a reliable form of value. In my view, the material or immaterial objects which serve as the matter of money tokens need not have any value for us prior to being "positioned" as money.[34] This difference in our views is crucial when it comes to cryptocurrency, since the bits or blocks of data which are "positioned" as crypto coins arguably have no prior value for us. Thus, whereas my view can accommodate cryptocurrency, Lawson's view arguably cannot.[35]

---

of the dollar bill but not the piece of paper. It is unclear whether Guala's view has the resources to likewise explain the non-identity of the dollar bill and the piece of paper. For arguments in favor of the non-identity of social objects and their constituting matter, see Passinsky (2021: §3.1).

[33] See chapter 1 in this volume and Hindriks (2012, 2013).

[34] Of course, in some cases the matter of money tokens will have value for us prior to being "positioned" as money. Examples include the sorts of cases discussed by Smith (e.g. cattle in antiquity, shells in some parts of India, dried cod in Newfoundland, tobacco in Virginia, and sugar in some of the West India colonies).

[35] Lawson acknowledges that bitcoin appears to pose a challenge to his view. See Lawson (2016: 974, n. 16).

8. Conclusion

In this chapter, I argued that neither the commodity theory nor the credit theory on its own can accommodate cryptocurrency into its ontology of money. I then proposed a novel hybrid hylomorphic account of money which draws on aspects of both the commodity and credit ontologies. This hybrid account, I argued, can accommodate cryptocurrency. In conclusion, I want to acknowledge the possibility that some credit theorists may be happy to embrace my hybrid ontology under the banner of the credit theory, on the grounds that this ontology makes an abstract credit relation central to the identity of money. Likewise, I want to acknowledge the possibility that some commodity theorists may be happy to embrace my hybrid ontology under the banner of the commodity theory, on the grounds that this ontology construes tokens of money as things and allows for these things to be constituted by commodities. Since the commodity and credit theories have many different versions and interpretations, I ultimately view this as a largely verbal issue. The substantive issue is whether the proposed hybrid ontology is viable. I hope to have shown that it is—particularly when it comes to the new forms of money of the twenty-first century.

Acknowledgments

I would like to thank audiences at the Ontology of Finance Workshop at SUNY Buffalo and the 2022 Social Ontology/Collective Intentionality Conference at the University of Vienna, where versions of this material were presented. For helpful comments and discussion, I would also like to thank Olivier Massin, Joakim Sandberg, Lisa Warenski, and an anonymous referee. I am especially grateful to Graham Hubbs for extremely helpful written comments and discussion, and for helping me to navigate the vast literature on the nature of money. Lastly, I want to thank my dear late friend and colleague David Dick, who introduced me to the philosophy of money and encouraged my interest in this area. This chapter is dedicated to his memory.

References

Ashford, Kate. (2023) "What Is Cryptocurrency?" *Forbes*. https://www.forbes.com/advisor/investing/what-is-cryptocurrency/.

Correia, Fabrice. (2006) "Generic Essence, Objectual Essence, and Modality." *Noûs*, 40, 753–67.

Eich, Stefan. (2019) "Old Utopias, New Tax Havens: The Politics of Bitcoin in Historical Perspective." In Philipp Hacker, Ioannis Lianos, Georgios Dimitropoulos, and Stefan Eich (eds.), *Regulating Blockchain: Techno-Social and Legal Challenges* (pp. 85–98). Oxford: Oxford University Press.

Evnine, Simon J. (2016) *Making Objects and Events: A Hylomorphic Theory of Artifacts, Actions, and Organisms*. Oxford: Oxford University Press.

Fine, Kit. (1982) "Acts, Events and Things." In Werner Leinfellner, Eric Kraemer, and Jeffrey Schank (eds.), *Language and Ontology, Proceedings of the Sixth International Wittgenstein Symposium* (pp. 97–105). Vienna: Hölder-Pichler-Tempsky.

Fine, Kit. (1994) "Essence and Modality." *Philosophical Perspectives*, 8, 1–16.

Fine, Kit. (1999) "Things and Their Parts." *Midwest Studies in Philosophy*, 23, 61–74.

Graeber, David. (2011) *Debt: The First 5000 Years*. Brooklyn: Melville House.

Guala, Francesco. (2020) "Money as an Institution and Money as an Object." *Journal of Social Ontology*, 6, 265–79.

Hazlett, Peter K., and William J. Luther. (2020) "Is Bitcoin Money? And What That Means." *The Quarterly Review of Economics and Finance*, 77, 144–9.

Hindriks, Frank. (2012) "But Where Is the University?" *Dialectica*, 66, 93–113.

Hindriks, Frank. (2013) "The Location Problem in Social Ontology." *Synthese*, 190, 413–37.

Hubbs, Graham. "Only Two Theories Deserving of the Name: Explanations of the Ontology of Money." Unpublished manuscript.

Ingham, Geoffrey. (2004) *The Nature of Money*. Cambridge: Polity Press.

Investopedia. (2021) "Legal Tender: Definition, Economic Functions, Examples." https://www.investopedia.com/terms/l/legal-tender.asp.

Johnston, Mark. (2006) "Hylomorphism." *Journal of Philosophy*, 103, 652–98.

Kelton, Stephanie. (2020) *The Deficit Myth: Modern Monetary Theory and the Birth of the People's Economy*. New York: Public Affairs.

Keynes, John Maynard. (1930/2013) *A Treatise on Money: The Pure Theory of Money*. In Austin Robinson and Donald Moggridge (eds.), *The Collected Writings of John Maynard Keynes*, Volume 5. Cambridge: Cambridge University Press.

Knapp, Georg Friedrich. (1905/1924) *The State Theory of Money*. London: Macmillan & Company. Abridged edition. Translated from the fourth German edition by H.M. Lucas and J. Bonar.

Koslicki, Kathrin. (2008) *The Structure of Objects*. Oxford: Oxford University Press.

Koslicki, Kathrin. (2012) "Essence, Necessity, and Explanation." In Tuomas E. Tahko (ed.), *Contemporary Aristotelian Metaphysics* (pp. 187–206). Cambridge: Cambridge University Press.

Koslicki, Kathrin. (2018) *Form, Matter, Substance*. Oxford: Oxford University Press.

Lawson, Tony. (2016) "Social Positioning and the Nature of Money." *Cambridge Journal of Economics*, 40, 961–96.

Lioudis, Nick. (2023) "Commodity vs. Product: What's the Difference?" *Investopedia*. https://www.investopedia.com/ask/answers/021615/whats-difference-between-commodity-and-product.asp.

Marx, Karl. (1867/1906) *Capital: A Critique of Political Economy*. New York: Random House. Translated from the third German edition by Samuel Moore and Edward Aveling. Edited by Frederick Engels. Revised and amplified according to the fourth German edition by Ernest Untermann.

Menger, Karl. (1892) "On the Origin of Money." *The Economic Journal*, 2, 239–55.

Mitchell Innes, Alfred. (1913) "What Is Money?" *Banking Law Journal* (May), 377–408.

Mitchell Innes, Alfred. (1914) "The Credit Theory of Money." *Banking Law Journal* (January), 151–68.

Nakamoto, Satoshi. (2008) "Bitcoin: A Peer-to-Peer Electronic Cash System." Available at: https://bitcoin.org/bitcoin.pdf.

Passinsky, Asya. (2021) "Norm and Object: A Normative Hylomorphic Theory of Social Objects." *Philosophers' Imprint*, 21, 1–21.

Schumpeter, Joseph. (1917) "Das Sozialprodukt und die Rechenpfennige." *Archiv für Sozialwissenschaft und Sozialpolitik*, 44, 627–715.

Searle, John R. (1995) *The Construction of Social Reality*. New York: Free Press.

Smith, Adam. (1776/1981) *An Inquiry into the Nature and Causes of the Wealth of Nations*, Volume 1. Indianapolis: Liberty Classics.

Thomasson, Amie L. (2014) "Public Artifacts, Intentions, and Norms." In Maarten Franssen, Peter Kroes, Thomas A.C. Reydon, and Pieter E. Vermaas (eds.), *Artefact Kinds: Ontology and the Human-Made World* (pp. 45–62). Synthese Library, 365. Cham: Springer.

Yermack, David. (2015) "Is Bitcoin a Real Currency? An Economic Appraisal." In D.L.K. Chuen (ed.), *Handbook of Digital Currency: Bitcoin, Innovation, Financial Instruments, and Big Data* (pp. 31–43). Boston: Elsevier.

3

How Many People Does It Take to Make a Dollar?

David G. Dick[†]

> It may be a dubious and even dangerous sort of money, but even the worst sort must be included in the theory. Money it must be, in order to be bad money.
>
> G. F. Knapp, *The State Theory of Money*, 1924

1. Introduction

How many people does it take to make a dollar? Suppose I wanted to create a new currency that was real money just as much as the dollar is. How many other people would I have to recruit to my project, and what would I have to have them do?

If the US dollar is my model, it seems I might need the help of an absolutely huge number of people to make my new currency become real money, since the US dollar is recognized and used as money by many millions (perhaps billions) of people. By contrast, the thousands of new cryptocurrencies that have emerged in the last decade or so seem like they might not count as money, precisely because there are not enough people who recognize and use them as money. Whatever the minimum threshold is for the necessary number of people, it seems it must be pretty high, since for even the most famous and popular cryptocurrency, Bitcoin, it is still an open question whether it counts as money or not (Passinsky 2020b).

So how could we determine when one of those new cryptocurrencies does or does not succeed in being money? Any attempt to establish a precise threshold of how many people are required to create money looks like it will be arbitrary: If 1,000 people are enough to make a currency real money, then why not 999?

Drawing on recent work in the ontology of money, I will argue that there is a non-arbitrary threshold number of people required to create money, and that this

---

[†] David G. Dick passed away suddenly in November of 2022 as he was completing his work on this chapter.

David G. Dick, *How Many People Does It Take to Make a Dollar?* In: *The Philosophy of Money and Finance.*
Edited by: Joakim Sandberg and Lisa Warenski, Oxford University Press. © Oxford University Press 2024.
DOI: 10.1093/oso/9780192898807.003.0004

threshold is nowhere near triple digits. Instead, I will argue that the number of people required to make money is just two. This will mean that, for some communities at least, both Bitcoin and many other new cryptocurrencies do succeed in being money, since many of them have at least two people doing all it takes to turn them into money. This seems to imply that there is no difference between the US dollar and an obscure cryptocurrency accepted by just two people. As an ontological matter, that may well be, if both the crypto and the dollar meet the requirements for being money. But that does not mean there is no difference between the two. While they might equally be money, the crypto and the dollar will not be equally good money for all purposes, and so we can understand the differences between them in normative terms, if not ontological ones.

To show all this, I will devote the next section to discussing the accounts of money that insist that it is attitudes that are crucial for the creation of money. Then I will examine the accounts of money that instead privilege function as the crucial element in creating money, concluding that the correct account of money will require elements of both attitude and function. Since these elements can be instantiated when there are no more than two people, I argue that this is the minimum number required to create real money. Finally, I will argue that this conclusion should be a welcome one, since it allows us to separate the ontological requirements for being money from the normative standards we may wish to apply to money.

2. Attitude Accounts of Money

Money is sometimes thought to work like Tinkerbell, the fairy in the Peter Pan story, who exists just as long as someone believes that she does. In the fictional story, Tinkerbell's existence depends on human beliefs. But in the real world, money is often thought to work in just the same way, with its existence being held up by the attitudes that humans direct toward it.

Asya Passinsky points out that the attitude holding up money cannot be belief, since humans can simply decide at will to create money, but they cannot simply decide to believe something at will. Instead, Passinsky thinks that the crucial attitude is one of "acceptance," and when the relevant agents hold this attitude toward a given material object, they can thereby turn it into a social object like money (2020a: 437–9). It is with this arrangement that Passinsky explains the "response dependence" that money has on us and our attitudes. She notes further that this is the same relationship that Euthyphro thought piety was in with respect to the love of the gods. In the Platonic dialogue bearing his name, Euthyphro thought that something was pious only because the gods loved it, and Passinsky thinks some material object can become money only because some agents accept it as such (Passinsky 2020a: 435).

Eyja Brynjarsdóttir also invokes Euthyphro to explain the way money depends on human attitudes, and even names the distinctive property it has after him:

> Euthyphro's account describes the direction of dependence for subjective properties: An object has a subjective property because of a subject's attitude toward it. Thus we might as well call such properties *Euthyphronic*.   (2018: 51)

What this means roughly "is that it is 'up to us' that the property is instantiated. It was not 'already there' to be discovered" (Brynjarsdóttir 2018: 50).

Both Passinsky and Brynjarsdóttir aim to capture the way people create the fact that something is money instead of merely discovering it. By holding the right sort of attitude toward something, people have the power to create money that was not there before. So, if these attitudes are powerful enough to bring things into existence, could a single person adopt the right one and thereby create money all by themselves?

Perhaps this is possible for some social objects, but not for money. This is due to the kind of attitude involved in creating money. A humble ashtray might become a beloved family heirloom if just one family member loves it, but that is because the attitude required to make it beloved can be held by just one person. By contrast, money must be endowed with exchange value in order to be money, and exchange value will always require more than one party to exist. To actually have exchange value, at least one agent must think that another agent regards something as acceptable in trade, and that other agent must think so too. Where sentimental value can be brought into the world by the attitudes of just one person, exchange value always requires another agent to recognize it in order for it to exist.

While neither Passinsky nor Brynjarsdóttir argues that the attitudes of a single agent are actually sufficient to create money, no attitude account of money is as explicitly committed to the requirement of at least two agents for the creation of money as is John Searle's. Searle's account is still the most prominent attitude account of social institutions like money, and it takes the relevant attitude that creates all social objects, not just money, to depend crucially on no fewer than two agents.

The attitude in question is "collective intentionality," which is "a biologically primitive phenomenon that cannot be reduced to or eliminated in favor of something else" (Searle 1995: 24). When it comes to money, the actual fact that makes it true that some bits of paper are really money is an "institutional fact." An institutional fact is a particular kind of social fact that agents can create by directing their intentions in a particular way. Searle defines a social fact as "any fact involving the collective intentionality of two or more agents" (2005: 6).

The creation of exchange value requires two agents because it only exists when the attitudes of at least two individuals coincide in the right way, but this coincidence might arise out of the unrelated activities of these individuals. Collective intentionality is different. It is not simply the sum of the individual intentions of agents in a given group, and it cannot be broken down into the individual intentions of its members. Collective intentions are different in kind from individual attitudes. It is the difference between two violinists deliberately playing a piece together in an orchestra and those violinists merely happening to play their parts synchronized with each other in separate rooms (Searle 1995: 25). In the orchestra, the violinists do something together, while in the building they do separate things that just so happen to align with each other. No amount of stacking individual activities can amount to the collective decision to do something, however much they end up intertwined. The building blocks necessary to create a social object like money, Searle thinks, can be achieved only through the deliberate orchestration of a group's collective intentionality, not the accidental harmonizing of individual agents.

What agents must collectively do to create the institutional fact that constitutes money is to grant something the "status function" of money. Status functions are distinctive because they are unlike other functions that can be performed by an object "solely in virtue of the object's intrinsic physical features," such a when a log performs the function of being a bench. But a status function is performed by an object independently of its intrinsic physical features and works "only in virtue of collective agreement or acceptance" (Searle 1995: 39). For example, a high wall can perform the function of being a barrier in virtue of its intrinsic physical features alone, but even once it is worn down to nothing more than a line of stones, it can still perform the function of being a barrier if granted the status function of being a boundary by collective agreement (Searle 1995: 39–40). Money works the same way as the line of stones, according to Searle, since it performs its function simply in virtue of the fact that it is agreed to have it.

Searle's example shows the tremendous power that our attitudes can have, creating an effective barrier where there is no physical obstacle at all. But just because Searle thinks that a social object like money or a boundary can perform its function in virtue of attitudes alone, he does not therefore think that social objects must perform their intended functions in order to be what they are.

Though he does not always appear to be committed to this conclusion,[1] in at least some places, Searle seems wedded to the claim that social objects exist in virtue of attitudes alone, regardless of how they function. In a striking passage, Searle insists that a group of agents who collectively decide to have a cocktail party that somehow "gets out of hand, and it turns out that the casualty rate is greater than the Battle of Austerlitz" do not thereby alter what kind of activity they are pursuing. Despite this turn of events, "it is not a war; it is just one amazing cocktail party" (Searle 1995: 33–4).

This commitment is the logical conclusion of any attitude account that takes social objects to be determined by attitudes alone. These conceptions are "united

---

[1] See Guala (2016: 165–6) for a discussion of this.

in the belief that something's being money is not so much a matter of what we *do* with it... but rather a matter of how we *think* or *talk* about it" (Passinsky 2020a: 287).

On such an attitude view, the number of people required to create the specific social object of money is only two. Two people are enough to instantiate the distinctive kind of exchange value that money must have in order to count as money. Two people are probably also necessary for something to count as a store of value, though it might take only one person to use something as a unit of account. If money can be created out of nothing more than attitudes, it appears that all three of money's canonically distinctive features can be instantiated by attitudes that require no more than two people to exist. Whether this comes about through the deliberate collective intentionality that Searle requires, or through an accidental constellation of individual attitudes, it is still the case that only two agents are required to meet the necessary and sufficient conditions to create money. All it takes to create real money on this pure attitude view is for at least two people to decide to accept that something is money, and then it thereby is.

This will mean that my wife and I could capriciously decide to accept jellybeans as money, and it would be true that they were even if we were the only two people in the world to accept it. We could endow them with exchange value on this view simply by deciding that they were acceptable for payments of debts between us, and a way of keeping track of what we owe each other. We could even give the jellybeans denominations, making red jellybeans (which are obviously the most valuable) worth twenty green ones. Furthermore, on any view that creates money out of attitudes alone, this is all we would have to do. Simply making this decision and accepting that jellybeans have this status is enough to make them a currency as real as the US dollar. We would never need to trade them, hoard them, or measure values in terms of them for them to be full and genuine money.

This is clearly absurd. Something has gone wrong with any view that would let my wife and I turn jellybeans into money in this way. There could be several diagnoses of the error here, but one thing is clear and that is that attitudes alone, unconstrained by any requirements on behavior or function are not enough to create a social object like money. To put it in Passinsky's terms, money must also be "a matter of what we *do* with it" and *not* just "a matter of how we *think* or *talk* about it" (2020a: 287). This commitment is what drives the functional views of money, which will also permit it to be created by very small groups of people, but for very different reasons.

3. Function Accounts of Money

Building money out of nothing but the attitudes of agents leaves us with the absurd entailments of Searle's cocktail party and my jellybean money. These results are not only intuitively absurd, they also make social objects opaque and epistemically inaccessible to anyone who cannot read the minds of the agents creating them. Thinking that social objects consist solely in how we think and talk about them disregards the crucial feature of how they function, and so will mislead us in understanding and categorizing all manner of social objects.

Insisting that social objects like money depend on our thoughts about them is what Francesco Guala calls "the dependence thesis," which asserts that "institutional entities depend for their existence on our representations" (2016: 163). This would mean that in order for something to be money, we would have to represent it to ourselves as money, and think and talk about it as such. But such representation is neither necessary nor sufficient to make something function as money, and so will leave out a crucial feature required for something to successfully become money.

Guala illustrates that recognizing and identifying something as money will not ensure it is treated as money with the case of the now dead Roman *sestertii* coins:

> Perhaps when people see a coin, they say "it's money," even though they do not actually use it for trade. Suppose that they prefer to use shells as a medium of exchange instead. When asked what that thing they hold in their pockets is, they say "this is a shell," not "this is money." But functionally speaking, the shells are money and the coin is just copper.
>
> The point is that one thing is to be recognized as money in a system of folk classification; quite another is to be money.   (2016: 169–70)

To be money, something must not just be thought and said to be money, it must function as money, at least some of the time. In his solo work and in work with Frank Hindriks, Guala makes it clear that the function that money must have is conceived of in two distinct but related ways (Guala 2016; Hindriks & Guala 2015). First, something must function as money in the sense that it must behave like money. That is, it must actually be used in exchanges, accounting, and storing value. But it further must function as money in the sense that it must behave this way because that is its function, in the sense of its purpose or explanation for existence. Money, like all institutions, according to Hindriks and Guala, must behave like money because it serves the purpose of solving a distinctive kind of coordination problem. In the case of money, this constituting coordination problem is the double coincidence of wants. This is just the problem that if you are to successfully trade with someone, they must want what you are offering in exchange if you are to get what you want in exchange for it. When it comes to specific goods, wants may often not coincide, and trade will thereby not occur. Money is the solution to this coordination problem because it is generically appealing to nearly everyone in trade. Not having to depend on the specific charms of its use value, like bread or beer must, money can be traded far more widely since it carries more generic exchange value instead. Those who take money in trade can be confident they will be able to trade it to someone else later on, since money is appealing to pretty much everyone.

This kind of function is described as an "etiological function" by Hindriks and Guala, and they note that those sorts of functions:

> are widely used for classificatory purposes. A particular *type* of institution is defined by the particular coordination or cooperation problem it solves. We illustrate this for the case of money. As compared to monetary economies, barter economies are notoriously inefficient. To the extent that an economy involves some division of labor, it faces the problem of the double coincidence of wants . . . [money solves this problem]. Thus, money confers considerable cooperative benefits on a society. One of its functions is to solve the problem of the double coincidence of wants. It does this by serving as a means of exchange.
>
> (2021: 2033)

Thus, in order to be money, this kind of functional view demands not only that it behave in a particular way, but that it also behaves that way for a particular reason. It is not enough to make something money simply for it to be used as a medium of exchange, it must also be used this way because doing so confers cooperative benefits and solves the problem of the double coincidence of wants.

J. P. Smit, Filip Buekens, and Stan du Plessis describe the existence of this problem in terms of incentives, and stress how it can explain the phenomenon of money without positing an extra ontological level, as Searle's account does. That ontological excess is their primary target, claiming "that Searle's theory, while ingenious, is wrong on all counts" (Smit et al. 2011: 1).

In particular, they "deny that institutional facts are irreducible" and provide an account that "explains the same facts, but without postulating a new ontological realm, and hence should be preferred" (Smit et al. 2011: 3–4). Where Searle thinks money is an instance of a group of agents collectively accepting it to be money in a given context, Smit et al. instead think that money exists whenever a particular subject is incentivized to treat it as money. Their formulation for all institutional objects, money included, is therefore "S is incentivized to act in manner Z toward X" (Smit et al. 2011: 5). An X counts as money on this view when someone (S) is incentivized to treat it as a medium of exchange (manner Z), rather than as valuable for consumption or some other reason.

Thus, something like mackerel tins can become money without any group of people collectively accepting them as Searle envisions. Instead, such a process:

> can start with some individual realizing that such tins are both generally popular and durable. This then leads the person to acquire them with the intention of

exchanging rather than consuming them. Other individuals, either independently, or by picking up the idea from others, then realise that the incentives operative in the local economy are such that they have good reason to act similarly. (Smit et al. 2014: 1827)

Crucially, this all comes about through "a series of individuals being incentivized to act in a certain way" and so can be explained in terms of actions and incentives of a group of individuals, without needing to appeal that group's collective agreement about anything (Smit et al. 2014: 1827).

In later work, Smit et al. propose a view of money on which it is, strictly speaking, a sophisticated mathematical object, but they describe the things we ordinarily point to and take to be money (bills, coins, etc.) as having a distinctive functional role, which is to serve as a medium of exchange. More precisely, they describe what we ordinarily think of as money as just whatever "is typically acquired in order to realise the reduction in transaction costs that accrues in virtue of such agents coordinating on acquiring the same thing when deciding what thing to acquire in order to exchange" (Smit et al. 2016: 330–1).

Smit et al. think something becomes money when a particular agent is incentivized to treat it as having exchange value. If one agent notices that the only other agent on the island is willing to trade for mackerel tins, this is to notice the incentive to treat mackerel tins as having exchange value, which is what is required to make them count as money. To be clear, it is the presence of these incentives, not the recognition of them that Smit et al. think is necessary for the mackerel tins to become money. The one agent was incentivized to treat the mackerel tins as having exchange value before the other agent noticed that she was. (How else could she notice?) But the more agents who notice and act on these incentives, the stronger they become. Widespread acceptance of something as money "is simply the end of a continuum that starts with a point where one person recognizes the existence of an incentive to act in a certain way" (Smit et al. 2014: 1828). But this acceptance is not what makes the money, it is the incentives instead that do. Smit et al.'s account allows people to create money without ever deliberately intending to and without ever really understanding that they have, since the processes and attitudes that create it need not be deliberate or transparent to the agents on whom the money depends.

Both Smit et al. and Hindriks and Guala present accounts of money on which it can be created unintentionally, without anyone thinking or talking about something as money, but only in response to a distinctive kind of problem. The problem of the double coincidence of wants is what generates the incentives that Smit et al. take to be constitutive of money, and so their view can be understood in largely the same way as Hindriks and Guala's. Both views require the existence of the same coordination problem in order to create money, so both views will also require a group of people large enough to generate this problem in order to create money. Therefore, to determine how many people are required to create money, we must determine how many people are required to generate the problem that defines it. So, how many people does it take to face the problem of the double coincidence of wants? It will depend on how we understand the contours of the problem, and different conceptions track a development across Smit et al.'s work.

If the problem occurs just whenever an agent has an incentive to gather and keep something for trade rather than consumption (as Smit et al. claim in their earlier work), then it can arise in systems as small as those with only two agents. Suppose I found myself on an isolated island with just one potential trading partner. Had I been alone on this island, I would have had no incentive to gather any of the coconuts on it, since I hate their texture (and assuming I had other things to eat). But if I have a potential trading partner on this island who loves coconuts and is willing to trade with me for them, I have thereby become incentivized to treat these coconuts as having exchange value, whether this fact consciously occurs to me or not. The mere presence of these incentives is enough to make the coconuts money on Smit et al.'s earlier view. And if all that is required is that an agent is incentivized to treat something as a medium of exchange, then this could occur between just two people, since incentives to exchange require at least one other trading partner, but not more than that.

But notice that in this system my trading partner might not have an incentive to also gather and keep coconuts to use as trade objects with me. Perhaps since I detest them so much, I would not accept them in trade and would be eager to rid myself of them in exchange for things I value more immediately as soon as I can. In this case, my trading partner would not be incentivized to treat coconuts as having exchange value when trying to appeal to me in trade, though they might be incentivized to treat something else that way. Suppose they were allergic to the mangoes I loved to eat, they would then have reason to treat mangoes as having exchange value, though I would not. In a system with only two agents, the problem of double coincidence of wants can be faced and solved without ever converging on the same thing as having exchange value.

This is not the case in any system with more than two agents, and it might seem wrong to think of the use of coconuts and mangoes in this two-agent system as the creation of money, rather than a kind of specialized barter. So, we might insist, as Smit et al. do in later work, that money requires convergence on "the same thing" to "realise the reduction in transaction costs" as part of the solution to a coordination problem (2016: 330–1). To be incentivized to treat something as having exchange value only requires one other person with whom you can exchange, but there is no pressure for both traders to converge on the same thing if each only has to worry about trading with one other partner. There, each could just keep a supply of what the other is willing to trade for. The pressure to coordinate and converge on the same thing can only begin to arise in a group of three, where there are inefficiencies and transaction costs in keeping exchange objects that appeal to each of your potential trading partners. Such a coordination problem can only arise when an agent has more than one potential partner to trade with, and these coordination problems are constitutive of what creates money on both Smit et al.'s later account and on Hindriks and Guala's as well.

Guala explicitly builds on the work of Smit et al. and presents an account that follows their later work in terms of how many people are required to get something to successfully function as money. Only when there are multiple potential trading partners is there pressure to converge on something appealing to all of them. Obviously, these pressures can intensify as the number of trading partners increases, but Guala explicitly allows them to exist in groups as small as three. In his chapter discussing money, Guala tells a simplified version of the commodity theory of money using only three agents (Alice, Bob, and Carol). They begin by producing meat, vegetables, and fruit, respectively, and end up converging on gold as a medium of exchange equally appealing to all of them (Guala 2016: 36–7). A group of three like this is the minimum size of a group where convergence on a single thing is the equilibrium solution to the coordination problem of the double coincidence of wants, since a system with two agents might be solved just by each gathering what the other one tends to desire, and those might well be different.

Should we therefore conclude that the smallest possible group that can create money is therefore three instead of two? No, and not because we should think that the problem of the double coincidence of wants can coherently be faced by groups as small as two. Instead, we should not be led to think that real money requires at least three people, because we should reject the idea that it can only arise in the context of a distinctive sort of problem. Of course, money can arise in response to the existing inefficiencies and other economic pressures, but that is no reason to think that it must always do so.

First of all, defining money as the solution to a specific problem will mean that it cannot arise where that problem is already solved. If money depends for its existence on being the solution to the problem of the double coincidence of wants, this will mean that when apparently new kinds of money or currency arise to replace the old, they cannot count as real money. In such cases, there is no problem of the double coincidence of wants for them to solve. This will bring the troubling conclusion that the only real monies are those that originally arose out of barter, and any that came after that are not money at all. This conclusion gets worse if, as Alexander X. Douglas (2015) and David Graeber (2012) argue, it turns out that as a matter of historical fact no money actually ever arose out of the inefficiencies of barter. This would mean that, contrary to appearances, our world contains no actual money at all.

Beyond this worry about making etiology part of the ontology of money, there is the further and deeper concern that it leaves out a distinctive feature of money, and that is our ability to create it at will. Passinsky calls this "creation by fiat" and takes it to be a defining feature of social objects in comparison with ordinary material objects. As she puts it, "under appropriate circumstances, social objects can apparently be created by acts of agreement, decree, declaration, or the like" (Passinsky 2020a: 439). This is something that cannot be done with ordinary material objects, but it can certainly be done with money. In the twentieth century, the United States, United Kingdom, and Canada all took their currencies off the gold standard, and so by decree changed what counted as money for political and economic reasons, not because the problem of the double coincidence of wants had not been solved.

What this indicates is that money can be created for many reasons and not only as the solution to a single, distinctive kind of problem. Whether the move off the gold standard was done for *good* reasons is a matter of considerable debate, but the new fiat currencies did not fail to be money, because the reasons they arose were in response to political and economic pressures beyond the simple inefficiencies of a barter economy.

This is not to say that function plays no role in the ontological requirements for money, but it is function in the sense of behavior, not in the sense of purpose. Since money can be created by fiat, it can be created for any number of reasons, not just as a response to a single kind of economic inefficiency. The problem with the jellybean money mentioned earlier was not that it was created on a whim in a context where the problem of the double coincidence of wants was already solved; it was that my wife and I decided that jellybeans were money but then never behaved in any way that treated them as such. Social objects unmoored from any behavioral constraints lead to absurdities like cocktail parties that act like wars but are still just cocktail parties. Function matters in creating money, but only in terms of the way the institution behaves, not in terms of the purpose for the institution, as Hindriks and Guala claim.

But this does not mean that money requires only a distinctive kind of behavior and nothing more. Insisting on that will also generate problems. As Sarah Vooys and I have argued, money involves a distinctive motivation, as well as a distinctive behavioral pattern. In order to distinguish barter transactions from monetary transactions, which could be behaviorally identical, they point to the "sake" for which the object is gathered or traded. Barter objects are traded for the sake of their use value, while monetary objects are traded for the sake of their exchange value, and consequently something can only count as money, according to Vooys and myself, when the party either giving or receiving it does so for the sake of its exchange value (Vooys & Dick 2021: 3448–9). An account that attempts to build money out of nothing more than behavior will not be able to distinguish money from barter, just as an account that builds it out of nothing more than attitudes will mistake a battle for a cocktail party. The correct account of the ontology of money, then, will be one that requires both attitudes of the right sort and behavioral patterns of the right kind.

Even without providing the complete and final account of what these attitudes and behaviors are, and what the balance between them must be, it still seems clear given all we know from work done in the ontology of money that they can be instantiated by groups of people no larger than two, since only two people are required to both accept and behave as if something is a medium of exchange, unit of account, and a store of value. Whenever at least two people have both these attitudes and behaviors, there is money. Whether this comes about by accidental coincidence or deliberate design, as the response to urgent economic pressures or just on the whims of these two agents, this is all that is needed to create real money.

4. Bitcoin and Bad Money

To answer our original motivating question, it takes just two people to make a dollar, since just two people are enough to instantiate the attitudes and exhibit the behaviors that money consists in. This will mean that Bitcoin is almost certainly real money, as are a great many other cryptocurrencies, since it is safe to assume that they have at least two people holding the attitudes and exhibiting the behaviors necessary to turn them into money. This is enough to make them money no less real than the US dollar, since the US dollar is money just because at least two people do the same thing for it. This might seem like a troubling conclusion for the view I am promoting here, because it flies in the face of both strong intuitions and recent scholarship. The intuition is the one that we began with, namely, that it is simply obvious that money must have a great many adherents in order to be real money. The scholarship focuses on Bitcoin specifically, but it can be applied to all cryptocurrencies or other candidate monies.

David Yermack (2013) concludes that Bitcoin is not a real currency, because, inter alia, it is not widely used as a medium of exchange and functioning as a medium of exchange is a condition for being a bona fide currency. Likewise, Smit et al. conclude that Bitcoin is not money, because it is not typically used as a medium of exchange. In their later work, they require both convergence on a single thing, and that the "typical" use of that thing be a medium of exchange (Smit et al. 2016: 330). Their statement on this is nuanced, however, and is worth quoting at length:

This question now becomes the question as to whether bitcoin is generally used as a medium of exchange, i.e., is mainly used in order to realise the reduction in transaction costs that arises in virtue of social coordination. The data is murky, but it is reasonably clear that the answer is no. At present, the vast majority of bitcoin is traded as a speculative investment, not as a means of lowering transaction costs. We could say that bitcoin may become money at some point, and we could say that bitcoin is already money among those who use it to transact. If asked, however, whether bitcoin as such is money at present, the least misleading thing to say is that it is not. (Smit et al. 2016: 333)

This passage neatly encapsulates two ways to approach the question of whether something is money or not, and it allows us to see that only one of these approaches is correct. When Yermack and Smit et al. consider the question of whether Bitcoin is money in terms of its "worldwide commercial" or "typical" use, they approach it from the wrong direction. The question of whether something is money is always the question of whether there is someone *for whom* it is money, and simply examining the sum total of all the uses of something obscures this matter. If the ontology of a social object must account for all the thoughts about and uses of it, then it will be extraordinarily difficult for anything to count as any particular social object, given all the thoughts and uses possible for any given thing. If this is what is required for an ontology of money, then perhaps not even gold counts as money, if it turns out that too much of it is filling teeth or being worn as jewelry instead of being used in exchange. Approaching the question in this way also obscures the fact that something only ever counts as money in some contexts and among some populations. Even the mighty US dollar is not accepted everywhere, and the currencies of small nations, like the Icelandic króna, can only be spent among a smallish group of people, but both are still money nevertheless. If, in order to be money, something must be accepted as money everywhere, then nothing can be money anywhere.

Smit et al. are aware of the other, correct way to approach this question, which is to ask if there are any groups of people who have turned this thing into money. That is how their own theory explains how the Americans have turned their dollar into money and how the Icelanders have turned their króna into money, and it is how their own theory can acknowledge that relative to some populations, Bitcoin and other cryptocurrencies are absolutely money. To their credit, they acknowledge this by saying "we could say that bitcoin is already money among those who use it to transact," but then go on to answer the more common, albeit mistaken version of the question as it is usually asked (Smit et al. 2016: 333).

Distinguishing these two different ways of approaching the question of whether Bitcoin or another small cryptocurrency can be money addresses the scholarship that rejects the idea that two people are enough to create money, but it may not unseat the nagging intuition that surely something must be wrong with a money accepted by only two people in comparison with a currency accepted by as many people as the US dollar is.

This intuition can be explained as a response to a failure relative to a normative standard rather than to an ontological requirement. A money accepted by only two people may be money as much as the US dollar is, but this does not entail that it is money equally as good as the US dollar is. A standard goal we might hope for in our money is for it to enable exchange with as many potential trading partners as possible. Relative to this standard, a money accepted by only two people is much worse money than one accepted by many millions.

This is not to say, however, that the best money is always the money with the widest scope of acceptance.[2] Just pragmatically, the fact that many millions of people accept the US dollar in trade is no help to you if you are in a country that does not include any of those people. A currency that is only acceptable in a small locality can be far preferable in some cases to a currency with a much wider scope of application, so supposing that the single normative standard for money is "widest acceptance" is a mistake.

Other philosophers have noted that there can also be moral and political reasons to prefer such limited currencies, beyond just immediate pragmatic ones. Nations might have good reasons for their currencies to have smaller scopes of application, and to not be usable beyond their national borders. This could permit them greater control of their national economies and shield them from volatility in the global economy. As Tobey Scharding (2019) argues, Johann Fichte saw such exclusively national currencies as morally necessary for a nation to fulfill its obligations to its citizens. Furthermore, advocates for even smaller local currencies that might only be usable inside a single city or town see them as ways to support initiatives that the outside economy would not, and to keep wealth from being removed from the local community (Hudon & Meyer 2019). It is therefore very plausible to think that there are many scenarios where having a smaller group of people recognize and use a currency is better than a larger one.

This is all to say that there can be a great many differences between a tiny cryptocurrency and a giant national currency like the US dollar, but as long as at least two people do what it takes to make them into money, these will be normative differences, not ontological ones.

We ought to be careful not to conjoin the ontological requirements for money with the various normative standards that we might apply to it. Yermack does this when he rejects Bitcoin as a currency because it fails to behave in the way a "successful currency typically functions" (2013: 9). But if something must line up to the normative standards we apply to money in order to count as money at all, then all money is good money, and the category of "bad money" becomes conceptually impossible. This commits us to both the ontological error of mis-classifying all bad money as no money at all, and to the normative limitation of not being able to criticize bad money. If bad money simply fails to be money, on what grounds can we insist it live up to the normative standards for money?

All the recent work in the ontology of money discussed here permits it to be created by very small groups of people, and this should be seen as a virtue of all these accounts, rather than as a drawback. This is because it allows each of them to

---

[2] See Dick (2020) for a detailed version of the argument that money should not be thought to be automatically governed by a single normative standard.

easily identify something that counts as money but that can nevertheless be criticized as bad money, relative to the normative standards we should apply to money. This is as it should be, since as the great chartalist G. F. Knapp observed almost one hundred years ago, "Money it must be, in order to be bad money" (1924: 1).

Acknowledgments

David G. Dick passed away suddenly in November of 2022 as he was completing his work on this chapter. The editors thank Erin Dick-Jensen for her kind permission to publish David's chapter posthumously. We publish it as an homage to a jovial colleague and a brilliant philosopher who made a distinctive contribution to the field.

References

Brynjarsdóttir, E. M. (2018). *The Reality of Money: The Metaphysics of Financial Value*. London: Rowman & Littlefield.

Dick, D. G. (2020). 'What Money Is and Ought to Be'. *Journal of Social Ontology*, 6(2), 293–313.

Douglas, A. X. (2015). *The Philosophy of Debt*. Abingdon, Oxon and New York: Routledge.

Graeber, D. (2012). *Debt: The First 5000 Years*. Brooklyn, NY: Melville House Publishing.

Guala, F. (2016). *Understanding Institutions: The Science and Philosophy of Living Together*. Princeton: Princeton University Press.

Hindriks, F., & F. Guala (2015). 'Institutions, Rules, and Equilibria: A Unified Theory'. *Journal of Institutional Economics*, 11(3), 459–80.

Hindriks, F., & F. Guala (2021). 'The Functions of Institutions: Etiology and Teleology'. *Synthese*, 198(3), 2027–43.

Knapp, G. F. (1924). *The State Theory of Money*. London: Macmillan.

Meyer, C., & M. Hudon (2019). 'Money and the Commons: An Investigation of Complementary Currencies and Their Ethical Implications'. *Journal of Business Ethics*, 160(1), 277–92.

Passinsky, A. (2020a). 'Social Objects, Response-Dependence, and Realism'. *Journal of the American Philosophical Association*, 6(4), 431–3.

Passinsky, A. (2020b). 'Should Bitcoin Be Classified as Money?'. *Journal of Social Ontology*, 6(2), 281–92.

Scharding, T. (2019). 'National Currency, World Currency, Cryptocurrency: A Fichtean Approach to the Ethics of Bitcoin'. *Business and Society Review*, 124(2), 219–38.

Searle, J. R. (1995). *The Construction of Social Reality*. Simon & Schuster.

Searle, J. R. (2005). 'What Is an Institution?'. *Journal of Institutional Economics*, *1*(1), 1–22.

Smit, J. P., F. Buekens, & S. Du Plessis (2011). 'What Is Money? An Alternative to Searle's Institutional Facts'. *Economics and Philosophy*, *27*(01), 1–22.

Smit, J. P., F. Buekens, & S. Du Plessis (2014). 'Developing the Incentivized Action View of Institutional Reality'. *Synthese*, *191*(8), 1813–30.

Smit, J. P., F. Buekens, & S. Du Plessis (2016). 'Cigarettes, Dollars and Bitcoins—An Essay on the Ontology of Money'. *Journal of Institutional Economics*, *12*(2), 327–47.

Vooys, S., & D. G. Dick (2021). 'Money and Mental Contents'. *Synthese*, *198*(4), 3443–58.

Yermack, D. (2013). 'Is Bitcoin a Real Currency? An economic appraisal' (Working Paper No. 19747). Retrieved from http://www.nber.org/papers/w19747.

4

Truth in Financial Accounting

Christopher J. Cowton

1. Introduction

During the twentieth century, the accounting profession and its associated practices grew increasingly prominent, as the provision of financial information became central to the organization of a wide range of activities. As Burchell et al. (1980, p. 6) remarked in an influential paper, accounting is no longer viewed as "a mere assembly of calculative routines," but "it now functions as a cohesive and influential mechanism for economic and social management."

However, with increased influence has come greater visibility, and recent decades have witnessed many episodes that have undermined confidence in accounting numbers and weakened trust in the processes by which they are generated and then verified by auditors. Some of those episodes—such as WorldCom, Tyco, and Enron (the failure of which led to the demise of one of the "Big Five" audit firms, Arthur Andersen) in the US, Parmalat in Italy, Olympus in Japan, and Carillion in the UK, to name just a few—became public "scandals," with politicians and regulators feeling impelled to address a crisis of confidence in a key aspect of the business world's operation.

The unexpected collapse of firms that had reported sound financial numbers, and the specter of many other firms "restating" previously reported results (usually downwards), fuel concerns about the accuracy of accounts. Terms such as "earnings manipulation," "creative accounting," "economical with the truth," "misrepresentation," "cheating," and even "fraudulent" are readily deployed in public debate. At the core of such criticisms lies the idea that the accounts were not telling "the truth." The commonsense intuition appears to be that financial reports should present the financial facts about things like firms' annual profits; accounts are supposed to reflect some selected portion of the world, and when they are subject to manipulation (or incompetence), they fail to be true. I take this kind of understanding to be widespread.

However, to anyone who understands how accounting operates, the idea that it is capable of simply reflecting economic reality is misleadingly naïve. Accounting numbers may appear factual after they have been presented, but the process of constructing them is contested and opaque, and accounting "facts" are "not as straightforward as they might seem" (Gill, 2009, p. 139). Yet, as Gill (2009) shows

Christopher J. Cowton, *Truth in Financial Accounting* In: *The Philosophy of Money and Finance*. Edited by: Joakim Sandberg and Lisa Warenski, Oxford University Press. © Oxford University Press 2024. DOI: 10.1093/oso/9780192898807.003.0005

in his study based on interviews with 20 young, male chartered accountants employed in the UK, accountants nevertheless tend to describe their work as if it were straightforward and technical, which "creates a discrepancy between their discourse and their practice" (p. 1). Thus they "bracket the question of truth out of everyday consideration" (p. 135).

In this chapter I will attempt to explore the relationship between truth and accounting. In doing so, I do not intend to defend a settled position on truth that satisfactorily resolves familiar debates on its nature. Nor is it my aim to debunk accounting as a worthwhile endeavor. Instead, I hope to offer the prospect of holding onto as much (of some form of) truth as possible without making any obvious category errors or highly contentious claims. The question is: In what sense or senses, if any, can accounting statements be said to be true?

I will pursue this agenda in three further sections. In section 2, I prepare the philosophical ground by saying some things about truth. This is a short section about a big subject. I present three broad accounts of truth, without seeking to adjudicate definitively between them or picking out some particular position within them. Instead, the hope is that a broad understanding of each will be sufficient to prove useful in my analysis of accounting in terms of truth. Section 3 then turns to accounting itself. This is not just an overview for readers who know little about the subject. Rather, I provide a description of conventional accounting to identify certain themes and issues that are pertinent to the consideration of accounting in terms of truth. Some of this discussion might be unfamiliar even to those with a working knowledge of accounting. In section 4, the characterization of accounting thus developed is related to the three views of truth outlined in section 2. By this stage in the argument, it is clear that a simple correspondence view, that figures such as profit pick out some feature of the world and can be judged true or untrue, will not do. Nevertheless, resonances between accounting and correspondence, coherentist and pragmatist accounts of truth can be found in aspects of accounting practice and thought, so we have at least some reason to resist the idea that "anything goes" with respect to financial accounting. Finally, section 5 presents concluding remarks.

2. On Truth

In this section I will provide three short sketches of accounts of truth that, individually, display a degree of family resemblance: correspondence theory, coherence theory, and pragmatist approaches to truth. The sketches are crude and no doubt do many injustices to individual philosophers (more extensive overviews can be found in David (2020), Glanzberg (2021), Horwich (1995), Lowe (2005), and Young (2018)), but hopefully they capture enough of the different views to open up a profitable exploration of the relationship between accounting and truth.

The commonsense intuition that the outputs of the accounting process should reflect the world as it is, independent of our accounting for it, accords with what Horwich (1995, p. 812) describes as "perhaps the most natural and widely held" account of truth, namely correspondence theory. According to this, a statement[1] is true if it successfully describes, or corresponds to, some aspect of the world. Correspondence "theory" might be viewed as a set of different accounts of truth that share a family resemblance in—metaphorically speaking—being concerned with "depicting" or "picturing" reality. Some of those strands are more convincing than others, perhaps because of their metaphysical underpinnings.

Much discussion of the correspondence theory of truth takes place in relation to general propositions about material things, often in the context of the philosophy of science—natural science, that is. This type of discussion does not always recognize that there are different sorts of statements that might, or might not, be capable of being true or false. It's one thing to make general statements (or propositions) about the movement of billiard balls, but it's another thing to make a statement about whether Billy has just potted the red ball; and it's still another to say that Belinda's billiard hall made a profit of £65,000 last financial year. Thus, even if there is merit in the correspondence theory of truth in the context of natural science, that does not necessarily mean that it sits comfortably with accounting statements as depictions of economic phenomena. After all, where can I find a profit and check that the number describing it is accurate or that the attribution of the number to describe the profit is true?

A prominent alternative, often motivated by the perceived difficulties of correspondence theory, is coherence theory. Broadly speaking, it identifies truth with verifiability, where a statement is verified when it stands in a suitably strong relation to, or "coheres" with, a wider set of statements. Coherence theory thus focuses on the relation of statements to one another rather than to the world. Different versions tend to turn on alternative accounts of that relation, but there would seem to be an opening for an application to accounting, given its systematic nature. The metaphor here might be the "dovetailing" of statements or numbers, rather than the "picturing" associated with correspondence theory.

However, for any system of statements that is not purely axiomatic but refers to the world in some way, it might be objected that coherence theory is problematically relativistic about truth. To make any sense—for anyone other than a thoroughgoing idealist—there would appear to be a need to "get things going" by some sort of connection to the world. If so, coherence does not appear to be a sufficient criterion for truth, and coherence theory does not succeed in stating

---

[1] It might be more common in discussions of truth to refer to "beliefs" or "propositions," but with my interest in accounting, I will keep things simple and refer to "statements."

what truth consists in. Coherence might be necessary—or at least strongly desirable—for a system of statements to be true, but for many, it still begs the question of how to assess the truth value of at least one statement.

Pragmatism offers a different approach by highlighting that true beliefs are a good basis for action. Knowledge is therefore considered instrumental; and, like other concepts, pragmatists understand truth in terms of practice. For a practical, information-providing endeavor such as accounting, this looks like a promising perspective. What is useful becomes the pragmatic criterion for judging truth. Although different pragmatists offer different accounts of what it means for knowledge to be useful, it cannot be something that simply suits the moment.

Critics note that, while actions based on true belief will tend to promote success, they do not always do so; and false beliefs may also produce good results. At its worst, such an account seems to have ends that trump truth-value. For critics of pragmatism, usefulness might be an attractive feature of truth, but it does not appear a sufficient criterion, nor does it succeed in providing a convincing account of what truth consists in. It is not even clear that it is necessary, except in a very general sense. Like coherentists, who select a prominent property of truth and consider it to be the essence, the same could be said of pragmatists. Then again, such criticisms sometimes seem to proceed from an assumption that there is something available to us in correspondence theory.

In concluding this very short overview, it must be acknowledged that what truth consists in, and what it means for a statement to be true, are issues that have exercised the time and talents of many philosophers, resulting in sophisticated arguments and nuanced positions. In contrast, I have offered highly simplified overviews of some of the principal philosophical accounts of truth. Nevertheless, I hope that these provide a sufficient basis for getting a discussion of truth and accounting going.

In keeping with this, I have focused on historically prominent, "substantive" theories of truth (Lowe, 2005; Young, 2018), rather than other accounts, such as deflationary theories, that seem to have less to offer in terms of understanding the practical endeavor that is accounting. Statements in accounting can be disquotationally true, so there is no special question about what truth in account-ing is on a deflationary theory of truth. Questions about objectivity remain; however, in this chapter, I explore these within my discussion of substantive theories of truth.

In suspending judgement on the three approaches that I describe, my account is implicitly pluralistic. However, while I am sympathetic to the notion that the plausibility of theories of truth varies across different domains, I am not offering a form of alethic pluralism, in which particular accounts of the truth property might align, say, with particular discourses (Pedersen et al., 2018). This means, inter alia, that readers can bring their own preferred understanding of truth to my analysis and accept, reject, or develop as appropriate the openings for truth that I offer.

An explanation of the essential features of accounting statements, sufficient to engage with the views of truth just sketched, is presented in the next section.

3. On Accounting

The history of accounting can be traced deep into antiquity (Edwards, 1989), where writing was early used to keep lists of things such as goods, money, and debts. The most sophisticated version for many centuries was the charge and discharge statement, often in the context of stewardship, where someone was "charged" with responsibility for the opening amount of some category of items and subsequent additions received, and then "discharged" that responsibility by means of legitimate outgoings and being in a position to surrender the closing balance. Cash might be the subject of a charge and discharge statement, but it might equally be some other property, such as head of cattle or even slaves (Cowton and O'Shaughnessy, 1991). In contrast, modern accounting statements, built on the foundation of double entry bookkeeping, use money as the unit of measurement.[2] Having money as the common denominator makes it possible to combine disparate items arithmetically.

3.1 Double Entry Bookkeeping

Although there is some debate regarding its origins and precursors, double entry bookkeeping became established (but not necessarily dominant) in the context of the merchant capitalism of the Italian city states of the Renaissance. Unlike earlier approaches to accounting, double entry provides an interlinked set of accounts, all expressed in monetary terms. A key characteristic is that every transaction affects at least two accounts, in such a way that the amount debited within the system equals the amount credited. For this reason, total debits must always equal total credits, which can be checked by extracting a "trial balance" from the books of account. If this does not balance, an error must have been made. Conversely, although a "balancing" trial balance might provide a degree of reassurance, it does not necessarily mean that the books are correct; for example, transactions might have been entered in the wrong accounts, or there could be compensating errors.

---

[2] Multiple international currencies bring practical challenges relating to "currency translation," particularly during an era of floating exchange rates. Inflation also creates challenges for the informativeness of traditional accounting, and various forms of "inflation accounting" (Whittington, 1983) have been proposed and sometimes implemented. Neither issue significantly affects the argument that will be developed.

3.2 Accruals Accounting, Costs, and Profit

One component of a double entry bookkeeping system is the profit and loss account, but the practice of calculating profit on a regular basis was comparatively rare until the growth of industrial capitalism. The requirement for companies to regularly disclose their financial performance and financial position became widely established during the twentieth century, and companies listed on major stock exchanges now publish lengthy annual reports, which contain vast amounts of information, as well as interim financial reports.

The profit and loss account or "income statement" (henceforth "profit and loss account"), which focuses on the company's revenues, expenses, and profit during a particular period, is a key component of corporate reporting. It is based on "accruals accounting" (explained below) and stands in contrast to the cash flow statement, which focuses more straightforwardly on cash inflow and outflows.

The other major financial statement is the balance sheet or "statement of financial position" (henceforth "balance sheet"), which summarizes the company's assets, liabilities, and shareholder equity at the financial year end. This is a statement at a point in time rather than a summary for a period. It is sometimes described as a financial "snapshot"—although that pictorial metaphor, while understandable, has some shortcomings, as we shall see. It is commonly thought that the balance sheet "values" the company, but this is misleading, as a simple comparison of the net asset value of a publicly listed company with its market capitalization will quickly show. Balance sheets provide information that might be useful in the valuation of companies, and in some respects they have been amended in the name of doing so better, but in the main they are simply a list of balances from the accounts—as their traditional name implies. Some resources that earn a company significant financial returns—such as its brands or reputation—will usually not appear on its balance sheet at all, and other company "assets" might be worth far more than the carrying figure shown in the accounts.

In drawing up the profit and loss account and the balance sheet, accountants engage in "accruals" accounting. This is why commonsense intuitions—such as that, when a company has made a large profit, it must have plenty of cash at its disposal—can be so wide of the mark. In accruals accounting, the financial impact of a transaction (and some other events) is recognized as it occurs; or, in the case of losses or liabilities, as they are anticipated.[3] This is often not when the associated cash flows take place. In this approach to accounting, there is a shift from a focus on cash "receipts and payments" to "income and expenditure." These may sound like synonymous terms, but they mean rather different things. I will

---

[3] This bias toward the recognition of losses and liabilities is the application of "prudence," which will be returned to later.

give some examples by way of elucidation. The first example is inventory (or stock), which we count as a cost when we use it, not when we buy it or pay for it.

Consider the following scenario. Retailer X purchases 100 units of some item for £10 each in cash during the current period. It sells 60 of them, at £25 each, giving revenue of £1,500. The cash surplus is £500 (£1,500 − £1,000). Now consider a second scenario, in which Retailer Y's sales are the same. However, this time the 100 units have been obtained by Retailer Y on credit, with the debt to the supplier, a trade creditor, still outstanding at the end of the accounting period. In this case the cash surplus is the whole £1,500 receipts, because there have been no cash outgoings—yet.

Comparing the two scenarios, Retailer Y's net cash flow is three times that of Retailer X, but it hasn't done any more business; the difference in cash flow is simply a reflection of delaying the settlement of the debt to the supplier. Even if a fine distinction could be made between their economic performance (I'm not sure it can), Retailer Y's success is not three times better than Retailer X's. Therefore, although it is often said in business that "cash is king" (alternatively gendered monarchs are available), net cash flow appears not to be a reliable way of judging performance. It is just one component, albeit an important one, not least because of the importance of liquidity to business survival.

To come to an overall assessment of performance, one needs to take account of how the two businesses have fared across the various dimensions—assets (including cash) and liabilities—during the period. In the first scenario, the cash surplus is only £500, but Retailer X is also now 40 units of inventory better off than it was at the beginning of the period, being the unsold (closing) inventory that is available to use during the next accounting period. If the inventory is valued at cost, which is usual, the overall surplus (profit) is £500 (cash increase) plus £400 (increase in inventory), or £900 in total. Undertaking the same exercise for Retailer Y works as follows: £1,500 (cash increase) plus £400 (increase in inventory) minus £1,000 (increase in trade creditors, a liability)—or £900 in total again. Thus, following a kind of "mental accounting," recognizing all the relevant changes between the opening and closing positions in the scenarios gives the same profit, in spite of the difference in cash flow. Although done quite intuitively here, this could be considered a "balance sheet" view of accounting, in which profit reflects the differences between opening and closing balance sheets. It is in line with what accruals accounting effectively does.

Having established, in an intuitive fashion, why it makes sense to move beyond just cash flow when evaluating business performance, the basics of the more conventional way of calculating profit can now be shown. This is quite simple. The sales revenue was £1,500 (60 units at £25 each) and the cost of those sales was £600 (note: 60 units at £10 each), giving the established profit of £900. The "matching" of inventory used, rather than purchased, to the relevant sales is the obverse of noticing the increase in unused inventory and is unaffected by whether the inventory has been paid for (cash outflow) or the invoice is still outstanding (increase in total trade creditors). In accruals accounting, supplies are counted as a cost when they are used, not when they are paid for or even when they are purchased.

Things get much more complicated in real life, of course. For example, in times of changing prices, the figures charged to the profit and loss account relative to those appearing on the balance sheet could be affected by different accounting methods that make different assumptions about the way that the inventory moves—for example FIFO (first in, first out), LIFO (last in, last out) or average cost. And in a manufacturing operation, raw materials and bought-in parts are worked on, which leads not only to the addition of labor cost to the figures for closing inventory and work in progress, but also to choices about how to allocate a share of overhead costs to those units (Tayles and Drury, 2020).

I will provide one further instructive example to demonstrate why it makes sense to go beyond cash flows when assessing business performance and what is involved when accruals accounting is undertaken. Imagine that you decide to start a taxi business (cf. Sterling and Thomas, 1979). You begin the business with £25,000 and purchase a vehicle with it. Suppose that, during the year, total fares minus costs, all in cash, amount to £20,000, which is therefore your closing cash balance. In overall cash terms, it looks like a significant setback; a year in the taxi business has brought about a net cash outflow of £5,000. Nevertheless, you persevere. Next year, trade is just the same—but this time the cash surplus is £20,000, because you haven't had to buy a car.

Of course, you might well have done some "mental accounting" before embarking on the second year of business. One form might have been to distinguish between ordinary ("operating") and special ("investment") cash flows before reacting to the first year's cash deficit (something similar happens in real cash flow statements published by companies). Another way of thinking about the situation is more like the treatment of inventory under the earlier retail scenarios. At the end of Year 1, you might console yourself that you are better off than you were at the beginning of the year, because you were "down" only £5,000 on cash, but you now have a motor vehicle that cost £25,000 and has plenty of years' use left in it. So far, so good: but you then realize that the car, with a good number of miles "on the clock," is no longer in mint condition. Similarly, your joy at the £20,000 operating cash flow made in Year 2 might be tempered by the recognition that your car has deteriorated further. This is a kind of non-cash cost, like using up last year's leftover inventory in the earlier retail scenarios.

Accruals accounting moves beyond the one-off cash outflow figure to "match" portions of the cost of the asset—the car—to the revenue it helps generate. This annual cost is called "depreciation." In capturing the intuition described in the previous paragraph, the profit and loss account thus gives a more rounded picture of the economic performance of the business. In turn, the balance sheet shows the depreciated figure for the asset, or its "net book value." This is not necessarily the value of the asset if it were to be sold or what it would cost to buy a replacement in the same condition.[4]

To calculate the annual depreciation charge, four things need to be determined:

(a) The cost of the asset: This might seem straightforward, but there is often more to getting an asset working productively than simply buying it. For example, expenses such as design fees or commissioning costs might be capitalized as well, though there is an element of judgment in this.

(b) The asset's forecast useful life: This will often be shorter than its technological life. Many pieces of equipment are expected to be replaced by cheaper alternatives or a later generation of technology while they still work. In practice, a decision is usually made to treat certain classes of asset in the same way.

(c) The asset's estimated salvage or terminal value at the end of its useful life: If the asset is simple scrapped this might be zero, or even negative if there are decommissioning costs. However, some assets are sold to third parties for significant sums while they are still working.

(d) The depreciation method which will be used to write off the net cost of the asset ((a) *minus* (c)) over its assumed life (b).

3.3 The Centrality of Judgment

The above list displays two types of judgment that accountants constantly face in implementing accruals accounting. The first is readily apparent in item (d): that accountants often need to choose between different methods of calculating their figures. In the case of depreciation, the "straight line method" is the most common method. It involves charging the same proportion of the original (net) cost of the asset for each year of its useful life. Annual reports therefore often refer to depreciating in "equal annual instalments." If the taxi were expected to be used for three years, then sold for £13,000, the annual profit in both Year 1 and Year 2 would be £16,000, after charging £4,000 depreciation [i.e. 1/3 x (£25,000 – £13,000)]. Also popular is the reducing or declining balance method, which involves charging a constant proportion, not of the net cost, but of the opening net book value (original cost less accumulated depreciation) each year. (For the taxi case, the figure is just under 25%.) It results in a relatively high depreciation charge in the early years, and much lower charges toward the end of the asset's useful life. One

---

[4] I should acknowledge that there are forms of financial reporting, which tend to be explored in times of inflation, that permit or mandate the substitution of more "realistic" valuations (on a variety of possible bases) for asset "book" numbers.

advantage of this method is that, for assets like motor vehicles, it tracks the way their second-hand value tends to decline—though the aim isn't actually to value them. However, if an asset's expected terminal value is zero or relatively small, only a very high rate will work, which has the effect of charging all or most of the depreciation in the first year—which misses the point of depreciation compared to using the cash figure.

Other depreciation methods exist, including double declining balance and sum of years' digits. The details of them need not concern us. The important point is that the choice of method affects the annual profile of profits of the business and the state of its balance sheet over the useful life of the asset; and identical businesses may have dissimilar annual accounting statements simply because of the choice of method. The world is the same, but the accounting numbers are different.

It should be noted that different choices of method and assumptions about the future usually result in "timing differences" rather than having a permanent impact on profit; a cost not recognized now will have to be put through the books at some point in the future. Nevertheless, this still leaves considerable scope for the practice of making the figures appear as you wish them to, sometimes referred to as "income smoothing." Furthermore, different firms set different thresholds for determining whether a putative asset is to be "capitalized" and depreciated or just treated as an expense for the period. This is a further source of "accounting" rather than "real" difference.

This issue is not limited to depreciation. We have already noted that different methods of inventory accounting are possible. Indeed, many aspects of accounting can be undertaken in different ways. For many decades, the published financial statements of UK companies were governed by an evolving legislative framework that specified an increasing number of things to be disclosed but left the methods of calculation of the numbers to the accountants. The overriding requirement was for the accounts to give a "true and fair view," which had little to do with the kinds of truth considered in this chapter. Instead, accountants seemed to work according to a loose set of conventions, which bore some similarity to the idea of Generally Accepted Accounting Principles (GAAP) in the US. Beginning in the late 1960s, public concern led to attempts to reduce the variety available to accountants, and many accounting/financial reporting standards have been issued since the 1970s by bodies such as the International Accounting Standards Board (IASB) and the Financial Accounting Standards Board (FASB); the primary purpose of the latter is "to establish and improve US GAAP." However, either because of options that remain within standards, or because certain areas have not been standardized, there is still considerable choice open to accountants in how they treat various items in the accounts. Part of the difficulty is deciding what interests or criteria to prioritize when standardizing to one method and hence ruling out others. Both the IASB and the FASB have long-running "conceptual framework" projects that are intended to "provide a structure for thinking about what is 'better' accounting and financial reporting" (Macve, 1981, p. 9).

Even if all areas of accruals accounting were standardized, a second important type of subjective judgment would still be required of accountants. Returning to what is needed to calculate depreciation: of the four things to be determined, two—the useful life and the net terminal value—involve predicting the future. Thus, in the example of your taxi business, the calculation of a depreciation charge requires a forecast of when you will cease to use the taxi and how much you will be able to realize from its sale at that time.

The need to predict, or make assumptions about, the future is explicit or implicit in many aspects of accounting for the past. Some of these are, in effect, a kind of counterfactual. For example, returning to inventory, it is usual, as in the earlier retail scenarios, to value it at cost. However, the standard rule is to carry inventory at the lower of cost and net realizable value. In other words, if it is believed that the inventory might not be sold for as much as was paid for it, the potential loss should be recognized and the transaction-based inventory figure replaced by an assumed future value. This is in accordance with accountants' convention of "prudence" or conservatism, which means that the threshold of confidence required for a revenue or asset to be recognized in the accounts is considerably higher than that for a cost or liability. This leads to a pessimistic bias rather than best estimate in profit figures, which might be problematic regarding notions of accuracy and hence truth. There is also the issue that this future hypothetical thinking might be applied differently by different accountants to identical circumstances and hence could result in different numbers. The most fundamental judgment of this kind is whether to account for the business as a "going concern." If the business became bankrupt or close to it, assets would be worth far less than the figures at which they are shown in the balance sheet and, per prudence, should be revalued accordingly. Two auditors might look at the same data regarding a company facing potential financial difficulties, and yet come to different judgments about whether assets now needed to be carried at liquidating value; and even if they were of the same mind on this issue, they might come to different judgments about what those (currently hypothetical) liquidating values might be.

4. Accounting and Truth

The chapter began with the observation that there is a widespread intuition that accounting numbers are veridical insofar as they describe or reflect some portion of the world and wrong or inaccurate insofar as they fail to do so. This intuition resonates with more general popular notions of truth that find expression in correspondence theory, which therefore seems a good starting point for considering how accounting numbers might be veridical.

However, the account of conventional accruals accounting in section 3 should have made it clear that accounting numbers do not pick out features of the world in some straightforward sense—if any. Even if correspondence theory possesses merit as, say, a view of propositions in natural science, it seems hard to make the case that the same is true of accounting statements. "Correspondence" looks like an inappropriate description of accounting numbers' relationship with the world. A comparison with another "applied," quantitative endeavor—engineering— should help to clarify the challenge for accounting.

Consider a civil engineer who accepts an assignment to assess the condition of a bridge. In addition to expert visual inspection, he will take various measurements to describe the condition of the bridge. Now, suppose that, for whatever reason, the clients have some concerns following submission of the report, which had concluded that all the measurements were within standard tolerances. They therefore decide to call in a second, independent engineer, who not only checks the first engineer's calculations but also visits the bridge to "see" for herself, making her own measurements in the process. The clients are presumably reassured if the second engineer's figures accord with those of the first, but not if they significantly fail to do so.

Contrast this with accounting, where different accountants can take the same underlying transactions data that have been recorded in the books of account and legitimately come up with very different profit figures, because of their different choices about how to account for particular items and through making different assumptions about the future. Similarly, while the auditors can provide an expert view of the draft accounts, a "clean" or "unqualified" audit report is compatible with a wide range of possible profit figures. The auditors can object to obviously wrong practices and express concern over dubious or "aggressive" techniques, but they cannot say that a given profit figure is "true" or "right" in the usual sense of the words.

The problem for accountants is that, when it comes to that key number, profit,[5] there is nothing "out there" for them to observe and then measure. Indeed, I would suggest that reference to "measuring" profit is inappropriate. Accountants do not measure profit; they calculate it. When measurement is held up by the profession as fundamental to accounting, such as being a key element of the IASB and FASB "conceptual frameworks," the misleading impression is given that "true" measurements are the likely outcome of "proper" accounting.

In calculating a profit figure, accountants are not so much reflecting the world as creating a picture of it from the raw material of transactions data. The term "creative accounting" is sometimes used as a euphemism for dishonest

---

[5] If you look at company accounts, you might see several different profit or income figures disclosed. This is to do with the costs have been taken off up to that point; various subtotals are presented. This is nothing to do with the way in which different accountants can calculate different profit figures and is not relevant to the argument here.

accounting. For example, the distinguished British journalist, Katharine Whitehorn, once remarked: "With 'creative accountancy,' who needs cheating?" However, there is a sense in which all accruals accounting is "creative." Accounting is not a mirror. It does not so much make *visible* as *make* visible (cf. Miller and O'Leary, 1987) and so constructs reality rather than reveals it (Hines, 1988).

This is an important milestone in the argument of the chapter, but there is a risk that this social construction card, once played, ceases to have any real purchase. For example, paper money is a classic example of social construction in action, possessing value only because people have agreed that this should be so. Our response, if this insight is new to us, might be to say, "Oh yes, so it is!" Parallels with M. Jourdain (in Molière's *Le Bourgeois gentilhomme*) learning that he has been speaking prose all his life without knowing it suggest themselves. But like M. Jourdain continuing to speak prose, we proceed to use money just as before. For everyday purposes, nothing significant seems to hang on the information that money is socially constructed (see Hacking (1999) for a robust perspective on the limits of social constructionism).

Accounting relies on this socially constructed thing called money to provide the units in which its statements are expressed. However, I would suggest that, in the case of accounting, something extra is going on. Accounting, as a set of techniques and procedures, is not just socially constructed, like money. Rather, its application constructs; it *creates* pictures of the world that are not tightly constrained by independently existing features of the world. It might be said to be constitutive rather than, *pace* mirrors, reflective.

Nevertheless, the conclusion should not be drawn from the social constructionist perspective on accounting—as it sometimes appears to be—that "anything goes."[6] It is still the case that accounting numbers depend, in some way, on how the world is. For the retail and taxi business examples outlined earlier, it is possible to calculate different legitimate profit figures, but not *any* total profit. The transactions data, which provide the raw material for accruals accounting calculations, provide some sort of world-relative constraint on the profit figures that can be produced. A silk purse cannot be made out of a sow's ear, and a billion pounds sterling profit can't be calculated for our one-person taxi business.

We are now also in a position to say something about a possible coherentist notion of accounting truth. It was implied in section 2 that some critics might be more sympathetic to something like coherence theory if there were some sort of connection to the world to help "get things going." Transactions data would appear to be a source of relation to the world that can get going a coherence

---

[6] The malleability of numbers is taken by some social constructionist scholars as enabling accountants to construct their truth just as they (or their masters) please (Rutherford, 2017). A well-known joke comes to mind. At a job interview, an interviewer asks, "What does two plus two equal?" Quick as a flash, back comes the reply, "What do you want it to equal?" The interviewee is immediately offered the role of chief accountant.

version of accounting truth that is not problematically relativistic. In this context, it is notable that Anscombe bases her 1958 paper "On Brute Facts" on an extended example in which she owes money to her grocer, who has delivered a quantity of potatoes to her home (Anscombe, 1958).

If there were some way of proceeding in a coherent, deterministic process from transactions data to a single profit figure, then that profit could be said to be "true and accurate" in the correspondence sense of truth. However, as we have already established, accounting calculations do not run along such tracks. Probably the best that can be said is that a given profit figure is not obviously wrong or unreasonable. This parallels an earlier point about the tightly integrated double entry bookkeeping system: an unbalanced trial balance reveals that there is a problem, but a balanced one is only necessary, not sufficient, for forming a belief that what is in the ledgers is accurate.

The preceding paragraph, like several others in this chapter, has referred to transactions data in the context of calculating profit. A focus on profit is not unreasonable, given its importance and prominence. It might be viewed as the accounting number *par excellence*. However, as a residual, it is affected by all the choices that have been made to account for the individual elements of cost and revenue (Gill, 2009). Therefore, it is especially sensitive to assumptions. For example, if the profit margin (profit as a proportion of revenue) were 10% and a change in accounting methods or assumptions were to increase total costs as a proportion of revenue by just five percentage points, the profit margin would halve. Recognizing this, one question might be: can we identify a meaningful degree of "world-relatingness" in accounting numbers other than profit?

Some clues to answering this question can be found in "events theory," which blossomed briefly in the academic accounting literature around 1970. Conscious of the way in which accountants took simple data arising from events (principally transactions) and processed them in contestable ways, events theorists were interested in the idea that accountants could do less processing and allow users of accounting data to do more (Sorter, 1969), in line with their needs and wants. Seeking to take this agenda forward, Johnson (1970) distinguished between three types of meaningful (i.e. not arbitrary) "summation" of accounting numbers: first, the simple addition or "aggregation" of the same characteristic of the same kind of "happening"; second, the addition or "combination" of numerous measurements of the same characteristics of different kinds of happenings; and, third, the addition or "composition" of numerous measurements of different characteristics of the same or different kinds of happenings.

Rather than pursuing the events theory agenda further here, the important point is that "compositions" tend to be the kind of "summations" that do not correspond to something in the world. On the other hand, "aggregations" do (or at least can). To give an example, if it is possible for Anscombe's debt to her grocer to be a brute fact, then it is possible for both the total of all her personal debts and the total of all the sums owed by creditors to the grocer to be factually true. Whether "combinations" could be said to be world-relating is less clear, but we may conclude from this brief excursion into events theory that there is more correspondence associated with some accruals accounting numbers than a broad argument or my earlier focus on profit might imply.

Finally, events theory can be seen as part of a wider "user" approach which supplanted much of the earlier discourse on accounting theory that focused on things like "principles" and, in its more extended versions, included terms such as "axioms" and "postulates" too. Although the conceptual frameworks of the IASB and FASB still contain material on what accounting *is* (or should be), there is a strong strand that is concerned with usefulness, or what accounting is *for*.

The appeal to usefulness has clear resonances with the underlying instrumental orientation of pragmatism; as mentioned in section 2, what is useful becomes the pragmatic criterion for judging truth. Perhaps pragmatism could therefore provide a suitable grounding for developing an account of what it might mean for financial reports to be true. Given that different pragmatists offer different accounts of what it means for knowledge to be useful, it would probably be necessary to pick a particular form of pragmatist thought. However, it would also require a clear view of what usefulness means in the context of accounting. Although there has been much thinking and writing on the user approach, by both policymakers and academics, I'm not sure we have that. I will provide the briefest of sketches here.

In accounting, usefulness is generally conceived of in terms of enabling users to make better decisions (Staubus, 1977). However, if usefulness is to be the overriding criterion, the questions arise: Which users? Which decisions? Perhaps the most systematic scheme for approaching these questions—at least in principle—was developed by Peter Bird (1975), who set out a procedure, in the form of a flow diagram, for identifying users, their objectives, their decisions, and the information inputs required to make those decisions. Given what we know from a variety of conceptual and empirical research, the outputs that would emerge from such a procedure would entail many incommensurable accountings rather than a single approach capable of yielding, for example, unambiguous profit figures. This was recognized by the events theorists, just discussed, who were keen for accountants to stop taking a one-size-fits-all approach.

Moreover, Bird's procedure is focused on determining relevant information, whereas relevance is just one characteristic (albeit perhaps the most important one) identified in a different tradition of thinking within the user approach, which seeks to identify the desirable attributes of accounting information. Others often found in lists of desirable attributes include, for example, reliability, objectivity, timeliness, and understandability—but, interestingly, not truth or accuracy. However, while such lists are not without merit, they are not conceptually robust, and they are limited in their capacity to determine how accounting should be undertaken.

Much more could be said about the user approach; the aim here has been to give just a flavor. Hopefully, though, this brief introduction not only confirms that there are signs of resonance with pragmatist accounts of truth, but also shows that employing the user approach to build a systematic account of accounting truth on such a foundation would be a challenging task.

5. Concluding Remarks

The question posed at the beginning of this chapter was: In what sense or senses, if any, can accounting statements be said to be true? To that end, in section 2, I sketched three historically prominent substantive approaches to truth. At the risk of doing a serious disservice to many detailed arguments and debates, I provided brief introductions to correspondence theory, coherence theory, and pragmatist approaches to truth. I tried to avoid making any particular commitments, but I suggested that correspondence theory seems to be reflected in the intuitions that are frequently displayed in public discussion of the perceived shortcomings of accounting practice.

In section 3, I presented a rather more detailed—though necessarily still constrained—account of the nature of accounting numbers. This should have been sufficient to demonstrate that figures like "profit" are not world-relating in a correspondence sense. Because of the possibility of treating similar items in different ways and the need to incorporate subjective assumptions about the future when accounting for the past, different accountants can legitimately come up with different profit figures. Although they might start with "brute facts" in the form of transactions data, they do not measure profit so much as calculate it. Financial accounting comes not to reflect reality but rather to construct it. Accountants might be said to *create* pictures rather than *take* snapshots.

Nevertheless, the notion of correspondence does have some resonance with what accountants do. Not only do transactions data describe aspects of the world and provide a limit to the profit figures that can be calculated, but certain summations of those data, less complex and subjective than others that end up in the residual profit figure, might also possess some world-relative content. Thus, while profit figures cannot be said to correspond to features of the world, there are some world-relative features of accounting that speak against the idea that "anything goes" in calculating the numbers found in financial reports.

It might have been expected that coherence theory would also resonate with accounting, given its calculative nature. As Rutherford (2017) suggests, it would certainly be better if researchers and policymakers could improve the coherence of accounting knowledge and systems.[7] However, the optionality open to accountants, even after significant standardization over the past five decades or so, means that the figures that are not obviously world-relative cannot be said to be "true" in

---

[7] Rutherford writes from a "neo-pragmatist" perspective, but his philosophical positioning would be seen as alethically pluralist in this chapter.

a strongly coherentist sense, even ignoring the impact of assumptions about the future—which is not possible with accruals accounting anyway. Nevertheless, there are features of accounting, such as the way debits and credits work in double entry bookkeeping, that have a coherentist quality and again speak against the idea that "anything goes" in calculating things like profit.

Part of the difficulty for accounting regulators, when it comes to a broader conception of coherence in accounting, is that it is difficult to impose uniformity of approach for its own sake when different techniques have their own rationales and champions. The establishment of "conceptual frameworks" to provide guidance has helped less than hoped. Nevertheless, it is interesting that they contain content, not only on the nature of accounting (e.g. reference to measurement, which I suggest is largely misguided), but also on how accounting might be useful. The notion of usefulness resonates with a pragmatist view of truth, albeit one that is difficult to work through convincingly in a manner that would be acceptable to all parties. Nevertheless, from a pragmatist perspective, it is an interesting turn that accounting has taken, to move away from the traditional focus on "good" accounting in abstract to "good" accounting in its effects.

In conclusion, accounting numbers such as profit cannot be true in the sense of correspondence theory, but resonances with correspondence, coherentist and pragmatist accounts of truth can be found in aspects of accounting practice and thought. It seems that accounting might have different forms of truth-aptness, even if none is capable of providing all that might be hoped for.

Future work might build on this by exploring the links in greater detail, perhaps by working with particular correspondence theories, coherence theories or pragmatist accounts. Such a suggestion is implicitly pluralist; and it follows that particular accounts of alethic pluralism might also be usefully explored in relation to accounting, following some of the lines mentioned in this chapter. In making this suggestion, I finish with an observation. In pluralist accounts, it is common to argue that the truth property varies across domains or discourses. However, in the case of accounting, which would generally be regarded as a single domain of discourse, resonances with more than one version of the truth property seem to be in play.

References

Anscombe, G. (1958). On Brute Facts. *Analysis*, 18(4), pp. 69–72.

Bird, P. (1975). Objectives and Methods of Financial Reporting: A Generalised Search Procedure. *Accounting and Business Research*, 5(19), pp. 162–167.

Burchell, S., Clubb, C., Hopwood, A., Hughes, J., and Nahapiet, J. (1980). The Roles of Accounting in Organizations and Society. *Accounting, Organizations and Society*, 5(1), pp. 5–27.

Cowton, C. and O'Shaughnessy, A. (1991). Absentee Control of Sugar Plantations in the British West Indies. *Accounting and Business Research*, 85, pp. 33–45.

David, M. (2020). The Correspondence Theory of Truth. In: E. Zalta, ed., Winter 2020 ed. *The Stanford Encyclopedia of Philosophy*. Available at: https://plato.stanford.edu/archives/win2020/entries/truth-correspondence/ (accessed June 20, 2021).

Edwards, J. (1989). *A History of Financial Accounting*. London: Routledge.

Gill, M. (2009). *Accountants' Truth: Knowledge and Ethics in the Financial World*. Oxford: Oxford University Press.

Glanzberg, M. (2021). Truth. In: E. Zalta, ed., Summer 2021 ed. *The Stanford Encyclopedia of Philosophy*. Available at: https://plato.stanford.edu/archives/sum2021/entries/truth/ (accessed June 20, 2021).

Hacking, I. (1999). *The Social Construction of What?* Cambridge, MA: Harvard University Press.

Hines, R. (1988). Financial Accounting: In Communicating Reality, We Construct Reality. *Accounting, Organizations and Society*, 13(3), pp. 251–261.

Horwich, P. (1995). Truth. In: R. Audi, ed., *The Cambridge Dictionary of Philosophy*. Cambridge: Cambridge University Press, pp. 812–813.

Johnson, O. (1970). Toward an "Events" Theory of Accounting. *Accounting Review*, 45(4), pp. 641–653.

Lowe, E. (2005). Truth. In: T. Honderich, ed., *The Oxford Companion to Philosophy*, 2nd ed. New York: Oxford University Press, pp. 926–927.

Macve, R. (1981). *A Conceptual Framework for Financial Accounting and Reporting: The Possibilities for an Agreed Structure*. London: Institute of Chartered Accountants in England and Wales.

Miller, P. and O'Leary, T. (1987). Accounting and the Construction of the Governable Person. *Accounting, Organizations and Society*, 12(3), pp. 235–265.

Pedersen, N., Linding, J. and Wright, C. (2018). Pluralist Theories of Truth. In: E. Zalta, ed., Winter 2018 ed. *The Stanford Encyclopedia of Philosophy*. Available at https://plato.stanford.edu/archives/win2018/entries/truth-pluralist/ (accessed April 10, 2022).

Rutherford, B. (2017). New Pragmatism and Accountants' Truth. *Philosophy of Management*, 16(2), pp. 93–116.

Sorter, G. (1969). An "Events" Approach to Basic Accounting Theory. *Accounting Review*, 44(1), pp. 12–19.

Staubus, G. (1977). *Making Accounting Decisions*. Houston, TX: Scholars Book Co.

Sterling, R. and Thomas, A., ed. (1979). *Accounting for a Simplified Firm Owning Depreciable Assets*. Houston, TX: Scholars Book Co.

Tayles, M. and Drury, C. (2020). *Management and Cost Accounting*, 11th ed. Boston, MA: Cengage.

Whittington, G. (1983). *Inflation Accounting: An Introduction to the Debate.* Cambridge: Cambridge University Press.

Young, J. (2018). The Coherence Theory of Truth. In: E. Zalta, ed., Fall 2018 ed. *The Stanford Encyclopedia of Philosophy.* Available at: https://plato.stanford.edu/arch ives/fall2018/entries/truth-coherence/ (accessed June 20, 2021).

PART II
EPISTEMOLOGY

5

Are Financial Markets Epistemically Efficient?

Lisa Herzog

1. Introduction

In many democratic societies, citizens receive financial market updates in the main news programs, day in, day out. Businesses make decisions in anticipation of the impact on stock prices, and politicians are evaluated, at least in part, according to how financial markets develop while they are in office (see also Kay 2015, 4, 248–50). But what justifies these practices? What is it that financial markets can tell the democratic public? The assumption seems to be that they provide a kind of real-time assessment of the economy, which incorporates all relevant news, the moment they are released, and anticipates future developments. But there are numerous instances in which this assumption seems difficult to justify. The latest one was the rally of the US stock markets in 2020, when the Covid 19 pandemic had led to a dramatic rise in unemployment and there were good reasons to expect a recession (see also Schlingemann & Stulz 2020, 1).

Economic doctrine has provided a theoretical justification for treating financial markets as assessment tools for the real economy and its developments. The core idea is that asset price developments tell us something about economic fundamentals because they contain information about current and future profits, adjusted by estimations about risks. It is an old argument in favor of markets that they facilitate the "use of knowledge in society," as F. A. Hayek had famously put it (Hayek 1945).[1] A version of this argument that applies to financial markets is the "Efficient Market Hypothesis" (Fama 1970). It summarizes the idea that asset prices incorporate all publicly available knowledge about future risk-adjusted income streams, and we can therefore interpret them as telling us something about where the economic system is going.[2] If true, the efficient market hypothesis

---

[1] On the history of the information argument in favor of markets, see, e.g. Heath 2014, 219–24. See also recently Boldyrev 2021 on the role of how uncertainty was incorporated in the relevant models.

[2] To be sure, this is not the only function of the Efficient Market Hypothesis. Another one is to provide a benchmark for evaluating the work of fund managers: do they do better than the market as a whole? For reasons of space, I here cannot discuss this point in detail; on "passive investment," see fn. 10 below.

Lisa Herzog, *Are Financial Markets Epistemically Efficient?* In: *The Philosophy of Money and Finance*. Edited by: Joakim Sandberg and Lisa Warenski, Oxford University Press. © Oxford University Press 2024.
DOI: 10.1093/oso/9780192898807.003.0006

justifies the epistemic role of financial markets that is ascribed to them in many societies. Arguably, it has contributed to the general narrative about the benefits of finance that has been predominant in recent decades, especially in the years before the Great Financial Crisis (see, e.g. Turner 2016, 37). But this hypothesis, and the underlying picture of financial markets, have always been controversial. Heterodox economists, but also economic sociologists and practitioners, have provided insights that lead to a very different account of what happens in financial markets.

In this chapter, I discuss how to think about this epistemic feature of financial markets:[3] their alleged ability to "mirror" the real economy and its future developments (although the metaphor of a "mirror" is in fact limited, because it suggests a focus on the present and thus does not capture the anticipatory capacity ascribed to financial markets). I use the term "epistemic efficiency" to describe the idea that a system (here, financial markets) represents the properties of another system (here, the real economy) with two conditions in place: (1) it represents those properties of the object that are most central for our epistemic needs, and (2) these properties are represented accurately, i.e. without systematic distortions.[4] The epistemic need in question is to understand where the economic system as a whole is going, and the representation that is suggested as offering insights about this are trends in financial markets. To be sure, expecting a *completely* undistorted picture from any representation is a mere logical possibility. But for the sake of my argument, it is nonetheless possible to work with this notion of epistemic efficiency because, as I hope to make clear, there are so many distortions that even a rough idea of what financial markets *without* these distortions would look like is sufficient as benchmark.

I draw on research from critical political economy, economic sociology, and behavioral economics inspired by evolutionary biology, to integrate their insights into the philosophical discussion about financial markets. On this basis, I argue against a picture according to which financial markets would be *automatically* epistemically efficient, because all epistemic inefficiencies would be removed by savvy arbitrageurs. Instead, epistemic efficiency should be understood as a principle (one among others) for the *design and regulation* of financial markets. Thus, I suggest turning the argument about the nexus of markets and knowledge on its head: instead of assuming that *in order* to process knowledge efficiently, financial

---

[3] My arguments apply most directly to stock markets, but of course in modern financial systems, other markets (e.g. those for bonds) are directly connected to them, while credit markets are related to them through securitization.

[4] Another topic that one could treat under the theme of "epistemology" and "markets" are prediction markets (for accounts, see, e.g. Wolfers and Zitzewitz 2004, Sunstein 2006, Arrow et al. 2008; from the perspective of epistemology, see Bragues 2009, Landemore 2013, 173–84, or Servan-Schreiber 2018). For reasons of space, I will not discuss these here; an interesting parallel, however, is that the design and regulation of prediction markets are crucial for them to function well, epistemically speaking—a claim that I defend, in parallel, about financial markets.

markets should be deregulated as much as possible, we should ask *which regulation is needed* in order to achieve epistemic efficiency, or at least to prevent the greatest obstacles to epistemic efficiency.[5] However, this is not a matter of "more" or "less" regulation, but rather one about *how* the regulatory framework assigns rights and responsibilities, and what incentives this in turn creates for market participants.[6]

I complement this argument by reflections about the relation between some broader features of an economic system and the epistemic efficiency of financial markets. If there are epistemic distortions in *other* parts of the economy, financial markets will reflect these—so condition (2) would be fulfilled, but condition (1) would fail, because these distortions distract attention away from the most salient features. Some of reasons for why financial markets as we currently see them are no good indicators of where "the economy" is doing are issues located outside of the financial realm. To illustrate this point, I contrast the current situation with a hypothetical situation in which some proposals for improving economic and ecological justice would be realized. Doing so makes clear why we should not be surprised that stock markets rallied in summer 2020, despite a global pandemic, prospects of a global recession, and the ongoing climate crisis.

Thus, I am writing against the assumption—widespread in many capitalist countries and underlying practices such as the constant broadcasting of financial market trends in the news—that financial markets, as we currently see them, should be understood as a heuristic for understanding how the "real economy" develops. As the sociological literature on "financialization" (see Carruthers 2015 for an overview) shows, in many societies financial markets have gained ever more importance in recent years. This trend had, for a long time, been supported by academic economists: Large parts of the economic profession were convinced that ever more "financial deepening," as it was called, would lead to ever more efficient allocations of assets and risks (Turner 2016, chap. 1). And the more the financial system expands and the more risks from the real economy are expressed in asset prices, the more financial markets reflect where the real economy is going, or so this argument ran. But if the assumptions on which the "efficient market hypothesis" is based do not hold, it is not at all clear whether "financial deepening" is always beneficial, epistemically or otherwise (see also Turner 2016, 46).

I hasten to add that this is a very "non-ideal" approach: it starts from a rather dire "here and now." I remain agnostic on the question of whether an ideally just society would contain financial markets at all. But it seems unlikely that we will get to such a world very soon—and as long as we *do* have financial markets, it is better

---

[5] I have provided a similar argument with regard to global markets for goods in Herzog 2020; see also Herzog 2023, chap. VII.

[6] For reasons of space, I will not discuss the regulation of monetary institutions and banks. See, e.g. recently Dietsch 2021 for reflections from a perspective of justice.

to have epistemically efficient than inefficient ones. Ultimately, the justification of their existence is that they are instruments that serve to allocate scarce capital— and as such, they need to be calibrated to correspond to societal values, reflecting what matters about the development of the real economy, and doing so without systematic biases.

It is worth noting, however, that at least one strand of liberal–egalitarian theorizing does seem to think that a perfectly just society would contain financial markets, even though I am not aware of any explicit discussion.[7] "Property-owning democracy" is a proposal for a just society in which the ownership of the means of production is dispersed widely among all members of society (e.g. Thomas 2017). It seems at least possible that such a society would contain financial markets. For those who hold this vision, it should therefore also be of interest for "ideal theory" how to think about the epistemic efficiency—together with other normatively desirable features—of financial markets.

The structure of the chapter is as follows. I start by contrasting different views of financial markets: the one suggested by mainstream economics, which imply automatic epistemic efficiency through arbitrage, and the one suggested by heterodox economists and economic sociologists, who describe various reasons for skepticism, concluding with a brief account of the new synthesis that is emerging under the label of "adaptive markets" (Lo 2012, 2019). I then discuss how regulatory measures that minimize behavior driven by emotions, reduce the blind reliance on metrics, and prevent conflicts of interest, could improve the epistemic efficiency of financial markets by reining in some sources of systematic distortion (speaking to condition (2)). This is followed by some reflections on how changes in other part of the economy system could help align financial markets with epistemic aims that are worth pursuing from a broader societal perspective (speaking to condition (1)). I conclude with some brief notes on how the picture of epistemically efficient financial markets that emerges from these reflections connects to other desirable features of financial markets.

2. Different Views of Financial Markets

In markets as neoclassical economics imagines them, fully rational agents trade with each other in order to realize win–win situations, which leads to Pareto-efficient outcomes (as expressed, for example, in the general equilibrium model, Walras 1870; Arrow & Debreu 1954). In markets for goods and services— mediated by money—individuals create win–win situations because they have different preferences, and trading helps exploit all possible opportunities for

---

[7] Some discussions about market socialism point in that direction, see, e.g. Roemer 1994.

improved allocations. In financial markets, the reason for why individuals trade is slightly different: the point is not so much that different individuals *prefer* to hold, say, Walmart or Volkswagen shares. Rather, they hold different *assumptions* about the future income streams and risk profiles of these assets (see also Kay 2015, 60, 64–5). But the basic idea that trading eliminates inefficient allocations has been applied here as well: if all opportunities for trading are used, no market participant can improve their position without another one worsening their position, i.e. Pareto efficiency is reached.

The key notion here is arbitrage: traders can make profits if there are opportunities for eliminating inefficiencies, which can arise because certain pieces of information have not yet been incorporated into market prices. If one assumes that there are rational arbitrageurs in markets, then assets with the same risk-and-return profiles must be traded at the same price. This is the key assumption that underlies many influential models of financial markets (see MacKenzie 2006 for an account of their historical development). For my purposes, the central one among them is "Efficient Market Hypothesis."[8] It holds that financial markets incorporate all available information and adapt prices accordingly. Therefore, "prices always 'fully reflect' available information" (Fama 1970, 383). For example, if news break about a slowing down of the demand for cars, this shows immediately in a drop in the stock prices of car companies.

The status of the "efficient market hypothesis" is notoriously contested (on the historical origins, see, e.g. Lo 2019, chap. 1; for critical discussions, see, e.g. MacKenzie 2006, 29–30, 65–6; Kay 2015, 68–70). Various attempts to empirically test it (or to test models based on similar assumptions) have tended toward its rejection as a *general* description for financial markets (for a survey, see, e.g. Lim & Brooks 2010). The empirical work here runs into complicated methodological problems (MacKenzie 2006, 89–94). But even if certain financial markets, especially more developed ones (Jiang et al. 2019, 72–4), are weakly Fama efficient over certain periods of time, in the sense that past price patterns cannot be used to explain current price movements, this, as such, is a rather weak statement. Logically speaking, the *negative* statement that one cannot beat the market on the basis of past data does not entail the *positive* statement that this is the case because prices incorporate all relevant information about the risk-adjusted returns of the traded assets. Moreover, one can imagine differently designed financial markets that are all close to weak Fama efficiency, but would achieve different degrees of efficiency concerning the use of societal resources or other goals.[9]

---

[8] It comes in different versions (weak, medium, and strong), which have been summarized in Fama's famous 1970 paper. For reasons of space, I bracket all questions about insider trading, or indeed other forms of rogue trading (e.g. Ponzi schemes), that might also affect the epistemic efficiency of financial markets.

[9] I thank an anonymous reviewer for pushing me to acknowledge this point.

One might respond that the "efficient market hypothesis" should be understood as a kind of ideal type, which reality approaches to a greater or lesser extent in different markets, and at different points in time (Lo 2012, 18). But it is this model that reality needs to approximate for the idea of financial markets as "mirrors" of developments in the real economy to make sense. If this were true, however, a paradox arises: no (risk-adjusted) profits could ever be made by trading, because financial markets would always already be efficient, and the most profitable strategy would be to simply follow the market as a whole.[10] But this cannot be true: *someone* has to do the trading that incorporates new information into market prices. There is thus a "logical contradiction" here, as John Kay puts it: "If all information were already in the price, what incentive would there be to gather such information in the first place?" (2015, 70; see also Grossman & Stiglitz 1980; for a discussion, see also Lomansky 2011, 150–1). And as a matter of fact, trading does happen, and some traders make profits, sometimes spectacular ones.

In the very act of trading, however, agents in financial markets use models— often the very models that economists had developed to *describe* financial markets—in order to grasp the realities that they are dealing with. Human beings have limited cognitive capacities, so they standardly use heuristics and mental shortcuts, including models that they know not to be fully adequate (see also MacKenzie 2006, 265; Graham et al. 2006, 5).[11] As Donald MacKenzie describes in a fascinating study, theoretical models, especially for option pricing, in fact helped to create the very markets in which they would be applied (MacKenzie 2006, esp. chaps. 5 and 6). The complexity of today's financial markets, with their many forms of derivatives and artificially constructed assets, would have been unthinkable without the theoretical tools provided by modern portfolio theory (and the power of modern computing). As MacKenzie puts it: "Financial economics . . . was an "engine" . . . an active force transforming its environment, not a camera passively recording it" (2006, 12).

In other words, there can be performative effects in financial markets, in the sense that economic theories affect the very phenomena they describe. Sometimes, they create the conditions under which the assumptions of a model hold, but sometimes they can also undermine them, so that the conditions that have been modelled disappear over time (MacKenzie 2006, chaps. 1 and 9). Such performativity is hard to incorporate into mainstream models; it has its roots in the fact that

---

[10] Indeed, in recent years one of the big trends in investing has been the rise of passive investment: investment vehicles that are tied to market indexes, without any active trading (e.g. Kay 2015, 201–3; MacKenzie 2006, 30). From the point of view of the epistemic efficiency of markets, it is a parasitic strategy: it leaves the work of checking the fundamentals to other traders.

[11] On the pre-history of such models and the role of Gaussian assumptions, see also Walter 2001. Bronk (2011) discusses what is problematic about the assumption of the knowability (at least in probabilistic terms) of the future.

human beings, in contrast, to, say, physical particles, can understand theories about their own behavior and change it in reaction to them (Taylor 1985).

In fact, the performativity of financial markets is not just an internal matter. The fact that financial markets are taken to be indicative of the success of companies also has an effect on the latter. For example, as Graham et al. (2006) show in a study based on a survey and interviews with financial executives, companies regularly massage their numbers, sometimes even sacrificing economic value, in order to deliver a smooth earnings curve, which is what stock markets like best. Earnings per share are the key indicator that traders in financial markets pay attention to (Graham et al. 2006, 2), which is why 78% of the executives in the survey were willing to "destroy economic value in exchange for smooth earnings" (Graham et al. 2006, 12). This can happen by lowering discretionary spending in areas such as research and development, or by delaying projects (Graham et al. 2006, 8; on the problems of short-term pressures on companies, see also Kay 2015, 109–10). The pressure to reduce what stock markets would perceive as excessive volatility of earnings leads to decisions that are otherwise economically irrational. However, from the perspective of a CFO who has to report to a board that anxiously watches share price developments, such a decision is not irrational at all.[12]

This pattern—apparently irrational behavior that is rational from the perspective of a specific social position—can be found at many points in financial markets. They are, after all, inhabited by real human beings in institutional and social settings. What we call "financial markets" are complex socio-technological arrangements. In a study based on extended ethnographic fieldwork and interviews, Diane-Laure Arjaliès and her co-authors describe these as the "chains" of intermediation, which "'sit between' savers and companies/governments" (2017, 1). The elements of this chain include financial advisers, pension and other funds, investment management firms, investment banks and other brokers, and "the market"; all of them are also influenced by raters, consultants, analysts, and legal regulators (2017, chaps. 1 and 2). As the metaphor of a "chain" implies, these social structures have both enabling and constraining features (2017, 14–15). They make complex interactions possible, but they also limit the influence of investors—and, at every step, money is siphoned off through fees or commissions (2017, 2–3, 11–12).

Another phenomenon, which also underlies the smoothing of earnings mentioned above, is the use of metrics to simplify complex decision-making processes. This can give rise to "Campbell's law" problems: situations in which individuals try to manipulate the metrics or the reality that underlies them, in order to achieve better-looking results (Campbell 1976). Or it can lead to constellations in which

---

[12] For a more general critique of the "hollowing out" of firms as a result of financial market pressures, see also Baker et al. 2020.

individuals blindly rely on metrics, often "because everyone does that," instead of doing their epistemic due diligence, checking the relevant fundamentals themselves. The most notorious instantiation of misguided reliance on metrics, in recent years, has been the role of rating agencies in the build-up of the 2008 financial crisis. After having built up a reputation as reliable raters of "plain vanilla" shares, in a period in which they faced hardly any conflicts of interest, rating agencies could use this reputation for continuously attracting clients. They falsely rated many complex derivative assets as being low risk, in constellations that often *did* contain conflicts of interests. But given their past reputation, and also government regulation that incorporated mandatory reliance on rating agencies, many traders relied blindly on these evaluations (Akerlof & Shiller 2016, chap. 2, for a discussion, see, e.g. de Bruin 2017).

There are also other ways in which these layers of intermediation can create epistemic distortion. One problem is that fund managers have incentives to trade "too much," focusing on short-term price movements and collecting fees for it (Arjaliès et al. 2017, 67–8; Kay 2015, 205–7). If these trades cancel out, as white noise, they might not be too epistemically harmful (although they are arguably unfair to investors who must pay higher fees). But in their trades, these intermediaries—and also investors who trade directly—often do not only look at the underlying assets. Instead, they look to each other, as it were, in ways that introduce a high degree of self-referentiality into financial markets. Intermediaries often see each other's behavior as benchmarks for what counts successful or unsuccessful strategy (Arjaliès et al. 2017, 54–6, 61, 67, 132–4, 165–6). Their career prospects might be tied to industry benchmarks (Arjaliès et al. 2017, 17–18), and they might be influenced by narratives that are shared along the investment chain (Arjaliès et al. 2017, 89–90, see also Kay 2015, 71).[13]

This self-referential nature of financial markets has been aptly described as the logic of a "beauty contest" by John Maynard Keynes: a contest in which one is supposed to guess who the most beautiful person is, and the latter is determined by who gets most votes. Therefore, it matters what the other participants think—not what a "true" judgment would be (Keynes 1936, 156; see Kay 2015, 1–3, 73, 87, 97 for discussions). Kay, one of the most outspoken critics of this feature of today's financial system, puts it sharply: "The industry mostly trades with itself, talks to itself and judges itself by reference to performance criteria that it has itself generated" (2015, 5). His main reason for complaint is that the financial industry thereby fails to serve the needs of other industries and of society as a whole, but of

---

[13] An interesting example, which Linsi & Schaffner (2019) have analyzed, is the use of heuristics such as the "BRIC" concept (for countries that are seen as promising for investors). As they show, while foreign direct investment was not influenced by the introduction of this concept (presumably because these investors were more interested in investigating the fundamentals), short-term portfolio equity investments were massively influenced by it (presumably because the managers of these funds had incentives to "go with the crowd" when BRICs became fashionable).

course, there is also a loss of epistemic efficiency. The "beauty contest" logic explains why there can be booms and busts that may be completely disconnected from underlying developments in the real economy, or at least massively exaggerate them (see also Kindleberger 1978).[14] Keynes (1936, 161) had also described the "animal spirits," the highly contagious psychological afflictions that can hold financial markets in their grip in such periods. But even if a trader is not affected by them, it can be *individually* rational to "go with the market," as long as one thinks one can get out of the market before the tide turns.

These various considerations show that real financial markets are at quite some distance from the smooth models of the rational-choice approach: they are populated by real, socially embedded agents who are not always fully rational; they are highly mediated; and they are influenced by (or sometimes indeed only came about by help of) the very theories that economists have developed about them. The lack of "rationality" in real instantiations of financial markets is not only—and maybe not even in the first instance—a matter of individual lack of rationality (as rooted in individual psychology, and as explored by behavioral economics), but also of the complex forms of social embeddedness and the incentives that socially situated individuals face.

In recent years, a new approach has attempted to synthesize the insights from mainstream and behavioral economics: the "adaptive markets hypothesis," developed by Andrew Lo and his collaborators (Lo 2012, 2019). Taking inspiration from evolutionary biology, Lo suggests seeing markets as biological systems in which individuals adapt their behavior to changing circumstances. However, evolutionarily hard-wired traits, e.g. certain emotional reactions such as "fight or flight" reactions, are not well-suited to all circumstances: while not per se "irrational," they are "maladaptive" in many contexts of financial markets (Lo 2019, 189). This perspective on markets is compatible with many empirical findings, e.g. about different periods in which prices show different patterns (Lo 2012, 18–20). It suggests that regulation should take a similar "adaptive" perspective, learning from past incidents and adapting regulatory parameters to evolving circumstances (Lo 2019, 378–84). In future research, this perspective will, hopefully, increase our understanding of how human behavior in financial markets works; for that purpose, it would probably benefit from collaboration with sociological research that analyzes the social embeddedness of human behavior in the financial system. Nonetheless, the "adaptive markets" perspective as such is purely descriptive; it is compatible with different underlying goals and principles that financial markets could be geared toward.

All these phenomena throw serious doubts on the ways in which democratic publics currently treat stock markets as indicators of how the real economy is

---

[14] A bigger question, from which I here abstract, is whether the *whole* capitalist economic system is necessarily, or in tendency, prone to booms and busts, as Minsky (1986) for example has argued.

doing. Kay, for one, holds that it "is time to query whether the stock markets that consume so much resource and receive so much attention any longer serve an important economic function" (2015, 209). In a recent paper on the US stock market, Schlingemann and Stulz (2020) show that in contrast to the 1970s, today there is a disconnect between the companies that are traded highest on stock markets and those that provide most employment or score highest on indicators for contributions to GDP. As they note, a main reason for this is the decline of manufacturing; manufacturing companies both had reasons to be listed on the stock market (to raise capital) and employed considerable amounts of people. For other industries, it may not be necessary or advantageous to raise capital on stock markets. From that perspective, one might wonder whether stock markets as we know them might wither away and be replaced by other mechanisms in the future. But I take it that for the foreseeable future, financial markets will continue to exist. Hence, in the next section I ask what it would take to make sure that financial markets are sufficiently epistemically efficient.

3. What, If Anything, Makes Financial Markets Epistemically Efficient?

The neoclassical model of financial markets assumes that they are epistemically efficient because if they were not, arbitrageurs could gain from moving prices, and they would thereby correct any anomalies. But as the previous section has shown, real-life financial markets are at quite some distance from the models based on these assumptions. If one wants them to be epistemically efficient, what matters is regulation that removes, or at least minimizes, the systematic distortions that can drive asset prices away from economic fundamentals. It is in conjunction with careful regulation that arbitrage can then have epistemically beneficial effects. In this section, I discuss some regulatory steps that might increase epistemic efficiency by reducing systematic deviations: (1) the minimization of herding, (2) the reduction of blind reliance on metrics, and (3) the minimization of conflicts of interest in the chain of intermediation. Together, they could help to make financial markets more boring, as it were—reducing sophisticated trading strategies that ultimately siphon off money without making epistemic contributions, and that are prone to exuberances—and thereby bring them closer to their role as a tool for efficient capital allocation.

3.1 The minimization of herding

The self-referential nature of financial markets—the "beauty contest" logic— means that the incentives for market participants with regard to knowledge acquisition only partly concern knowledge about fundamentals. At least as important, especially for short-term traders, is knowing what the "herd" is doing, and seeing whether one can ride the wave. To put it metaphorically: such investors or traders look sideward to their fellow market participants, instead of downward to the underlying assets. In addition, they are likely to be infected by the "moods" of markets, and the narratives that prevail in them. This kind of herding-behavior is epistemically harmful, in the sense that it has little to do with information about the underlying assets, and that it can create the misleading impression that the economy has better or worse prospects than is actually the case.[15]

Regulation that slows trading down and prevents mere "momentum trading" can reduce these epistemic distortions (whether or not it can ever be *completely* prevented is a question on which I here remain agnostic).[16] On the mainstream picture, fast trading is epistemically beneficial because it allows the quick integration of new information. But the question is how much of it actually *is* the integration of new information—and how much is the anticipation of how *other* market participants might integrate it.

Slower trade could be enforced in various ways. A "Tobin tax" would make trades that react to minimal price differences unprofitable, which could help reduce herding (Tobin 1978, for discussions, see, e.g. Reddy 2005; Kay 2015, 273–4). The empirical evidence on the effects of a Tobin tax are, admittedly, uncertain (see Turner 2016, 45–6), so much would depend on the concrete design of specific markets. But arguably, a general slowdown of trading could create better conditions for traders to take well-informed, controlled decisions, instead of being driven by irrational emotions (see also Lukomnik & Hawley 2021, 52). If the research on "adaptive markets" proceeds, it might also, in the future, be possible to flexibly adapt regulations, with restrictions or tax levels following the level of emotional exuberance.

Another strategy would be to require minimum holding periods for certain kinds of assets. It is hard to believe that the relevant information about, say, a company or a government, could ever change at the speed in which their shares or bonds are traded—what changes are the perceptions by different market participants, in a potentially self-reinforcing dynamic.[17] While market participants could still follow trends (though more slowly), it is likely that the kind of instinctual reactions that are driven by the excitement, or fear, of very fast trading, would then play a lesser role in determining their behavior.

---

[15] And of course, it is also harmful in a broader sense if there are financial crises that trigger economic crises or otherwise harm the economy.

[16] This might to a considerable extent depend on whether or not researchers can find reliable early signs of bubbles. If so, the relevant metrics would certainly receive attention from traders—and regulators could also use them as a basis for intervention, e.g. slowing down trading in markets in which the likelihood of a bubble hits a certain threshold.

[17] Kay (2015, 93) remarks that from the perspective of the "real economy," trading could in fact take place on much slower timescales.

Another question is whether certain financial instruments that allow traders to "ride the wave," and thus add momentum in upswings or downswings, should be banned; an example where this has already happened is naked short selling, which was banned in many countries after the Great Financial Crisis. While this financial instrument is now widely recognized to be mostly harmful, for other classes of financial instruments, this question is more difficult to answer. Some trading that could be characterized as "speculative" might be needed in order to make sure that traders with legitimate trading interests, e.g. to hedge against future price movements, find counterparties.

It would require a separate discussion to decide which types of instruments should be admitted and which ones banned. My only point here is that the default position of such a discussion should *not* be that *more* trading is always better. This had been the assumption in the phase in which "financial deepening" was seen as generally beneficial, because it was seen as leading to an ever more efficient allocation of risks, with rational market actors incorporating ever more information into market prices (see, e.g. Turner 2016, chap. 1). But if a more complex picture of financial markets is taken as the starting point, the risks and potentials for epistemic inefficiencies (and other forms of inefficiency, in fact) become visible as well. The potential benefits of financial instruments need to be weighed against the potential risks of market distortions, which are harmful from an epistemic perspective and often also in other ways.[18]

3.2 The reduction of blind reliance on metrics

A second set of questions concerns the use of metrics in financial markets and the risk that these are either not suited for reflecting the underlying reality, or, relatedly, that agents might try to game them in order to bring about certain desired effects. The judgments by rating agencies, mentioned above, were a case in point: traders relied on them (and were legally required to do so), and therefore did not ask many questions about the underlying assets. Because the percentage of those who did so was sufficiently large, the upswing movement could go on for a considerable time. De Bruin (2017) suggests that the mandatory reliance on rating agencies should be abolished in its current form, because the "epistemic responsibilities" for evaluating credit risks should be carried by financial institutions themselves (and also because of the obvious conflict of interest—a point to which I return below). Even if it were not mandatory, however, financial market actors would probably continue to rely on *some* metrics. The "outsourcing of epistemic

---

[18] The same holds for the regulation of *algorithmic* trading, which often seems to be purely momentum-driven. The legitimacy of algorithmic trading would require a discussion of its own, but my arguments about epistemic efficiency can be applied to it as well.

responsibilities" is a feature of many markets, in the sense that key information is processed through regulatory frameworks, e.g. via product labels, instead of being processed directly by market participants.[19] Where this happens, great care needs to be taken to make sure that the relevant agencies are independent from pressures by the very agents whose behavior they are supposed to regulate.

3.3 The minimization of conflicts of interests

This leads us to the third point: the avoidance of conflicts of interest. Financial intermediation as we currently see it is rife with conflicts of interest, and it often puts epistemic trustworthiness at risk, because parties may not have the right incentives to acquire and/or share information neutrally and objectively. The fact that rating agencies are paid by the institutions that issue assets, not by those who trade them, is a case in point—would they bite the hand that feeds them by being overly critical of these assets? (see also de Bruin 2017, 257–62; Kay 2015, 249–50). Another obvious case is the inherent conflict of interest in broker-dealers, who trade for others but also for themselves (e.g. Kay 2015, 29, 198–9, 283, 287). In the aftermath of the financial crisis, these and many other problematic practices were revealed, for example when bankers created the impression of being fair and independent advisors to clients while at the same time shortchanging them (see, e.g. Tenbrunsel & Thomas 2015 on the ensuing ethical problems).

Insofar as intermediation in financial markets is needed, so that clients can draw on the expertise of specialized agents,[20] the institutional framework must be such that conflicts of interest are avoided. Only then can clients rely on the "guardianship" or "stewardship" of financial institutions.[21] As many commentators have emphasized, this also requires a change of culture, away from a short-term focus on profits, toward a long-term focus on relationships.[22] This is certainly correct—formal rules alone are unlikely to achieve this goal. Nonetheless, the formal rules should, as far as possible, align the incentives of different parties, such that distortions in the transmission of information are avoided. This is an ethical imperative, but also an epistemic one: some arrangements reward honesty, while others make it difficult for honest players to survive competitive pressures. In the latter scenario, it should not come as a surprise that the epistemic features of the institution in question are unreliable.

Regulatory steps in these directions would help reduce obvious epistemic distortions that mar financial markets today and reduce their epistemic efficiency.

---

[19] See Herzog 2020 on the "epistemic infrastructure" of many markets; on labels, see, e.g. Bullock 2017.

[20] Kay (2015, e.g. 206) calls for a radical shortening of the chain of intermediation; Arjaliès et al. 2017 (chapter 8), however, skeptically ask whether this is realistic given the need for expertise.

[21] See, e.g. the chapters in Morris & Vines (eds.) 2014.   [22] Salz 2013; Kay 2015.

Admittedly, they can be taken in ways that would more or less effective in achieving this goal, e.g. by either allowing or preventing sidestepping reactions by market participants.[23] If Lo's hypothesis about the adaptive nature of financial market behavior is taken seriously, then it is likely that regulation will have to be regularly updated, to take into account new insights about how market participants adapt to regulatory changes.

However, the obstacles to epistemic efficiency addressed by such regulation are *internal* to financial markets. In addition, we also need to see financial markets in the context of the economy as a whole. In the next section I discuss epistemic inefficiencies that have their causes outside financial markets but are reflected within them, thereby leading to deviations of the first condition of epistemic efficiency, i.e. failing to reflect the epistemically most relevant features of the "real economy."

4. Reflecting Information that Matters

The epistemic efficiency of financial markets is not an end in itself. Ultimately, it is meant to help to understand where the economy is going, and for market participants to efficiently allocate capital and distribute risks. Capital allocation needs to be in line with societal needs and values. For example, at this point, an urgent societal need is the development of alternative, climate-friendly energy technologies (see also Lo 2019, 416; he also mentions finding cures against cancer and fighting poverty). But in order to contribute to such goals, financial markets need to be embedded in economic systems that are in turn not prone to distortions, epistemic or otherwise. Or to put it differently: insofar as financial markets can ever be "mirrors" of economic developments, they will also be "mirroring" the ways in which these economic developments are out of sync with our alleged societal values. Given that our current economic systems are at a huge distance from the assumptions that enter the abstract models about the role of financial markets in the economy, many arguments in favor of financial markets need to be taken with a generous grain of salt.

Understanding these distortions helps explain why current financial markets seem to be such bad "mirrors"—in part, that is because the economic reality itself badly deviates from some of the idealization assumptions in our economic models and the values embedded in them. In this section, I focus on two such distortions, which are recognized as problematic by a broad range of commentators: massive economic inequalities, and market failures with regard

---

[23] An obvious challenge is the problem of international regulatory arbitrage, which I here cannot discuss. Ideally, governments would move in lockstep to introduce such regulation.

to environmental externalities with ensuing unfair distributions of burdens.[24] For each of them, I contrast a more just society—for example a "property-owning democracy"—with the current situation in order to illustrate the epistemic problems.

The ultimate aim of "efficiency," in markets or otherwise, is to satisfy human needs with as few resources as possible—at least that seems to be the implicit assumption in many arguments in favor of markets. But in market societies, these human needs are mediated by purchasing power.[25] In an egalitarian society, all human needs would be undergirded by roughly the same purchasing power, so that markets in products and services would react to them evenly (and many abstract models of markets seem to implicitly assume that all market participants have the same purchasing power and differ just with regard to preferences, which would indeed lead to that result). In highly unequal societies, in contrast, markets in goods and services prioritize the needs (or whims) of those with higher purchasing power. A well-known example of this phenomenon is the global market for pharmaceutical innovations, in which widespread but relatively harmless health problems of groups with high purchasing power (e.g. male erectile disorders) attract much higher R&D investments than far graver diseases that prevail in the Global South (many "tropical" diseases).[26] The same pattern can be observed in numerous other retail markets, and it translates into the valuation of companies on stock markets.

The claim that stock markets help allocate capital to firms that provide innovations is thus at best partially true—it helps allocate capital to firms that provide innovations *for those with sufficient purchasing power*. Whether or not these innovations also benefit society as a whole depends on a plethora of factors (e.g. whether jobs are created, whether the technologies will be more widely adopted, or whether companies contribute to society through taxes or not), but it cannot be simply taken as given. This was the fallacy of "trickle-down" economics, which has been clearly refuted (see, e.g. Stiglitz 2016). There is thus a real question about the extent to which financial markets—even hypothetical ones for which obviously distorting factors would be minimized through regulation, as suggested above—in highly unequal societies could be described as epistemically valuable: they continue to reflect a highly distorted economic system, and push many other questions, which concern those with little purchasing power, to the margins of our field of vision. In a more egalitarian society, they would better reflect the contribution of firms to the needs of all members of society, because the distribution of

---

[24] This list of areas is not exhaustive. For example, questions about the epistemically dysfunctional structures *within* firms, or about the regulation of financial companies and about the monetary system (which I here cannot discuss for reasons of space—see fn. 6 above) would also play a role in making sure that financial markets reflect "what matters."

[25] I abstract from the question of how to treat those with special needs, e.g. because of disabilities, who should obviously need to get more resources for satisfying the same preferences (e.g. for mobility) as others.

[26] See, e.g. Pogge & Hollis 2008.

purchasing power would be more even. In such a society, e.g. a property-owning democracy, they would presumably also include a broader range of risk profiles, and more epistemic diversity, because more individuals would have the means for trading in them.[27]

Second, a more just society would not allow companies to benefit from market failures.[28] I will focus on one of the most obvious examples in the current situation: the failure to adequately price climate and other environmental externalities.[29] Because companies can pollute largely for free, it is very difficult for more climate-friendly innovations to be competitive. In our current economic systems, the very notion of "efficiency" is thus massively distorted; in fact, it fails to capture one of the key dimensions in which more efficiency would be urgently needed, namely the reduction of CO_2 emissions. Therefore, many figures that claim to be about efficiency fail to measure what really matters—and financial markets in turn reflect these failures.

More and more investors have started to take these issues into account, divesting from fossil fuel companies or paying attention to environmental criteria in their portfolios.[30] While this is laudable under the current non-ideal circumstances, it is, in a way, the wrong systematic place for these measures. If emissions were adequately priced, then market prices would reflect companies' successes or failures in reducing them, and investors could focus directly on market prices.[31] But because of the lack of legal regulation—which would, ideally, happen at the global level—it is better than nothing that some investors have started to pay attention to this issue (maybe in the anticipation that legal regulation will one day arrive). From an epistemic perspective, however, it remains unclear whether it will adequately reflect the values of different companies, not least because it remains unclear what percentage of investors will join these efforts. Legal regulation of market failures, such as externalities, would force *all* companies to pay for emissions, which would in turn mean that *all* investors would have to take them into account—and in this way, financial markets would no longer fail to reflect this crucial feature of our economies.

---

[27] Unless, that is, these individuals all participate through intermediaries—then their epistemic diversity will not play any role, because the gathering and evaluation of information will all happen within these chains of intermediation.

[28] On the moral duty to prevent market failures, see, e.g. Heath 2006. However, I here deal with market failures that *can* be legally regulated.

[29] See, e.g. IMF 2016 on emissions as externalities and the need to put a price on them.

[30] See, e.g. https://gofossilfree.org/divestment/commitments/ (accessed October 19, 2020).

[31] Does this mean that all environmental (and maybe also other societal) problems should be solved by market processes? Certainly not, market processes are unlikely to be sufficient solutions. But given the way in which our capitalist systems currently function, putting a price on certain behaviors (e.g. CO_2 emissions, measures that destroy biodiversity) is the most realistic way of changing these behaviors. Therefore, I take it to be an important element in the fight against climate change and other environmental problems.

5. Conclusion

In this chapter I have argued that the epistemic efficiency of financial markets is not something that can be expected to come about automatically, through the work of arbitrageurs. Instead, careful regulation is needed to abolish or at least reduce various epistemic distortions internal to financial markets. Moreover, financial markets as they currently exist reflect many distortions of the economic system caused by extreme inequality and environmental externalities. For all these reasons, paying so much attention to the epistemically inefficient financial markets we currently have is a problematic strategy for democratic societies. It means that all the distortions and irrationalities that I have discussed get transported into discussions about economic policy, obscuring the matters at stake and biasing the choices to be made.

It is worth emphasizing once more that the criterion that I have focused on in this chapter, epistemic efficiency, is not the only one that should be used to evaluate financial markets and to guide their regulation. It only partially overlaps, for example, with the prevention of unfair profiteering (cf. Arjaliès et al. 2017, 11–13 on the high costs of intermediation) or optimal functionality from the perspective of the "real" economy (Kay 2015, e.g. 93). Another imperative is to minimize the risk of finance-induced economic crises. I take it, however, that all these normative criteria are at least *related* to epistemic efficiency.

A more radical approach would be to ask whether we need financial markets at all, or whether their epistemic (and other) functions could be fulfilled in other ways, e.g. based on big data analyses.[32] In fact, the challenges to epistemic efficiency I have discussed might be understood as a pro-tanto argument in favor of the complete abolition of financial markets. I take it that in order to be part of a just society, e.g. a property-owning democracy, financial markets would have to be massively constrained by regulation that prevents internal epistemic efficiencies. If they were thus regulated, and other problems such as inequality and environmental externalities were also addressed, maybe, just maybe, financial markets could play a justifiable and even positive role in supporting economic innovation toward a greener economy. Until then, we should treat their "judgments" with a healthy dose of skepticism.

References

Akerlof, George A., & Shiller, Robert J. 2016. *Phishing for Phools. The Economics of Manipulation and Deception*. Princeton: Princeton University Press.

---

[32] Phillips & Rozworksi 2019 argue that the logistical capacities of a company such as Walmart suggest that computing facilities might help allocation tasks also for a socialist government.

Arjaliès, Diane-Laure, Philip Grant, Iain Hardie, Donald MacKenzie, & Ekaterina Svetlova. 2017. *Chains of Finance: How Investment Management is Shaped*. Oxford: Oxford University Press.

Arrow, Kenneth J. & Gérard Debreu. 1954. "The Existence of an Equilibrium for a Competitive Economy." *Econometrica* 22(3), 265–90.

Arrow, Kenneth J., Robert Forsythe, Michael Gorham et al. 2008. "The Promise of Prediction Markets." *Science* 320 (5878), 877–8.

Baker, A., Haslam, C., Leaver, A. et al. 2020. *Against Hollow Firms: Repurposing the Corporation for a More Resilient Economy*. Report. Centre for Research on Accounting and Finance in Context (CRAFiC), University of Sheffield.

Boldyrev, Ivan. 2021. "The Ontology of Uncertainty in Finance: The Normative Legacy of General Equilibrium." *Topoi* 40, 725–31.

Bragues, George. 2009. "Prediction Markets: The Practical and Normative Possibilities for the Social Production of Knowledge." *Episteme* 6(1), 91–106.

Bronk, Richard. 2011. "Epistemological Difficulties with Neoclassical Economics." *LSE e-prints*, http://eprints.lse.ac.uk/39423/.

Bullock, Graham. 2017. *Green Grades. Can Information Save the Earth?* Cambridge, MA: MIT Press.

Campbell, Donald T. 1976. "Assessing the Impact of Planned Social Change." Public Affairs Center, Dartmouth College. Hanover.

Carruthers, Bruce G. 2015. "Financialization and the Institutional Foundations of the New Capitalism." *Socio-Economic Review* 13(2), 379–98.

de Bruin, Boudewijn. 2017. "Information as a Condition of Justice in Financial Markets: The Regulation of Credit-Rating Agencies," in Lisa Herzog (ed.), *Just Financial Markets? Finance in a Just Society* (Oxford: Oxford University Press), 250–70.

Dietsch, Peter. 2021. "Money Creation, Debt, and Justice." *Politics, Philosophy & Economics* 20(2), 151–179.

Fama, Eugene F. 1970. "Efficient Capital Markets: A Review of Theory and Empirical Work." *Journal of Finance* 25(2), 383–417.

Graham, John R., Campbell R. Harvey & Shiva Rajgopal. 2006. "Value Destruction and Financial Reporting Decisions." Available at: https://ssrn.com/abstract=871215

Grossman, Sanford J., & Stiglitz, Joseph E. 1980. "On the Impossibility of Informationally Efficient Markets." *American Economic Review* 70(3), 393–408.

Hayek, Friedrich August von. 1945. "The Use of Knowledge in Society." *American Economic Review* 35(4), 519–30.

Heath, Joseph. 2006. "Business Ethics without Stakeholders." *Business Ethics Quarterly* 16(4), 533–57.

Heath, Joseph. 2014. *Morality, Competition, and the Firm: The Market Failure Approach to Business Ethics*. New York: Oxford University Press.

Herzog, Lisa. 2020. "The Epistemic Division of Labor in Markets. Knowledge, Global Trade, and the Preconditions of Responsible Agency," *Economics & Philosophy* 36, 266–286.

Herzog, Lisa. 2023. *Citizen Knowledge. Markets, Experts, and the Infrastructure of Democracy*. New York: Oxford University Press.

IMF. 2016. "Fact Sheet: Climate, Environment, and the IMF," available at https://www.imf.org/external/np/exr/facts/pdf/enviro.pdf

Jiang, Zhi-Qiang, Wen-Jie Xie, Wei-Xing Zhou, & Didier Sornette. 2019. "Multifractal Analysis of Financial Markets: A Review." *Reports on Progress in Physics* 82(12), 125901.

Kay, John. 2015. *Other People's Money. Masters of the Universe or Servants of the People?* London: Profile Books.

Keynes, John Maynard. 1936. *The General Theory of Employment, Interest and Money*. London: Palgrave Macmillan.

Kindleberger, Charles P., 1978, *Manias, Panics, and Crashes: A History of Financial Crises*. London: Macmillan.

Landemore, Hélène. 2013. *Democratic Reason: Politics, Collective Intelligence, and the Rule of the Many*. Princeton: Princeton University Press.

Lim, Kian-Ping, & Brooks, Robert. 2010. "The Evolution of Stock Market Efficiency over Time: A Survey of the Empirical Literature." *Journal of Economic Surveys* 25(1), 69–108.

Linsi, Lukas, & Schaffner, Florian. 2019. "When Do Heuristics Matter in Global Capital Markets? The Case of the BRIC Acronym." *New Political Economy* 24(6), 851–72.

Lo, Andrew W. 2012. "Adaptive Markets and the New World Order (Corrected May 2012)." *Financial Analysts Journal* 68(2), 18–29.

Lo, Andrew W. 2019. *Adaptive Markets: Financial Evolution at the Speed of Thought. Adaptive Markets*. Princeton: Princeton University Press.

Lomansky, Loren E. 2011. "Liberty after Lehman Brothers." *Social Philosophy & Policy* 28(2), 135–65.

Lukomnik, Jon, & Hawley, James P. 2021. *Moving Beyond Modern Portfolio Theory. Investing That Matters*. New York: Routledge.

MacKenzie, Donald. 2006. *An Engine, Not a Camera: How Financial Models Shape Markets*. Cambridge, MA: MIT Press.

Minsky, Hyman P. 1986. *Stabilizing an Unstable Economy*. New Haven: Yale University Press.

Morris, Nicholas, & David Vines (eds.). 2014. *Capital Failure. Rebuilding Trust in Financial Services*. Oxford: Oxford University Press.

Phillips, Leigh & Michal Rozworksi. 2019. *The People's Republic of Walmart How the World's Biggest Corporations Are Laying the Foundation for Socialism*. London: Verso.

Pogge, Thomas & Aidan Hollis 2008. *The Health Impact Fund: Making New Medicines Accessible for All*. New Haven: Incentives for Global Health.

Reddy, Sanjay G., 2005, "Developing Just Monetary Arrangements," in Christian Barry & Thomas W. Pogge (eds.), *Global Institutions and Responsibilities: Achieving Global Justice*. Oxford: Blackwell, 218–34.

Roemer, John E. 1994. *A Future for Socialism*. Cambridge, MA: Harvard University Press.

Salz, Anthony. 2013. "Salz Review. An Independent Review of Barclay's Business Practice." http://online.wsj.com/public/resources/documents/SalzReview04032013.pdf

Schlingemann, Frederik P. & René M. Stulz. 2020. "Has the Stock Market Become Less Representative of the Economy." NBER Working Paper No. 27942, https://www.nber.org/papers/w27942

Servan-Schreiber, Emile. 2018. "Prediction Markets. Trading Uncertainty for Collective Wisdom," in Hélène Landemore & Jon Elster (eds.), *Collective Wisdom: Principles and Mechanisms*. Cambridge: Cambridge University Press, 21–37.

Sikka, Prem & John Stittle. 2017. "Debunking the Myth of Shareholder Ownership of Companies: Some Implications for Corporate Governance and Financial Reporting." *Critical Perspectives on Accounting* 63 Article 101992.

Stiglitz, Joseph E. 2016. "Inequality and Economic Growth," in *Rethinking Capitalism*. Wiley-Blackwell, 134–55.

Sunstein, Cass R. 2006. "Deliberating Groups versus Prediction Markets (or Hayek's Challenge to Habermas)." *Episteme* 3(3), 192–213.

Taylor, Charles. 1985. "Self-interpreting animals," in *Philosophical Papers*, vol. II, Cambridge: Cambridge University Press, 45–76.

Tenbrunsel, Ann, & Jordan Thomas. 2015. "The Street, The Bull and the Crisis: A Survey of the US & UK Financial Services Industry." University of Notre Dame and Labaton Sucharow LLP (May).

Thomas, Alan. 2017. *Republic of Equals: Predistribution and Property-Owning Democracy*. New York: Oxford University Press.

Tobin, James. 1978. "A Proposal for International Monetary Reform." *Eastern Economic Journal* 4(3–4), 153–9.

Turner, Adair. 2016. *Between Debt and the Devil. Money, Credit, and Fixing Global Finance*. Princeton: Princeton University Press.

Walras, Léon. 1870 [1954]. *Elements of Pure Economics*. Irwin.

Walter, Christian. 2001. "The Efficient Market Hypothesis, the Gaussian Assumption, and the Investment Management Industry." EFMA 2001 Lugano Meetings, available at: https://ssrn.com/abstract=267443 or http://dx.doi.org/10.2139/ssrn.267443

Wolfers, Justin, & Eric Zitzewitz. 2004. "Prediction Markets." *Journal of Economic Perspectives* 18(2), 107–26. https://doi.org/10.1257/0895330041371321.

6

Financial Economics: What Kind of Science Is It?

*Conrad Heilmann, Marta Szymanowska,
and Melissa Vergara-Fernández*

Financial economics has been steadily maturing as a subfield of economics for many decades now. Finance scholars have received some of the most prestigious research awards in economics, and the key finance journals belong to the most respected outlets in economics as a whole. Financial economics is also a research field that is—there can be no doubt—of enormous practical importance and consequence. Its models and theories inform actors on financial markets, in financial regulation, and in central banking.

The practical influence of financial economics is especially important in asset pricing. Asset pricing is a core component of financial economics and in many ways also one of its most popular and successful parts: it accounts for Nobel Prizes in economics, and its models and theories are important for many questions in micro- and macroeconomics. At the heart of asset pricing is the CAPM—the Capital Asset Pricing Model. Conceived by Treynor (1962), Sharpe (1964), Lintner (1965), and Mossin (1966), it is one of the major frameworks in financial economics for analysing investor behaviour under risk. The CAPM is also inextricably linked to important trends in financial markets. Consider the growing relevance of index funds and passive investment more generally, which by the end of 2020 accounted for \$15tr in assets (Wigglesworth, 2021). The roots of this financial innovation can be traced directly the CAPM (Bernstein, 1993, ch. 12; Mehrling, 2005, ch. 4).

Despite the theoretical and practical importance of financial economics, there has not been a lot of specific and sustained engagement with its models and theories by philosophers of science. Indeed, the *Stanford Encyclopedia of Philosophy* entry on money and finance observes: 'only a few philosophers of science have considered finance specifically' (de Bruin et al., 2018). In similar vein, Vergara-Fernández and de Bruin (2021) characterize financial economics as 'terra incognita' for philosophers of science.[1]

---

[1] While the literature that examines financial economics is small, there are a number of significant contributions on which our chapter builds. First, there is a sizable literature in the sociology of science, especially with regard to the theme of "reflexivity" or "performativity" of financial models and theories

Conrad Heilmann, Marta Szymanowska, and Melissa Vergara-Fernández, *Financial Economics: What Kind of Science Is It?*
In: *The Philosophy of Money and Finance*. Edited by: Joakim Sandberg and Lisa Warenski, Oxford University Press.
© Oxford University Press 2024. DOI: 10.1093/oso/9780192898807.003.0007

In this chapter, we provide a roadmap for how philosophers of science can engage more with financial economics. We argue that financial economics is best characterized by its use of *models* and its *performative* nature. We show that the model-based and performative character of financial economics is: (1) visible in the history of its emergence and its current scientific practice; (2) central to the kind of insights it aims to generate; and (3) key to understand what kind of ethical values are at play. We do so by focusing on the CAPM. As a model that is both theoretically and practically important, it is a good starting point for asking how philosophers of science should go about assessing the epistemic performance of financial economics.

We proceed as follows. Section 1 tells an abridged story of the emergence of financial economics, outlining how it became its own branch of economics. Section 2 makes the case for characterizing financial economics particularly by its focus on the use of *models* and by its *performative* nature. To do so, we focus on asset pricing and analyse the kind of claims that are made in asset pricing research. Specifically, we analyse models that originate in the CAPM, the centre-stage model at the emergence of the field. With its multiple extensions, it continues to play an important role in financial economics as well as in industry practice. Section 3 comments on the significance of analysing the role of ethical values in financial economics. Section 4 concludes.

1. The Emergence of Financial Economics: From 'Old' to 'New' Finance Research

Financial economics is a branch of economics concerned with the allocation and redistribution of financial resources (capital).[2] The key feature of financial economics is its focus on financial assets that represent claims to future uncertain payoffs. In his Nobel lecture, Robert C. Merton (1997) described financial economics as 'the study of allocation and deployment of economic resources, both spatially and across time, in an uncertain environment' (p. 85).

(see MacKenzie, 2006a; Boldyrev and Svetlova, 2016; and a special issue in the *Journal of Economic Methodology* on reflexivity e.g. Davis, 2013; Hommes, 2013; Soros, 2013). Second, there are contributions from a philosophy of science perspective that are focused on models and theories in financial economics (e.g. Walter, 2000, 2016, 2021; Vuillemey, 2014; Mangee, 2015; Jovanovic, 2018; Svetlova, 2018; Delcey, 2019; Miotti, 2021; Vergara-Fernández and de Bruin, 2021) and reflections on highly specific questions (e.g. Brav et al., 2004; Greene, 2019; Boldyrev, 2021). Some attention is paid to models of finance, such as Black–Scholes or Modigliani–Miller (Hindriks, 2008, 2013; Pfleiderer, 2014; Brisset, 2018; Vergara-Fernández and de Bruin, 2021). There is recent interest in models of econophysics by some philosophers of science (e.g. Rickles, 2007; Jhun et al., 2018) as well as behavioural finance (e.g. Greene, 2019). Ippoliti (2021a, 2021b) reflects on the epistemology and ontology of finance and also touches on issues in the philosophy of science.

[2] Financial economics studies both capital and money markets.

The history of financial economics as a distinct branch of economics is recent. It starts around the mid-twentieth century, with the emergence of 'new' finance research.[3] 'New' finance research, as much of the rest of economics, starts with the setting of two of its most significant concerns,[4] *asset pricing* and *corporate finance*, on a model-based footing. Asset pricing and investment theory is concerned with the determinants of the value of financial assets and the financial decisions of investors. Corporate finance is concerned with the financial decisions within corporations, which are the main users of funds, and their impact on corporate valuations.

In contrast to 'new finance,' 'old finance' had mostly a descriptive character. The *Journal of Finance*, which appeared in 1945, published articles which mostly described Federal Reserve policy, taxation, corporate finance, insurance, accounting, and the impact of money on prices and business activity (Bernstein, 1993, ch. 2). There was also little interest in the stock market as an object of study. The market crash of 1929 and the Great Depression were only in the recent past. In the minds of academics, the stock market was almost comparable to gambling (Bernstein, 1993, ch. 2). Corporate finance, in turn, which was exemplified by Arthur Stone Dewing's handbook *The Financial Policy of Corporations* (1919), centre on the history of corporations, their relation to other financial institutions, particularly regarding their funding, and the effects of regulation on their rise and survival. According to a review of its fifth edition published in 1954, its two volumes constituted 'a short encyclopedia of the conception, birth, life and death of a corporation' (Forer, 1954, p. 889).

At least two important efforts by both individuals and institutions led to the transformation of 'old' finance research into 'new' model-based research in finance. The first set of efforts was aimed at bringing rigor to research in *asset pricing*. The second set of effort concerns *corporate finance*.

The first set of efforts, on *asset pricing*, advanced from within the Cowles Commission, particularly during the directorships of Jacob Marschak and Tjalling Koopmans in the late 1940s and early 1950s. The Cowles Commission aimed to establish a solid foundation for economics in which economic theory, mathematics, and statistics would come together (Dimand, 2019). The research at the Commission built on the theory of expected utility by Von Neumann and Morgenstern and focused on addressing uncertainty in decision-making

---

[3] "New finance" is an informal term to mark the watershed in the field, which historians have characterized as a "revolutionary idea" (Mehrling, 2005); the "origins of modern Wall Street" (Bernstein, 1993); and the emergence of the scientific community of financial economics (Jovanovic, 2008). With "old finance" (see further below) we refer to the period prior to this watershed.

[4] There are other subfields of finance research, such as personal and public finance. Notably *banking* is sometimes described as a separate subfield of finance research. Banking is concerned with the financial intermediaries including (trans)national and private banks, it studies their activities, related risks, and their impact on the economy. As such, it touches on both asset pricing and corporate finance.

(Herfeld, 2017). This development was also crucial for the models of financial decision-making.

In 1952, Harry Markowitz published 'Portfolio Selection' (Markowitz, 1952), the article that does for capital markets what the Cowles Commission project called for: to establish how rational agents, in this case investors, should make decisions in the face of uncertainties. In his article, Markowitz provided a decision rule for selecting investment portfolios. This decision rule, contrary to what was customary in the industry, established that investors should maximize expected return, instead of just return. This involved accounting for the risk involved in investing. To do this, Markowitz characterized expected return as mean and risk as variance, and offered a geometrical proof. It established that there was an efficient frontier of portfolios that either maximize return for a given level of risk or minimize risk for a given level of return. Investors should choose portfolios on the efficient frontier.

William Sharpe took Markowitz's decision rule as an input for his CAPM (Sharpe, 1964). The CAPM uses the portfolio choices of individual investors to represent investors' demands for financial assets. By aggregating the investor demands and equating them to asset supplies, equilibrium asset prices are determined. Although the CAPM has been shown unable to account for all the data well (Black et al., 1972; Banz, 1981; Fama and French, 1992, 1996) and has been called untestable (Roll, 1977), the ideas it espouses about the functioning of financial markets continue to play a crucial role in the analysis of these markets (see section 2). It is also used in analyses in corporate finance. For example, the CAPM expected returns are used to estimate firms' costs of capital (Graham and Harvey, 2001; Brounen et al., 2004).

At around the same time, at the University of Chicago, Eugene Fama published his work on the Efficient Market Hypothesis (1965a, 1965b, 1970). The Efficient Market Hypothesis postulates that prices fully reflect all available information. It explained the randomness of the prices (Kendall and Hill, 1953) and the inability of financial analysts to forecast them (Cowles, 1933) in terms of competition between rational agents in markets where prices converge to fundamental values. Hence, the randomness of price variation is attributed to the random arrival of new information.[5] Consequently, the only source of returns in efficient markets is the compensation investors receive for bearing the risk (i.e. equilibrium expected returns). And so, investors are not able to earn extra returns by trading on new information, but only by subsuming higher risk on their investments. And yet, Fama's work, as much of the work at Chicago at the time, was empirical in nature,

---

[5] At the same time, in an independent contribution, Paul Samuelson has also linked the randomness of prices to the competitive markets (Samuelson, 1965). The two contributions: Fama's and Samuelson's differ, however, in their approach, in particular in the assumptions about the statistical model describing the price process (Delcey, 2019).

fuelled by the establishment of the Center for Research in Security Prices (CRSP) at the University of Chicago in 1960.[6] Fama did not take a stance on a particular theory of expected returns. William Sharpe's CAPM arrived just in time to fill that gap.

These first efforts to set finance research on a more scientific footing have led to a proliferation of model-based research in *asset pricing*. We now turn to the second set of efforts, which concerned *corporate finance*.

The second efforts, on *corporate finance*, came from scholars in finance at Carnegie Tech (later Carnegie Mellon). Like the economists at the Cowles Commission, they were equally interested in bringing rigor to their discipline. Towards the end of the 1940s there was dissatisfaction among some scholars about the business education in the United States. In the words of Herbert Simon, it was a 'wasteland of vocationalism that needed to be transformed into science-based professionalism, as medicine and engineering had been transformed a generation or two earlier' (Simon, 1996, p. 139). From this project emerged one of the most remarkable contributions to corporate finance: the Modigliani and Miller propositions, also known as the Modigliani and Miller theorem, or the principle of the irrelevance of capital structure (Modigliani and Miller, 1958).[7] The Modigliani and Miller theorem states the following. In equilibrium, the market value of a company is determined by the value of its future earnings discounted at the market rate that reflects the riskiness of those earnings. Crucially, the market value of a company is thus independent of how a company finances its operations—its capital structure. That is to say, the Modigliani and Miller theorem set firms' capital structure, an aspect that would traditionally be studied by corporate managers—and thus not economists—under the economics framework of studying markets in equilibrium.[8] (For a detailed review of the relevance of the Modigliani and Miller theorem, see Vergara-Fernández and de Bruin (2021).)

---

[6] Other important work in this empirical effort was that of Benjamin King, whose dissertation "The Latent Statistical Structure of Security Price Changes," was supervised by James Lorie, director of the CRSP (see Mehrling, 2005, ch. 3).

[7] On the basis of these propositions, Merton Miller was awarded the Nobel laureate in 1990, together with Markowitz and Sharpe. Modigliani was awarded the Nobel Prize in 1985, for his pioneering studies of saving and financial markets.

[8] In their article, Modigliani and Miller, under a set of stringent assumptions, demonstrated that the decisions of a firm about how to fund its activities, be it by issuing debt or equity, are irrelevant for the firm's market valuation. Contrary to what was thought at the time, that there had to be an optimal balance between debt and equity issuance for minimizing the cost of capital, the choice, in fact, has no effect on the market's valuation of the firm. There is much literature that discusses the contribution to corporate finance of the Modigliani and Miller propositions (e.g. Bhattacharya, 1988; Miller, 1988; Ross, 1988; Knoll, 2018). For our story, however, one is particularly relevant. It is that the financial structure of firms was treated in a way that aimed to solve the larger macroeconomic problem of firm investment decisions for economic fluctuations. This involved addressing the problem "from the macroeconomic perspective" (Miller, 1988, p. 101). In other words, a problem that was previously addressed as exclusive of the corporate manager—viewed from within the firm—was now treated from the larger perspective of capital markets in equilibrium.

The question Modigliani and Miller addressed is perfectly complementary to the question addressed by the CAPM. Whereas Modigliani and Miller solve the problem of the corporate manager by claiming that all that matters for the firm valuation is market valuation—not its capital structure—the CAPM claims that all that investors care about is the undiversifiable risk (market risk) and not the individual risk of corporations. The two models solve the same problem. One does it for the corporate manager and the other for the investor. More generally, both models highlight the transformation from descriptive, vocationalist 'old' finance research to model-based 'new' finance research.

In the following section, we focus on the CAPM—as it is still the central modelling framework for asset prices. Studying it will allow us to get a more specific insight into the kind of claims financial economics makes today.

2. Financial Economics as a Model-Based and Performative Science

We now turn to the topic of assessing the epistemic performance of financial economics. We continue with a narrowed focus on asset pricing and use the CAPM as the main example.

First, what is the content of the claims made in asset pricing research, and which strategies are employed to make them?

The methodology of financial economics is similar to other areas in economics; it is also a model-based science. The models, while often partial rather than general equilibrium models, are based on the prevailing paradigm of neoclassical economics.[9] The story of asset pricing models and the CAPM in particular shows how much financial economics is driven by models. Indeed, the very fact that asset pricing has developed by considering a multitude of variants and extensions of the CAPM highlights this fact. Here, we comment on some peculiarities of the ecology of models that have developed from the original CAPM.

Claims made on the basis of the CAPM centre on its core idea: an equilibrium in which the mean-variance efficiency of the market portfolio is derived from aggregate investor demand. As such, the CAPM offers insights into the determinants of the returns of assets, and can explain differences in asset returns in terms of their relation to market risk in equilibrium. To do so, the CAPM makes a series of assumptions that describe (i) investors' preferences, (ii) the investment universe

---

[9] In parallel to many other subfields in economics, where the models and insights of behavioural economics play an increasingly important role, there is also an emerging literature on behavioural finance (for an overview, see e.g. Hirshleifer, 2015).

based on the mean-variance portfolio choice, (iii) the availability of the risk-free rate for borrowing and lending, and the (iv) homogeneity of investors' expectations (i.e. all investors agree on expected values, variances, and correlations of assets).

Specifically, the CAPM assumes that all investors have the same information about the investment universe, face the same risk-free rate, and follow Markowitz's mean-variance portfolio rule. Under these assumptions, the optimal portfolio of all investors should consist of the risk-free asset and the single mean-variance portfolio of all risky assets. The portfolio of risky assets is chosen such that it offers maximum return above the risk-free asset per unit of risk.[10] Investors' portfolios, thus, differ only in the proportion of wealth allocated to risk-free versus risky assets, but the relative proportions of risky assets are identical across the investors. Because the market portfolio is the sum of all the risky assets held in the economy by all investors, it is thus the sum of identical mean-variance portfolios of risky assets that each investor holds. Hence, the market portfolio is mean-variance efficient. Consequently, there is a linear relation between the asset's expected return and its quantity of market risk. The quantity of the market risk is measured with the so-called market (or CAPM) beta (β), which captures how much the returns on a given asset co-move with the market.[11] According to the CAPM, the riskier the asset is—i.e. an asset with higher market risk—the higher the expected return investors will demand to hold that asset. So, an asset that has a high market beta is a very risky asset. Holding this asset will pay off well when the market is doing well, and badly when the market is doing poorly. Therefore, there would be little demand for this asset. In equilibrium, such an asset would have to offer high expected returns to convince investors to hold it.

The four contributions that make up the original CAPM have been extended in various ways. The CAPM extensions comprise both theoretical and empirical models. They vary in the way they extend the CAPM: some models vary only some parameters and assumptions, while others depart more fundamentally and add components, as we show below.

What can be said about the strategies employed in asset pricing? First, asset pricing is model based. Second, the centre stage example of the CAPM shows that there is a model with a main core, extended in various ways, and subjected to empirical tests. Let us now delve a bit deeper into the CAPM extensions and empirical tests.

---

[10] It is also referred to as the portfolio that maximizes Sharpe ratio in the economy or the optimal tangency portfolio.

[11] Fama (1968) provides the well-known beta-form of the CAPM:

$$E[R_{i,t+1} - R_{f,t+1}] = \beta E[R_{m,t+1} - R_{f,t+1}], \tag{1}$$

where $R_{i,t+1}$ is the return on asset i, $R_{f,t+1}$ is the risk-free rate, $R_{m,t+1}$ is the return on the market, and $\beta = \frac{Cov[R_{i,t+1}, R_{m,t+1}]}{Var[R_{m,t+1}]}$.

The claims made on the basis of the CAPM and its extensions centre on explaining the determinants of asset prices, notably with relation to market risk and other aspects, which depend on the specific extension of the CAPM used. In that sense, there is a broad similarity in terms of the content of the claims they make: they are aimed at explaining the determinants of asset prices. At least that much can be said about the original CAPM and its theoretical extensions.

However, even among the theoretical extensions of the CAPM we can further identify notable differences in the content of the claims made. For example, the original CAPM identifies a single determinant of asset prices, namely assets' market risk. The intertemporal extension by Merton (1973) allow for other determinants of stock prices (that are different from market risk). The Consumption CAPM of Breeden (1979) also aims at explaining the determinant of asset prices and points towards consumption risk rather than the market risk.

There are also empirical extensions of the CAPM that seem to be less geared towards explanatory import and more closely related to improving on the predictive power of the original CAPM. Fama and French (1992, 1996) introduced the three-factor model where next to the market factor of the CAPM they added size and book-to-market factors. The three-factor model is an empirical extension to the CAPM, because the additional two factors are not a result of a theoretical extension of the CAPM (i.e. relaxation of the CAPM assumptions), but are motivated by the observed differences between the CAPM predictions and the observed cross-section of stock market returns (the so-called CAPM anomalies, as mentioned in section 1 (Black et al., 1972; Banz, 1981)). The main goal of this model is to summarize the differences in return across assets, rather than providing the determinants of their prices.

While such characterizations can be made, at least provisionally, our main contention is that it is difficult to make more precise the content of the claims and their differences between the different CAPM-related models (for a more detailed analysis of this point, see Vergara-Fernández et al. (2023a)). Our brief review suggests that the persistent proliferation of slightly varied empirical and theoretical extensions of the CAPM has resulted in a scientific practice that is complex. As such, model-based asset pricing is fertile ground for the exploration of model-based inquiry more generally in practice-oriented philosophy of science, not only regarding financial economics, but also other disciplines such as biology.

Second, what is the practical import of the claims typically made in asset pricing?

Let us now move from analysing the *content* of the claims that are made in CAPM-based asset pricing to their *practical import*. Here, it is striking that—despite the differences between the various CAPM extensions—the close interrelation with financial practice is a common theme. We briefly highlight two aspects of these interrelations. First, there is overwhelming evidence that the

CAPM plays a central role in financial practice. Graham and Harvey (2001) show that the CAPM is the most popular method for estimating cost of capital (i.e. 73.5% of CFO use CAPM). Brounen et al. (2004) claim that CAPM is consistently more popular among large firms in estimating the cost of capital (45% in Europe and 73% in the US). Similar evidence exists for firms in the UK (McLaney et al., 2004), the Netherlands and China (Hermes and Yao, 2007), Australia (Truong and Peat, 2008), and Iceland (Khalfan and Sturluson, 2018). Berk and van Binsbergen (2016, 2017) show that the CAPM is the closest approximation to the model that mutual fund investors use to make their capital allocation decisions. Blocher and Molyboga (2017) show that the CAPM best models sophisticated investors' preferences and that this model dominates all other known multifactor models. This evidence suggests that—despite the complex picture of CAPM extensions, and despite the empirical failures of CAPM—the CAPM plays a significant role in financial practice. What precisely such surveys show remains unclear, though: the CAPM might be used as one of many tools, as a baseline model, or as one ingredient in a complex decision calculus.

A second aspect of the practical import of the CAPM we have already mentioned in the introduction to this chapter. One of the biggest trends on financial markets in the past decades is the advent of 'passive investment'. In contrast to active investment, there is no discretionary strategy by an investment manager in passive investment. Passive funds simply follow a predetermined rule, which can generally be carried out by computers. They invest in publicly listed stocks or bonds that are liquid, or easy to buy and sell. The most popular are 'index' funds that track benchmark stock and bond indices (e.g. S&P 500). Passive investing is cheaper: there are no expensive portfolio managers. As such, it has 'democratized investment' by opening up the possibility for institutional investors to market investment opportunities to individual households. As mentioned in the introduction to this chapter, index funds accounted for $15tr in assets at the end of the year 2020 (Wigglesworth, 2021), and the roots of this financial innovation can be traced to the theories of financial markets proposed in the 1960s and 1970s (Bernstein, 1993, ch. 12; Mehrling, 2005, ch. 4).

The emergence of financial economics shows deep and complex interrelations with financial practice. This 'reflexivity' or 'performativity' of financial economics has been analysed with tools from sociology of science already. Notably, MacKenzie (2006a, 2006b) and MacKenzie et al. (2007) have investigated how Black-Scholes modelled option pricing. While this is a significant contribution, the challenge for the philosopher of science is to ascertain what the performative aspect of financial economics has to do with the epistemic performance of this scientific field: is it (partly) constitutive of it, independent of it—or even detrimental to it in some sense? It is in this sense that observing 'performativity' forms a question and not an answer. For a more detailed elaboration of this point, see Vergara-Fernández et al. (2023b).

To sum up: the scientific practice of the CAPM and its extensions is complex, and analysing the content of the claims made is an intriguing task for philosophers of science. Moreover, the CAPM and its extensions are generally important for practice and also 'performative'. In particular the performative aspect of financial economics presents a pervasive challenge for the philosopher of science who is interested in analysing the content as well as the epistemic and non-epistemic import of the claims made in this field.

Third, what are the main problems related to obtaining adequate evidence for the claims made in the asset pricing literature?

As we have seen before, the empirical record of the CAPM is mixed: various empirical extensions of the CAPM have been proposed in order to deal with the CAPM anomalies (Black et al., 1972; Banz, 1981; Fama and French, 1992, 1996), that is, the observed differences between the CAPM predictions and the observed cross-section of stock market returns. But what are the main elements and problems in the empirical work in asset pricing in the first place?

In a seminal contribution Roll (1977) asserted that the CAPM is testable in principle, but that no correct test has been provided in the literature. Moreover, he claims that 'there is practically no possibility that such test can be accomplished in the future' Roll (1977, p. 129f.). The problem arises because the implication of the CAPM that betas are linearly related to expected returns is not an independent proposition. The only testable implication of the CAPM is that the market is mean-variance efficient. Betas will be linearly related to expected returns if and only if the market is mean-variance efficient. Moreover, the market portfolio, being the sum of all the risky assets held in the economy by all investors, is not observable. In any sample, there are always a number of mean-variance efficient portfolios. There will be a linear relationship between the betas of these portfolios and the expected returns. So, the relation between beta and expected return will be satisfied exactly irrespective of whether the true market portfolio is efficient or not. Therefore, at least in principle, the CAPM is not testable unless the true market portfolio is observed.

Now, problems of indirect observation, proxies, and auxiliary assumptions are familiar problems in all the empirical sciences, and the fundamental challenges described here are a classic case of theory being underdetermined by the evidence. And so, the question arises how the CAPM literature deals with these challenges. Simply put, they use a proxy to capture the true unobserved market portfolio. This is a sound empirical strategy, but still defeasible in two ways (Roll, 1977). First, the proxy might be mean-variance efficient when the true market is not. Or the chosen proxy might be inefficient, again implying nothing about the efficiency of the true market portfolio. Second, all the proxies will be highly correlated and correlated with the true market portfolio, which makes it seem that the exact composition is not important whereas two proxies (one efficient the other not) will lead to the opposite conclusions.

Asset pricing scholars debate the prospects for progress in empirical testing in the face of these challenges. Consider that the three-factor model of Fama and French (1992, 1996) mentioned earlier became a new state of the art model and started a large (perhaps even the biggest) literature on more so-called 'factor models' in finance: Harvey et al. (2016) document 315 such factors and characteristics, and Harvey and Liu (2019) document more than 400 of them. The question thus arises whether this 'factor zoo' can be tamed (Feng et al., 2020). Cochrane (2008, 242f.) is pessimistic that the strategy pursued by factor models will be fruitful: 'The only content to empirical work in asset pricing is what constraints the author put on his fishing expedition to avoid rediscovering Roll's theorem. The instability of many 'anomalies' and the ever-changing nature of factor models that 'explain' them (Schwert, 2003) lends some credence to this worry'. This debate about the empirical research strategies in asset pricing presents a further angle from which to formulate interesting questions from the philosophy of science. For instance, are spurious findings in asset pricing an indication of a replication crisis, or could they also partially reflect changing causal relations? More generally, what kind of accomplishments can reasonably be expected from a branch of scientific inquiry that researches a phenomenon that changes and fluctuates as much as financial markets do?

3. Ethical Values in Financial Economics

We now turn from the epistemic assessment of financial economics to the role of non-epistemic values. To what extent does financial economics take into account and discuss ethical, political, and social values?

First, it is interesting to ask which role the so-called 'value-free ideal' might play for financial economics. Here, we think that the existing literature in the philosophy and methodology of economics has much to offer in order to reflect about some issues related to this question. To what extent is or can a part of financial economics be value-free? We think it is fruitful to analyse this question from the point of view of the longstanding fact–value debate regarding economics (e.g. Mongin, 2006; Putnam and Walsh, 2012; Su and Colander, 2013; Małecka, 2021).

Second, a specific value topic of recently emerging relevance in the literature in financial economics is *sustainability*. Contributions related to sustainability are scattered across different topics that include, among others, the analysis of (i) Corporate Social Responsibility (CSR) policies of firms, (ii) Socially Responsible Investments (SRI), sometimes also called ethical or sustainable investments, (iii) Environmental, Social and Governance factors (ESG) and their relation to risk and performance, and (iv) climate finance.

In the asset pricing literature, Heinkel et al. (2001) were the first one to propose an equilibrium model with 'green' investors. Later, Bauer et al. (2005) and Renneboog et al. (2008) found no significant difference between risk-adjusted returns of sustainable and conventional mutual funds, while Geczy et al. (2005) report a worse performance of the portfolio of SRI funds compared to the unconstrained portfolio of all the funds. Statman and Glushkov (2009) compare the performance of firms with high and low ESG scores and find that investing in companies with high ESG scores can have a positive impact on portfolio value provided that investors do not shun stocks of companies associated with the so-called sin industries (i.e. tobacco, alcohol, gambling, firearms, military, and nuclear operations). More recently, Pedersen et al. (2021) attempt to solve the problem of incorporating costs and benefits of ESG into investors' portfolio choice.

Regarding climate finance, Beatty and Shimshack (2010) examine the impact of climate-related ratings of firms on their stock returns, Balvers et al. (2017) examine the impact of temperature shocks on firms cost of equity, and Bernstein et al. (2019) examine how housing markets price long-run risk related to sea level rise.

The results across these different studies are pointing in multiple directions. In general, the literature on all the aforementioned aspects of sustainability in financial economics (i-iv) has only been emerging recently, and there is no clear trend yet as to which kinds of claims about sustainability and its relation to performance and risk can be made.

The topic of sustainability also poses a deeper methodological question to financial economics: is it enough to estimate the impact of sustainability-related aspects on risk and performance? Or does financial economics itself need to change? Schoenmaker (2017, p. 8) answers the latter question in the affirmative and calls for a more fundamental methodological shift in the outlook of financial economics: 'Traditional finance focuses on financial return and regards the financial sector as separate from the society of which it is part and the environment in which it is embedded. By contrast, sustainable finance considers financial, social, and environmental returns in combination'. Critically examining these new developments, their methodological implications, and the role of ethical values in financial economics more generally presents a further opportunity for philosophy of science research into financial economics.

4. Conclusions

This concludes our threefold analysis of financial economics from a philosophy of science perspective. To summarize: First, we provided what we take to be a faithful description of how financial economics matured as a research field.

Second, we investigated how asset pricing establishes its claims. The model-based and performative character of asset pricing as depicted here by focusing on the CAPM and its extensions paints a complex and intriguing picture. We have shown that there is a multitude of models in CAPM, which are at the same time closely related as well as slightly different from each other. Due to this, the content of the claims they make are difficult to analyse conclusively. What is more, the CAPM enjoys both enduring popularity in financial practice, and many claim that it has even played an important role in shaping financial reality through facilitating the growing importance of passive investment. In addition, there are some concrete debates about how to resolve the evidential challenges in asset pricing, as well as principled doubts about the eventual success of any such strategy.

Third, we emphasized that analysing the role of ethical values—and sustainability in particular—is another important, and potentially fruitful topic for the philosophy of science of financial economics.

In general, we think that the degree of complexity of the scientific practice that emerges from our analysis may be a reason for why analysis of financial economics has so far mainly proceeded by investigating single models, or not taken up as enthusiastically as other economic subfields by general philosophers of economics. It is our hope that some of the issues we outline in this chapter can be taken up in the emerging field of the philosophy of science of financial economics.

Acknowledgements

We thank Robert Northcott, William Peden, Jack Vromen, two anonymous referees, and the editors of this volume for their insightful comments on a previous draft of this chapter. We also thank Vince Rijnberg for his research assistance and the Erasmus Initiative 'Dynamics of Inclusive Prosperity' at Erasmus University Rotterdam for supporting the 'Values in Finance' research project.

References

Balvers, R., Du, D., & Zhao, X. (2017). Temperature shocks and the cost of equity capital: Implications for climate change perceptions. *Journal of Banking and Finance, 77*, 18–34.

Banz, R. W. (1981). The relationship between return and market value of common stocks. *Journal of Financial Economics, 9*(1), 3–18.

Bauer, R., Koedijk, K., & Otten, R. (2005). International evidence on ethical mutual fund performance and investment style. *Journal of Banking and Finance, 29*, 1751–67.

Beatty, T. K. M., & Shimshack, J. P. (2010). The impact of climate change information: New evidence from the stock market. *B.E. Journal of Economic Analysis and Policy, 10*.

Berk, J. B., & van Binsbergen, J. H. (2016). Assessing asset pricing models using revealed preference. *Journal of Financial Economics, 119*(1), 1–23.

Berk, J. B., & van Binsbergen, J. H. (2017). How do investors compute the discount rate? They use the CAPM (corrected June 2017). *Financial Analysts Journal, 73*(2), 25–32.

Bernstein, A., Gustafson, M. T., & Lewis, R. (2019). Disaster on the horizon: The price effect of sea level rise. *Journal of Financial Economics, 134*, 253–72.

Bernstein, P. L. (1993). *Capital Ideas: The Improbable Origins of Modern Wall Street.* Simon & Schuster.

Bhattacharya, S. (1988). Corporate finance and the legacy of Miller and Modigliani. *Journal of Economic Perspectives, 2*(4), 135–47.

Blocher, J., & Molyboga, M. (2017). The revealed preference of sophisticated investors. *European Financial Management, 23*(5), 839–72. https://doi.org/10.1111/eufm.12128

Boldyrev, I. (2021). The ontology of uncertainty in finance: The normative legacy of general equilibrium. *Topoi, 40*(4), 725–31. https://doi.org/10.1007/s11245-019-09646-5

Boldyrev, I., & Svetlova, E. (eds.). (2016). *Enacting Dismal Science.* Palgrave Macmillan US. https://doi.org/10.1057/978-1-137-48876-3

Brav, A., Heaton, J., & Rosenberg, A. (2004). The rational–behavioral debate in financial economics. *Journal of Economic Methodology, 11*(4), 393–409.

Breeden, D. T. (1979). An intertemporal asset pricing model with stochastic consumption and investment opportunities. *Journal of Financial Economics, 7*, 265–96.

Brisset, N. (2018). Models as speech acts: The telling case of financial models. *Journal of Economic Methodology, 25*(1), 21–41. https://doi.org/10.1080/1350178X.2018.1419105

Brounen, D., de Jong, A., & Koedijk, K. (2004). Corporate finance in Europe: Confronting theory with practice. *Financial Management, 33*, 71–101.

Cochrane, J. H. (2008). Financial markets and the real economy. In R. Mehra (Ed.), Handbook of the equity risk premium. Elsevier. https://doi.org/10.1016/B978-0-444-50899-7.X5001-5

Cowles 3rd, A. (1933). Can Stock Market Forecasters Forecast? *Econometrica, 1*(3), 309–24. https://doi.org/10.2307/1907042

Davis, J. B. (2013). Soros's reflexivity concept in a complex world: Cauchy distributions, rational expectations, and rational addiction. *Journal of Economic Methodology, 20*(4), 368–76. https://doi.org/10.1080/1350178X.2013.859407

De Bruin, B., Herzog, L., O'Neill, M., & Sandberg, J. (2018). Philosophy of money and finance. In E. N. Zalta (ed.), *The Stanford Encyclopedia of Philosophy* (Winter 2018). Metaphysics Research Lab, Stanford University.

Delcey, T. (2019). Samuelson vs Fama on the efficient market hypothesis: The point of view of expertise. *Œconomia. History, Methodology, Philosophy, 9–1*, 37–58. https://doi.org/10.4000/oeconomia.5300

Dewing, A. S. (1919). *The Financial Policy of Corporations.* Ronald Press Company.

Dimand, R. W. (2019). The Cowles Commission and Foundation for Research in Economics. *Cowles Foundation Discussion Paper No. 2207*. https://dx.doi.org/10.2139/ssrn.3495952

Fama, E. F. , & French, K. (1992). The cross-section of expected stock returns. *Journal of Finance, 47*(2), 427–65.

Fama, E. F. (1965a). Random walks in stock market prices. *Financial Analysts Journal, 21*, 55–9.

Fama, E. F. (1965b). The behavior of stock-market prices. *The Journal of Business, 38*(1), 34–105. http://www.jstor.org/stable/2350752

Fama, E. F. (1968). Risk, return and equilibrium: Some clarifying comments. *Journal of Finance, 23*(1), 29–40. https://doi.org/10.1111/j.1540-6261.1968.tb02996.x

Fama, E. F. (1970). Efficient capital markets: A review of theory and empirical work. *Journal of Finance, 25*, 383–417.

Feng, G., Giglio, S., & Xiu, D. (2020). Taming the factor zoo: A test of new factors. *Journal of Finance, 75*, 1327–70.

Forer, M. L. (1954). Dewing: The financial policy of corporations. *Yale Law Journal, 63*(6), 10.

Geczy, C. C., Stambaugh, R. F., & Levin, D. (2005). Investing in socially responsible mutual funds. Working Paper, Wharton School.

Giang Truong, G. P., & Peat, M. (2008). Cost-of-capital estimation and capital-budgeting practice in Australia. *Australian Journal of Management, 33*, 95–121.

Graham, J. R., & Harvey, C. R. (2001). The theory and practice of corporate finance: Evidence from the field. *Journal of Financial Economics, 57*.

Harvey, C. R., & Liu, Y. (2019). A census of the factor zoo. Working Paper, Duke University.

Harvey, C. R., Liu, Y., & Zhu, H. (2016). . . . and the cross-section of expected returns. *Review of Financial Studies, 29*, 5–68.

Heinkel, R., Kraus, A., & Zechner, J. (2001). The effect of green investment on corporate behavior. *Journal of Financial and Quantitative Analysis, 36*(4), 431–49. https://doi.org/10.2307/2676219

Herfeld, C. (2017). Between mathematical formalism, normative choice rules, and the behavioural sciences: The emergence of rational choice theories in the late 1940s and early 1950s. *European Journal of the History of Economic Thought, 24*(6), 1277–317.

Hermes, N., Smid, P., & Yao, L. (2007). Capital budgeting practices: A comparative study of the Netherlands and China. *International Business Review, 16*, 630–54.

Hindriks, F. (2008). False models as explanatory engines. *Philosophy of the Social Sciences, 38*(3), 334–60. https://doi.org/10.1177/0048393108319414

Hindriks, F. (2013). Explanation, understanding, and unrealistic models. *Studies in History and Philosophy of Science Part A, 44*(3), 523–31. https://doi.org/10.1016/j.shpsa.2012.12.004

Hirshleifer, D. (2015). Behavioral finance. Annual Review of Financial Economics, 7, 133–159.

Hommes, C. (2013). Reflexivity, expectations feedback and almost self-fulfilling equilibria: Economic theory, empirical evidence and laboratory experiments. *Journal of Economic Methodology, 20*(4), 406–19. https://doi.org/10.1080/1350178X.2013.859426

Ippoliti, E. (2021a). Introduction: Philosophy for finance. *Topoi, 40*(4), 707–13. https://doi.org/10.1007/s11245-021-09759-w

Ippoliti, E. (2021b). Mathematics and finance: Some philosophical remarks. *Topoi, 40*(4), 771–81. https://doi.org/10.1007/s11245-020-09706-1

Jhun, J., Palacios, P., & Weatherall, J. O. (2018). Market crashes as critical phenomena? Explanation, idealization, and universality in econophysics. *Synthese, 195*(10), 4477–505.

Jovanovic, F. (2008). The construction of the canonical history of financial economics. *History of Political Economy, 40*(2), 213–42.

Jovanovic, F. (2018). A comparison between qualitative and quantitative histories: The example of the efficient market hypothesis. *Journal of Economic Methodology, 25*(4), 291–310.

Kendall, M. G., & Hill, A. B. (1953). The analysis of Economic Time-Series-Part I: Prices. *Journal of the Royal Statistical Society. Series A (General), 116*(1), 11–34. https://doi.org/10.2307/2980947

Khalfan, T., & Sturluson, J. T. (2018). Corporate finance approaches of Icelandic private firms after the financial crisis. *Managerial Finance, 44*, 1274–91.

Knoll, M. S. (2018). The Modigliani–Miller theorem at 60: The long-overlooked legal applications of finance's foundational theorem. *JREG Bulletin, 36*, 1.

Lintner, J. (1965). The valuation of risk assets and the selection of risky investments in stock portfolios and capital budgets. *Review of Economics and Statistics, 47*(1), 13–37. https://doi.org/10.2307/1924119

MacKenzie, D. (2006a). *An Engine, Not a Camera: How Financial Models Shape Markets.* MIT Press.

MacKenzie, D. (2006b). Is economics performative? Option theory and the construction of derivatives markets. *Journal of the History of Economic Thought, 28*(1), 29–55. https://doi.org/10.1080/10427710500509722

MacKenzie, D., Muniesa, F., & Siu, L. (2007). *Do Economists Make Markets? On the Performativity of Economics.* Princeton University Press.

McLaney, E., Pointon, J., Thomas, M., & Tucker, J. (2004). Practitioners' perspectives on the UK cost of capital. *European Journal of Finance, 10*, 123–38.

Małecka, M. (2021). Values in economics: A recent revival with a twist. *Journal of Economic Methodology, 28*(1), 88–97.

Mangee, N. J. (2015). A Kuhnian perspective on asset pricing theory. *Journal of Economic Methodology, 22*(1), 28–45.

Markowitz, H. (1952). Portfolio selection. *Journal of Finance, 7*(1), 77–91. https://doi.org/10.2307/2975974

Mehrling, P. (2005). *Fischer Black and the Revolutionary Idea of Finance.* Wiley.

Merton, R. C. (1973). An intertemporal capital asset pricing model. *Econometrica*, *41*(5), 867–87. https://doi.org/10.2307/1913811

Merton, R. C. (1997, December 9). Applications of option-pricing theory: Twenty-five years later [Nobel Lecture].

Miller, M. H. (1988). The Modigliani–Miller propositions after thirty years. *Journal of Economic Perspectives*, *2*(4), 99–120.

Miotti, G. (2021). Model building and problem solving: A case from Libor market derivatives. *Topoi*, *40*(4), 783–91. https://doi.org/10.1007/s11245-019-09652-7

Modigliani, F., & Miller, M. H. (1958). The cost of capital, corporation finance and the theory of investment. *American Economic Review*, *48*(3), 261–97.

Mongin, P. (2006). Value judgments and value neutrality in economics. *Economica*, *72*(290), 257–86.

Mossin, J. (1966). Equilibrium in a capital asset market. *Econometrica*, *34*(4), 768–83. https://doi.org/10.2307/1910098

Pedersen, L. H., Fitzgibbons, S., & Pomorski, L. (2021). Responsible investing: The ESG-efficient frontier. *Journal of Financial Economics*, *142*(2), 572–97.

Pfleiderer, P. (2014). Chameleons: The misuse of theoretical models in finance and economics. *Revista de Economía Institucional*, *16*(31), 23–60.

Putnam, H., & Walsh, V. (2012). *The End of Value-Free Economics*. Routledge.

Renneboog, L., Horst, J. ter, & Zhang, C. (2008). The price of ethics and stakeholder governance: The performance of socially responsible mutual funds. *Journal of Corporate Finance*, *14*, 302–22.

Rickles, D. (2007). Econophysics for philosophers. *Studies in History and Philosophy of Science Part B: Studies in History and Philosophy of Modern Physics*, *38*(4), 948–78.

Roll, R. (1977). A critique of the asset pricing theory's tests Part I: On past and potential testability of the theory. *Journal of Financial Economics*, *4*(2), 129–76. https://doi.org/10.1016/0304-405X(77)90009-5

Ross, S. A. (1988). Comment on the Modigliani–Miller propositions. *Journal of Economic Perspectives*, *2*(4), 127–33.

Samuelson, P. (1965). Proof that properly anticipated prices fluctuate randomly. *Industrial Management Review*, *6*, 41–9.

Schoenmaker, D. (2017). *From Risk to Opportunity: A Framework for Sustainable Finance*. Rotterdam School of Management, Erasmus University, Rotterdam.

Schwert, G. W. (2003). Anomalies and Market Efficiency, In: George Constantinides, Milton Harris, and René Stulz (eds.), *Handbook of the Economics of Finance* (Ch. 15, pp. 937–72). North-Holland.

Sharpe, W. F. (1964). Capital asset prices: A theory of market equilibrium under conditions of risk. *Journal of Finance*, *19*(3), 425–42. https://doi.org/10.1111/j.1540-6261.1964.tb02865.x

Simon, H. A. (1996). *Models of My Life*. MIT Press.

Soros, G. (2013). Fallibility, reflexivity, and the human uncertainty principle. *Journal of Economic Methodology*, *20*(4), 309–29. https://doi.org/10.1080/1350178X.2013.859415

Statman, M., & Glushkov, D. (2009). The wages of social responsibility. *Financial Analysts Journal*, *65*, 33–46.

Su, H.-C., & Colander, D. (2013). A failure to communicate: The fact–value divide and the Putnam–Dasgupta debate. *Erasmus Journal for Philosophy and Economics*, *6*(2), 1–23.

Svetlova, E. (2018). *Financial Models and Society: Villains or Scapegoats?* Edward Elgar.

Treynor, J. (1962). *Toward a Theory of Market Value of Risky Assets*. Online: Available at SSRN: https://ssrn.com/abstract=628187 or http://dx.doi.org/10.2139/ssrn.628187

Vergara-Fernández, M., & de Bruin, B. (2021). Finance and financial economics: A philosophy of science perspective. In C. Heilmann & J. Reiss (eds.), *The Routledge Handbook of Philosophy of Economics* (pp. 198–207). Routledge.

Vergara-Fernández, M., Heilmann, C., & Szymanowska, M. (2023a). Describing model relations: The case of the capital asset pricing model (CAPM) family in financial economics. *Studies in History and Philosophy of Science*, *97*, 91–100.

Vergara-Fernández, M., Heilmann, C., & Szymanowska, M. (2023b). Contextualist model evaluation: Models in financial economics and index funds. *European Journal for Philosophy of Science* *13*, 6.

Vuillemey, G. (2014). Epistemological foundations for the assessment of risks in banking and finance. *Journal of Economic Methodology*, *21*(2), 125–38.

Walter, C. P. (2000). The efficient market hypothesis, the Gaussian assumption, and the investment management industry. EFMA 2001 Lugano Meetings. https://dx.doi.org/10.2139/ssrn.267443

Walter, C. P. (2016). The financial logos: The framing of financial decision-making by mathematical modelling. *Research in International Business and Finance*, *37*, 597–604. https://doi.org/10.1016/j.ribaf.2016.01.022

Walter, C. P. (2021). The Brownian motion in finance: An epistemological puzzle. *Topoi*, *40*(4), 1–17. https://doi.org/10.1007/s11245-019-09660-7

Wigglesworth, R. (2021). *Trillions: How a Band of Wall Street Renegades Invented the Index Fund and Changed Finance Forever*. Portfolio.

7

JPMorgan Chase's "London Whale" Trading Losses

A Tale of Human Fallibility

Lisa Warenski

1. Introduction

We are fallible reasoners, prone to error in various ways. Yet we have the capacity to recognize and correct our errors. We are likewise capable of improving the ways in which we make decisions and arrive at judgments. Practices that promote good reasoning and veridical judgments and, further, are suitable for widespread adoption are what I call "good epistemic practices." Epistemic practices are norms, policies, procedures, and methodologies that have been or could be adopted. Good epistemic practices are practices that generate cognitive successes and minimize cognitive failures. They include practices that anticipate and correct for ways in which we are prone to error.

Good epistemic practices are important for groups as well as individuals. My concern in this chapter will be with good epistemic practices for a particular kind of group: financial institutions. Epistemic failings were implicated in the 2008 global financial crisis (De Bruin 2015; Warenski 2019 and forthcoming), and one way for financial institutions to avoid future epistemic failings is by developing and adopting institutional good epistemic practices. These will include practices that promote good judgments generally as well as methodologies that are specific to particular lines of business within an organization. Making judgments about relative risk and reward, and managing for risk, are central to the business of banking; good epistemic practices are implicit in these core functions. My focus in this chapter will be on the risk management function.

In 2012, JPMorgan's notorious "London Whale" trading losses roiled the financial markets and raised concerns about the presence of ongoing systemic problems in the credit derivatives market. The losses were all the more alarming because JPMorgan was (and is) widely considered to be an industry leader in risk management (US Senate Subcommittee Report 2013, p. 154). In this chapter, I explain some of the key breakdowns in the Bank's risk management function that led to the London Whale trading losses. I argue that some of these failures of

Lisa Warenski, *JPMorgan Chase's "London Whale" Trading Losses: A Tale of Human Fallibility* In: *The Philosophy of Money and Finance*. Edited by: Joakim Sandberg and Lisa Warenski, Oxford University Press. © Oxford University Press 2024.
DOI: 10.1093/oso/9780192898807.003.0008

risk management were epistemic in character and might have been prevented by anticipating and taking steps to counter potential errors of reasoning. Ergo, taking up the epistemic point of view with the aim of identifying good epistemic practices could support the risk management function.

In Section 2, I further explain what good epistemic practices are. In Section 3, I explain how good epistemic practices are components of risk management, and I illustrate with an example. I then present a summary of the circumstances that led to the London Whale trading losses in Section 4. Section 5 discusses some of the distinctively epistemic failings that were implicated in the London Whale trading losses and suggests some precautions that might have been taken to guard against them. Section 6 concludes with a few lessons to be learned from the case.

2. Good Epistemic Practices

The notion of "best practices" or "good practices" is widely used in industry and professions such as medicine and accounting. Statements of best or good practices are guidelines that have been shown, or can reasonably be expected, to produce good results. An example is provided by the accounting profession. Accounting best practices are established by the International Accounting Standards Board (IASB) for most parts of the world and by the Financial Accounting Standards Board (FASB) for the USA. Accounting best practices are a common set of principles, standards, and procedures that are designed to provide useful information to the users of financial statements and reports by focusing on the relevant and faithful representation of financial information (FASB 2014, pp. 2–3).[1]

The Boards issue both general and specific guidelines that are designed to cover the full range of financial reporting circumstances. For example, FASB's Concepts Statements are general guidelines that set the objectives and concepts that guide the selection of economic phenomena to be included in financial reporting (FASB. org, Concepts Statements). The Concepts Statements inform the Board in their development of specific accounting guidelines. The accounting guidelines in their totality are under continuing review in order to reflect changes in methods of doing business and changes in the economic environment (FASB 2014, p. 3).

Another example of a statement of good practices is the ICH–GCP, an international set of ethical and scientific standards that governs research involving human subjects. The ICH–GCP guidelines provide a framework for the fair and scientifically sound conduct of clinical trials involving human subjects (European

---

[1] See Chapter 4 in this volume, for discussion of some of the complexities involved in achieving this aim.

Medicines Agency 2002). The current system of good clinical practices evolved, in part, in response to past abuses of research participants.[2]

Similarly, statements of good *epistemic* practices are guidelines that prescribe actions and encode values. A good epistemic practice is one that furthers an epistemic aim or realizes an epistemic value. I understand epistemic aims and values to be truth-oriented cognitive aims and values. Taking epistemic aims and values to bear some essential relation to truth does not require taking true belief to be the only non-instrumental epistemic good: we also value goods such as understanding, explanation, and coherence. But these epistemic goods do not stand in opposition to true belief; they arguably have their epistemic value in virtue of a relation that they bear to truth (see Alston 2005, ch. 3 and Pritchard 2014 for discussion).

Like other good practices in industry, good epistemic practices are adopted methodologies or candidates for adoption. Examples of good epistemic practices include checking one's work for accuracy, considering and evaluating possible alternative explanations for a set of observed facts, and utilizing a method of assessment that has been shown to be reliable. Like other good practices, they are, in principle, subject to ongoing evaluation and improvement. In what follows, I will speak of "good" rather than "best" epistemic practices because I do not want to imply that a particular suggested epistemic practice is uniquely best.

In addition to task-specific methodologies, good epistemic practices may include general norms of reasoning. A central project of epistemology from Antiquity onward has been the effort to identify good deductive rules, inductive rules, and governing norms of belief formation. For example, the logic of Chrysippus encompassed the analysis of argument forms; Descartes's *Discourse on Method* (1637/1985) laid down rules for belief formation; and modern-day Bayesians study epistemic rationality and probabilistic inference.

An example of a general epistemic norm that we might adopt as a good practice is the norm of coherence. We may employ coherence as a component of our standards of evaluation for a proposed strategy or an explanation of a set of apparently interrelated facts or events. Another example of a general norm that we might adopt is the requirement that a sample be sufficiently large and free of bias before making an inductive generalization based on the sample. For professionals who are engaged in the collection and statistical analysis of data, this general norm will generate sampling techniques that are designed to minimize bias. For individual reasoners, adhering to the norm may mean being sensitive to the pitfalls of hasty generalization.

---

[2] The ICH–GCP was developed by the International Council for Harmonisation of Technical Requirements for Pharmaceuticals for Human Use (the "ICH"). The ICH–GCP has its roots in the Nuremberg Code (1947) and is based on principles in the Declaration of Helsinki (1964). See Vijayananthan and Nawawi (2008) for discussion.

By way of supporting good reasoning and our epistemic goals, some good epistemic practices will be designed to anticipate the ways in which we are fallible reasoners and to guard against potential errors. One source of error that will feature in the discussion to follow is failure of imagination. We may fail to consider relevant alternative explanations or fail to identify possible risks and their likely consequences. Misdiagnoses in medicine, erroneous economic predictions, and unexpected ways in which algorithms reflect and perpetuate bias are outcomes that may reflect failures of imagination.

Cognitive biases are another important source of error. We often employ heuristics in reasoning. Heuristics are problem-solving processes—mental shortcuts—that make efficient use of limited resources. Heuristics produce intuitive judgments in which difficult questions are answered by substituting easier ones (Kahneman and Frederick 2002). While heuristics enable us to sometimes make accurate approximations (Arkes 1991; Gigerenzer 2002, 2008), they also tend to generate biases, namely systematic deviations from optimal standards of reasoning (Kahneman and Tversky 1972; Tversky and Kahneman 1974; Bishop and Trout 2005). Being aware of potential cognitive biases and taking steps to correct them in circumstances where they may have materially adverse effects potentially improves our epistemic performance.

The causes of epistemic failings are varied. In addition to the epistemic causes mentioned above, epistemic failings may have non-epistemic causes. Epistemic failings may be the result of willful disregard, circumstantial interference with the free exercise of reason, or having limited resources to carry out an epistemic function such as computation or inquiry. A given epistemic failing may be the result of a complex of contributing factors, and arriving at a good explanation of it will be a matter of teasing out the different factors. The development of good epistemic practices is often a response to past epistemic failings.

Articulating good epistemic practices for industry and the professions is an endeavor to answer epistemic "ought" questions of practical significance. In this respect, articulating good epistemic practices is applied epistemology. Applied epistemology brings epistemological theorizing along a range of dimensions to issues of practical, social, and political concern (Coady 2012; Coady and Chase 2019; Lackey 2021).

3. Good Epistemic Practices in the Financial Services Industry

Many of the judgments that professionals in the financial services industry make are about relative risk and reward, and good epistemic practices will support the making of these judgments. For example, a large bank will be engaged in a range of financial services that include investment banking, retail banking, consumer and corporate lending, financial transaction processing, and asset management.

Engaging in these activities requires, among other things, making judgments about credit and market risk. A credit risk is the risk of default by a borrower on a contractual financial obligation. A market risk is the risk of loss arising from factors in the financial markets, namely marketplaces where securities are traded. Factors in the marketplace that pose market risks include changes in interest rates, foreign exchange rates, equity prices, commodities prices, and credit spreads. In addition to making judgements about risk when entering into a transaction, banks and other financial institutions also need to manage the risks relating to their existing assets and liabilities.

An illustration of good epistemic practices in banking is provided by the approval process for a corporate loan. A request for a loan will go through a credit approval process during which the creditworthiness of the borrower will be evaluated. The initial request is typically considered by a credit analyst, who evaluates the credit risks associated with the requested loan. Some of these risks will be risks that are routinely evaluated and which analysts will know to consider in virtue of their training. Such risks include, but are not limited to, possible loss of market share due to competition, product obsolescence, and a high level of debt relative to equity. Other risks will be particular to the loan request. These may pertain to the nature of the company's lines of business; the structure, terms, and conditions of the contracts that the company has entered into; or any number of circumstantial factors that could potentially have an adverse effect on the company's ability to repay the loan on the agreed-upon terms and conditions.

A good analyst will think through the credit request and identify the materially significant risks, whether routine or novel, and consider the factors that mitigate these risks. As part of this evaluation, the analyst will likely ask questions of the company's management and consult with the account officer in charge of the bank's relationship with the company. If the analyst and the account officer conclude that the prospective borrower's credit strengths outweigh its weaknesses and that the proposed loan facility is a good risk for the bank, they will recommend approval of the loan facility. The proposal will then go through a formal approval process during which more senior credit and lending experts in the bank will review it and have the opportunity to ask further questions. If the request is approved and the loan is made, the loan will be monitored on an ongoing basis by the bank for its duration.

The good epistemic practices here include (1) the training of the credit analyst to identify and evaluate certain well-known credit risks, (2) the directive to the analyst to look for and evaluate novel risks that are particular to the request, and (3) the implementation and maintenance of a structured review process whereby the analyst's work is subjected to critical evaluation by increasingly senior and experienced experts. These practices do not ensure that the loan will be repaid as agreed—there is always the possibility that a previously identified or unforeseen risk will materialize, but a decision arrived at via this process will represent the best-considered judgments of all of parties to the decision.

In addition to evaluating risks pertaining to new transactions, financial institutions will manage risk for their assets, liabilities, and operations on an ongoing basis. The risk management function in a bank is an internal system of regulation and control. The "three lines of defense" risk model, originally advocated by the Institute of Internal Auditors, distinguishes three functions involved in effective risk management: operational managers who own and manage risk (first line of defense), risk management functions that oversee the operational units (second line of defense), and the internal audit function (third line of defense) (Institute of Internal Auditors 2013). The London Whale case, which I discuss in the next section, illustrates a breakdown in risk management.[3] The case illustrates the importance of good epistemic practices.

4. JPMorgan Chase's "London Whale" Trading Losses

In early 2012, JPMorgan Chase took massive positions in a complex set of synthetic credit derivatives that resulted in losses to the Bank of at least $6.2 billion. The trades were so large that they roiled the world credit markets. The trades came to be known as the "London Whale" trades because of their size and the fact that they were made by the London branch of the Bank's Chief Investment Office. Prior to the events of the London Whale trading losses, JPMorgan was widely regarded as having among the best risk management practices in the financial industry (US Senate Subcommittee Report 2013, p. 154). The Bank did not need to be bailed out in the 2008 financial crisis, but CEO Jamie Dimon agreed to participate in the Troubled Asset Relief Program (TARP) in order to support the government's efforts to stabilize the banking system. In a message to his employees on the tenth anniversary of the collapse of Lehman Brothers, Mr Dimon wrote, "JPMorgan Chase did not want or need TARP money, but we recognized that if the healthy banks did not take it, no one else could—out of fear that the market would lose confidence in them" (JPM annual report 2019, p. 28).

In 2012 and 2013, an investigation of the circumstances that led to the trading losses was conducted by the US Senate. The summary below is drawn from this investigation and an internal review by a special task force at JPMorgan,[4] which is incorporated in the US Senate Subcommittee's report (US Senate Subcommittee Report 2013). I will abbreviate in-text citations of the review by the Bank's task force and the Senate Subcommittee investigative report, as "TF" and "SSR," respectively.

---

[3] I recount the story of the London Whale trading losses and discuss it in more detail in my "Organizational Good Epistemic Practices" (Warenski 2024). That paper focuses on the development of specific good epistemic practices for organizations.

[4] Cited page numbers are for the original report, which was subsequently incorporated in Volume One of the US Senate Subcommittee Report.

In 2005, JPMorgan's Chief Investment Office (CIO) was created as a separate unit to manage the Bank's excess deposits. The Bank has excess deposits because its businesses take in more deposits than the Bank makes in loans. The CIO invested the bulk of JPMorgan's excess cash in high-quality, fixed-income securities. In 2007, the CIO launched a portfolio of investments called the Synthetic Credit Portfolio, the purpose of which was to offset credit risk within the CIO and for the Bank in its capacity as lender (TF, pp. 21–23).

The Synthetic Credit Portfolio offset credit risk by investing in complex indices comprising credit default swaps. A credit default swap is a contract between two parties that allows the buyer of the swap to transfer or "swap" the credit risk associated with a particular corporate debt instrument to the seller of the swap. The buyer of the swap is essentially buying insurance against the event of a credit default, and the seller of the swap is selling that insurance. The buyer of the swap, who is buying credit protection in the event of a default, is said to be the "short" party, and the seller of the swap, who is selling the credit protection, is said to be the "long" party (SSR, p. 30).

At its inception, the aim of the Synthetic Credit Portfolio was to maintain a position that was net "short" (meaning that the bank was buying credit protection) in order to protect the CIO portfolio and the Bank against adverse credit scenarios. Loans and debt securities tend to perform well when credit markets perform well, and borrowers meet their obligations as agreed. However, in adverse credit markets, loans and debt securities tend to suffer declines in performance. In 2009, during the worst recession in generations, JPMorgan Chase's performance was buoyed by more than $1 billion in profits from protection afforded by the Synthetic Credit Portfolio (SSR, p. 154).

As the recession brought on by the global financial crisis of 2008 began to ease, credit markets began to improve. Accordingly, the CIO traders reduced the size of the Synthetic Credit Portfolio. However, in June 2011, the CIO thought that the credit markets were once again at risk of deteriorating, and it once again started buying credit protection.

The traders wanted to have a more cost-effective way of buying credit protection, so they implemented a new "smart short" strategy that required the purchase of long as well as short credit derivatives. The traders, in effect, sold insurance on the lower-risk investment grade indices and used the proceeds to help fund the purchase of insurance on the higher-risk, higher-yield indices (SSR, p. 51). By taking this strategy, the traders expanded the net notional positions in the Synthetic Credit Portfolio from $4 billion at the beginning of 2011 to approximately $51 billion by the end of the year. (The notional value of a credit default swap refers to the face value of the underlying contract.[5] A net notional position

---

[5] See Wen and Kinsella (2016) for an introduction to credit default swaps, including credit default swap pricing.

offsets, against each other, the amounts of a buy and sell position that reference the same name.)

In late 2011, the Bank's senior management, including the head of the CIO, determined that the global economy was improving. This meant that there was less of a need for the kind of macro-level credit protection that the Synthetic Credit Portfolio had been providing. Also, as part of a Bank-wide effort to comply with new Basel Accord[6] requirements for risk-based capital, senior management directed the CIO to reduce its risk-weighted assets. (Risk-weighted assets are a dollar measure of the bank's assets in the aggregate, where the component assets are weighted by credit risk.[7] It is used to calculate the bank's minimum risk-based capital for which a greater ratio of equity-based capital is required for higher risk-weighted assets.)

The Synthetic Credit Portfolio had a high level of risk-weighted assets. At the end of 2011, the Bank's chief financial officer asked the CIO to evaluate the impact of additional reductions of risk-weighted assets in the Synthetic Credit Portfolio. However, these reductions would have been expensive: the traders estimated that a 35% proportional unwind of the positions in the Synthetic Credit Portfolio would result in a $10 billion reduction to the Portfolio's risk-weighted assets but that the unwind could cost slightly more than $500 million (TF, p. 28).

The head of the CIO, Ina Drew, then asked the traders to see if it was possible to reduce risk-weighted assets without "holding a fire sale."[8] Ultimately, the Bank required the CIO to make only the originally budgeted reductions to their risk-weighted assets. When even these reductions proved to be costly, Drew signaled to the traders that the CIO might have some flexibility in achieving the required reductions, and she ultimately directed them to reduce risk-weighted assets in a way that maximized profits to losses (TF, pp. 28–29).

In late 2011, the traders had begun to unwind some of their short positions in line with the directive to scale back the credit protection component of the portfolio. But in mid-January, a large US corporation filed for bankruptcy. The traders were exposed to this company on the long side, but they had let their credit default protection on the company expire, and the Synthetic Loan Portfolio suffered a loss of $50 million. Also, in January, economies were strengthening in the United States and elsewhere, so worldwide credit markets rallied. This meant that the value of the short credit positions (the protection on the high-risk companies) fell. The result was that the Synthetic Loan Portfolio experienced

---

[6] The Basel Accord standards are banking regulation agreements that are set by the Basel Committee on Bank Supervision.

[7] Risk-weighted assets are calculated by multiplying each individual asset by the weight percentage that corresponds to it risk level and summing the individual risk-weighted assets. Riskier assets such as unsecured loans to non-investment grade companies are given a higher weight than lower-risk assets such collateralized loans or loans to companies with investment-grade ratings.

[8] Subcommittee interview of Ina Drew, CIO (9/7/2012), SSR, p. 62, fn 394.

nine straight days of losses in the second half of January because of the declining value of their short positions (SSR, pp. 65–66).

By mid-January 2012, the CIO traders were confronted with a set of complex and apparently conflicting objectives: stem the losses in its credit portfolio, reduce the Synthetic Credit Portfolio's risk-weighted assets, and maintain default protection to take advantage of any large corporate defaults (SSR, p. 72). In an effort to simultaneously achieve these goals, the traders resumed their strategy of purchasing additional long credit derivatives to finance their short derivative positions, and they engaged in a series of increasingly complex and risky trades.

Market conditions continued to go against the Synthetic Credit Portfolio's positions, and the losses in the Synthetic Credit Portfolio accelerated. By the end of March 2012, the losses had reached $719 million, and the size of the portfolio had increased from net notional $51 billion at the end of calendar year 2011 to $157 billion (SSR, pp. 4, 84, 87).

During the period in which the losses occurred, the Synthetic Credit Portfolio breached a number of its internal limits. At JPMorgan Chase, a breach of a limit is intended to trigger a discussion and analysis of the reasons for the breach and of the rationale for the limit itself (TF, p. 76). However, in the case of the Synthetic Credit Portfolio, two of the limits that were breached were in the process of being revised, and a third was for a new metric that was still in the process of being refined.[9]

Beginning in late January, the London CIO's head of equity and trading directed the senior trader of the portfolio (who became known as the "London Whale") to mark the values of the Portfolio's positions in such a way as to minimize the losses.[10] Moreover, the London CIO did not provide prompt and current trading data to the CIO Head, Ina Drew. As a result, she did not become aware of the full extent of the Synthetic Credit Portfolio's losses and its dramatic increase in size until a fourth and key limit was breached. Once she became fully informed of the changes in late March, she ordered the traders to stop trading. The head of the CIO's London office then solicited the help of the Firm's senior risk managers because he had "lost confidence" in his team. But it was too late to reverse the course of the losses that subsequently ensued (SSR, pp. 83–86).

In early April, the market risk officer of the CIO received a call from a reporter at the *Wall Street Journal* informing him that the paper was planning to run a story on the trading activities of JPMorgan's CIO. The Bank's senior managers first became aware of problems in the Synthetic Credit Portfolio when they were informed of this planned story. Shortly thereafter, both the *Wall Street Journal* and *Bloomberg* ran stories about the large positions in credit default swap market

---

[9] The limits that were breached are identified and discussed in Section V (D) of the Senate Subcommittee Report, pp. 164–210.

[10] I discuss the mismarking of the Synthetic Credit Portfolio in Warenski (2024).

that were taken by a JPMorgan trader, whom the *Wall Street Journal* dubbed the "London Whale" (SSR, p. 91).

On April 13, 2012, JPMorgan Chase hosted an earnings call during which Jamie Dimon agreed with an analyst's characterization of the publicity surrounding the Synthetic Credit Portfolio's trading activities as a "tempest in a teapot." However, the losses in the CIO ultimately forced the Bank to restate its earnings for the first quarter of 2012, and the Bank went on to incur losses of approximately $6.2 billion for the year (SSR, p. 156).

5. Epistemic Failings and Some Possible Remedies

The circumstances and events that led to the London Whale trading losses exhibit a number of epistemic failings. Some of these were violations of the Bank's own endorsed practices for managing risk. For example, the Task Force notes in their report that the Bank expected the traders to subject trading strategies to rigorous questioning and analysis prior to their implementation, and to understand the risks inherent in the trading strategies (TF, p. 85). Another example was the absence of a robust risk management infrastructure within the CIO. The CIO risk function had been historically understaffed; its management team met infrequently; and it failed to perform its intended role as a forum for constructive challenge of practices, strategies, and controls (TF, p. 12).

Other epistemic failings were of a more general nature, reflective of the ways in which we can go wrong, individually and collectively, in our reasoning. These general faults of reasoning are the topic of this section. I will identify three such sources of error that may have been implicated in the Whale trading losses and some of their potential remedies.

5.1 Underreaction to Evidence

The Bank's senior managers were slow to recognize and respond to the changing profile of the Synthetic Credit Portfolio. The original purpose of the Synthetic Credit Portfolio was to generate revenue for the Bank during adverse credit scenarios by buying credit default protection; however, it morphed from a portfolio of net protective positions to an increasing complex and risky portfolio of both long and short positions.

The managers of both the CIO and the Bank may have been slow to heed the signs of the changes in the Synthetic Loan Portfolio because it had performed well in the past. As Jamie Dimon explained, "there was a little bit of complacency about what was taking place [in CIO] and maybe overconfidence." Also, the more conservative nature of the CIO's portfolio, of which the Synthetic Credit

Portfolio was a part, may have suggested to senior Bank management that the CIO did not present significant risks (TF, pp. 94–95).

Given the historically low-risk profile of the Synthetic Credit Portfolio, some signs of escalating risk may have been reasonably discounted. Breaches of limits that were in the process of being revised would have been expected to be cured via the revision. Similarly, the CIO's breaches of value-at-risk, a dollar measure of potential losses over the course of a day, were expected to be rectified upon the immanent approval of a new model for the calculation of value-at-risk.[11]

But other signs of escalating risk should have sounded an alarm. The exponential growth in the notional size of the Synthetic Credit Portfolio, not only in early 2012 when the trading losses began but during the prior year, should have triggered an investigation into the trading strategies that led to the growth. Relatedly, the large spike in early 2012 to the CIO's Comprehensive Risk Measure, a dollar measure of potential losses over the course of a year, was a clear sign of trouble. CIO senior management, firm-wide risk management, and persons in both the CIO and firm-wide finance functions presumably would have been in a position to be aware of these changes. Also, the trading strategies of the Synthetic Credit Portfolio had become increasingly complex and risky for some time prior to the implementation of the strategy that directly led to Whale losses, and senior management should have taken steps to confirm their beliefs that the prevailing risk limits and oversight for the CIO were appropriate (TF, p. 96).

Being slow to recognize change and adjust our belief system accordingly is one way in which we may be prone to error. Systematic underreaction to evidence in complex probabilistic reasoning is a form of cognitive bias, namely a systematic tendency to deviate from correct reasoning about probabilities or Bayesian updating. Underreaction to evidence in laboratory settings is an empirically robust phenomenon that has been well-documented, primarily by studies conducted in the late 1960s and early 1970s. (For reviews of this literature, see Benjamin 2018, Edwards 1968, and Slovic and Lichtenstein 1971.) A leading candidate explanation for systematic underreaction to evidence is *conservatism bias* (Phillips and Edwards 1966; Edwards 1968). Expressed in Bayesian terms, conservatism bias is the systematic tendency to underweight likelihood ratios when updating to posterior beliefs. A likelihood ratio expresses the conditional probability of some observed data, given a hypothesis H; what's relevant to the confirmation of H is the extent to which the observed data is more (or less) probable according to H than according to alternative hypotheses. The utilization of Bayesian reasoning as a standard of correctness is an idealization, however, and it is generally understood that agents who make inferences in the real world and in real time will be making approximate inferences.

---

[11] The new value-at-risk model turned out to be flawed and was later discovered to have been rushed through the Bank's approval process (SSR, pp. 179–180).

The notion of conservatism bias was introduced and studied by Ward Edwards and his students.[12] To illustrate the problem, Edwards asks the reader to consider a hypothetical problem:

> This bookbag contains 1,000 poker chips. I started out with two such bags, one containing 700 red and 300 blue chips, the other containing 300 red and 700 blue. I flipped a fair coin to determine which one to use. Thus, if your opinions are like mine, your probability at the moment that this is the predominantly red bookbag is 0.5. Now, you sample, randomly, with replacement after each chip. In 12 samples, you get 8 reds and 4 blues. Now, on the basis of everything you know, what is the probability that this is the predominantly red bag? Clearly it is higher than 0.5.
>
> (Edwards 1968, pp. 21–22; excerpted in Edwards 1982)

Edwards goes on to report that the intuitive answer for most people is 70–80%, but the appropriate calculations yield an answer of 97%.

However, people do not always underreact to evidence. They sometimes overreact: people sometimes exhibit *base rate neglect*, namely the tendency to underweight the prior probability of an event or the distribution of a characteristic in a population when making a judgment based on incoming evidence. People may underreact or overreact depending on the situation. Daniel Benjamin (2018) notes that the interesting question concerns the conditions that predispose people to do one or the other. Benjamin suggests that people tend to underreact, except in particular cases of signal alignment (Benjamin 2018, Sect. 10.a). Ishita Dasgupta et al. (2020) hypothesize that people put more weight on either the prior or the likelihood ratios, depending on which of the two has been historically more informative about the true posterior.

Much of the evidence for underreaction and overreaction is provided by tightly controlled laboratory studies. The problem structure of laboratory experiments may differ from that of real-world problems, and this raises concerns about the generalizability of laboratory results. Yet some biases, for example, base-rate neglect, have been relatively well-documented in field settings (Benjamin 2018, p. 167). If conservatism bias similarly generalizes to field settings, then it may have been operative in the failure of managers to update their beliefs about the risk profile of the Synthetic Credit Portfolio.

To guard against the pitfalls of underreaction, a first step is to recognize that we may fall victim to it. For situations in which updating our standing beliefs in a

---

[12] See Phillips and Edwards (1966) and Edwards (1968). As Ishita Dasgupta et al. (2020, p. 414) note, the literature on underreaction to evidence faded away without a satisfactory resolution, in part, because research was driven toward the study of base-rate neglect (and concomitant overreaction to evidence) in the early work of Daniel Kahneman and Amos Tversky.

timely fashion is important, we might adopt a review process in which we deliberately ask ourselves: Is there any new information that bears on my existing degrees of belief, and if so, what might it signify? Directing our attention to incoming evidence and deliberating about its possible significance is a first step toward giving due consideration to the hypothesis (or hypotheses) that the evidence supports.

Individual attempts to compensate for bias may be insufficient, however, and some form of external check is often needed. In the case of monitoring a bank's portfolio of assets, asking and answering questions about what has changed as part of a regularly scheduled review process would be an external check that addresses the problem of slow updating of beliefs. Constructing systems of metrics that track changes of potential significance, for review by both initial decision makers and persons who serve in an audit function, is a further measure that is often taken to guard against underreaction. The role of a system of metrics in cases where expert judgment is generally reliable would be to augment rather than replace human judgment.[13]

The Bank, in effect, went on to adopt some epistemic practices along these lines in response to management's failures to recognize and respond to the changes in the Synthetic Credit Portfolio. Specifically, the Bank (1) put in place more stringent requirements for when a breach of a limit must be escalated to senior management, (2) expanded senior management's participation in CIO risk committee meetings and increased their frequency, and (3) created a new firm-wide risk committee to conduct periodic reviews of the Firm's business activities (TF, pp. 115–116).

5.2 The Flip Side of Cognitive Diversity

Having some measure of cognitive diversity within decision-making groups in corporations is generally understood to be desirable. A cognitively diverse group can bring a broader range of perspectives to deliberation than a more cognitively homogenous group. This broader range of perspectives will often lead to better-grounded and more robust judgments.[14]

However, cognitive diversity comes with its own risks. Given the possibility of divergent judgments, operative decision makers in a group need to take steps to ensure that the group arrives at joint decisions that are aligned with group goals.

---

[13] See Kahneman and Klein (2009) for discussion of the role of algorithms in augmenting human judgment and a discussion of skilled intuitions generally.

[14] Diversity within a group can have negative as well as positive effects, however. For a group to benefit from diversity, diversity must be matched by appropriate processes in order for the group to benefit (Simons et al. 1999). See also van Knippenberg and Schippers (2007).

In December 2011, Jamie Dimon and the Bank's chief financial officer directed the CIO to reduce its risk-weighted assets. The chief financial officer, whose background was in investment banking, had assumed that the most direct way for the Synthetic Credit Portfolio to reduce risk-weighted assets would be to unwind its positions (SSR, pp. 61–62). But this would have resulted in large losses to the Portfolio. Accordingly, Ina Drew directed the traders to achieve the reduction in a way that minimized losses. The traders then adopted a strategy whereby they took positions in the market that were designed offset each other in an effort to reduce risk-weighted assets.

The failure to vet the decision to reduce risk-weighted assets without unwinding the Synthetic Credit Portfolio was the crucial misstep that led to the ill-fated trading strategy. Had the strategy been vetted by senior management, either it could have been rejected or its implementation could have received appropriate oversight. From the perspective of a trader, a strategy of offsetting positions was preferable to unwinding positions, if the latter would result in significant losses to the Bank. From the perspective of a former investment banker who was not informed of the costs involved, unwinding the positions would be the natural course to take. Each course of action was justified from one of the two perspectives, but neither party appeared to have considered the possibility that their judgment about how best to proceed was not shared by other decision makers.

The Task Force faulted Ina Drew for failing to tell the members of the operating committee that CIO was not pursuing "the expected course of action" and was instead "embarking on a more complicated and different strategy that entailed adding significantly to the size of the positions" (TF, p. 38). But for whom was reducing the positions in the Synthetic Credit Portfolio the expected course of action? When asked whether bank management had provided any instruction to the CIO about how to proceed, Jamie Dimon told the Senate Subcommittee that his only expectation had been that the reduction be done "wisely" (SSR, p. 62).

It is often natural to assume that one's colleagues share one's point of view; however, a failure to anticipate the possibility that they don't may lead to a decision that does not reflect what the operative members of an organization would have arrived at through a process of deliberation. Mishaps can be avoided by anticipating the possibility of there being differing perspectives on how to solve a problem and taking steps to ensure that these perspectives are brought into some form of alignment before action is taken. A good epistemic practice for important group decisions would be to adopt a policy whereby individual solutions to a problem are required to be communicated to the other members of the group before the solutions are adopted. Corporations often do follow this practice in order to coordinate and manage the implementation of a strategy or project. But it is also needed to manage cognitive diversity within a group.

5.3 Structural Soundness vs. Individual Talent

There were structural weaknesses in the risk management function of the CIO. The CIO had been operating without a chief risk officer prior to the commencement of the trades that led to the losses. During this time, the market risk officer had been serving as the de facto chief risk officer; however, he viewed his responsibility as that of reporting risk as opposed to enforcing risk limits (SSR, p. 159, fn 891). The CIO Risk function was not staffed with as many experienced or strong personnel as it should have been (TF, p. 96).

Ina Drew was essentially doing the job of the chief risk officer as well as serving as the CIO's business lead. As business lead, her primary responsibility was to generate profits rather than police risk, yet she was the person most responsible for managing the CIO's risk profile.[15] The CIO had a staff of approximately 400, including 140 traders, and by 2012, it was managing a portfolio of approximately \$350 billion. According to the US Office of the Comptroller of the Currency, the enormous size of this \$350 billion portfolio would have made the CIO alone the seventh largest bank in the country (SSR, p. 22, fn 51). The CIO did not have the risk management staffing that it needed, and Ina Drew was clearly overextended.

Why was the CIO not given more support? One reason, no doubt, was the perception that the CIO's portfolio was low risk. Another problem was that it had been difficult to find and hire a chief risk officer. A search had been initiated by early 2011, but the position was not filled until early 2012 (SSR, p. 162, fn 909). Yet presumably the Bank could have arranged for some form of interim coverage.

Perhaps it was Ms. Drew's very competence that blinded senior management to the need for additional structural support in the CIO. She had significant experience in CIO's core functions. Senior management viewed her as a highly skilled manager and executive with a strong and detailed command of her business, and she was someone in whom they had a great deal of confidence (TF, p. 20). The Senate Subcommittee observed that she was afforded great deference by Mr Dimon and the other members of the bank's operating committee and that she exercised "nearly unfettered discretion" as a manager (SSR, p. 155, 214). If Drew was deemed to be inter alia a capable risk manager, members of the operating committee may have assumed that she had things under control from a risk management perspective, and so failed to see an urgent need to provide additional support for the CIO risk functions.

But a talented individual is not a substitute for a structural system of checks and balances. In the case of the CIO, a system of check and balances would have been one that ensured the critical evaluation of trading strategies and the transmission

---

[15] Soon after the extent of the CIO's losses became apparent, Drew voluntarily retired from the Bank and voluntarily agreed to return or waive the amount of her compensation that the Bank deemed subject to a clawback (TF, p. 14).

of important information to key decision makers. Although the CIO had been performing well prior to the events that led to the trading losses, it lacked an adequate risk management structure. In addition to the epistemic elements of systems of checks and balances themselves, a good epistemic practice would be to look beyond the well-functioning of a unit to consider whether appropriate systems are in place.

6. The Moral of the Story

JPMorgan's London Whale trading losses were a direct result of breakdowns in risk management. In response to the trading losses, the Bank restructured components of its risk management function to explicitly increase its focus on identifying and implementing good practices across the firm (TD, pp. 17, 116). Some of these "good practices" were epistemic in character. As illustrated by some of the examples discussed in this chapter, identifying good epistemic practices in risk management is not always a matter of making explicit what is already implicit: A good epistemic practice may be a way of anticipating and taking steps to counteract a vulnerability to error in reasoning processes more generally.

In seeking to identify and develop good epistemic practices, we take up the epistemic point of view, namely a perspective within which we consider our epistemic values and goals. Taking up the epistemic point of view enables us to do (at least) two things: (1) make the epistemic elements of good practices in industry and the professions explicit, and (2) identify novel epistemic practices that could support good reasoning in industry and the professions. The aim in identifying good epistemic practices—as is the aim for good practices generally—is to be able to take them as guides. Good epistemic practices are in principle subject to further refinement and revision. Although they guard against epistemic failings, they are not failsafe. There is always a possibility of error, despite our best efforts to prevent it.

In thinking about how to promote the healthy functioning of financial institutions, the case of JP Morgan's London Whale trading losses suggests that we would do well to consider the challenge from the epistemic as well as the ethical perspective.

Acknowledgments

I am grateful to Hartry Field, Shelley Yu, and two reviewers for this volume for helpful comments on earlier drafts of this chapter. I thank the participants in the Gothenburg Financial Ethics Workshop of September of 2021 for helpful questions and comments.

References

Alston, W. (2005). *Beyond Justification*. Ithaca, NY: Cornell University Press.

Arkes, Hal R. (1991). "Costs and Benefits of Judgment Errors: Implications for Debiasing." *Psychological Bulletin* 110(3): 486–498.

Benjamin, D. (2018). *Errors in Probabilistic Reasoning and Judgment Biases*. Cambridge, MA: National Bureau of Economic Research.

Bishop, M., and J. D. Trout (2005). *Epistemology and the Psychology of Human Judgment*. New York: Oxford University Press.

de Bruin, Boudewijn (2015). *Ethics and the Global Crisis: Why Incompetence Is Worse than Greed*. Cambridge: Cambridge University Press.

Coady, D. (2012). *What to Believe Now: Applying Epistemology to Contemporary Issues*. Chichester: Wiley-Blackwell.

Coady, D., and J. Chase (2019). "The Return of Applied Epistemology." In D. Coady and J. Chase (eds.), *The Routledge Handbook of Applied Epistemology*. New York: Routledge, pp. 3–12

Dasgupta, I., E. Schulz, J. B. Tenenbaum, and S. J. Gershman (2020). "A Theory of Learning to Infer." *Psychological Review* 127(3): 412–441.

Descartes, René (1637/1985). *Discourse on the Method for Rightly Conducting One's Reason Well and for Seeking the Truth in the Sciences*. In J. Cottingham, R. Stoothoff, and D. Murdoch (eds.), *The Philosophical Writings of Descartes*. Cambridge: Cambridge University Press, 1985.pp. 111–115.

Edwards, W. (1968). "Conservatism in Human Information Processing." In B. Kleinmuntz (ed.), *Formal Representation of Human Judgment*. New York: Wiley, pp. 17–52.

Edwards, W. (1982). "Conservatism in Human Information Processing." In D. Kahneman, P. Slovic, and A. Tversky (eds.), *Judgment under Uncertainty: Heuristics and Biases*. Cambridge: Cambridge University Press, pp. 359–369.

European Medicines Agency (2002). *ICH Harmonised Tripartite Guideline E6: Note for Guidance on Good Clinical Practice (PMP/ICH/135/95)*. London: European Medicines Agency.

Financial Accounting Standards Board (FASB). Concepts Statements. In FASB.org/ Standards. https://fasb.org/page/PageContent?pageId=/standards/concepts-statements. html. Retrieved September 16, 2023.

Financial Accounting Standards Board (FASB) (2014). *Rules of Procedure, Amended and Restated through December 11, 2013*. Norwalk, CT: FASB.

Gigerenzer, G. (2002). "The Adaptive Toolbox." In G. Gigerenzer and R. Selten (eds.), *Bounded Rationality: The Adaptive Toolbox*. Cambridge, MA: MIT Press, pp. 37–50.

Gigerenzer, G. (2008). "Why Heuristics Work." *Perspectives on Psychological Science* 3(1): 20–29.

Institute of Internal Auditors (2013). "The Three Lines of Defense in Effective Risk Management and Control." https://theiia.fi/wp-content/uploads/2017/

01/pp-the-three-lines-of-defense-in-effective-risk-management-and-control.pdf. Retrieved January 12, 2023.

JPMorgan Chase & Company (2013). *Report of JPMorgan Chase & Co. Management Task Force regarding 2012 CIO Losses*, January 16, 2013. JPMorgan Chase & Company, New York. In *JPMorgan Chase Whale Trades: A Case History of Derivatives Risks and Abuses: Hearing before the U.S. Senate Permanent Subcommittee on Investigations*. Government Printing Office, Washington, DC, S. Hrg. 113–96, vol. 1: 963–1094.

JPMorgan Chase & Company (2019). *2018 Annual Report*. New York: JPMorgan Chase & Company.

Kahneman, D., and S. Frederick (2002). "Representativeness Revisited: Attribute Substitution in Intuitive Judgment." In T. Gilovich, D. Griffin, and D. Kahneman (eds.), *Heuristics and Biases: The Psychology of Intuitive Judgment*. Cambridge: Cambridge University Press, pp. 103–119.

Kahneman, D., and G. Klein (2009). "Conditions for Intuitive Expertise: A Failure to Disagree." *American Psychologist* 64(6): 515–526.

Kahneman, D., and A. Tversky (1972). "Subjective Probability: A Judgment of Representativeness." *Cognitive Psychology* 3(3): 430–454.

Lackey, J. (2021). *Applied Epistemology*. Oxford: Oxford University Press.

Phillips, L. D., and W. Edwards (1966). "Conservatism in a Simple Probability Inference Task." *Journal of Experimental Psychology* 72(3): 346–354.

Pritchard, D. (2014). "Truth as the Fundamental Epistemic Good." In J. Matheson and R. Vitz (eds.), *The Ethics of Belief: Individual and Social*. Oxford: Oxford University Press, pp. 112–129.

Simons, T., L. H Pelled, and K. A. Smith (1999). "Making Use of Difference: Diversity, Debate, and Decision Comprehensiveness in Top Management Teams." *Academy of Management Journal* 42(6): 662–673.

Slovic, P., and S. Lichtenstein (1971). "Comparison of Bayesian and Regression Approaches to the Study of Information Processing in Judgment." *Organizational Behavior and Human Performance* 6(6): 649–744.

Tversky, A., and D. Kahneman (1974). "Judgment under Uncertainty: Heuristics and Biases." *Science* 185(4157): 1124–1131.

US Senate Permanent Subcommittee on Investigations (2013). *JP Morgan Chase Whale Trades: A Case History of Derivatives Risks and Abuses*. Report by the Permanent Subcommittee on Investigations Majority and Minority Staff. Government Printing Office, Washington, DC, S. Hrg. 113–96, Vol. 1: 150–510.

van Knippenberg, Daan, and Michaéla C. Schippers (2007). "Work Group Diversity." *Annual Review Psychology* 58: 515–541.

Vijayananthan, A., and O. Nawawi (2008). "The Importance of Good Clinical Practice Guidelines and Its Role in Clinical Trials." *Biomedical Imaging and Intervention Journal* 4(1): e5. https://doi.org/10.2349/biij.4.1.e5

Warenski, L. (2019). "Disentangling the Epistemic Failings of the 2008 Financial Crisis." In D. Coady and J. Chase (eds.), *The Routledge Handbook of Applied Epistemology*. New York: Routledge, pp. 196–201.

Warenski, L. (2024). "Organizational Good Epistemic Practices." Forthcoming in *Journal of Business Ethics*.

Wen, Y., and J. Kinsella (2016). "Credit Default Swap-Pricing Theory, Real Data Analysis and Classroom Applications Using Bloomberg Terminal." *Journal of Finance and Economics Education* 16(3): 68–78.

8

Climate Change and Reflexive Law

The EU Sustainable Finance Action Plan

Boudewijn de Bruin

1. Introduction

This chapter studies legislative initiatives around sustainable finance deriving from the Action Plan: Financing Sustainable Growth (also called "Sustainable Finance Action Plan," "Action Plan" henceforth), published by the European Commission ("Commission") in 2018 (Communication 2018/97). I investigate the appropriateness of various instruments proposed in the Action Plan, using a reflexive law approach coupled with insights from epistemology that, as I have elsewhere argued, can be fruitfully applied in business ethics (De Bruin 2013) and financial ethics (De Bruin 2015). I point to the challenges a reflexive law approach encounters, and offer suggestions on how to address them.

The study of reflexive law is part of a tradition in legal scholarship that goes back to the German legal sociologist Gunther Teubner (1989). Reflexive law has made its appearance in the study of environmental law in the works of various legal scholars and philosophers (Farber 1994, Farmer & Teubner 1994, Hess 1999, Orts 1995). These scholars acknowledge the limits of law as an instrument to realize social or political goals, and stress the need to encourage self-reflection and transparency among stakeholders through procedural rather than through more traditional "command-and-control" legislation. Typical reflexive law instruments involve disclosure, reporting, and labeling.

Examining the Action Plan and the policy document in which it finds its main inspiration, a report by the EU High-Level Expert Group on Sustainable Finance ("HLEG"), I show that the main legislative instruments it puts forward are reflexive. I use empirical and theoretical arguments challenging the effectiveness of such instruments, and suggest an alternative grounded in business ethics and epistemology.

I give some background information on reflexive law and the Action Plan first. I then show how the Action Plan is reflexive law par excellence. Finally, I consider the challenges, and offer suggestions of how to overcome them.

Before I start, a few disclaimers are in place. First, the argument I develop in this chapter could be read as a critique of reflexive law approaches. While I believe

Boudewijn de Bruin, *Climate Change and Reflexive Law: The EU Sustainable Finance Action Plan* In: *The Philosophy of Money and Finance*. Edited by: Joakim Sandberg and Lisa Warenski, Oxford University Press. © Oxford University Press 2024. DOI: 10.1093/oso/9780192898807.003.0009

that interventionist regulation in the realm of climate change mitigation and adaptation is sorely needed, specifically at the global level, that is not the point I develop here (see, e.g. De Bruin 2022a). Rather, I argue that once a regulator opts for a reflexive law approach, a richer notion of information should be deployed. I call this "epistemic" instead of "reflexive" law. It is inspired by work in business ethics and epistemology paired with insights drawn from empirical research.

Second, as of this writing, parts of the Action Plan are being implemented, others parts are being changed, still others have been postponed or discarded. Financial regulation is in constant flux, underscoring the sense of urgency among legislators. The risk is that the legal details that underlie this chapter change continuously. This does not, however, undermine the relevance of studying financial regulation through the lens of reflexive law, business ethics, and epistemology. The analysis I offer in this chapter holds *mutatis mutandis* for a large share of present (and future) regulatory instruments just as well.

2. Reflexive Law

2.1 Background: An Alternative to Market-Based and Command-and-Control Regulation

To position reflexive law, it is useful to briefly consider the typical development of environmental law in the second half of the twentieth century. Up until the 1960s most environmental issues were resolved through private law, for instance by conceiving them by way of principles of tort. In this "market-based" approach (as Orts 1995 calls it in a paper that informs the present treatment), nuisance laws and rights of ownership were deployed to develop a rule-oriented mechanism of regulation, which could involve Pigouvian taxation (e.g. in water pollution regulation in a number of European countries), or tradable pollution rights (e.g. the American acid rain permit trading program).

The 1970s witnessed an increase in knowledge about environmental degradation. It was the time of the Club of Rome report (Meadows et al. 1972). Legislators started to realize that nuisance law and other private law instruments were fairly ineffective mechanisms against more large-scale environmental issues that were gaining attention, such as toxic waste disposal, and this made legislators move toward administrative law. Orts (1995) provides an ideal-typical characterization of such approaches as "command-and-control" regulation, stressing administrative law and bureaucratic strategies.

About a decade later, the feeling was that these administrative law instruments had been insufficient, and—a second and independent point—that they were not fully consonant with the then-popular sentiment that states should step back and advance deregulation.[1] Moreover, the command-and-control approach was claimed to have caused considerable environmental "juridification," a concept going back to Habermas's (1981) theory of communicative action. Environmental law was accused of having developed in such a way as to create a situation in which, because of sheer cognitive limitations, no one is in the position to oversee the entire legal landscape. It was also observed that administrative law often entailed a considerable degree of outsourcing of decision-making from the judiciary to the executive, for instance when powers are delegated to administrative agencies, which—despite possibilities for judicial review of administrative decisions—bears a latent threat to democratic legitimacy, and sits uneasily with the ideas of separation of power and checks and balances. In these circumstances, reflexive law was seen as an attractive and welcome alternative.

The point of departure of a reflexive law approach is the view that law should not be seen as primarily proscribing and prescribing behaviors in an attempt to regulate society, but rather as offering guidance to actors by means of processes and procedures. Grounded in the concept of "autopoiesis" (Gr. self-making), Teubner (1989) maintained that legal instruments should be used to stimulate internal reflection and learning among interested parties. Applied to environmental law, there should be "a law of ecological self-organization using strong external pressures for internal self-regulation" (Farmer & Teubner 1994, p. 8).

2.2 Example: The Eco-Management and Audit Scheme

It is important to appreciate that the contrast between reflexive law, on the one hand, and market-based and command-and-control approaches, on the other, is not fully black and white. Orts (1995) in fact explains in detail the reflexive elements in *both* approaches. His key example of reflexive law is the EU Eco-Management and Audit Scheme ("EMAS," Council Regulation 1836/93) of 1993. This regulation includes three elements that make it distinctively reflexive: proactive management (in contrast to reactive compliance), auditing, and disclosure. It contains environmental management policies and programs that, for instance, describe the activities a company must deploy to protect the environment at a given site. It proposes an environmental auditing system. And it contains provisions on public environmental disclosure statements. The rules on disclosure Orts calls the "backbone" (1995, p. 1323) of the EMAS. It involves such things as environmental reviews and subsequent alterations of policy, education and training, procedures for investigation and communication, keeping a register

---

[1] This argument for reflexive law lost its force in the 2008 financial crisis. It has become painfully clear that the aims of financial institutions and supervisory agencies are not fully aligned. See De Bruin (2015).

of environmental effects, and *ex ante* assessment of the environmental impact of products and services.

The big question that confronts such regulatory approaches is, however: What should make us believe that the EMAS leads to the intended goals? Orts (1995, p. 1311) writes:

> the success of the EMAS will... turn on... market and social forces: pressure from within the corporate governance process; political and economic pressure from suppliers, distributors, banks, and insurance companies; and perhaps moral pressure on top managers of large enterprises. Its success will turn also on whether the EMAS is administered fairly, flexibly, and professionally.

In other terms, the thought is that the reflexive law instruments—disclosure, reporting, and review in particular—create pressures for businesses to change behavior in the desired and intended way.[2] As Orts (1995, p. 1313) writes, "[t]he reflexive EMAS aims at fundamental structural change in the everyday life of business institutions. It aims at nothing less, in the end, than the transformation of business culture."

2.3 Mechanism: Reflection and Behavior Change

But how do you change "business culture"? And will the monetary and financial pressures that businesses face not be much stronger than the moral and other pressures referred to above?

One way to argue would be to establish that specific reflexive law instruments change the decision situation of a profit-maximizing organization in such a way that profit maximization and environmental sustainability coincide. One might think of pressure exerted by consumers or employees in the face of negative press coverage, forcing the firm to change its course of action. A second way to think of reflexive law is to look at the way it changes the internal workings of a business. A process of disclosure, reporting, and continual review stimulates employees and other stakeholders to think about environmental issues, and this influences individual and corporate behavior for the better, often in less tangible and explicit ways. Such thinking may lead existing businesses to develop new technology, and may stimulate innovation. A further argument is to the effect that environmental reports would enable sustainable investors and non-governmental organizations

---

[2] An example of non-reflexive law is, for instance, a building decree according to which buildings that do not have a specific energy label shall not be used as office buildings. Clearly once such a decree is in force, this has sweeping consequences for the balance sheet of banks owning commercial real estate.

better to track the environmental performance of companies, which would stimulate businesses to assume their responsibilities.

A host of work in business ethics attests to the fact that changing culture is difficult, to say the least. My plan is, however, not so much to use that literature, but rather to start from a slightly more abstract point of view, and to consider the dynamics of reflexive regulation at the level of the individual decision-maker. I use the traditional belief–desire framework of action, according to which human action is explained by a combination of "mind-to-world" attitudes that give a purported description of reality and "world-to-mind" attitudes such as desires that give a description of what the decision-maker would prefer the world to be (see, e.g. Davidson 1963).

Using this framework, the first question to ask is how people get to their beliefs and desires, and, in particular, how they change as a result of obtaining information. This is relevant, I think, because to the extent that reflexive law fosters recruiting, processing, disseminating, receiving, and evaluating such information, it may be seen as exploiting exactly this aspect of human agency. In fact, with its focus on reflection, reflexive law, I argue, is close to views of human agency grounded in autonomy, often loosely inspired by Kant (see, e.g. Christman 1991). According to such a view, a person's actions are determined by beliefs and desires that have been formed autonomously. For Christman (1991, p. 347) this means—in brief—that conditions of "non-resistance" and "self-reflection" apply to the formation of desires: the agent is in a position to reflect on the formation of the desires, and does not resist them. Similar rationality conditions can be postulated for belief formation (see, e.g. Zagzebski 2012). To the extent that it is the aim of the reflexive law approach to "encourage thinking and behavior in the right direction" (Orts 1995, p. 1264) by way of stimulating self-reflective and self-critical processes, the underlying view of human agency is plausibly construed by way of an autonomy-based belief–desire model. This is not to say that decision-makers are always fully conscious of their reasoning, for instance when they copy the behaviors of others. To the extent that reflexion is an intended outcome of reflexive law, however, it entails at least a modicum of autonomous belief and desire formation.

3. The EU Action Plan: Financing Sustainable Growth

It is estimated that to finance the climate and energy ambitions of the European Union (EU) that follow from the Paris Agreement and the United Nations Agenda 2030 Sustainable Development Goals, the EU faces an investment gap of around 180 billion euros annually.[3] To bridge that gap is among the aims of the 2018

---

[3] The estimate is continuously adjusted upwardly. The 180 billion euros estimate underlies the Action Plan.

Action Plan that lies at the bottom of ongoing EU legislative initiatives such as the EU Taxonomy (Regulation 2020/852), the Sustainable Finance Disclosure Regulation (Regulation 2019/2088), and the Benchmark Regulation (Regulation 2019/2089).[4] The thought behind this mountain of legislative efforts is that without further action being taken, there will not be enough money to pay for the measures needed to make sure that global warming remains well below the Paris Agreement goal of two degrees (see generally, Beekhoven van den Boezem et al. 2019).

The Action Plan is based on recommendations from the EU High-Level Expert Group on Sustainable Finance, which was established by the Commission in 2016 to develop two things: a set of policy recommendations about the challenges and opportunities of sustainable finance, and a program of reforms of EU financial policy to stimulate the flow of capital toward environmentally sustainable investments (Commission Decision 2016/6912). The HLEG published a report entitled *Financing a Sustainable European Economy* in 2018.[5] The recommendations of the HLEG were to establish a taxonomy singling out climate-change-relevant areas where investments are most needed; a clarification of the duties of investors regarding time horizon and environmental, social and governance factors; improving sustainability disclosure rules; and to set up sustainability standards for assets, such as official EU standards for bonds meeting certain sustainability requirements.

The Action Plan adopts a large number of suggestions of the HLEG. It puts forward ten Actions meant to contribute to the realization of three main aims. The first aim follows directly from the observation of the investment gap. It is to direct capital flows toward sustainable investment. To realize this aim, the Action Plan envisages the development of a taxonomy to classify sustainable activities; a system of labels and norms for "green bonds"; the inclusion of sustainability as a parameter in the suitability assessment that is part of financial advice provided by investment firms and insurance distributors; and the development of sustainability benchmarks.

The second aim of the Action Plan pertains to financial stability and the financial risks due to climate change and other sustainability threats. The motivation is that global warming of two degrees or more will have a negative effect on

---

[4] The Action Plan is an integral part of the Capital Markets Union Action Plan, launched by the Commission in 2015 (Communication 2015/0468). The latest version of that plan is from 2020 (Communication 2020/590). See Busch et al. (2019) for details about the Action Plan and its history. The three regulations should also be seen in combination with the Non-Financial Reporting Directive (Directive 2014/95/EU), which already requires large companies to report on environmental factors in the director's report. Unlike the EU Taxonomy and the Benchmark Regulation, the Sustainable Finance Disclosure Regulation does not explicitly refer to the Action Plan.

[5] Some of the HLEG's recommendations are indebted to the Task Force on Climate-Related Financial Disclosure (2017), an industry-led task force not discussed in the present chapter, established by the Financial Stability Board in 2015 in response to a request from the G20 finance ministers and central bank governors.

financial stability in Europe, and that the financial sector fails to take that effect into sufficient account.[6] Proposed actions include measures to integrate sustainability in credit rating and market research in a better way; a clarification of the relevant duties of institutional investors and asset managers in this regard; and the inclusion of sustainability in prudential regulation, for instance in capital requirements.

The third aim of the Action Plan is to promote transparency and long-termism in finance and business. This aim arises out of the observation that transparency is crucial for the financial sector to function well, and for participants to judge value creation in the long term. Currently, market parties have too much of a short-term frame of mind. The two proposed actions here are to extend disclosure rules concerning sustainability reporting; and the promotion of sustainable corporate governance.

4. Reflexive Law in the Action Plan

How do the Action Plan and the HLEG report on which it is based reflect a reflexive law approach?

4.1 Investor Ignorance and Preferences

Developing a taxonomy is the first and foremost recommendation made by the HLEG and the Action Plan. The expert group sees it as the top priority to establish a taxonomy that describes various asset types in terms of their sustainability contributions or performance, and relatedly puts forward the idea of developing a system of labels for sustainable assets. In essence, this suggestion is taken over by the Commission in the Action Plan, namely, in Actions 1 (taxonomy) and 2 (labels). The Commission gives it the same high priority as the HLEG.

These two actions are very much in the spirit of reflexive law. The idea of a taxonomy is based on the assumption that a "lack of clarity among investors regarding what constitutes a sustainable investment is a contributing factor behind [the] investment gap" (Action Plan, 1.1). In other words, the key diagnosis the Commission puts forward here is that the investment gap of an estimated 180 billion euros annually for reaching the EU's climate and energy goals is (at least partly) the result of investor ignorance. If investors knew what assets or projects

---

[6] Climate risk is typically analyzed as a combination of physical risks (e.g. extreme weather events), transitions risks (stranded assets), liability risks (the risk of facing climate litigation), and reputational risk. For financial institutions, these risks translate to traditional risks such as credit risk (clients may no longer be able to repay) and operational risks (a bank's physical infrastructure may collapse). I thank an anonymous reviewer for raising this point.

were sustainable, they would, the thought is, move their capital to such projects. This diagnosis is reiterated in the motivation underlying Action 2 (labels). There it is assumed that "EU standards and labels for sustainable financial products... enable easier access for investors seeking those products," particularly for "retail investors who would like to express their investment preferences on sustainable activities" (Action Plan 2.2).

A further form of investor ignorance that the Action Plan aims to address concerns the information retail end-investors or beneficiaries have about the duties of asset managers regarding sustainability. Action 7 aims to address that form of investor ignorance. Rather than establishing new duties concerning sustainability, the idea is that when a large group of retail end-investors become familiar with existing duties of asset managers this provides an incentive for these managers to incorporate environmental and climate-change-related risks to a greater degree. In the words of the Commission (Action Plan 3.2):

> End-investors may, therefore, not receive the full information they need, should they want to take into account sustainability-related issues in their investment decisions. As a result, investors do not sufficiently take into account the impact of sustainability risks when assessing the performance of their investments over time.

When discussing investor ignorance, it is important to realize that both the HLEG and the Action Plan aim to make sure that institutional investors, asset managers, retirement scheme providers, and other financial services providers are sufficiently knowledgeable about the sustainability preferences of their clients. Currently, investment advisers and portfolio managers are required under Article 25(2) of the Markets in Financial Instruments Directive II to solicit information about their clients' "knowledge and experience" about investing, their financial situation and ability to bear losses, and their investment objectives and risk tolerance. The aim is to allow the adviser to recommend only those services or instruments that are "suitable" for their clients. Similar provisions are included in the Insurance Distribution Directive, for insurance companies.

So far, the suitability of financial services and products has not, however, been thought to depend on the sustainability preferences of the client. The HLEG recommends the view that the adviser's obligations not only include soliciting information from clients about their sustainability preferences, but also include providing information about sustainability risks to clients, and to explain their approach to investing in a "clear and understandable manner" (HLEG 2018, p. 23). Advisers should be required "to ask about, and then respond to, retail investors' preferences about the sustainable impact of their investments, as a routine component of financial advice" (HLEG 2018, p. 28). In Action 4 of the Action Plan, the Commission adopts this suggestion, and sets out to amend the respective Markets in Financial Instruments Directive II and Insurance Distribution Directive delegated acts.

4.2 Long-Termism and the Fit-and-Proper Test

As we saw, the Action Plan's third set of actions is meant to increase long-termism in the financial services industry. This idea is very prominent in the HLEG report. To put things in relief, the current focus in finance is generally a time frame of no more than three to five years. Consequently, the HLEG's approach to stimulating long-termism may still be a far cry from what philosophers have started calling by that name (Greaves & MacAskill 2021; Tarsney 2022), which easily stretches into the thousands of years.[7]

The way in which the HLEG approaches long-termism—which the Commission follows to some extent—is indebted to reflexive law. The idea is that investors should be led to gather information about the long-term effects of their investments. This is to be evaluated in light of such observations as that, at the time of writing the report, only 5 percent of EU pension funds had gathered information about the impact of climate change on their portfolio (HLEG 2018, p. 20), and that despite increased attention, investors still tend to downplay the risks attached to "stranded assets." If, for instance, due to changes in law, or as a result of climate-related physical events, particular oil fields can no longer be used by a refinery, the value of these assets will decrease, and ultimately may end up "stranded." The HLEG therefore includes an investor duty to examine the materiality of such and other sustainability risks in an attempt to orient the investor's view to the long term (HLEG 2018, p. 22).

The approach put forward here is in fact even more decidedly reflexive than one might think at first sight, focusing as it does on the epistemic prerequisites of autonomous reflection—knowledge and competences. The HLEG recognizes that long-termism in the financial world requires massive changes in corporate governance, culture, and leadership. Among others, it therefore suggests strengthening the so-called "fit-and-proper" tests that supervisory authorities use to assess individual candidates for board positions. According to DNB, the Dutch central bank and supervisor, for instance, "fitness" has to do with whether the

---

[7] See also former Governor of the Bank of England, Mark Carney, "Breaking the Tragedy of the Horizon: Climate Change and Financial Stability," Lloyd's of London, September 29, 2015, London, at 4:

> The horizon for monetary policy extends out to 2–3 years. For financial stability it is a bit longer, but typically only to the outer boundaries of the credit cycle—about a decade. In other words, once climate change becomes a defining issue for financial stability, it may already be too late.
>
> (https://www.bankofengland.co.uk/-/media/boe/files/speech/2015/breaking-the-tragedy-of-the-horizon-climate-change-and-financial-stability.pdf)

prospective candidate possesses "relevant knowledge and skills," a question answered on the basis of an evaluation of his or her "education, work experience and competencies."[8] "Propriety," in turn, pertains to a host of traits or qualities including veracity, openness, sincerity, prudence, and punctuality—which all have a decidedly epistemic flavor.[9]

The boost that the proposed instruments are meant to give to long-termism is embodied in the recommendation of the HLEG that fit-and-proper tests should explicitly examine whether the prospective candidate understands long-term risks to do with climate change and sustainability. Directors should be vested with a duty to be well-informed about the impact of the company's business on the environment, and to participate in adequate education and training in this respect (HLEG 2018, p. 41). They should develop their own respective competences so as to ensure that there is an "internal awareness" concerning sustainability (HLEG 2018, p. 73). Probably much to the regret of advocates of long-termism, the Commission does not follow the HLEG here, except perhaps in a very general sense that Action 10 of the Action Plan aims to foster sustainable corporate governance.

4.3 Scenario Analysis

The Commission does, however, adopt a related suggestion put forward by the HLEG. The HLEG proposes to stimulate long-termism not only through the procedural sorts of principles requiring minimum levels of expertise and knowledge, but also by way of more substantive instruments, namely, a recommendation to use specific types of evidence or data for financial forecasting. It is, in effect, a plea for a different methodology to identify long-term risks, providing a different evidential basis for long-term assessments.

The starting point is the observation that currently historical data are still by far the most important source of evidence for financial forecasting, despite their alleged shortcomings when it comes to determining the probability of events that have no likes in the recent past, climate change being the prime example here. What the HLEG suggests is that European financial supervisors should extend burgeoning initiatives around scenario analysis to detect non-cyclical, non-linear risks that the financial industry faces as a result of climate change. The Commission seconds that suggestion (Action Plan 5).

---

[8] https://www.dnb.nl/en/sector-information/supervision-stages/prior-to-supervision/fit-and-proper-assessments/initial-assessment/initial-assessment-assessing-fitness/

[9] https://www.dnb.nl/en/sector-information/supervision-stages/prior-to-supervision/fit-and-proper-assessments/initial-assessment/initial-assessment-propriety-assessment/

4.4 Accounting Standards

Another related example of more substantive epistemic instruments concerns accounting standards. The HLEG recommends an upgrade of existing disclosure regulations for companies so as to make their climate change and sustainability opportunities and risks more transparent, and recommends requiring credit rating agencies to disclose how they incorporate environmental, social, and governance factors in their risk analysis, noting that the current lack of standardization of sustainability accounting standards leads to very different levels and kinds of evidence about sustainability performance being provided by companies. According to the Commission, there are "growing concerns" that the current accounting rules are "not conducive to sustainable investment decision-making" (Action Plan 4.1).

5. Epistemic Law

We could summarize the preceding thoughts by calling the type of approach to legislation identified in the Action Plan not only "reflexive," but also "epistemic"; for the thought is that encouraging individuals and organizations to gain, process, store, and communicate information—that is, making them engage in epistemic activities—leads them or their stakeholders to reflect, and consequently to change their behavior in ways that the legislator deems desirable. And we could, then, make a useful distinction between "procedural" and "substantive" epistemic instruments, as already hinted at in passing above. Procedural epistemic instruments may stimulate the ways or procedures through which knowledge is gained, processed, stored, and communicated, without, however, adopting a view on what should count as knowledge in the first place. Substantive epistemic instruments, by contrast, stipulate what in some particular case should be counted as sufficient justification, warrant, or evidence for something to count as knowledge the way philosophers think of it. Examples of procedural epistemic instruments include regulations concerning transparency and reporting, or duties to request or to provide information. Examples of substantive epistemic instruments are accounting standards prescribing what should count as evidence, regulations about the specific type of models that credit rating agencies should use, or rules about the use of scenario analysis.

But do these epistemic instruments lead to reflection? And does reflection lead to behavior change? In 2021, the Commission put it thus:

> while the EU Taxonomy can guide market participants in their investment decisions, naturally it does *not* prohibit investment in any activity. There is no obligation on companies to be Taxonomy-aligned, and investors are also free to choose what to invest in.   (Communication 2021/188 II, 1, emphasis added)

To allay charges of unjustified optimism, the Commission notes that implementing Action 4 (including sustainability preferences in the Markets in Financial Instruments Directive II and Insurance Distribution Directive suitability assessments) makes sure that:

> everyone will have a chance to make a tangible positive impact on the climate, environment and society if they desire to do so [and this will] increase the demand for financial instruments and products with sustainable investment strategies.   (Communication 2021/188 VI)

To evaluate the cogency of such a line of reasoning, empirical and conceptual questions should be asked. What does behavioral economics tell us about the impact of the mere provision of information on consumer behavior? Something like this: it depends on the type of decisions we are talking about, on the level of complexity of the information, on the cognitive capacities of the decision-makers, on the search costs they have to make, on the importance they assign to the decision, and on whether decision-makers really care about sustainability (see generally, Kahneman 2013). I cannot do full justice to all these intricacies in this chapter, so my plan for the remainder of this section is to argue that the relevant scholarly literature should be interpreted as suggesting that we must exercise great care not to overstate the effects that information provision will have on behavior.

A disclaimer is in order here: it may well be that with the EU Taxonomy and other instruments in place, Member States may require specific investors to invest in particular asset classes, and private parties may do the same. A system of disclosure, reporting, and labeling would then be used as "input" to a command-and-control approach, thereby leaving the idea of reflexive law behind. This applies, for instance, to NextGeneration EU, the European stimulus package. My focus here below is on genuine reflexive law, though.

5.1 Belief Revision and Preference Change

So, to begin with, I want to consider the question of how the potential success of a reflexive law approach to sustainable finance might be explained within the belief–desire framework of human agency set out above. This is particularly useful because it is an attractive aspect of this framework that it allows us to explain changes in behavior in terms of changes in preferences and/or beliefs.

An example shows how. I am walking in the direction of the railway station. I look at my mobile phone, and turn back. What happened? Perhaps I learnt about construction works that will cause significant delays, and hence I am walking back to catch the bus. Or, in another scenario, I received a message from an old friend who happens to be in town, and has invited me for dinner. So in that scenario

I will be walking to the restaurant. I changed behavior in the first scenario due to a change in beliefs (I still want to leave town, but opt for a different strategy), and, in the second, due to a change in preferences (I no longer want to leave town). I received information that made me change my beliefs and/or preferences, and upon reflection I realized it was rational for me to change my course of action.

As we saw, it is among the stated aims of the Action Plan to close the investment gap of 180 billion euros annually by tempting investors to move their funds to sustainable projects. The question now is what mechanisms explain how the strategies envisaged by the HLEG and the Commission would change the beliefs and/or desires of such investors in ways that make it rational for them to move their funds to the respective projects. It is useful here to distinguish behavioral changes that result from belief revision and those that result from preference change.[10]

5.1.1 Belief Revision

The HLEG report and the Action Plan are built on the assumption that investors lack reliable information about sustainable projects, or at least that investors have difficulties accessing such information. They lack information about what should be considered as "sustainable," and that is why a taxonomy or classification scheme is put in place. They lack information about the performance of sustainable assets, and that is, among others, why benchmarks should be developed. And they lack information about alleged sustainable companies and projects, which motivates the Commission's taking further steps to develop disclosure regulations and accounting standards.

It cannot be sensibly denied that presently this sort of information is lacking in the ambitious and systematic form envisaged by the Commission. All the same, however, we should ask ourselves which investors will be persuaded by this information to move their money to more sustainable projects.

It may be helpful, or even a precondition, that such an investor already has a preference for sustainability; for recall, we are here exploring the mechanism of a projected behavioral change that is due to belief revision, not preference change. Given the wealth of opportunities for sustainable investing that such an investor presently has, it may, however, be somewhat unlikely that there are many investors who, despite their preferences for sustainable investing, have so far decided to postpone reorienting their investments, and wait until they receive information about sustainable projects. Moreover, even if such "wait-and-see investors" did exist, a further question is why we should expect them to take a particular interest in information provided on the basis of EU legislation, rather

---

[10] These two mechanisms do not cover all there is to the reflexive elements in the Action Plan. For reasons of space, I focus on investor ignorance and preference, and only touch upon the other elements (fitness and propriety, scenario analysis, accounting standards) in passing.

than, say, information provided through global initiatives, or initiatives from non-governmental organizations.

5.1.2 Preference Change

The typical investor we should imagine when we consider preference change is not yet fully concerned about the climate emergency. They may care about other things (say, the coverage ratio of their pension fund or other retirement-planning-related things), or they may not care about anything in particular, and just invest for the thrill of it (and see the stock and bond market as an occasion to play games); climate change is at least *not* what comes to mind when they reflect on their portfolio.

What would taxonomy, labels, disclosures, or all other bits of information provision do to change this investor's attitudes toward sustainability? Here, again, it is unlikely that such information will sway this type of investor. The provided information mostly concerns issues such as whether a company should be considered as sustainable, how well it scores on various sustainability factors, and whether it uses scenario analysis in addition to traditional methods involving historical data. Providing such information does not help the investor understand why sustainable investing is needed in the first place, unless they are also exposed to information about the risks of climate change as such, or about the need to fund climate mitigation and adaptation. So, if an investor has the belief that fossil energy is unproblematic, the mere provision of information concerning taxonomies, labels, benchmarks, risk-management methods, and the like, will not help them understand their error.

5.2 Salience and the Value of Knowledge

Let us go back to belief revision. One mechanism that might persuade wait-and-see investors we encountered there is that the choice between "green" and "brown" assets becomes more salient to them as a result of implementing the Action Plan's initiatives. The EU Taxonomy and other reflexive law instruments may help add, so to speak, a dimension to the investors' decision situation that so far they had failed to perceive, just as the mere perception of the train as a sensible means of transportation among European academics may gradually change the way we think about flying. Rather than addressing investor ignorance as the Commission has it, we should then describe what the Action Plan does as suggesting measures that provide a novel perspective on already available information.

Similarly, turning to preference change: here too a possible mechanism might be one in which the climate emergency is made more salient to investors. It may be that at the moment of investing, climate change does not enter the reflection, just as one does not always think of global warming while taking a shower. Confronted with tangible consequences of the EU Taxonomy and other instruments, investors' awareness might be raised, which might lead them to include climate-related risks in their decisions.

Salience is a notoriously hard to model notion. One way to understand the role salience may play in reflexive law uses some insights from work in epistemology on the value of knowledge. Starting point is the traditional philosophical distinction between knowledge and belief. The main idea is that if you "know" something, you have some evidence for it, which is to say, there are reasons that justify it, or make it rational for to you to hold it. If you merely believe something, by contrast, your attitude toward the proposition is nothing more than a guess. Getting an answer right does not show you knew it, for you may just have been lucky. Ever since Plato's *Meno*, knowledge has been credited with being more stable, and therefore more valuable than a mere true guess. If you get confronted with some purported piece of counterevidence, you may quickly discard your mere belief; you will naturally give up your wild guess. But if you have knowledge, you may find out that the purported counterevidence is fake. Another way to put this is to observe that you will not lose knowledge as easily as belief, because knowledge is embedded in further evidence, that is, in further bodies of knowledge. This explains why knowledge is more valuable than mere belief.

The analysis of the value of knowledge has made great progress in philosophy recently (Pritchard 2018), and has also been taken up in legal scholarship, for instance in debates on freedom of speech (Blocher 2019, see also De Bruin 2022). The main claim I want to put forward here now is the following: for reflexive law to be effective and to lead to the intended reflection and behavior change, the information provision should generate knowledge in decision-makers. It is unlikely to sway the as yet unconvinced investor that a particular asset counts as sustainable as long as such information does not saliently cohere with a wider body of knowledge concerning global warming, climate change mitigation, the investment gap, and so forth. This is essentially meant to be an uncontested claim: as long as you are unaware of a problem, you do not realize it needs a solution.

One might object that by now everyone knows about the climate emergency. But the knowledge required to motivate the investor may need to be more detailed than a general sense of impending disaster, and moreover, it needs to be activated at the moment the investor acts. One only saves water if one sees it is worth saving water and if one reflects on water consumption just when one is taking a shower.

I take this observation about the relevance of knowledge as a source of salience to develop a sketch of how reflexive law might incorporate this. I connect here with the view of law as an instrument to steer and encourage the epistemic processes of self-reflection and thinking. In a sense, however, I suggest an even more self-critical approach, because I also acknowledge that the success of the instruments depends on whether the epistemic processes actually materialize, whether the self-reflection actually happens, and whether epistemic processes and self-reflection then lead to the desired behavior. My approach, then, is to observe that considerable care must be taken to ensure that information does what it needs to do to become knowledge. As I suggested above, one could call this "epistemic law."

6. Epistemic Law in Practice

What these observations mean for practical purposes is that policymaking is largely a matter of "piecemeal engineering," to use Karl Popper's (1957) well-known phrase. It will always require research and practical experience to see what is needed, and where it is needed, typically resting on insights from behavioral economics and cognate disciplines. Yet it is also possible to gain some more general insights from that body of scholarship. I summarize these insights in two slogans: provide different information, and provide information differently.

6.1 Provide Different Information

One approach is to provide different information. There is some evidence that demand for socially responsible investing decreased as a result of the Covid-19 pandemic.[11] As Döttling and Kim (2021) show, demand for funds with higher sustainability rankings dropped more intensely during the pandemic than for funds with lower rankings. On the other hand, environmental disasters may have the opposite effect: they may temporarily increase demand for sustainable finance (Marshall et al. 2021). The explanation is that such disasters make climate change salient to sustainability minded investors, thereby deepening the investor's sense of knowledge in such a way that when they make investment decisions, the knowledge is "activated." The salient event gives the investor a very genuine sense of urgency vis-à-vis the climate emergency, resulting in belief revision and/or preference change supporting a more intense focus on sustainable investing. The event has led to reflection, and to behavioral change.

This leads to the following concrete suggestion: the sort of information that the Action Plan seeks to provide investors with may have to be complemented with a different type of information: non-financial information about the climate emergency. To simplify a bit, sustainable investors may be moved to action more effectively by providing them with information about concrete climate-related events than with information about the EU Taxonomy, labels, and benchmarks.

---

[11] I acknowledge the risks inherent in the use, in this section, of work in progress that has not yet gone through peer review.

6.2 Provide Information Differently

Another approach is to provide information differently. An experimental study by Isabella Kooij and colleagues (2021) provided investors with the opportunity to retrieve and read a sustainability report. About 40 percent of participants requested the report. But the answer to the question of whether these investors changed their investment behavior turned out to be negative. Other studies, by contrast, do show that investors sometimes change behavior after receiving information. An often-cited article by Hartzmark and Sussman (2019), for instance, found that after the US financial services firm Morningstar adopted a simple visual system to communicate sustainability rankings, demand for sustainable finance rose significantly. What this suggests is that policymakers expecting to generate particular forms of behavior through self-reflection and critical thinking have to experiment with ways in which information is provided. A lengthy report may not boost salience. A nice visual system may have that effect. What works will depend on context, so what I am saying here is that it is very much the task of policymakers and social scientists to discover what works and what not.

7. Conclusion

In his seminal article on reflexive environmental law, Orts (1995, p. 1336) claimed that "[i]t is not overstating the situation to say that the future of the human race may depend on developing an effective legal strategy to address [such] issues" as global climate change. A generation later, this claim rings even more true. The climate emergency has come much nearer, but global inaction has brought us not much closer to a solution. Waves of climate legislation and litigation reflect the deep frustration of many citizens with the lack of progress that businesses and governments make. So, it may indeed be law that will save the planet.

But when law takes over, important questions must be asked: What is the power of legislation and litigation, and what legal instruments and tactics are appropriate? This chapter's aim was to contribute to this debate. I zoomed in on legislative initiatives around sustainable finance deriving from the Action Plan: Financing Sustainable Growth published by the European Commission in 2018. I investigated the appropriateness of various instruments proposed in the Action Plan, using a reflexive law approach coupled with insights from behavioral economics and epistemology. I pointed to the challenges such an approach encounters, and gestured at some tentative suggestions of how to address them.

My assessment has not been fully positive. When I started working on this chapter, the finer details of the EU Taxonomy were still under construction. I finished this chapter a month or so after the European Commission decided that, contrary to earlier views, natural gas and nuclear power must also be considered activities that are aligned with the EU Taxonomy, undermining its status of independent and "objective" classification. Second, it is important to stress the relatively high level of abstraction at which the Action Plan discusses these matters. The real content of regulation is in the EU Taxonomy, the Sustainable Finance Disclosure Regulation, and the Benchmark Regulation, and even more, as the example of gas and nuclear energy underscores, in the respective delegated and implementing acts. I have largely ignored these issues. Clearly, more research is needed in this direction, and among others due to reasons of space, my ambitions in this chapter have been fairly modest. But I hope I have at least succeeded in sharing some insights that may support the reflexive law approach of the Action Plan as well as the legislative initiatives that follow in its wake.

Acknowledgements

Portions of this chapter were presented at the Wharton Business School, the Financial Ethics Workshop at the University of Gothenburg, and the Phinance Online Seminar in 2021. I am grateful to the audiences collectively for their feedback. I am particularly grateful to Stephen Barrie, Brian Berkey, Olha Cherednychenko, Philipp Dapprich, Geert Demuynck, Richard Endörfer, Brian Feinstein, the late Gwen Gordon, Robert Hughes, Emiliano Ippoliti, Ronald Jeurissen, Julian Jonker, Jens van 't Klooster, Louis Larue, Quintus Masius, Marco Meyer, Helen Mussell, Philip Nichols, Barend de Rooij, Amy Sepinwall, Christian Walter, and Raymond Zaal, to two discussants, Joakim Sandberg and Arnaud Van Caenegem, to two anonymous reviewers for Oxford University Press, and to Joakim Sandberg and Lisa Warenski for excellent editing. All errors are attributable to the author alone and not to these helpful commentators. I finished this chapter in early 2022, and have not taken into account any later developments.

References

Beekhoven van den Boezem, F. E. J., Jansen, C., & Schuijling, B. (eds.) (2009). *Sustainability and Financial Markets.* Deventer: Wolters Kluwer.

Blocher, J. (2019). Free Speech and Justified True Belief. *Harvard Law Review*, *133*(2), 439–96. https://harvardlawreview.org/wp-content/uploads/2019/12/439-496_Online-1.pdf.

de Bruin, B. (2013). Epistemic Virtues in Business. *Journal of Business Ethics*, 113, 583–95. https://doi.org/10.1007/s10551-013-1677-3.

de Bruin, B. (2015). *Ethics and the Global Financial Crisis: Why Incompetence Is Worse than Greed.* Cambridge: Cambridge University Press.

de Bruin, B. (2022). *The Business of Liberty: Freedom and Information in Ethics, Politics, and Law*. Oxford: Oxford University Press.

de Bruin, B. (2022a). Against Nationalism: Climate Change, Human Rights, and International Law. *Danish Yearbook of Philosophy*, 55, 173–98. https://doi.org/10.1163/24689300-20221060.

Busch, D., Ferrarini, G., & van den Hurk, A. (2019). The European Commission's Sustainable Finance Action Plan. In Beekhoven van den Boezem, F. E. J., Jansen, C., & Schuijling, B. (eds.), *Sustainability and Financial Markets*. Deventer: Wolters Kluwer, 35–58.

Christman, J. (1991). Liberalism and Individual Positive Freedom. *Ethics*, *101*(2), 343–59. https://doi.org/10.1086/293292.

Commission Decision 2016/6912. Commission Decision on the creation of a High-Level Expert Group on Sustainable Finance in the context of the Capital Markets Union. European Commission. https://ec.europa.eu/info/sites/default/files/161028-decision_en.pdf.

Communication 2015/0468. Action Plan on Building a Capital Markets Union. https://eur-lex.europa.eu/legal-content/EN/TXT/?uri=CELEX%3A52015DC0468.

Communication 2018/97. Action Plan: Financing Sustainable Growth. European Commission. https://eur-lex.europa.eu/legal-content/EN/TXT/?uri=CELEX:52018DC0097.

Communication 2020/590. A Capital Markets Union for people and businesses-new action plan. https://eur-lex.europa.eu/legal-content/EN/TXT/?uri=COM:2020:590:FIN.

Communication 2021/188. EU Taxonomy, Corporate Sustainability Reporting, Sustainability Preferences and Fiduciary Duties: Directing finance towards the European Green Deal. https://eur-lex.europa.eu/legal-content/EN/ALL/?uri=CELEX:52021DC0188.

Council Regulation (EEC) No. 1836/93 of 29 June 1993 allowing voluntary participation by companies in the industrial sector in a Community eco-management and audit scheme. https://eur-lex.europa.eu/legal-content/EN/TXT/?uri=CELEX%3A31993R1836.

Davidson, D. (1963). Actions, Reasons, and Causes. *Journal of Philosophy*, *60*(23), 685–700. https://doi.org/10.2307/2023177.

Directive 2014/65/EU of the European Parliament and of the Council of 15 May 2014 on markets in financial instruments and amending Directive 2002/92/EC and Directive 2011/61/EU. https://eur-lex.europa.eu/legal-content/EN/TXT/?uri=CELEX%3A32014L0065.

Directive 2014/95/EU of the European Parliament and of the Council of 22 October 2014 amending Directive 2013/34/EU as regards disclosure of non-financial and diversity information by certain large undertakings and groups. https://eur-lex.europa.eu/legal-content/EN/TXT/?uri=CELEX:32014L0095.

Directive (EU) 2016/97 of the European Parliament and of the Council of 20 January 2016 on insurance distribution. https://eur-lex.europa.eu/legal-content/EN/TXT/?uri=CELEX:32016L0097.

Döttling, R., & Kim, S. (2021). Sustainability Preferences under Stress: Evidence from Mutual Fund Flows during Covid-19. https://ssrn.com/abstract=3656756.

EU High-Level Expert Group on Sustainable Finance [HLEG] (2018). *Financing a Sustainable European Economy*. https://ec.europa.eu/info/sites/default/files/180131-sustainable-finance-final-report_en.pdf.

Farber, D. A. (1994). Environmental Protection as a Learning Experience. *Loyola of Los Angeles Law Review*, 27, 791–808. https://digitalcommons.lmu.edu/cgi/viewcontent.cgi?article=1836&context=llr.

Farmer, L., & Teubner, G. (1994). In Teubner, Gunther, Farmer, Lindsay, & Murphy, Delcan (eds.), *Environmental Law and Ecological Responsibility: The Concept and Practice of Ecological Self-Organization*. Chichester: Wiley, 3–13.

Greaves, H. & MacAskill, W. (2021). The Case for Strong Longtermism. Global Priorities Institute Working Paper Series. GPI Working Paper No. 5–2021. https://globalprioritiesinstitute.org/wp-content/uploads/The-Case-for-Strong-Longtermism-GPI-Working-Paper-June-2021-2-2.pdf.

Gunningham, N., Grabosky, P. N., & Sinclair, D. (1998). *Smart Regulation: Designing Environmental Policy*. Oxford: Oxford University Press.

Habermas, J. (1981). *Theorie des kommunikativen Handelns: Band II: Zur Kritik der funktionalistischen Vernunft*. Frankfurt am Main: Suhrkamp.

Hartzmark, S. M., & Sussman, A. B. (2019). Do Investors Value Sustainability? A Natural Experiment Examining Ranking and Fund Flows. *Journal of Finance*, 74(6), 2789–837. https://doi:10.1111/jofi.12841.

Hess, D. (1999). Social Reporting: A Reflexive Law Approach to Corporate Social Responsiveness. *Journal of Corporation Law*, 25(1), 41–84. https://heinonline.org/HOL/P?h=hein.journals/jcorl25&i=51.

Kahneman, D. (2013). *Thinking, Fast and Slow*. New York: Farrar, Straus and Giroux.

Kooij, I., Kapraun, J., & Krakow, J. (2021). Sustainability Information and Investment Decisions. Paper presented at Behavioural Finance Working Group Conference 2021. https://www.qmul.ac.uk/busman/media/sbm/research/researchcentres/behavioural-finance-working-group/Sustainability-Information-and-Investment-Decisions.pdf.

Marshall, B. R., Nguyen, H., Nguyen, N. H., Visaltanachoti, N., & Young, M. R. (2021). Salient Climate Information and Mutual Fund Flows: A Note. https://ssrn.com/abstract=3788390.

Meadows, D. H., Meadows, D. L., Randers, J., & Behrens III, W.W. (1972). *The Limits to Growth: A Report for the Club of Rome's Project on the Predicament of Mankind*. New York: Universe Books.

Orts, E. W. (1995). A Reflexive Model of Environmental Regulation. *Business Ethics Quarterly*, 5(4), 779–94. https://doi.org/10.2307/3857414.

Popper, K. R. (1957). *The Poverty of Historicism*. Boston: Beacon Press.

Pritchard, D. (2018). The Value of Knowledge. In Zalta, E. (ed.), *Stanford Encyclopedia of Philosophy*. https://plato.stanford.edu/entries/knowledge-value/.

Regulation (EU) 2019/2088 of the European Parliament and of the Council of 27 November 2019 on sustainability-related disclosures in the financial services sector. https://eur-lex.europa.eu/legal-content/EN/ALL/?uri=CELEX:32019R2088.

Regulation (EU) 2019/2089 of the European Parliament and of the Council of 27 November 2019 amending Regulation (EU) 2016/1011 as regards EU Climate Transition Benchmarks, EU Paris-aligned Benchmarks and sustainability-related disclosures for benchmarks. https://eur-lex.europa.eu/legal-content/EN/TXT/?uri=CELEX%3A32019R2089.

Regulation (EU) 2020/852 of the European Parliament and of the Council of 18 June 2020 on the establishment of a framework to facilitate sustainable investment, and amending Regulation (EU) 2019/2088. https://eur-lex.europa.eu/legal-content/EN/TXT/?uri=celex:32020R0852.

Tarsney, C. (2022). The Epistemic Challenge to Longtermism. https://philpapers.org/archive/TARTEC-2.pdf.

Task Force on Climate-Related Financial Disclosures (2017). Recommendations of the Task Force on Climate-Related Financial Disclosures. https://assets.bbhub.io/company/sites/60/2020/10/FINAL-2017-TCFD-Report-11052018.pdf.

Teubner, G. (1989). *Recht als autopoietisches System.* Frankfurt am Main: Suhrkamp.

Zagzebski, L. T. (2012). *Epistemic Authority: A Theory of Trust, Authority, and Autonomy in Belief.* Oxford: Oxford University Press.

PART III
ETHICS

9

Is the Pursuit of Money Incompatible with Morality?

Some Historical and Philosophical Reflections

Adrian Walsh

1. Introduction

Financial ethics—which is the central theme of this part of the book—is focused upon exploring and providing solutions to the ethical dilemmas faced by agents in financial markets (Dobson 1993). One significant aim of such investigations is to instil public trust in the fairness of financial markets and financial transactions, thereby allowing them to function efficiently. Another aim is to enable competing business agents to harmonize their interest, as it were, and once again for the public to benefit. In general, ethical norms are considered by financial ethicists as necessary for maintaining stability in our social lives; hence, they defend forms of ethical education. However, in society at large there remains (unsurprisingly) a great deal of mistrust of financial operatives, be they individuals or institutions. People do not view such actors to be following appropriate ethical norms. One common cause of concern involves the motives of financial agents and, especially, the perception that they are driven only by financial imperatives. It is often thought that the craven pursuit of profit renders the very idea of financial ethics impossible. This I shall refer to as the *Incompatibility Thesis*, according to which morality and the pursuit of money are thought of as necessarily incompatible. But should the profit motive be treated with such suspicion? Is it in fact irreconcilable with the motives that one might think should animate a properly moral human life?

In this chapter I explore the moral status of the profit motive *as a motive*, in the first instance, from a historical perspective, for we find the clearest condemnations of the profit motive in the writings of earlier philosophers and religious moralists. By 'profit' I simply mean the term as it is commonly used when referring to the difference between what consumers pay for outputs (revenue) and what companies pay for inputs (costs) (Hussain 2012, p. 313). It is this sense of profit which is at issue. The question under discussion in this chapter is not whether following moral principles can also be profitable—which is the central question for many

Adrian Walsh, *Is the Pursuit of Money Incompatible with Morality? Some Historical and Philosophical Reflections* In: *The Philosophy of Money and Finance.* Edited by: Joakim Sandberg and Lisa Warenski, Oxford University Press.
© Oxford University Press 2024. DOI: 10.1093/oso/9780192898807.003.0010

contemporary business ethicists and which concerns the compatibility of morals and profits—but whether the profit motive is in itself morally dubious.

The concern herein is with the moral status of the profit motive and the implications of that for financial ethics. The profit motive is a significant driver in finance and, accordingly, in financial ethics. But it is often said that the profit motive is vicious. (A contemporary example of this is to be found in the work of G. A. Cohen (1991).) Our first question then is: can we reconcile the obvious consequential benefits of markets and thus of the profit motive with what some see as the essentially or necessarily vicious nature of pecuniary motives? We might well wonder whether morality and the profit motive are necessarily at odds with one another. Second: what are the assumptions underpinning the view that the profit motive and morality are incompatible? Third: can we develop a compatibilist model of economic activity in which the profit motive and morality are not necessarily at odds with one another? In responding to these questions, I develop a *compatibilist model* in which the *compossibility* of the profit motive and morality properly conceived is defended. In this compatibilist approach—and in stark contrast to the so-called Efficiency Argument for Profit Maximization (EAPM) and Joseph Heath's well-known Market Failures Approach (MFA)—the profit motive itself is regarded as having no singular normative content.[1] Instead, I develop a taxonomy of profit-motivational sets which identifies a variety of different ways in which our motivations for pecuniary gain and moral principles intersect. In the final section of the chapter, I consider the implications of this compatibilist approach for financial ethics.

2. A Brief Overview of Four Common Normative Objections to the Profit Motive

In order to analyse the classical antagonism directed towards the profit motive, it is helpful to distinguish between four somewhat different types of objections that have been leveraged against it. First, it is a commonplace of a great deal of public discourse about the profit motive (and the pursuit of wealth) that it involves the vice of greed. Put simply, the thought is that it is wrong to be motivated by greed; and the profit motive is seen as the prime example of what it is to be motivated by greed. In the Bible, the pursuit of money is referred to as the 'root of all evil' (Ecclesiastes 5:10). Plato and Aristotle both denounced those who were motivated by profit. In a famous passage in his late work *The Laws*, Plato is highly critical of the avaricious behaviour of various business people, most notably innkeepers. Aristotle not only agrees with Plato, but also provides an explanation as to why

---

[1] The argument is outlined in Jensen 2001. For a detailed and insightful discussion of the EAPM, see Hussain 2012.

commerce leads to avarice. It is, he says, a consequence of the nature of money and what is involved in pursuing it. Aristotle argues that seeking profit is an activity which does not have a *telos* (Baldwin 1959, p. 13). If I have the goal of building a house or a boat, there is an end point where I have achieved my goal, by producing a well-appointed house or a seaworthy boat. But this is not the case with money (Baldwin 1959, p. 13). It has no 'satisfaction conditions' and thus endlessly iterates. To wish to pursue profit represents, in this sense, a failure of practical reasoning.

A related but different objection to the profit motive that can be found in the literature is that it distorts the beliefs and desires that should underpin human interaction: When one engages with others, one should be animated by feelings of solidarity rather than personal gain. Unfortunately, the profit motive leads to the destruction of amity-based or fraternal relations.[2] This is a recurrent theme in the works of many writers both ancient and modern. For an example of the thesis defended by an ancient thinker, one need look no further than the Roman philosopher Cicero, who writes that 'if we each of us propose to rob or injure another for our personal gain, then we are clearly going to demolish what is more emphatically nature's creation than anything else in the whole human world: namely, the link that unites every human being with every other' (Cicero 1974, pp. 166–167). To profit from another person's loss would be to strike at the heart of human fellowship and undermine society as a whole. In the medieval period, the Franciscans took vows of poverty because of their belief that desire for profit was harmful to the ideal of universal amity (Coleman 1988, p. 631). More recently, the twentieth-century social theorist Karl Polanyi (1886–1964) has argued, in his magnum opus *The Great Transformation*, that the profit motive ensures orderly production and distribution of goods. The organization of production relies solely on the market and is, in this way, separated from society. Such an organization, driven by the 'motive of gain', is destructive to the fabric of society (Polanyi [1944] 2001, see also Gemici 2008). What unites these thinkers from vastly different cultures and historical periods is the thought that being animated by profit leads to the disintegration of the shared ideals on which human moral community ultimately depends.

A third commonly encountered objection to the profit motive is that it distracts one from more noble and elevated goals—that is from what J. S. Mill would have referred to as the 'higher pleasures' (Mill 1962, pp. 259–262). The poet and artist William Blake, for instance, suggested that the vocation of the artist was necessarily at odds with that of commerce. He claimed that one cannot serve Mammon and Art, for money distracts an individual from genuine creativity (Hughes 1990, pp. 387–388). This idea we might refer to as the Distraction Thesis.

---

[2] See Cicero (1974, pp. 166–167).

The Distraction Thesis is not simply a pretension of the artistic fraternity but is to be found in any other areas where the activity in question is thought of as a vocation. Indeed, it underpins some of the more traditional objections to both professional sport and to medicine understood as a commercial practice. Instead of being truly dedicated to the activity in question—which should be treated as an end in itself—we are tempted by the 'false promises' of money and profit.

A fourth and final objection to the profit motive involves the claim that it is to be condemned because of the temptations it provides to engage in dubious practices. This we might refer to as the Objection from Sharp Practice (Baldwin 1959, p. 14). Many critics of the profit motive have focused on lying, which they see as an integral part of merchants' lives. In De Officiis, Cicero claims that retail traders have little to gain unless they are dishonest (Cicero 1967, trans. Higginbotham, p. 92). One might thus object to the marketplace because of the tendency towards haggling and lies. There are also concerns with the fraudulent selling of goods which are not what they appear to be. Martin Luther objected to the selling of spiritual indulgences by the Roman Catholic Church on the grounds that those buying indulgences were being deceived.[3]

These four objections are some of the primary reasons why traditional moralists have found the profit motive, as a motive, morally pernicious. Of course, these are not exhaustive of the reasons one might object to the profit motive, but I suggest that they do provide a fairly comprehensive list. Let us now turn to the question of whether we should believe that virtue and the profit motive are necessarily at odds.

3. Mandeville's Challenge: The Benefits of the Market versus the Perfidious Nature of the Profit Motive

It is clear that markets generate tremendous material benefits and, furthermore, that those benefits are caused, in large part, by the actions of agents animated by the profit motive. This is one justification of markets (and, indirectly, of the profit motive), and it is consequentialist in nature. Many sympathetic commentators have noted the ways in which markets provide both (i) incentives for agents to produce and (ii) information about what it would be most advantageous for them to produce. In terms of incentives, the claim is that markets—at least in the absence of monopoly—encourage producers to generate a remarkable quantity of goods that would not be possible under any other incentive system. It is also

---

[3] In his pamphlet 'To the Christian Nobility of the German Nation on the Improvement of the Christian Estate', Luther writes that at Rome: 'there is a buying, selling, bartering, trading, trafficking, lying, deceiving, robbery, theft, luxury, whoredom, knavery, and every sort of contempt of God' (1952, pp. 138–139).

claimed that the incentives provided by the profit motive also encourage a level of innovation that is not found in any other system. Driven by the desire for profit—and being in competition with other market agents who also wish to obtain those profits—producers are forced to innovate and create better products more likely to attract customers. Despite the lack of any intrinsic concern for the welfare of those who consume their goods, the market system is so structured as to encourage agents to provide benefits for others. (This is in essence Adam Smith's 'Invisible Hand' at work.) There is also what we might call the Argument from Information, a different consequentialist argument that focuses on markets as information systems and, in particular, on the ways in which they provide information for the coordination of production and distribution.

Additionally, there are a number of influential deontological arguments about the freedom that one finds in markets or about the connection between fundamental human rights and markets, however, the least controversial justification concerns the consequential benefits. Herein, I shall focus simply on the consequential arguments in favour of markets and—by virtue of its intimate association with the markets—the profit motive. Let us assume, then, for the sake of this argument, that markets do indeed provide valuable material benefits and, further, that they are the best system known for doing so. At the same time, it must be acknowledged that market agents often engage in vicious behaviour in pursuit of profit. So, here is our dilemma: if we hold that markets give rise to great benefits, then what should we make of the fact that the profit motive is believed by many to be morally vicious? Should we reject the profit motive, as many have urged? Alternatively, should we reject morality?

One well-known (and perhaps notorious) response to this puzzle is to be found in Mandeville's *Fable of the Bees*. The idea is that we should accept the vicious motives as socially necessary. Mandeville writes that the benefits we receive in a commercial society are the result of fraud, luxury, and pride. To attempt to make the 'hive of bees' honest would be a fool's errand, a 'vain UTOPIA seated in the brain' (Mandeville 1957, pp. 36–37). According to Mandeville, then, the social basis of our well-being is to be found in vice. Mandeville here endorses a version of the Incompatibility Thesis, according to which profit-seeking and morality are in mortal conflict. Given the benefits markets provide and the incompatibility of profit-seeking and virtue, we must reject virtue.

An even stronger view would be that vice itself is a duty. Samuel J. Tilden, in 1877, made just this point at a testimonial dinner for John Pierpont Morgan's father, Junius Morgan. In this speech he warmed the hearts of his audience of industrialists with the following words:

> You are, doubtless in some degree, clinging to the illusion that you are working for yourself, but it is my pleasure to claim that you are working for the public. [Applause] While you are scheming for your own selfish ends, there is an

overruling and wise Providence directing that the most of all you do should inure to the benefit of the people. Men of colossal fortunes are in effect, if not in fact, trustees for the public.   (Canterbury 1980, p. 120)

Here Tilden is not just accepting or accommodating vice, but actually celebrating it: according to Tilden, one has a duty to be vicious. It follows from this reasoning that any person involved in business who chooses virtue over self-interest is not a paragon of moral virtue, but simply morally self-indulgent.

At the other end of the spectrum of the incompatibilists are socialists who also hold that the profit motive and morality are at odds and, accordingly, choose to side with virtue. An example of such incompatibilism can be found in the writings of the French socialist Charles Fourier (1772–1837), who held that the immorality of the market is such that we must reject markets and commercial values entirely.[4] Fourier wrote: 'I am a child of the marketplace, born and brought up in mercantile establishments. I have witnessed the infamies of commerce with my own eyes, and I shall not describe them from hearsay as our moralists do' (1971, p. 150). In his youth, Fourier writes, he discovered that commercial life was 'a cesspool of moral filth' and he vowed an eternal hatred of it (1971, p. 150). Fourier, in effect, argues that virtue and seeking profit are necessarily incompatible and, therefore, we should reject the profit motive.

While the views of Fourier and Mandeville stand in stark opposition to one another, there are some striking similarities. Both consider the profit motive to be at odds with morality, within an account in which it is assumed that morality must be a form of pure other-regarding altruism. Where they part company is with how they interpret the demand for altruism. Mandeville implores us to reject the calls of morality. His work is utilitarian in that it does not assess the quality of an individual's motives in performing this or that action, but rather evaluates it in terms of the efficacy of the individual's action in delivering general benefits. Mandeville takes this to mean that a commercial agent's pursuit of self-interest is morally legitimated because such pursuit non-accidentally produces wealth for the community of agents. Fourier, on the other hand, wants us to reject the market because of its necessarily vicious nature and because of what seeking profit impels us towards. For Fourier, commercial agents are to be condemned as immoral since to be animated by the profit motive is to ignore our obligations to

---

[4] I suggest that the Incompatibility Thesis finds its clearest socialist expression not, as one might expect, in the works of Karl Marx (1818–1883), but in the writings of Charles Fourier. While Marx subjected capitalism and market relationships to radical criticism, his determinist and progressivist philosophy of history also committed him to a certain historical and consequentialist justification for all the admitted sins of commercial life. This is because the communist utopia he envisaged depended on the provision of a material plenitude that could only emerge from the extraordinary productive capacities unleashed by market capitalism. Fourier saw no such role for capitalism.

others. If the Incompatibility Thesis is correct, then it would seem that we are forced to choose between the benefits of markets and moral virtue. But must we accept the Incompatibility Thesis? In the rest of this chapter, I argue that we need not do so.

4. Three Common Mistakes When Framing the Issue of the Relationship between Morality and the Profit Motive

One common feature of all of the radical critiques of the profit motive and of commerce listed in section 2 is the view—even if not expressed in explicitly modal terms—that the profit motive and morality are necessarily at odds. But why? How might one argue that it is necessarily at odds? I suggest that what underpins this idea of mutual exclusivity are mistaken views about the nature of self-interest, altruism, and selfishness: profit-seeking is understood as a form of self-interest, self-interest is conflated with selfishness, and finally, morality is defined in terms of selfless altruism. If we think in this way, then it is not surprising that we end up considering virtue and the profit motive as mutually exclusive. Instead, we need to acknowledge that self-interest does not rule out an other-regarding concern and, more specifically, that being driven by the profit motive does not necessarily rule out a concern for our fellow human beings.

G. A. Cohen (1941–2009) makes just this kind of mistaken argument about the incompatibility of profit-seeking and morality in his 1991 article entitled 'The Future of a Disillusion' (1991, pp. 5–20). He writes that markets 'motivate contribution not on the basis of commitment to one's fellow human beings and a desire to serve them while being served by them, but on the basis of impersonal cash reward'. He notes that in a market society the immediate motive to productive activity is usually some 'mixture of greed and fear'. Cohen's argument against the profit motive and markets can be reconstructed as follows:

(i) Markets motivate contribution on the basis of impersonal cash reward.
(ii) Our motivations should in some sense be solidaristic.
(iii) Thus, in a market, people fail to treat others in a solidaristic way.
(iv) Solidarity is a central human ideal.
(v) Therefore, the market is morally pernicious. It is a mixture of 'greed and fear' (Cohen 1991, p. 16).

(Notice the important role that the idea of solidarity—understood as a form of selflessness—plays in the argument. I shall say more about this below.)

There are three main mistakes made in these kinds of accounts—and of which Cohen's argument is a typical example—which involve:

1. The conflation of selfishness and self-interest: self-interest is treated as being identical to selfishness.
2. An altruism-only view of moral action: other-regarding moral concern is identified with altruism and must therefore be entirely selfless in order to be moral.
3. An avarice-only conception of the profit motive: the profit motive is understood as being animated by entirely selfish, avaricious motives that exclude the possibility of concern for others.

Let us consider some reasons to believe that these views are mistaken.

First, self-interest is not the same as selfishness. Indeed, it is wrong to assume that self-interest involves the exclusion of other-regarding concerns. Antony Flew observes, in his article on the profit motive, that when his daughters eagerly eat their respective evening meals, they are pursuing their own interests (1976, p. 314). The consumption of those meals is clearly self-interested. However, he notes that 'it would be monstrous to denounce them as selfish hussies' simply because of that. Flew dismisses the identification of self-interest with selfishness: 'For, although selfish actions are perhaps always interested, only some interested actions are selfish.' His point is that selfishness is always (and necessarily) out of order. What he calls 'interestedness' however is not out of order and, he says, scarcely could be. In many instances self-interest is an element of self-respect and as such is not objectionable, nor is it selfish. This explains why the Objection from Greed, at least as stated as an objection to all profit-seeking behaviour, is mistaken. The mere fact that one is pursuing profit does not mean that one is guilty of greedy, morally pernicious selfishness.

A second mistake is to think that genuinely moral action excludes any self-regarding components. This seems to be Cohen's assumption when he claims that in a market people interact with others only on the basis of impersonal cash rewards. We also find this erroneous view in the writings of the early modern philosopher Francis Hutcheson, who says, '[A]s to the love of benevolence, the very name excludes self-interest' ([1725] 2004, p. 103). Hutcheson argues that if there is to be such a thing as benevolence, it must be disinterested. But why think this? Altruism, of course, is normally thought of as selfless, but altruism is distinct from morality. I might assist a friend to landscape their garden because the work requires two people, if it is to be accomplished effectively and also because I enjoy my friend's company. But, it might also be the case that my garden will need landscaping in the near future, and I hope that if I help, then perhaps my friend might return the favour. This simply means that my motives are mixed, and the mere presence of self-interest does not mean my concern for my friend is not genuine. This suggestion should not be a surprise, since in many instances our motives are mixed or mingled. Our reasons for acting are rarely singular.

When we move our attention to the profit motive itself, we see that these considerations about self-interest demonstrate what is wrong with an avarice-only conception of the profit motive; and, further, why the Objection from Solidarity, if it is read as encompassing all profit-seeking activity, is mistaken.[5] It is simply not true that that the profit motive operates entirely independently of other-regarding concerns.[6] To take a rather unexceptional example, the fact that a nurse works for a living, and does so with the intention of making money, does not mean that the nurse's motive does not have an altruistic component. Indeed, the other-regarding element will often explain why the person chose to become a nurse, despite the fact that the financial reward is typically, relative to other occupations, rather low. To be sure, it might be objected that this is wage labour rather than commercial activity animated by the profit motive. But similar considerations apply if we move to the commercial realm proper, and consider the motives of a medical professional who has a business, and who is not a wage labourer. There is no reason to suppose that the mere existence of a profit motive means that other incentives are not live in an individual's all-things-considered judgements.

In summary, we need to distinguish between selfishness and self-interest. Self-interest is a form of self-respect and is neither selfish nor objectionable. Second, we need to acknowledge that moral action—or morally permissible action—can contain a self-regarding component. It is a mistake to hold that other-regarding moral action and moral concern must be altruistic, in the sense of being entirely selfless, in order to be genuinely moral. Third, the profit motive itself need not be avaricious. The avarice-only conception of the profit motive is mistaken because it is simply not the case that being animated by the profit motive necessarily rules out concern for others (even if this is typically the case).

5. Commercial Life and Varieties of Profit Motives: Towards Conditional Acceptability of the Profit Motive

If concerns for individual morality and for the benefits of the market are not necessarily mutually exclusive, the challenge then is to understand how they may come together, and, so, on occasion, come apart. The approach suggested herein involves developing a taxonomy of different profit motives and is predicated on the more general philosophical notion that in any single action the agent in question can have more than one motivation. It is based on the phenomenon of mixed motives and generates what I shall refer to as the *conditional moral permissibility* of the profit motive.

This idea of commercial activity and the profit motive being conditionally permissible is not without precedent in the philosophical literature. Indeed, we

---

[5] This is the model with which Cohen is working when he says that in the market people interact with others *only* if they can get something out of it.

[6] This point is not, of course, entirely novel. For a good example of earlier discussions (though not one I eventually endorse), see Keynes 1890, pp. 118–135.

can find antecedents of it in the work of Ancient and medieval philosophers. For instance, in the *Politics* Aristotle distinguishes between two forms of commercial exchange—namely, the *natural* and the *chrematistic* (Aristotle 1946, pp. 23–27). By 'natural exchange' Aristotle means transfers in which goods produced for household consumption are sold because they have a superfluity over and above the needs of a particular household. In contrast is the chrematistic which Aristotle condemns because the goods sold were produced for the purpose of sale alone. Profit is, in Aristotle's vision, only permissible as a mere happenstance. However, the medieval thinker Thomas Aquinas (the son, as it turns out, of a merchant) was far more sympathetic to seeking profit. Aquinas held that it was permissible to pursue profit as a goal so long as the money gained was a means to other morally acceptable ends (such as providing for one's family) (Aquinas, 1963).[7] However, neither of these two philosophers are willing to condone profit as an end in itself. In the model I proffer below, it is indeed permissible to have profit as an end or goal in itself, although this does not vindicate all forms of profit-seeking.

We find related—although distinct—views about the conditional compatibility of moral intentions and the profit motive in some contemporary writings in business ethics. Notably, Johan J. Graafland, in an article entitled 'Profits and Principles: Four Perspectives', outlines a variety of different approaches to the question of how principles and profits might coexist (2002, pp. 293–305). Some of what Graafland writes intersects with the categories I delineate below.[8] However, Graafland's attention is also fixed upon the question of whether the realization of profits is compatible with moral principles, rather than with the compatibility of profit-seeking with morally appropriate motives. Graafland is concerned in large part with the economic sustainability of businesses adopting and abiding by moral principles; that is, with the question of whether a firm can remain profitable while acting morally. But profitability itself is not my concern herein. Nonetheless, there are a number of points where he discusses the moral status of the profit motive as a motive and thus I shall note those points as they arise.

If one is worried about maintaining and sustaining an other-regarding moral concern, can one justify profit as an end in itself? First, as we have already noted, a person engaging in commercial activity need not be animated only by a desire for profit. Such a person might have a number of goals. A doctor running a commercial medical practice might, for instance, aim to heal the sick and comfort the

---

[7] A similar point was made (somewhat surprisingly) by the neoclassical economist Alfred Marshall, who suggested that we should not judge a businessman who maximizes his profits, without knowing to what purposes those profits are put (1907, pp. 7–29).

[8] Graafland outlines a taxonomic framework with four distinct ways in which profit-seeking and morality intersect. Some of these perspectives concern the putative compatibility of moral motives and profit motives; however, not all of them do so. However, his first category—the licence-to-operate perspective—is concerned with whether ethical behaviour is rewarded with a competitive advantage. In his list of possible perspectives there is a slide between whether ethical behaviour is profitable and whether the motivational structure of the profit-seeker is compatible with appropriate moral attitudes.

dying, and, simultaneously, to provide him- or herself with a reasonable standard of living. In fact, in commercial action it is possible to be animated by a variety of different motives, some of which are other-regarding. The second point turns on the distinct roles that motives can play in practical reasoning. Motives or reasons can function either as side-constraints upon, or goals of, action. The thinking here rests on the work of Robert Nozick, who distinguishes between the specific or particular goals of an action and those values or interests or ends which might place limits on what we are prepared to do in pursuit of our primary goal. These limiting factors Nozick refers to as 'side-constraints' (1975, pp. 28–33). (In a related discussion, the management theorist Sam Eilon refers to constraints as a form of goal that provide boundaries that you cannot or will not transgress (1971, pp. 292–303).)

Applied to commercial life, it follows that the pursuit of profit might either be (i) a goal of one's actions, or (ii) a side-constraint upon one's actions. In the former case, one is animated primarily by the pursuit of profit. In the latter, one is motivated primarily by some other consideration, but, nonetheless, one needs to make a profit in order to realize one's goals. Some readers might object that Nozick's side-constraints involve talk of 'rights' rather than 'motives' and, accordingly, raise doubts about whether a motive can be a side-constraint. The answer is quite simple—one might be motivated by the idea that any activity in which one engages must be profitable, but this is simply a threshold that the activity must pass. If the activity that one wishes to pursue is not profitable, then it cannot be undertaken, but that is the only role that profit plays in determining the appropriate course of action.

With these considerations in mind, it is time to turn to our framework, which is fundamentally a taxonomy of action types, based on a structural analysis of commercial motives. Notice that in this account, the talk is of profit motives in the plural rather than the profit motive in the singular form.⁹ This approach differs from that of Lankoski and Smith (with which it might be confused), who provide a taxonomy based on the various roles that social welfare plays in the objective function of firms (2018, pp. 242–262). In my model it is the role that morality plays in the goals of firms that matters.

1. The first category of profit-seeking involves cases where morality and profit-seeking are both conceived of as goals of action. Let us call this the *fully compatibilist* profit motive.¹⁰ It is equivalent for all intents and purposes to

---

⁹ The model outlined here is a development and modification of the taxonomy to be found in Adrian Walsh and Tony Lynch's *The Morality of Money* (2008). There are, on the model developed in this chapter, five main categories of profit motivational sets, rather than four, as was the case in Walsh and Lynch.

¹⁰ Some readers might well be sceptical about the extent, in practice, to which both goals can be successfully pursued simultaneously. Nonetheless it is certainly a conceptual possibility, and this is all that matters when arguing against the necessity that is embedded in the Incompatibility Thesis.

what Graafland calls the 'integrated perspective' in which a company attaches an intrinsic value to both profits and principles (2002, p. 300). To take our earlier example of the well-intentioned doctor, in this case the agent aims to engage in significant other-regarding action as well as to realize a genuine profit. Another example is provided by Waheed Hussain when he discusses instances where stakeholders agree to seek profits while also seeking to advance other ends. Hussain's example is of two friends, Ben and Jerry, who decide to set up an ice-cream company that will seek to make a profit, but will do so while looking to pay its workers above-market wages and benefits (2012, pp. 318–319).

2. The second category involves cases where profit-seeking is the only genuine goal, but where morality is a side-constraint. This is the *accumulative* profit motive. The agent's sole aim in their commercial activity is to make a profit, however, there are a range of things that this person would not do in pursuit of commercial gain. For instance, by way of example, they would not sell exploitative pornography. Morality here provides significant constraints on the ways in which profit might be pursued. Schoenmaker and Schramade in *Principles of Sustainable Finance* (2019) refer to activity structured in this way as profit maximization while avoiding 'sin' stocks; that is, not investing in companies with negative impacts (2109, p. 21). In the social domain, they suggest, this would include companies that sell tobacco, anti-personnel mines, and cluster bombs or those that exploit child labour. In the environmental domain, they suggest that companies engaged in waste dumping and whale hunting would count as sin stocks.

3. The third category—the *stipendiary* profit motive—involves cases where profit-seeking is a side-constraint and the goals are non-commercial. They might, for instance, be moral in the sense of being other-regarding or alternatively being guided by some valuable outcome the person wishes to realize. For instance, a person might be committed to assisting the needy or achieving a valued environmental goal. If the activity is commercial, then the profits made are simply a sideline and necessary in order to satisfy the person's fundamental needs (and also to guarantee the continuation of the activity). Additionally, there will also be cases where the goal is not so much moral, but oriented towards some activity which the agent finds intrinsically valuable. A good example of this would be a musician highly motivated to develop their artistic outputs and who needs to make money in order to continue doing so. In this case the profits made are really just what is required to sustain the musician in their artistic activity.

4. The fourth category—which is the most troubling—is the *lucrepathic* profit motive. This refers to cases where profit-seeking is unconstrained by any moral side-constraints. There is nothing that the lucrepath will not do in pursuit of profit. For the lucrepath, moral considerations are either rejected

explicitly or are simply not taken seriously in their all-things-considered judgements. Profit-seeking is the only motivation here.

5. Our final category is the *lucrephobic*, and it is not so much a profit motive as a rejection or repudiation of the practice of seeking commercial gain. In this case, profit is neither a side-constraint nor a goal. Lucrephobes accept the Incompatibility Thesis and thus reject profit-seeking. Lucrephobia is included in part for purposes of taxonomic completeness, but at the same time, this is a motivational set that one often encounters amongst various religious and radical anti-capitalist movements, so it is a real-life case.

Obviously, the interesting cases for our purposes with respect to rejecting the Incompatibility Thesis are 1, 2, and 3 because in each of these instances the pursuit of profit does not mean that other-regarding concerns are otiose or to be ignored.

The significance of this taxonomy for our understanding of the relationship between individual morality and commercial life should be clear. It is not that the pursuit of profit is necessarily immoral, but that the actions of the lucrepath are to be repudiated. When people complain about the morality of commercial life, their complaint is with the behaviour of the lucrepath, who will do anything for profit. The taxonomy outlined here shows that there is the moral and logical space for forms of profit-seeking activity that do take moral considerations into account, and if this is true, then the Incompatibility Thesis as stated at the outset is false. At the same time, the taxonomy demonstrates why the objections outlined in section 2 are not entirely mistaken and raise genuine concerns. The lucrepath is someone who is prone to greed, indulges in sharp practices, and is unlikely to appreciate the intrinsic non-monetary value of creative activities nor the desirability of 'solidaristic' action. However, at the same time there remain cases where the pursuit of profit is not objectionable from a moral point of view.

Notice some key ways in which this approach differs from two central approaches in the business ethics literature, namely, the EAPM (as developed most famously by Michael C. Jensen) and Heath's Market Failures Approach. Both models locate normativity within economic activity itself rather than treating it as an external and distinct constraint upon such activity. The basic idea of the EAPM is that companies are normatively required to maximize the total market value of the financial instrument through which people invest in the firm. According to Jensen—who is a leading advocate of this view—the objective function of the firm is the profit that firms are normatively required to maximize (Jensen 2001, p. 8; Lankoski and Smith 2018, pp. 242–243). What underpins such a normative obligation? Jensen's response is the standard Smithian argument concerning the maximization of social welfare (as conceived within welfare economics): 'The short answer to the question . . . is that 200 years' worth of work in economics and finance indicate that social welfare is maximized when all firms maximize total firm value' (2002, p. 239). The thought is that the profit motive is a normative phenomenon: it is not, as is the case in the model developed here, that morality is an external evaluative mechanism. However, as Hussain notes in some detail, this account of the normativity of the profit motive is in some considerable tension with our ordinary conception of morality. Hussain asks the reader to imagine that a company (which he calls *Beta Lending*) decides to seek reasonable—as opposed to maximal—profits and aim to provide home ownership to minorities. This would appear to violate the EAPM. As Hussain notes, pursuing minority home ownership as an end in itself contributes in some ways to the company's long-term profits but detracts in others. However, it would be odd, according to commonsense morality, to consider this as violating a normative requirement despite EAPM's demand that corporations always maximize their profits. Hussain provides a number of examples—including the aforementioned Ben and Jerry case—in which pursuing non-maximal economic strategies does not violate commonsense morality. In a similar vein, Lankoski and Smith (2018) argue that it is wrong to presume that profit maximization is the sole objective of companies.[11] Also, Colin Mayer's work on corporate responsibility undertaken for the British Academy emphasizes that corporations produce profits but profits are not per se the purpose of corporations (2018). This is all grist to my mill, since it would support the assumption that we treat normativity and profit-seeking as distinct phenomena: On the model developed here, the task is to determine the cases in which they are compatible.

The development of a moral system grounded in justificatory features of the market also animates the Market Failures Approach to Business Ethics. While EAPM focuses on aggregate social welfare, Heath's system grounds itself in the economic ideal of Pareto-efficient market outcomes. Heath believes the production of such efficient outcomes for consumers to be an irreducible moral principle (Heath 2014, p. 73). Indeed, Heath talks at times of 'efficiency imperatives'. Markets are justified, according to Heath, because they produce significant benefits for consumers; he is committed to rejecting what he believes is the anti-capitalism of much business ethics. Considerations of Pareto efficiency—which he calls the implicit morality of the market—provide the justificatory grounds for constraints and government regulation. The upshot, for our purposes, is that morality is not, as it is in my taxonomy, external to, or distinct from, economic activity; it is instead derived from the market. Both the justification of the market and the constraints upon it are said to spring from the market's efficiency benefits for consumers. Hence, on Heath's account we do not evaluate market phenomena, such as the profit motive, via distinct ethical criteria. On Heath's model it is not a matter of choosing between economic considerations and ethical ones (Cohen and Peterson 2019, p. 86).

---

[11] Lankoski and Smith (2018, p. 249). They also note that as a matter of fact firms do not typically operate as if profit were their sole concern.

Clearly this is different from my approach, in which the different ways that pecuniary motives intersect with moral considerations provide us with a taxonomy of distinct profit-motivational sets. It might be objected that this is a distinction without a difference, for in both instances ethical considerations are embedded in economic concepts. However, there is a significant difference between these models in that the source of morality in my profit-motivational taxonomy is external to the market—these are independent criteria. Furthermore, Heath is wary of intentions playing a role in business ethics, writing that: '[T]he virtues of competition, such as they are, are associated with the institutional structure (i.e., the set of rules) that constrains the participants' behavior, and not necessarily the intentions of the participants' (2007, p. 363). However, we should be highly sceptical of this idea that all of business ethics can be derived from the ideal of efficiency. As Cohen and Peterson argue, in an article which is largely sympathetic to Heath's work, this conception of business ethics overlooks too much. They suggest than an adequate business ethics 'must include normative considerations beyond the consequential optimization of preference satisfaction' (Cohen and Peterson 2019, p. 86). I suggest that this demonstrates the reasons for the maintenance, within business ethics generally, of a conception of morality whose source is independent of, and external to, the market and economic phenomena.

6. The Limits of Conditional Permissibility

If the Incompatibility Thesis is understood as the claim that the profit motive and other-regarding moral considerations are necessarily in conflict, then it would seem that the claim is false. Profit-seeking and morality are compossible, as it were, and commercial agents can and often do act with mixed motives of the kind outlined above. But what follows from this? Does this mean we can drop all of our moral concerns concerning the profit motive? Is the profit motive no longer a matter of moral concern? And can we rely simply on the motives of commercial agents in order to deal with the dangers of corruption and exploitation?

It is important at this point to point out the limits of such claims about compossibility. Mixed motives are possible, but as David Hume reminds us in his essay 'Of the Dignity or Meanness of Human Nature', '[W]here avarice or revenge enters into any seemingly virtuous action, it is difficult for us to determine how far it enters' (1964, p 156). Hume notes that it is quite natural to suppose avarice is the sole actuating principle. If we understand Hume to be saying that it is impossible simultaneously to pursue profit and to engage in morally virtuous other-regarding action, then the arguments outlined above show why Hume's arguments are wrong. But if we understand Hume's comment as a word of warning about the 'moral hazards' of the profit motive, then the point is well-taken. The dangers of profit-seeking becoming one's only motive in the market are ever-present. The point is that there will always be opportunities and temptations within a market context to engage in morally dubious but profitable activities. This is exactly what was at issue in the Objection from Sharp Practice, although on our model it is not framed as a necessary consequence of market activity. It is not that mixed motives are impossible, but that the temptations and pressures of commercial life mean that there is always the risk of 'lucrepathology'.

To see why the profit motive might be thought of as a moral hazard, let us begin by considering the problem of what the Swiss economist Bruno Frey referred to as 'crowding out' (1997). The idea here is that market ideals and values tend to push out non-market ones. There is a large body of evidence presented by writers such as Frey that this is, in fact, the case. Similarly, with respect to motives: non-commercial motives will often be crowded out by the desire for profit. Relatedly, there are dangers of self-deception when one is engaged in commercial activity. In order to see how we are capable of deluding ourselves, one need only read Daniel Kahneman and Amos Tversky's (1982) work on heuristics and biases where, on the basis of very little demonstrable evidence, human beings form excessively flattering views of themselves and far less flattering pictures of others. Equally, with respect to the profit motive, it is entirely possible to be self-deceived about the extent to which one's motives are actually other-regarding. This is all to say that markets are morally hazardous: conditional permissibility does not mean there are no moral dangers. There are also important questions—if our aim here is to ensure that commercial agents do in fact take moral considerations into account—how we motivate morality in the first place. This, of course, is the long-standing philosophical problem, which was raised by Plato in The Republic, of why we should be moral.

These are not the only hazards in the area: in addition, there are systematic pressures within market systems that often make acting on moral considerations—when those moral considerations undermine the maximization of profit—extremely difficult if not impossible. Competitive pressures within market systems mean that it is often a 'race to the bottom'. Those who act upon moral motives that, in effect, make them less competitive—when their rivals lack such scruples—will often find survival as a business difficult. Hence, the possession of moral motives alone cannot be relied upon. Political institutions that place constraints upon the excesses of profit-seeking are required to ensure that those who wish to act out of moral motives are not necessarily and inevitably forced out of business. This is but another way of saying that the conditional moral permissibility of the profit motive is predicated upon the existence of social institutions which make it financially possible for one's actions to be animated by what I earlier labelled accumulative profit motives.

7. Concluding Remarks

It is a mistake—as the Incompatibility Thesis claims—to view the profit motive and morality as being necessarily at odds, and it is wrong to characterize the relationship in such a way that there is no place for the moral evaluation of our pursuit of profit. In order to avoid the unenviable choice with which the Incompatibility Thesis presents us, we need to distinguish between different ways in which one might pursue profit. This involves developing a more nuanced account of the profit motive than the one standardly discussed in exchanges between anti-market socialists on the one hand and uncompromising defenders of laissez-faire on the other. The approach developed here draws on critiques of the profit motive which focus on its status as a motive and which then considers the different ways profit-seeking might intersect with the moral realm. Instead of treating the profit motive as a singular item of analysis to be condemned for its selfishness or praised for its social consequences, we need to distinguish between different profit motivational sets, according to the ends or goals pursued in commercial activities and whether other-regarding side-constraints on the pursuit of such ends are present. If we do so, then the dilemmas raised by the Incompatibility Thesis can be circumvented and we can turn to questions about how one might avoid commercial life being so organized, as to make the non-vicious forms of profit-seeking genuine possibilities. The model differs significantly from accounts such as EAPM and Heath's MFA, which treat economic phenomena as fundamentally normative. In this model, morality and seeking profit are distinct, but we can outline different profit motivational sets in which normative considerations play a variety of different roles.

What might be the significance of these conclusions for financial ethics? If we take a step back and reconsider the remit of financial ethics, we see that, in part, it is a necessary corrective to one dominant view in financial theory and financial practice that lionizes the so-called rational agent who is a self-interested profit-seeker (Bowie 1991, pp. 1–21). That specific view derives from orthodox economic theory, according to which rationality is to be understood in terms of what maximizes self-interest. Against this, financial ethicists argue for the necessity of ethics in order to (i) maintain public confidence in the financial system and (ii) to harmonize the interests of competing business agents. (These are, admittedly, rather instrumental utilitarian reasons for being ethical.) However, the very idea of financial ethics is often met with great suspicion from both (i) those who defend the financial system and (ii) those who are openly critical of it; and one common reason for such suspicion is adherence to something like the Incompatibility Thesis. The conclusions developed in this chapter aim to demonstrate why that particular reason for rejecting financial ethics is mistaken. In a sense this approach opens up the epistemic space for financial ethics by showing—at least with respect to our motives—why it is not logically impossible for ethical considerations to be present in financial transactions. Perhaps in providing a taxonomy of profit motivational sets, the chapter also provides a model for use in financial ethics education. The ideal financial operative would presumably be an accumulator who seeks profits with appropriate side-constraints—and the 'spectre of the lucrepath' would help explain how things can go awry. The application of the taxonomy to real-life ethical dilemmas in finance promises to be a fruitful line of inquiry for future research.

References

Aquinas, Thomas, 1963, *Summa Theologica*. London: Blackfriars Press.

Aristotle, 1946, *The Politics*, trans. E. Barker. Oxford: Clarendon Press.

Baldwin, John, 1959, 'The Medieval Theories of Just Price: Romanists, Canonists, and Theologians in the Twelfth and Thirteenth Centuries', *Transactions of the American Philosophical Society*, 49, part 4.

Bowie, Norman E., 1991, 'Challenging the Egoistic Paradigm'. *Business Ethics Quarterly*, 1(1), pp. 1–21.

Canterbury, E. Ray, 1980, *The Making of Economics*, 2nd ed. Belmont, CA: Wadsworth.

Cicero, 1967, *Cicero on Moral Obligations*, trans. John Higginbotham. Berkeley: University of California Press, p. 92.

Cicero, 1974, 'On Duties' III, *Cicero, Selected Works*. Harmondsworth: Penguin.

Cohen, G. A., 1991, 'The Future of a Disillusion', *New Left Review*, 190, pp. 5–20.

Cohen, Marc A., and Peterson, Dean, 2019, 'The Implicit Morality of the Market and Joseph Heath's Market Failures Approach to Business Ethics', *Journal of Business Ethics*, 159, pp. 75–88.

Coleman, Janet, 1988, 'Property and Poverty' in J. H. Burns, ed., *The Cambridge History of Medieval Political Thought*. Cambridge: Cambridge University Press, pp. 607–648.

Dobson, John, 1993, 'The Role of Ethics in Finance', *Financial Analysis Journal*, 49(6), pp. 57–61.

Eilon, Sam, 1971, 'Goals and Constraints', *Journal of Management Studies*, 8(3), pp. 292–303.

Flew, Antony, 1976, 'The Profit Motive', *Ethics*, 86(4), pp. 312–322.

Fourier, Charles, 1971, *Harmonium Man: Selected Writings of Charles Fourier*, edited with an introduction by Mark Poster. New York: Anchor Books.

Frey, Bruno, 1997, *Not Just for the Money*. Brookfield, VT: Edward Elgar.

Gemici, Kurtulus, 2008, 'Karl Polanyi and the Antinomies of Embeddedness', *Socio-economic Review*, 6(1), pp. 5–33.

Graafland, Johan J., 2002. 'Profits and Principles: Four Perspectives', *Journal of Business Ethics*, 35(4), pp. 293–305.

Heath, Joseph, 2007. 'An Adversarial Ethic for Business: Or, when Sun-Tzu Met the Stakeholder', *Journal of Business Ethics*, 74(2), pp. 359–374.

Heath, Joseph, 2014. 'Efficiency as the Implicit Morality of the Market' in J. Heath, ed., *Morality, Competition, and the Firm: The Market Failures Approach to Business Ethics*. Oxford: Oxford University Press, pp. 173–204.

Hughes, Robert, 1990, *Nothing if Not Critical: Selected Essays on Arts and Artists*. London: Collins Harvill.

Hume, David, 1964, 'Of the Dignity or Meanness of Human Nature' in T. H. Green and T. H. Grose, eds., *The Philosophical Works*, *Vol. 3*. Darmstadt: Scientia Verlag, pp. 150–156.

Hussain, Waheed, 2012. 'Corporations, Profit Maximization and the Personal Sphere', *Economics and Philosophy*, 28(2), pp. 311–331.

Hutcheson, Francis [1725] 2004, *An Inquiry into the Original of Our Ideas of Beauty and Virtue*, edited by Wolfgang Leidhold. Indianoplis: Liberty Fund.

Jensen, Michael C., 2001. 'Value Maximization, Stakeholder Theory and the Corporate Objective Function', *Journal of Applied Corporate Finance*, 14, pp. 8–21.

Jensen, Michael C., 2002. 'Value Maximization, Stakeholder Theory, and the Corporate Objective Function', *Business Ethics Quarterly*, 12, pp. 235–256.

Kahneman, Daniel, and Tversky, Amos, 1982. *Judgement Under Uncertainty: Heuristics and Biases*. Cambridge: Cambridge University Press.

Keynes, John Neville, 1890. *The Scope and Method of Political Economy*. London: Macmillan.

Lankoski, Leena, and Smith, N. Craig, 2018. 'Alternative Objective Functions for Firms', *Organization & Environment*, 3(13), pp. 242–262.

Luther, Martin 1952, *Reformation Writings of Martin Luther, Vol. 1*, translated with an introduction and notes from the definitive Weimar edition by Bertram Lee Woolf. London: Lutterworth Press, pp. 138–139.

Mandeville, Bernard, 1957, *The Fable of the Bees, Vol. 1*, ed. F. B. Kaye. Oxford: Clarendon Press.

Marshall, Alfred, 1907, 'The Social Responsibilities of Economic Chivalry', *Economic Journal*, 17, pp. 7–29.

Marx, Karl, 1950, *Capital Vol. 1*. Moscow: Progress Press.

Mayer, Colin, 2018, 'The British Academy, Reforming Business for the 21st Century', https://www.thebritishacademy.ac.uk/publications/reforming-business-21st-century-framework-future-corporation/

Mill John Stuart [1861] 1962, *Utilitarianism*, ed. M. Warnoch. London: Collins/ Fontana.

Nozick, Robert, 1975. *Anarchy, State, and Utopia*. New York: Basic Books.

Polanyi, Karl, [1944] 2001, *The Great Transformation: The Political and Economic Origins of Our Time*. Boston, MA: Beacon Press.

Schoenmaker, Dirk, and Schramade, Willem, 2109. *Principles of Sustainable Finance*. Oxford: Oxford University Press.

Smith, Preserved, 1911, *The Life and Letters of Martin Luther*. New York: Houghton Mifflin.

Walsh, Adrian, and Lynch, Tony, 2008, *The Morality of Money: An Exploration in Analytic Philosophy*. New York: Palgrave Macmillan.

10

Virtue Theory and the Ethics of Finance

Kate Padgett Walsh and Nolan Pithan

1. Introduction

The vices characteristically associated with finance are numerous: dishonesty, recklessness, and greed, to name a few. What light, then, does virtue theory, both historically and today, shed on the ethics of finance? In this chapter, we distinguish between two distinct virtue theoretic approaches to the ethics of finance today. First, virtue theory can be employed to assess the behavior of those engaged with finance in terms of the presence or absence of virtuous character traits such as honesty, moderation, and empathy. Second, virtue theory can be applied to evaluate the complex forms of activity that constitute finance in terms of how those activities contribute to or impede human flourishing in society more broadly. Both virtue theoretic approaches are of great relevance to the ethics of finance, we contend, because each emphasizes distinct dimensions of engagement with finance. More specifically, we argue that, alongside consideration of the character traits realized by individuals engaged in financial activities, the capabilities approach is a promising tool for evaluating those activities in terms of human flourishing. We conclude with an example that illustrates how the two modes of virtue theoretic analysis can be fruitfully integrated to generate nuanced assessments of both individual behavior within finance and forms of financial activity more broadly.

2. Early Virtue Theoretic Critiques of Finance

The early virtue theorists focused their remarks on finance exclusively on the ethics of lending. This focus reflects the fact that, for much of human history, the activities of finance consisted primarily of lending and collecting sums of money. Even the term "finance," from the French *fin*, originally referred to closing or paying off a debt. Today, finance is much more diverse, encompassing investing, trading, managing funds and assets, and various activities of forecasting, rating, securitizing, insuring, consulting, and accounting. However, debt remains a basic component of finance, with many debts additionally now securitized and sold as

Kate Padgett Walsh and Nolan Pithan, *Virtue Theory and the Ethics of Finance* In: *The Philosophy of Money and Finance.* Edited by: Joakim Sandberg and Lisa Warenski, Oxford University Press. © Oxford University Press 2024. DOI: 10.1093/oso/9780192898807.003.0011

financial products to investors. Debt also remains the primary way in which most individuals engage with finance, since more people are debtors than investors. Early virtue theoretic assessments of finance thus remain relevant, despite their narrow focus on the ethics of debt.

Early virtue theorists were on the whole quite critical of finance as they understood it. In *The Republic*, for instance, when the moneylender Cephalus attempts to define justice just as paying one's debts and telling the truth, Socrates counters by asking whether it is always the case that we should return what we borrow (Plato 2016, 1.331c). Imagine, for example, returning a weapon to someone who is in a murderous rage. The obligation to pay debts is far from absolute, Plato suggests, and depends at the very least upon facts about the actual lender or debt collector involved. He subsequently extends this implicit critique in *The Laws*, arguing that lending at interest should be prohibited altogether, on the grounds that doing so would increase both the stability of the *polis* and the virtue of its citizens (Plato 1992, 742). The business of moneylending is a key driver of inequality that creates and exacerbates excessive concentrations of wealth, he contends. The resulting inequality erodes honesty and friendliness between citizens, thereby harming their virtue, but it also has a destabilizing effect on the *polis* because it increases disagreement and the potential for political strife. By removing profit from lending, Plato concludes, both virtue and stability can thus be promoted.

Aristotle was also highly critical of moneylending, arguing both that it is parasitic upon productive economic activity and that it reflects vice rather than virtue. In his view, money itself produces nothing, but rather stores value and facilitates production and trade. Moneylending, in contrast, perverts the purpose of money "Money came into being for the sake of exchange, but interest makes the money itself increase" (Aristotle 2013, 1258b). The problem is thus not inequality per se, as Plato contends; rather, it is the way in which wealth is created. Profiting from interest allows lenders to accumulate wealth in a way that is divorced from the production and trading of goods, and thus undermines core economic activities. Moreover, Aristotle contends, those who make their living from moneylending display a specific kind of failure concerning the virtue of justice (Swanson 1994). More specifically, they exhibit the vice of meanness (*aneleutheria*), which Aristotle describes as both an excess in taking from others and a deficiency of generosity. Persons with this vice attribute more value to money and wealth than those things deserve, so much so that they take pleasure from the activity of taking from others. Meanness is such a deep character flaw, he contends, that it is "incurable" (Aristotle 1999, 1121b). Moneylenders display this vice both by taking excessively and by taking from those who cannot afford it. And they are typically indiscriminate in whom they lend to; they will take money from the rich, who have plenty, but also from the poor, even those who are desperate.

A third important critic in this tradition was Aquinas, who synthesized Aristotelian arguments with biblical prohibitions on moneylending.[1] Aquinas argues that it is both predatory and impious to lend money for the purpose of growing more money (Aquinas 1975). Lending is predatory insofar as it exploits the neediness of the poor for one's own advantage (Hirschfeld 2015). And it is impious in that it appropriates something that Aquinas regards as ultimately belonging to God, namely the debtor's labor and time that is required to pay interest. In contrast to Aristotle, however, Aquinas remains hopeful about the possibility of redemption, suggesting that those who have committed the sin of usury can make amends by returning the interest they collected from borrowers.

Common to these early virtue theoretic assessments of finance is the view that the activities of lending are in tension, and perhaps even incompatible, with flourishing together within society (Ahn 2017; Niewdana 2015; Padgett Walsh 2018). Each thinker also incorporates into their assessment of lending an evaluation of the character of lenders. Plato, for instance, argues both that moneylending drives inequality and that it reflects personal vice on the part of lenders. Similarly, Aristotle's contention that moneylending perverts the true purpose of money complements but does not reduce to a critique of the vices of lenders. And Aquinas emphasizes the harms suffered by impoverished debtors while also critiquing the impiety of lenders. The normative considerations discussed within these early virtue theoretic critiques thus simultaneously focus on assessing the character of those engaged in moneylending and on determining the broader implications of their activities for human flourishing within society.

3. Assessing Character in Finance

The intervening centuries have seen transformations of lending and debt, as well as the rise of new financial markets and increasingly complex forms of finance. They have also seen the rise to prominence of virtue ethics (VE), a virtue theoretic approach that focuses ethical analysis on individual character traits. In this section, we explore the implications of contemporary VE for the ethics of finance. VE builds upon but also diverges from early virtue theory by focusing more closely on the character of individual agents, emphasizing the cultivation of personal virtue and directing individuals to strive to act well by developing virtuous thoughts, feelings, and desires (Annas 2004). This focus serves to illuminate important aspects of the ethics of finance, but it can also limit the scope of ethical analysis.

---

[1] See especially Psalm 15, Ezekiel 18:8, Leviticus 25:36, Deuteronomy 23:19–20, and Nehemiah 5.

VE focuses ethical evaluation on character traits, and specifically on the virtues and vices that are realized in a person's actions. One very prominent version of VE has been developed by Rosalind Hursthouse, who asserts that actions are right if and only if they are those that virtuous agents would take in the circumstances (Hursthouse 1999). In order to evaluate and guide behavior, then, we must determine how a virtuous agent would act in a given situation by identifying the relevant virtues of character they would display. Applied to finance, this Aristotelian account directs us to identify as virtues the individual character traits that constitute a flourishing human life and then determine how well they are realized in finance. A fully virtuous agent, for instance, acts honestly and moderately, and thus so should those occupied in finance. A distinct version of VE developed by Michael Slote builds instead upon early modern accounts of virtue that emphasize moral sentiments such as benevolence (Slote 1995). Slote argues that empathy is the virtue that underlies all others, and so individual behavior can be assessed by determining the degree to which it is motivated by empathetic care. Applied to finance, this view implies that the vices characteristically associated with finance should be understood as rooted in failures of empathy.

VE's focus on how virtues and vices manifest in the behavior of individuals is of great relevance to the ethics of finance. Pedagogically, discussing virtues such as honesty and moderation with pre-professional students may especially serve to promote moral development (Dutmer 2022; Frey 2009). For instance, analyzing case studies and the actions of moral exemplars in terms of virtues and vices may help students become more reflective about their own character and give them practice in making moral decisions that realize virtues. VE can also contribute to the ethics of finance by providing a framework for examining how practices and cultures in finance shape the character, positively and negatively, of participants. For example, a practice or culture that accepts and encourages excessively risky behavior is clearly in tension with the virtue of moderation (Das 2011). In addition to focusing on how individuals might develop virtues such as moderation, VE can guide reforms to financial practices and cultures that encourage excessive risk by fostering relevant virtues throughout communities of financial professionals. This might be accomplished if leaders within financial organizations deliberately promote the realization of virtues within their organizations, but it may also require that they generate dialogue about the societal impacts of finance upon human flourishing more generally (Asher and Wilcox 2022). Regarded through the lens of VE, the task of advancing ethics within finance is thus one of both transforming financial practices and cultures so that the behavior of those in finance comes to more fully reflect that of fully virtuous agents, as well as encouraging the development of virtuous character traits among individuals.

VE also provides a mechanism for evaluating a wide range of behaviors in finance in terms of the underlying virtues and vices of individual agents (Ferrero et al. 2021). Consider again the ethics of lending. VE directs us to ask whether the provision of household debt, for instance, is inherently in tension with virtuous character traits, as earlier virtue theorists assert. Certainly, many examples of bad actors can be identified within the debt industry, including payday lenders, abusive mortgage lenders, and unscrupulous debt collectors. What makes the behavior of such actors unethical, according to VE, is that it is dishonest, excessively risky, or lacking in empathy for borrowers. Virtuous lending, in contrast, would at a minimum require refraining from pressuring vulnerable borrowers into risky mortgages and accurately representing loan characteristics to borrowers, investors, and ratings agencies, as occurred frequently in the run-up to the 2008 financial crisis (Griffin 2021).

VE can also, as Heidi Hurd and David Baum argue, recommend legal and regulatory reforms of finance (Hurd and Baum 2012). Focusing on bankruptcy law specifically, they argue that consumer bankruptcy protections should be expanded because doing so would serve to better aggregate and coordinate the personal virtue of forgiveness. Causing debtors to suffer by enforcing burdensome debt obligations reflects vice, they contend, but the practical problem is that any lender that wished to act virtuously by forgiving burdensome debts would thereby incur costs that would be passed on to shareholders or future borrowers. What is needed, then, is a mechanism for jointly relieving burdensome debts by spreading the costs of forgiveness across society so that individuals jointly exercise that virtue. Bankruptcy law is that mechanism, they propose, and consumer bankruptcy should ultimately be understood as a means of aggregating and coordinating the demands of individual virtue.

VE's focus on individual character traits is thus of great relevance to the ethics of finance. And yet, that focus can also serve to limit the scope of normative assessment, as thinkers going back to Hegel have argued. The problem is that individuals can be engaged in forms of activity that are ethically objectionable in ways that do not reduce to failures of personal virtue. Hegel puts the point this way: Focusing narrowly on individual character traits is ultimately insufficient for assessing complex activities within social structures (Hegel 1977). He has in mind early modern accounts of virtue, which, like Slote's version of VE today, emphasized the possession of virtuous sentiments such as benevolence (Yeomans 2015). Hegel contends that a narrow emphasis on character can lead to a version of the same error he ascribes to Kant, namely that of ignoring the extent to which elements of the social world shape and constrain deliberation, motivation, and character. In the case of Kant, the problem is that applications of the categorical imperative always depend upon assumptions about the underlying social and economic context, assumptions that are rarely examined and sometimes false (Padgett Walsh 2014). These assumptions effectively import content into what Kant understands as a purely formal principle. Similarly, Hegel argues that a narrow focus on individual character traits can obscure ethical questions about the social practices that frame individual behavior.

More recently, Susan Brison has argued that an exclusive focus on character traits is insufficient for evaluating and guiding behavior because some questions about the morality of our activities do not reduce to the level the individual (Brison 2012). One might fully possess empathetic concern for others, she argues, and yet be a participant in sexist or racist practices and institutions, for instance. Applied to finance specifically, the claim is that reducing the ethics of finance to a focus on character traits limits the scope of assessment. And while implementing legal and regulatory reforms can help to better coordinate the realization of the individual virtues, as Hurd and Baum propose, the further question remains of how to assess, ethically, the varied and complex activities in finance in which individuals are participants. Let us imagine, for example, a virtuous loan officer, one who strives to treat clients with honesty, moderation, and empathy. Such a person might nonetheless participate in redlining or sexist lending requirements as part of their work if such practices are standard and requisite. If it is possible to be possessed of a virtuous character and yet be party to financial activities that are flawed in such ways, then we also must look beyond the presence or absence of individual virtue to assess the activities of finance.

Slote has responded by noting that "someone doesn't demonstrate caring motivation in a given instance if they say that they want to help a given person, but don't do the relevant homework about how best to help that person" (Slote 2012, p. 41). Virtue, in other words, requires doing due diligence and being sensitive to ethically salient particulars; we cannot simply ignore realities about the potential impacts of our behavior on others. Yet, structural barriers to acting ethically extend beyond failures to express good character, especially when the activities in which we participate are highly complex, as in the case of finance today. Let us again imagine a virtuous loan officer who is empathetic and strives to act honestly with clients and help them avoid excessive risk. Such a person's actions are certainly commendable insofar as they reflect such virtues. However, the challenge persists because, as history reveals, it is possible for individuals who possess an abundance of honesty, moderation, and empathy to yet be caught up in and perpetuate practices that are discriminatory.

A second response would argue that a focus on character is sufficient so long as it is grounded in an independent conception of human flourishing, as Aristotelians such as Hursthouse propose. However, such a grounding is, alone, insufficient for fully engaging with the ethics of finance insofar as it centers ethical assessment just on the character of individuals. Consider, by way of analogy, Hursthouse's remarks on racism, which focus on the need for individuals to control their own racist emotional responses, which are often deeply ingrained (Hursthouse 1999). What remains unclear, however, is how to adequately account for the structural dimensions of racism, i.e. how it manifests at the level of shared practices and institutions, within the confines of this approach.[2] If individuals can participate in and perpetuate racist activities without being driven by racist emotions, then we must look beyond the level of individual character. And if it is possible for an individual to participate in financial practices that are flawed in such ways despite possessing key virtues, then we must again supplement VE with additional tools of analysis.

4. Assessing the Activities of Finance

How, then, might virtue theory shed light on the ethics of finance beyond assessing behavior in terms of individual character traits? Alasdair MacIntyre has, in recent years, directly taken up this question as part of his attempt to reclaim what he regards as the broader scope of early virtue theory (MacIntyre 2015). Drawing upon both Aristotle and Hegel, he proposes to assess forms of activity in terms of human flourishing more broadly so as to include, but not be limited to, considerations of individual character (MacIntyre 1984). And the activities of finance, he contends, are ultimately in conflict with flourishing together in society, so much so that they fail to rise to the level of what he defines as a social practice. This term is normatively laden, as MacIntyre uses it, since, in order to count as a social practice, a form of activity must systematically extend human excellence by realizing genuine rather than merely instrumental goods (MacIntyre 1984). The activities of finance, however, fail to realize genuine goods because they are dedicated solely to making money, a purely instrumental good that is not valued for its own sake.[3]

MacIntyre argues that finance's pursuit of money alone impedes human flourishing in two ways. First, its activities promote and elicit vice among those who participate in them (MacIntyre 1999). By way of example, he discusses financial traders specifically, highlighting four traits that he regards as essential to a successful career in trading, and all of which are in tension with personal virtue: first, traders are excessively confident and thus lacking in adequate self-knowledge; second, they are foolhardy and seek out high levels of risk; third, they exhibit insufficient care for others and the common good, failing to look beyond self-interest when weighing the consequences of their actions; and finally, they are overly focused on the present moment, at the expense of considering long-term impacts (MacIntyre 2015). Traders are thus prevented from flourishing by the activities that constitute their occupation, independent of whether they begin their careers as virtuous people.

---

[2] Tommie Shelby develops this critique at length in response to Jorge Garcia's more detailed virtue theoretic account of racism (Garcia 1996; Shelby 2002).

[3] As Aristotle contends, "wealth is evidently not the good we are seeking, for it is merely useful and for the sake of something else" (Aristotle 1999, I.5).

Second, MacIntyre contends that finance creates profit in a way that is parasitic, as Aristotle argued, on the true purpose of money. Finance siphons money away from those who actually make and sell things, allowing a relatively small number of investors, lenders, and financial professionals to reap the fruits of the labor of others, thereby driving inequality, as Plato observed. Echoing Aquinas, MacIntyre further argues that finance extracts much of its profit from the debt of people with modest means. Indeed, the rapid growth since 1980 of finance as a sector of the economy has been predicated in part upon the rise of mass indebtedness (Fuller 2016; Greenwood and Scharfstein 2013). The activities of finance broadly impede human flourishing, MacIntyre concludes, insofar as they create and promote debts that constrain the lives of masses of people, all to enrich a relatively small number of individuals.

MacIntyre's revival of the early virtue theoretic critiques of finance is important because it revitalizes broad questions about the activities of finance that extend beyond the scope of individual character traits. Is enriching the wealthy by extracting value from the labor of others truly essential to finance? Are the activities of finance unethical insofar as they drive inequality? Is finance fundamentally exploitative because it promotes and relies upon mass indebtedness? These questions have far-reaching implications for determining whether and how it is possible to participate ethically in finance. If the activities of finance are as deeply problematic as MacIntyre claims, then the best way to advance human flourishing with regard to finance would seemingly be to avoid or abolish those activities.

However, it is our contention that MacIntyre's critique does not adequately engage with the complexity and nuance of actual activities in finance. If it can be shown that, while there are vices associated with and even incentivized by some of the activities of finance, there are also virtues that are compatible with or encouraged by some of its activities, then perhaps the ethical prospects for those in finance are not as bleak as his critique implies (Bruni and Sugden 2013; West 2018). Similarly, the complex realities of financialized debt reveal a need for greater nuance than he offers. Indebtedness today certainly does constrain many people's life choices, requiring individuals to forfeit not only much of their time but also, in many cases, deeply held values and projects to pay burdensome debts (Lazzarato 2012; Porter 2012; Walker 2015). Debtor–creditor relationships existed in the earliest human societies, long before the invention of money (Mauss 2002), but it is the monetizing of debts, David Graeber argues, that has enacted a widespread violence upon human life by assigning a monetary value to all goods and values, including in some cases personhood (Graeber 2011). But, even so, there remains a pressing need to assess different forms and instances of debt, given that the burdens of debt are not shared equally among debtors. Some debtors are crushed by exploitative debts that were forced upon them by necessity, but others successfully utilize mortgages, for instance, to achieve stability and comfort that would otherwise be unattainable. Assessing debt today thus requires determining which specific forms and instances of debt are (most) unethical, rather than ignoring important differences between them.

More fundamentally problematic is MacIntyre's reliance on the distinction between genuine and instrumental goods to assess activities within finance. On his view, financial activities such as trading are ultimately at odds with human flourishing because their singular devotion to money prevents them from realizing genuine goods. Closer inspection, however, reveals this conclusion to be untenable. Consider an important class of genuine goods that MacIntyre identifies as intrinsic to complex activities such as chess: analytical skill, strategic imagination, and competitive intensity (MacIntyre 1984). Such goods of intellectual engagement make the activity of chess worthwhile in its own right and contribute to human flourishing, he contends, even when participants are also motivated by extrinsic rewards such as success or money. But similar goods are quite obviously also achieved within activities in finance, such as trading, that involve analysis, creativity, and competition. At least some genuine goods are realized through participation in finance, then, even if the activities of finance are also problematic in other ways. Moreover, at least some of the activities of finance also realize goods that contribute to human flourishing in society more broadly. Finance is, after all, a species of business more generally, and business activities can realize a variety of goods beyond that of making money. Some businesses create needed products and provide essential services, some realize goods of stable and adequate employment for employees, and some strengthen communities and advance research, for example. With regard to finance specifically, some of its activities may promote valuable goods, e.g. by making homeownership and retirement accessible, making insurance available, and facilitating the creation or expansion of businesses (Shiller 2013). The notion that finance utterly fails to realize any goods other than money is tenable only if we adopt an extremely narrow understanding of its activities. Finance does perhaps aim more directly at making money than, for example, manufacturing and service industries, but that does not imply that money is the only good it realizes.

The mere fact that a form of activity realizes some genuine goods does not, however, render it ethically supportable. The question, then, is how to assess such goods relative to the impediments to flourishing that finance also creates. What is needed is a way of operationalizing the notion of flourishing so as to make possible nuanced assessments of the complex activities of finance, above and beyond distinguishing between genuine and instrumental goods. It is our contention that the capabilities approach (CA) offers a promising theoretical tool for operationalizing assessments of finance in terms of human flourishing. The CA proposes to assess activities, practices, and institutions by determining how they contribute to or undermine human well-being. Capabilities are a person's capacities or opportunities to achieve states that one can reasonably value, such as physical and mental health, bodily autonomy, and educational achievement. As developed by Martha Nussbaum, this approach is rooted in Aristotle's project of ascertaining the components of a flourishing human life. Nussbaum identifies ten capabilities that she takes to be essential to well-being (Nussbaum 2011). Some capabilities pertain to the functioning of our physical selves: life, bodily health, and bodily integrity. Other capabilities pertain to our cognitive functioning: emotions, practical reason, and imagination. Yet others pertain to navigating the world as deeply social beings: affiliation and belonging, play and leisure, control over one's environment, and concern for other species. Because flourishing human beings exercise all of these capabilities in pursuit of their projects and life plans, Nussbaum contends, activities, practices, and institutions that support or build these capabilities thereby promote flourishing, whereas those that undermine them impede flourishing.

How might the CA be applied to assess the activities of finance? Consider again the critiques of finance developed by MacIntyre and the early virtue theorists. Each critique can be restated in terms of how financial activities affect capabilities that are essential to human flourishing. A high level of inequality, for example, is objectionable if it interferes with social capabilities such as affiliation and belonging, but also if it undermines bodily and cognitive capabilities (Case and Deaton 2020). Any activities of finance that are significant drivers of inequality, as Plato argued, can in this way be seen to impair or restrict human capabilities. Similarly, the CA can be used to assess Aristotle's claim that the activities of finance are parasitic on other economic activities. Financial trading, for instance, is an activity that MacIntyre critiques for its narrow focus on making money. According to the CA, this focus is objectionable insofar as it serves to impede the development and possession of physical, cognitive, or social capabilities. If forms of trading increase market volatility, thereby rendering the lives of various stakeholders more precarious, for instance, or if trading generally undermines productive economic activity by diverting resources away from those who make and sell things, it can thus be seen to reduce the capabilities of individuals throughout society. Finally, the CA can also be fruitfully applied to assess various forms of debt, including debt bondage, medical debt, educational debt, and mortgages, in terms of their impacts upon human capabilities (Padgett Walsh and Lewiston 2020). The CA can thus engage in a rich and nuanced way with the kinds of critiques of finance raised by MacIntyre and the early virtue theorists.

5. An Integrated Virtue Theoretic Approach

We conclude with an example that illustrates the need to integrate considerations of character in finance with assessments of financial activities in terms of human capabilities. Short selling is a financial activity that originated in the early seventeenth century but is increasingly commonplace today (Appel and Fos 2020), and it is often regarded as inimical to both individual virtue and the common good (Lotz and Fix 2013). At is most basic, a short is a bet that the price of a stock (or other security) will fall. This bet is placed by borrowing shares from a brokerage and selling them on the market. At the end of the loan period, the investor repurchases the same number of shares and returns them to the brokerage. The investor thus makes money if the share price falls during the loan period but loses money if the price rises or stays the same. Short selling is controversial for a number of reasons. First, it is seemingly a bet against prosperity, a way of making money at the expense of those who invest more optimistically in a company's long-term prospects. Second, short selling is risky because losses can be large if share prices rise or if brokerages modify loan terms. Third, short selling may have, historically, contributed to several economic crises, most notoriously in 1929. Out of concern that short selling would exacerbate instability during the financial crisis of 2008 and the market decline of March 2020, regulators throughout the world thus enacted temporary bans on short selling.

VE directs us to assess short selling by considering whether it reflects virtues or vices on the part of those involved. Does betting against a company's performance reflect empathy for other investors and participants in the economy? Does short selling reflect additional virtues, such as moderation and honesty, that are seemingly necessary for flourishing? On the face of it, short selling appears to conflict with moderation, empathy, and even honesty, since investors usually do not voluntarily disclose shorts. Yet, a closer examination of short selling reveals additional considerations that are ethically salient. Short selling need not involve excessive risk, for example, and some advisors recommend moderate inclusion of shorts in portfolios as a strategy for mitigating the risk of a market downturn or hedging against the risk of falling share prices. There similarly exist more and less honest and transparent ways to engage in short selling, and a trader who shorts a small amount of stock as part of a diverse portfolio is arguably engaged in a very different activity than a hedge fund that shorts a large portion of a company's shares without disclosing that activity to the public. Short selling also need not reflect a lack of empathy on the part of investors. An investor, for instance, might not actually wish for a company's share price to fall, but nonetheless believe it is likely to do so and thus decide to short the stock. Shorts can thus reflect realism rather than a lack of virtue, at least in some cases.

To further complicate matters, short selling has in recent years increasingly been coupled with acts of shareholder activism, especially on the part of institutional investors (Bliss, Molk, and Partnoy 2020). This activism can take a variety of forms, some of which are less compatible with virtues than others. Informational activism seeks to influence share prices by providing information to other investors. A short seller engaged in this kind of activism shorts a stock and then releases information in an attempt to cause the share price to decline by, for instance, uncovering misstatements or fraud. This sort of activism is at least consistent with the virtue of honesty, so long as it increases access to true information. And while such activism certainly may reflect a lack of empathy, it may also simply reflect a desire to benefit from the release of information that will eventually become known in any case. Operational activism, in contrast, seeks to influence share price by damaging a company's operations. A short seller engaged in this kind of activism shorts a stock and then tries to weaken the underlying state of the company by, for instance, challenging a patent or blocking the company from taking favorable actions. Seeking to profit by thus inflicting damage upon a company after shorting its shares seemingly indicates a failure of empathy because it inflicts harm upon a variety of stakeholders.

VE thus enables us to differentiate among instances of short selling according to the degree to which each realizes or fails to realize virtues such as moderation, honesty, and empathy. Hurd and Baum's extension of VE also has potential legal and regulatory implications for short selling. Consider the Security and Exchange Commission's 2022 proposal (13f-2) to require public disclosure of short selling by institutional investors. The rule emphasizes the importance of transparency, the idea being that large shorts should not be hidden from public view because of potential market effects. Regarded from the perspective of VE, as elaborated by Hurd and Baum, the proposed rule is seemingly justified because it offers a mechanism for aggregating and coordinating the virtue of honesty with regard to large shorts. Even if honesty did not require transparency with regard to all shorts, it is seemingly required when shorts are of a sufficient size to have significant market effects. Most short selling is unlikely to be voluntarily disclosed, however, in the absence of a strong norm or legal requirement to do so. The proposed rule, then, can be understood as a mechanism for jointly realizing the virtue of honesty in this domain, one which is necessitated by the presence of opposing market pressures.

VE thus sheds light on important ethical dimensions of short selling. Yet, the question remains of how to assess the activities of finance beyond the level of individual virtue and vice, and even beyond the question of how to best coordinate individual virtues within a legal and regulatory framework. Is short selling, for instance, an activity that contributes to flourishing within society more generally, or is it, as many believe, inherently in tension with the common good? This question can be fruitfully addressed in terms of the CA, which directs us to consider how short selling might undermine or enhance human capabilities. If short selling serves to exacerbate inequality or undermine productive economic activity in ways that impede human capabilities, for instance, then it is an objectionable activity even if some of the individuals who engage in it possess virtues such as honesty, moderation, and empathy.

One effect of short selling that has been extensively studied is increased liquidity within markets, meaning that shorts typically enable trading to occur fluidly and at more stable prices. This is important because when liquidity is low, investors may be unable to trade efficiently, which can cause market swings and thereby increase risks. Such volatility has the effect of negatively impacting capabilities by rendering more precarious the livelihoods of various stakeholders who are affected by market fluctuations. This suggests that some amount of short selling can positively contribute to human flourishing, at least during periods of normal market activity, and such potential contributions must be assessed in light of negative effects on capabilities. For example, during times of significant volatility, short selling may increase risk and exacerbate market declines. If so, the CA implies that it is unethical to engage in short selling, especially in large quantities, at moments of crisis because doing so is likely to undermine the capabilities of great numbers of people.[4]

Such an assessment of the activities of short selling in terms of human capabilities notably does not reduce to an assessment of the character traits of individuals in that activity. Consider again the distinction between informational and operational activism, as combined with short selling. An investor lacking the virtue of honesty might well choose to pursue a strategy of informational activism by researching and uncovering a company's misconduct in order to short its shares and profit from releasing the information. Such behavior, though not necessarily reflective of virtuous character, may nonetheless serve to enhance human capabilities by bringing to light information that assists other investors and halts misconduct. By assessing activities such as short selling in terms of how they impact human capabilities within society, we can thus assess those activities in a way that is distinct from assessments of the character traits of individual investors who engage in short selling.

Determining whether and how it is possible to ethically participate in finance ultimately necessitates a focus on both the character of individuals and on the broader implications of their forms of activity for human flourishing. We typically expect virtuous individuals to engage in activities that promote flourishing, whereas we expect individuals who lack virtues to engage in activities that fail to promote flourishing. Yet, virtuous individuals can engage in activities that fail to promote human capabilities, and individuals lacking in important virtues can nonetheless act in ways that do promote capabilities. An integrated virtue theoretic approach to the ethics of finance thus encompasses both modes of evaluation. There exist more and less virtuous ways of being a lender, investor, trader, and financial advisor, and these differences matter; so too, however, do the implications of financial activities for human flourishing beyond the realization of virtue or vice among the individuals in such roles.

---

[4] See Balakrishnan, Elson, and Heintz (2012) for an analysis of the harms of the 2008 financial crisis in terms of the CA.

References

Ahn, I. (2017) *Just Debt*. Waco, TX: Baylor University Press.

Annas, J. (2004) "Being Virtuous and Doing the Right Thing," *Proceedings and Addresses of the American Philosophical Association*, 78(2), pp. 61–75.

Appel, I. and Fos, V. (2020) "Active Short Selling by Hedge Funds," European Corporate Governance Institute (ECGI)—Finance Working Paper, 609.

Aquinas, T. (1975) *Summa Theologica*, tr. Lefebure, M. London: Blackfriars.

Aristotle. (1999) *Nicomachean Ethics*, tr. Irwin, T., Indianapolis, IN: Hackett.

Aristotle. (2013) *Politics*, tr. Lord, C. Chicago: University of Chicago Press.

Asher, A. and Wilcox, T. (2022) "Virtue and Risk Culture in Finance," *Journal of Business Ethics*, 179, pp. 223–36.

Balakrishnan, R., Elson, D., and Heintz, J. (2012) "Financial Regulation, Capabilities and Human Rights in the US Financial Crisis: The Case of Housing" in Elson, D., Fukuda-Parr, S., and Vizard, P. (eds.), *Human Rights and the Capabilities Approach: An Interdisciplinary Dialogue*. London: Routledge, pp. 153–68.

Bliss, B. A., Molk, P., and Partnoy, F. (2020) "Negative Activism," *Washington University Law Review*, 97(5), pp. 1333–95.

Brison, S. (2012) "On Empathy as a Necessary, but Not Sufficient, Foundation for Justice (A Response to Slote)" in Amaya, A. and Ho, H. L. (eds.), *Law, Virtue and Justice*. London: Bloomsbury, pp. 303–10.

Bruni, L. and Sugden, R. (2013) "Reclaiming Virtue Ethics for Economics," *Journal of Economic Perspectives*, 27(4), pp. 141–64.

Case, A. and Deaton, A. (2020) *Deaths of Despair and the Future of Capitalism*. Princeton, NJ: Princeton University Press.

Das, S. (2011) *Extreme Money: The Masters of the Universe and the Cult of Risk*. Hoboken, NJ: Wiley.

Dutmer, E. (2022) "A Model for a Practiced, Global, Liberatory Virtue Ethics Curriculum," *Teaching Ethics*, 22(1), pp. 39–67.

Ferrero, I., Roncella, A., and Rocchi, M. (2021) "A Virtue Ethics Approach in Finance" in San Jose, L., Retolaza, J. L., and Van Liedekerke, L. (eds.), *Handbook on Ethics in Finance*. Dordrecht: Springer, pp. 77–96.

Frey, W. J. (2009) "Teaching Virtue: Pedagogical Implications of Moral Psychology," *Science and Engineering Ethics*, 16(3), pp. 611–28.

Fuller, G. (2016) *The Great Debt Transformation: Households, Financialization, and Policy Responses*. Dordrecht: Springer.

Garcia, J. (1996) "The Heart of Racism," *Journal of Social Philosophy*, 27, pp. 5–45.

Graeber, D. (2011) *Debt: The First 5000 Years*. New York: Melville House.

Greenwood, R. and Scharfstein, D. (2013) "The Growth of Finance," *Journal of Economic Perspectives*, 27(2), pp. 3–28.

Griffin, J. M. (2021) "Ten Years of Evidence: Was Fraud a Force in the Financial Crisis?" *Journal of Economic Literature*, 59 (4), pp. 1293–321.

Hegel, G. W. F. (1977) *Phenomenology of Spirit*, tr. A. V. Miller. Oxford: Oxford University Press.

Hirschfeld, M. L. (2015) "Reflection on the Financial Crisis: Aquinas on the Proper Role of Finance," *Journal of the Society of Christian Ethics*, 35(1), pp. 63–82.

Hurd, H. M. and Baum, D. C. (2012) "The Virtue of Consumer Bankruptcy" in Brubaker, R., Lawless, R. M., and Tabb, C. J. (eds.), *A Debtor World: Interdisciplinary Perspectives on Debt*. Oxford: Oxford University Press, pp. 317–44.

Hursthouse, R. (1999) *On Virtue Ethics*. Oxford: Oxford University Press.

Lazzarato, M. (2012) *The Making of the Indebted Man: An Essay on the Neoliberal Condition*. Cambridge, MA: MIT Press.

Lotz, S. and Fix, A. (2013) "Not All Financial Speculation Is Treated Equally: Laypeople's Moral Judgments about Speculative Short Selling," *Journal of Economic Psychology*, 37, pp. 34–41.

MacIntyre, A. (1984) *After Virtue* (2nd ed.). Notre Dame: Notre Dame University Press.

MacIntyre, A. (1999) "Social Structures and Their Threats to Moral Agency," *Philosophy*, 74(3), pp. 311–29.

MacInytre, A. (2015) "The Irrelevance of Ethics" in Bielskis, A., Knight, K. (eds.), *Virtue and Economy: Essays on Morality and Markets*. Farnham: Ashgate.

Mauss, M. (2002) *The Gift: The Form and Reason for Exchange in Archaic Societies*. New York: Routledge.

Niewdana, L. (2015) *Money and Justice*. Abingdon: Routledge.

Nussbaum, M. (2011) *Creating Capabilities: The Human Development Approach*. Cambridge, MA: Harvard University Press.

Padgett Walsh, K. (2014) "Consent, Kant, and the Ethics of Debt," *Philosophy in the Contemporary World*, 21(2), pp. 14–25.

Padgett Walsh, K. (2018) "Transforming Usury into Finance: Financialization and the Ethics of Debt," *Finance and Society*, 4(1), pp. 41–59.

Padgett Walsh, K. and Lewiston, J. (2020) "Human Capabilities and the Ethics of Debt," *Journal of Value Inquiry*, 56(2), pp. 1–21.

Plato. (1992) *The Republic*, tr. G. M. A. Grube. Indianapolis, IN: Hackett.

Plato. (2016) *The Laws*, tr. T. Griffith. Cambridge: Cambridge University Press.

Porter, K. (2012) "The Damage of Debt," *Washington & Lee Law Review*, 69, rev. 979.

Shelby, T. (2002) "Is Racism in the 'Heart'?" *Journal of Social Philosophy*, 33, pp. 411–20.

Shiller, R. (2013) *Finance and the Good Society*. Princeton, NJ: Princeton University Press.

Slote, M. (1995) "Agent-Based Virtue Ethics," *Midwest Studies in Philosophy*, 20(1), pp. 83–101.

Slote, M. (2012) "Empathy, Law, and Justice" in Amaya, A. and Ho, H. L., and Pavlakos, G. (eds.), *Law, Virtue and Justice*. London: Bloomsbury, pp. 279–92.

Swanson, J. (1994) "Aristotle on Liberality: Its Relation to Justice and Its Public and Private Practice," *Polity*, 27(2), pp. 3–23.

Walker, C. ed. (2015) *Social and Psychological Dimensions of Personal Debt and the Debt Industry*. Dordrecht: Springer.

West, A. (2018) "After Virtue and Accounting Ethics," *Journal of Business Ethics*, 148(1), pp. 21–36.

Yeomans, C. (2015). *The Expansion of Autonomy: Hegel's Pluralistic Philosophy of Action*. Oxford: Oxford University Press.

11

On the Wrongfulness of Bank Contributions to Financial Crises

Richard Endörfer

1. Introduction

Financial crises are severely harmful events. The Global Financial Crisis of 2008 (GFC) demonstrated this forcefully: 35 million people lost their jobs, 19.1 million of which were citizens of developing nations (ILO 2009); 84 million people have been pushed below the extreme poverty benchmark of a daily income of $1.25 (World Bank 2010); more than one-quarter million excess cancer-related deaths resulted from the aftermath of the GFC (Maruthappu et al. 2016).

Private commercial and investment banks have often been identified as one of the main culprits of the GFC. Much of the philosophical literature agrees: The core of the problem were greedy, overly risk-friendly bankers who were part of a morally corrupt culture in banking (see for example de Bruin 2015; Graafland and van de Ven 2011; Moore 2012; Sison and Ferrero 2019). However, is it exclusively "greedy bankers," as Tooze (2018, 26) put it, who committed wrong-doing? This question is of particular importance, because the problem we identify to be at the center of past financial crises will have an impact on how we attempt to mitigate future financial crises. Greedy bankers require a different response than, for example, merely increasing capital requirements for banks, as suggested by experts in finance and economics (Admati et al. 2010).

In this chapter, I investigate what precisely makes it wrong for banks to contribute to financial crises in general and explore different ethical theories that try to provide an answer to this question. More specifically, I defend the view that the actions of banks which contribute to a financial crisis are wrong insofar as they collectively expose third parties to a severe risk of harm. The chapter is structured as follows. In section 2, I illustrate how banks can contribute to financial crises in reference to the best-known economic theory that explains how financial crises emerge, Hyman Minsky's Financial Instability Hypothesis (FIH). In section 3, I sketch out the general structure of collective harm cases and explain how this structure applies to the case of bank contributions to financial crises. I also argue here that we have a defeasible pro tanto reason to consider bank contributions to financial crises as wrong insofar as they expose third parties to a

Richard Endörfer, *On the Wrongfulness of Bank Contributions to Financial Crises* In: *The Philosophy of Money and Finance.* Edited by: Joakim Sandberg and Lisa Warenski, Oxford University Press. © Oxford University Press 2024. DOI: 10.1093/oso/9780192898807.003.0012

severe risk of harm. Section 4 discusses the virtue ethical perspective on individual bank contributions to financial crises. Virtue ethical theories can acknowledge that it is in some cases pro tanto wrong for banks to impose risks on third parties, but because of their insistence that only vicious conduct is wrongful, they fail to concede that even virtuous agents (including banks) can wrongfully contribute. Section 5 is dedicated to the consequentialist perspective on bank contributions. I argue that consequentialist theories can also acknowledge that bank contributions wrongfully impose risks onto third parties, but they fail to acknowledge important fairness considerations regarding risk impositions. In section 6, I demonstrate how Scanlonian contractualism can circumvent the problems of both virtue ethics and consequentialism. Section 7 concludes with a summary of the main arguments and an outlook on future research.

2. Financial Crises and Bank Contributions

In his book *Finance and the Good Society*, Robert Shiller emphasized that "finance remains an essential social institution, necessary for managing the risks that enable society to transform creative impulses into vital products and services" (Shiller 2012, xvi), while Ann Pettifor even speaks of banking as a public good (2016, 155). But the past decades have demonstrated that our financial system is periodically under threat of catastrophic failures, i.e. financial crises. Financial crises are states of affairs in which the financial system's functioning is catastrophically impaired; most centrally, the function of matching lenders with borrowers. Whether a financial crisis erupts or not is a matter of uncertainty. Economists refer to the risk of a financial crisis as Systemic Financial Risk (SFR), i.e. the risk that an endogenous or exogenous shock will unravel imbalances within the financial system which then results in significant economic losses (Smaga 2014, 1).[1] SFR builds up through the transactions of a multitude of market participants, until, if nothing is done to prevent the outcome, it culminates in a financial crisis. Banks are at the center of most financial crises.

In order to illustrate the role of banks in the emergence of a financial crisis, it pays to look a bit closer at the mechanisms by which such crises come about. For this, we require an explanatory model that tells us how individual lending operations of banks causally connect to the emergence of a financial crisis. One of the most prominent economic models of financial crises is Minsky's FIH.[2]

---

[1] Alternatively, one might define systemic risk not as the risk to the entire financial system, but instead as the contribution of a single individual firm to a financial crisis. See also Acharya et al. (2012).

[2] See for example Kindleberger and Aliber (2005), Brunnermaier and Oehmke (2012), Eggertson and Krugman (2012), Bhattacharya et al. (2015). Additionally, an excellent recent contribution in political economy on Minskian supercycles can be found in Gabor et al. (2020).

According to the FIH "[the] instability [of our financial system] is not due to external shocks or to the incompetence or ignorance of policy makers. Instability is due to the internal processes of our type of economy" (Minsky 2008, 11). The FIH states that an economy's financing structure is determined by the predominating financing structures of the individual firms within the economy. Minsky distinguishes three such structures: First, "hedge units," i.e. firms that are consistently able to meet their payment obligations without taking on further debt. Second, "speculative units," i.e. firms that have to roll over their debt to meet their payment commitments. Third, "Ponzi units," i.e. firms that constantly have to grow their debt in order to meet their payment commitments. The central contribution of the FIH is an explanation of how stable hedge economies transform into instable speculative and Ponzi economies.

The model begins with the boom phase of an economy, during which lenders grow less cautious about the debt structure of their borrowers, as most borrowers are hedge units. As a result, more and more firms thus enjoy a wider availability of credit (Minsky 1982, 65). But over time, debt becomes a significant production cost which diminishes profit margins, because once the demand for debt increases, so does its price: Interest rates rise (Minsky 2008, 239). Higher costs of debt diminish profits further and hence, the economy gradually is ever more characterized by the presence of speculative units and Ponzi units, which need to acquire additional credit in order to repay their old debts.

This process continues until the economy reaches an "upper turning point," i.e. a state of affairs in which production costs, financed by both internal (i.e. equity) and external (i.e. debt) sources, are greater than the value of goods produced (Minsky 2008, 239). Firms that were once hedge units are transformed into speculative and Ponzi units, which are highly sensitive to increases in interest rates. If interest rates rise, speculative and Ponzi units must find new sources of income to cover their increased costs. If they fail to do so, they might be pressured to desperately sell off their assets at only a fraction of their value. Such processes are known as "fire sales." Fire sales are one of the central transmission mechanisms by which SFR spreads through the financial system (ECB 2019). Eventually, some firms will go bankrupt due to some relatively small trigger event. As a result of increased bankruptcies, lenders refuse to offer credit as willingly, thereby provoking a sharp debt contraction, a so-called credit crunch. Many firms that survive the initial shock are likely to lose their credit lifelines over time. This is the beginning of a financial crisis.

Minsky's FIH does not stop here: Even if the current crisis can be overcome, a new boom phase might set the stage for the next crisis. But economies are not inevitably caught in a cycle of booms and busts. Appropriate policy interventions can help economies escape the grasp of instability (Minsky 2008, 324). Among these policies are, of course, also financial regulations that determine the degree to which financial institutions are permitted to contribute to the boom phase of a financial crisis. As Minsky notes: "the financial powers and practices of corporations are the starting points for policies to manage or contain instability" (Minsky 2008, 349). But unless appropriate regulations are thoroughly enforced, firms are free to contribute to the emergence of the next crisis.

On to the banks' impact on financial crises. In their highly influential book *This Time It's Different* (2009), Reinhart and Rogoff empirically confirm one of the central insights of the FIH: Financial crises are almost always precipitated by a credit expansion (Reinhart and Rogoff 2009, xxxiii). Credit expansions are driven by financial institutions of various kinds, but my focus here lies with banks.[3] Banks are most usefully characterized in terms of the functions they serve in an economy. Central to my arguments in this chapter is the banks' lending function, i.e. the provision of credit. The provision of credit is a vital source of economic growth. Credit is beneficial insofar as it allows consumers and firms to finance capital expenditures and overcome liquidity constraints, i.e. temporal difficulties in meeting one's payment obligations (Meyer 2018). But as Minsky points out, once credit becomes an essential source of funding for a firm's day-to-day operations, firms are rendered highly vulnerable to adverse changes in financial markets (Minsky 2008, 260). These credit expansions can increase an economy's growth rate for a while but can eventually lead to a financial crisis. Due to their lending function, banks are thus specifically important in their role of enabling credit expansions.

Just like their non-financial counterparts, banks are profit-maximizing firms. Banks generate profits from earning more on assets, i.e. loans and investments, than they pay for funds, i.e. their own debt (Admati and Hellwig 2013, 84). When a widespread erosion of margins of safety occurs, some banks might be incentivized to secure their profits by either increasing their net earnings per unit of assets or by increasing their net assets per unit of equity (Minsky 2008, 265).

The first option ultimately requires banks to extend riskier loans to extract higher risk premia from their bank or non-bank borrowers. A bank can demand a higher interest rate in order to compensate for excess risk. All things equal, this increases the bank's net earnings per asset (i.e. loan) and thereby their profit. Minsky specifies two types of particularly risky loans: Loans the repayment of which depends on increasing asset prices and loans the repayment of which depends on the increasing value of the underlying collateral (Minsky 2008, 261). Both kinds of loans are vulnerable to changes in financial markets and hence tend to introduce a "Ponzi-flavor" into the financial structure of an economy. In the

---

[3] In what follows, I will use the term "bank" somewhat loosely, as is usual in the economics jargon. What precisely institutions do that are legally declared as banks differs from jurisdiction to jurisdiction. Furthermore, with the age of financial liberalization, non-bank financial firms (for example mutual and hedge funds, commercial paper markets, and insurance companies) have moved their business activities onto the turf of banks and vice versa. Hence, the arguments I provide in this section will to some extent also apply to non-bank providers of credit.

next section, I provide an example (*Land Loan*) involving a loan the repayment of which is dependent on its underlying asset value.

The second option involves extending more, rather than riskier, loans by borrowing more. By taking on more debt (an increase in liabilities), banks are able to finance more loans and thereby generate more profits. Banks are speculative units in Minsky's sense of the term, but the more a bank's balance of debt and equity shifts toward debt, the more the bank itself becomes exposed to adverse developments in financial markets (Minsky 2008, 262).

In conclusion, the business model of banks itself creates incentives to drive credit expansions. Consequently, not all bank lending is increasing the risk of a financial crisis. But some specific kinds of loans can steer borrowers into speculative or Ponzi finance. Banks themselves can also increase their own vulnerability to changes in financial markets, for example, by borrowing excessively to fund their own lending operations. Because both methods of producing profit mentioned above increase the vulnerability of the financial system to financial crises, both constitute contributions to the risk of a financial crisis. In the next section, I explain the moral relevance of bank contributions in the context of collective harm cases.

3. Financial Crises as Collective Harm Cases

From the standpoint of moral philosophy, it is helpful to consider financial crises as collective harm cases. Collective harm cases are situations in which a group of individual agents engage in actions which collectively lead to an undesirable outcome.[4] Consider a variation of a famous example introduced by Derek Parfit for illustration:

> *The Harmless Torturers*: A victim is strapped to a table that is connected to a machine with a thousand buttons. Each button, once pressed, will imperceptibly increase the voltage of an electric shock received by the victim. A torturer is assigned to each button. Even though the victim does not perceive any pain when only few torturers press their button, once sufficiently many do so, the victim will be in unbearable pain.[5]

The example illustrates three morally relevant features of collective harm cases. First, it is obvious that the end result (the victim's suffering) is *undesirable*. Second, the undesirable result only comes about as a *combined effect* of (some, if

---

[4] For the sake of simplicity, I assume that even collectives such as firms qualify as agents in the relevant sense. For further discussion, see for example French (1979).
[5] For variations of the Harmless Torturer case, see Parfit (1986) and Spiekermann (2014).

not all) torturers pressing their respective buttons. Third, while the combined effect causes the victim's pain, it is unclear whether any individual torturer causally contributed to this outcome, since no button press on its own was sufficient or necessary to bring about the victim's pain (Sandberg 2011, 235).

Nonetheless, many of us will have the straightforward intuition that the torturers do not only do wrong as a collective by causing the victim severe pain, but that each individual torturer does wrong. I assume this assessment is correct: We have a reason to consider each of the individual actions as *wrongful, because each one causally contributes to a collective action that imposes significant harm onto the victim.*

Let me expand on the central concepts of this claim: First, having a reason to consider an action wrong does not entail that the action is all-things-considered wrong; we may have strong countervailing reasons. The kind of reasons I discuss throughout the course of this chapter are thus defeasible, pro tanto reasons. Second, the term "causally contribute to a collective action" serves as a placeholder here. Some contributors to the literature on collective harm cases doubt that individual actions are causally efficacious in bringing about collective harms (such as Sinnott-Armstrong 2005 and Sandberg 2011). But if there is no causal connection between individual contributions and a collective harm, it follows prima facie that there is no reason not to perform actions that only seem to, but do not actually causally contribute to a collective harm (Nefsky 2017, 2744). Solving this particular issue is not the focus of this chapter. Instead, the term "causally contribute to a collective action" stands as a placeholder for whichever account delivers the result that individual contributions do have a causal impact on the collective harm in question (such as the victim of the torturers being in pain).[6] To sum up: We have reason to consider each torturer pressing their button as wrong, because each torturer thereby *contributes to a collective action that exposes a third party to an undesirable outcome,* i.e. *the victim suffers severe physical pain.* I believe that this reasoning generalizes to other collective harm cases, including financial crises.

The analogy from *Harmless Torturers* illustrates why financial crises also constitute collective harm cases: First, financial crises tend to *cause significant risks of harm* and thereby threaten the livelihoods of those who were not participating in transactions that brought about the crisis.[7] This is doubtlessly an undesirable outcome. Second, the overall risk of a financial crisis (i.e. SFR) is the combined effect of an immense number of financial transactions. A large number

---

[6] The literature offers a wide variety of solutions to this problem. Due to space constraints, I refer readers to Kagan (2011), Braham and van Hees (2012), Kutz (2000), and Nefsky (2017).

[7] There is an ongoing debate on whether risk impositions constitute genuine harms (see for example Oberdiek 2017). I remain non-committal on this issue here. I merely assume that we have pro tanto reasons to consider risk impositions wrong. Readers put off by the term "collective harm cases" are hence invited to replace it with "collective risk cases."

of these transactions were the result of standard banking practices. Individual banks thus collectively contribute to the collective risk of SFR by engaging in these practices. Third, as discussed earlier, I assume each individual bank's contribution is causally efficacious in bringing about SFR. For illustration, consider the following case:

> *Land Loan*: Credit Bank (CB) is a medium-sized, domestic bank which, among other products, provides so-called land loans, i.e. loans that use land as collateral.[8] CB approves a land loan of $1 million to GTA Inc., a mid-sized automotive supplier. Because GTA Inc. is already heavily indebted, the loan contains an unduly significant default risk for CB. By providing the loan to GTA Inc., CB hence slightly increases the risk that the bank itself might not be able to meet its own payment commitments in time. This effectively constitutes a minimal increase in SFR (or, in Minsky's terminology, a minute shift toward a vulnerable Ponzi-type economy). A large number of banks approve similar loans. The combined loans destabilize the financial system sufficiently to cause a financial crisis.

Similar to each individual torturer's causal contributions to their victim's suffering, the increase in SFR produced by CB's loan approval is seemingly causally negligible in isolation. However, taken together, the collective contribution to SFR by CB and the other banks is one of the primary causes of the resulting financial crisis. CB causally contributed to a collective action that generated a significant risk of harm to third parties, just as each individual torturer contributed to the risk that the victim might suffer severe pain. If we have reason to consider the actions of each individual torturer as wrong, then we must also have reasons to consider the actions of each individual bank as wrong.

Notice that this line of reasoning adequately captures the outrage directed at the financial industry in the aftermath of the GFC: It was obvious to even the most casual observer that the GFC was caused in part by the excessive risks taken on by the financial industry (FCIC 2011, xviii). In acknowledgment of this fact, Barack Obama famously warned the financial community in 2014 that the USA would "not go back to the days of reckless behavior and unchecked excess at the heart of this crisis" (*New York Times* 2014). I believe the widespread consensus on risky financial activities should guide our moral evaluation of bank contributions to SFR. Any moral evaluation of risky activities by the financial sector should acknowledge that we have at least a defeasible, pro tanto reason to consider financial transactions that raise the risk of a financial crisis as wrong.

---

[8] As explained earlier, CB approves the loan in the hope that the value of the underlying collateral, the land, will increase. However, the loan is risky because the land on its own does not generate profits for GTA Inc.

However, there are also important disanalogies in *Harmless Torturers* and financial crises: First, that the degree to which each contributor increases SFR is not homogenous. All else equal, we have a stronger reason to consider larger contributions as wrong compared to smaller contributions. Second, the interests of the contributors are not homogenous either. Financial firms differ in their business models, their legal forms, the markets in which they operate etc. In this chapter, I focus exclusively on the case of bank lending, but there are other kinds of actions by which financial firms can increase SFR (developing misguided financial innovations, promoting subpar underwriting standards, etc.). Third, as has been mentioned earlier, even if there is reason to consider contributions to SFR as wrong, such reasons might be defeated. *Harmless Torturers* does not provide any such countervailing reasons. In the case of financial crises, however, one might (perhaps implausibly) argue that the benefits of excessive bank lending generally outweigh the costs of financial crises.[9]

In conclusion, I argued that financial crises can aptly be characterized as collective harm cases. The (defeasible) reason why we can consider contributions to collective harms as wrong is that they together constitute a collective action which imposes risks of severe harm onto third parties. If bank contributions to the risk of a financial crisis are structurally similar enough to the torturers' contributions in *Harmless Torturers*, they are also prima facie wrong. In the next section, I argue that a virtue ethical approach is unfortunately not fully congruent with the commonsense intuition that bank contributions are wrong because each contribution causally contributes to a collective risk imposition onto third parties.

4. Virtue Ethics

A disproportionately large number of authors in moral philosophy have discussed the role of banks in the wake of the GFC from the perspective of virtue ethics. All virtue ethical analyses point to failures of financial professionals or entire financial firms to act in accordance with a virtuous disposition.[10] Roughly, virtue ethical theories state the following:

> An action is wrong iff a virtuous agent had characteristically not performed it in the relevant circumstances.   (Hursthouse 1999, 28)

Some authors argue that financial firms failed to act in accordance with conventional virtues, such as honesty, prudence and instead displayed vices such as greed

---

[9] Quite interestingly, this seemed to have been the consensus among mainstream economists prior to the GFC (Besley and Hennesy 2009).

[10] For simplicity, I assume here that firms can be virtuous agents, as is commonplace in some of the virtue ethical literature on the GFC, see for example de Bruin (2015).

and an irrational appetite for risk (Moore 2012; Sison and Ferrero 2019). An exception worthy of mention from this standard is de Bruin (2015), who argues more subtly that a lack of epistemic virtues, such as epistemic courage and generosity, was a driver of incompetence among financial firms and regulators. In general, virtue ethical accounts offer a compelling narrative about why banks contributed to the GFC. But virtue ethical accounts also imply that bank contributions are morally wrong precisely because they resulted from a lack of virtue. The virtue ethicist would hence argue that in *Land Loan*, CB's loan approval is wrong, insofar as the loan would not have been approved by a virtuous agent.

But despite the initial appeal, the virtue ethical analysis has drawbacks. To see this, consider again the FIH. According to the FIH, banks' involvement in credit expansions is part of their business model. Far from being vicious, this is simply standard practice. Nonetheless, contributions to SFR are pro tanto wrong, even if it is not apparent that they are indeed vicious.

The main worry is thus that if only vicious conduct can in principle qualify as wrong, the virtue ethical analysis will fail to evaluate many apparently non-vicious bank contributions as wrong. For illustration, consider two variations of *Land Loan*:

Land Loan 1: Before being presented with the option to approve GTA Inc.'s loan, CB underwent significant change. Ethical counselors successfully changed the internal moral culture of the company, eliminating any traces of greed, psychopathy, incompetence etc. After long and careful deliberating on GTA Inc.'s loan, CB approves the loan with the same impact on SFR as in *Land Loan*.

Land Loan 2: Contrary to the case in *Land Loan 1*, CB did not receive any guidance by ethical counselors and exhibits a careless, greed-driven internal firm culture. Nonetheless, CB does not approve GTA Inc.'s loan out of sheer incompetence.

The examples show that we can conceive of cases in which the presence or absence of virtuous behavior is not correlated with the imposition of a risk onto a third party. There is no apparent lack of moral virtue in *Land Loan 1* (while there is an evident lack of both moral and epistemic virtue in *Land Loan 2*). Hence, the virtue ethicist will be hard-pressed to find any virtue-related reason to consider CB's loan approval morally wrong (vice versa in *Land Loan 2*). Examples like these demonstrate that "virtuous character is not sufficient to insure right action" (Adams 2006, 6). Even virtuous banks are doing wrong if they contribute to SFR in absence of any countervailing reasons. In short, what makes the approval wrong is not that it occurs due to a lack of virtue, it is simply that the approval constitutes a contribution to a collective risk imposition.

The virtue ethicist could object that problematic cases like *Land Loan 1* are inconceivable. Following Hursthouse's account of virtue ethics (1999), a virtuous agent would characteristically not approve the loan, hence CB must have made a mistake or acted out of a lack of virtue. But neither of these options establishes that we have reason to consider CB's approval of the loan as wrong on the virtue ethical analysis.

First, the virtue ethicist might well agree that when a virtuous agent makes a mistake and brings about a bad outcome, she might not be acting out of a lack of virtue, but we have reason nonetheless to consider her action wrong. But it is unclear whether the virtue ethicist has the resources to acknowledge any wrong-making feature of such a mistake, given the fact that a mistake has been made precludes any further reference to a lack of virtues. In short, the virtue ethicist is not able to acknowledge that we have reason to consider CB's mistake as wrong.[11]

Second, the virtue ethicist might then state that the loan could have only been approved due to a lack of virtue. But this is where the virtue ethical analysis opens itself up to what Das (2003) called the "circularity objection."[12] The virtue ethical analysis states that it is wrong to approve the loan because it would be uncharacteristic for a virtuous agent to approve the loan. But why would this be uncharacteristic for a virtuous agent? The virtue ethicist cannot respond that it is uncharacteristic for an agent to approve the loan because doing so constitutes a contribution to a collective risk imposition. This response effectively admits that the virtue ethical analysis adds nothing but redundancy to the original analysis; the real evaluative force of the virtue ethical analysis then comes from an "independent concept of right action" (Das 2003, 332). But neither can the virtue ethicist respond that a virtuous person would not approve the loan because doing so would be wrong simpliciter—this response would constitute straightforwardly circular reasoning, because the virtue ethicist needs to explain (instead of simply presuming) why wrongful behavior is uncharacteristic for virtuous agents (Das 2003, 332).

To sum up, unless the virtue ethical analysis can overcome the circularity objection, we must conclude that the virtue ethicist's assessment of bank contributions will falsely state that we only have reason to consider vicious bank contributions (for example, those involving fraud, deception, and incompetence) as pro tanto wrong. Conversely, this implies that if virtuous banks contribute to SFR, we have no reason to consider their contribution wrong. As I argued earlier, we do have such reasons irrespective of vice or virtue.

5. Consequentialism

An obvious alternative candidate to evaluate bank contributions is consequentialism. Consequentialist reasoning has become a staple of real-world policy decision-making in the form of cost–benefit analysis (Hansson 2007).

---

[11] For discussion, see van Zyn (2009).
[12] For similar objections, see Hooker (2002) and Johnson (2003).

Consequentialism states that:

> An action is wrong iff it does not bring about better expected consequences than all available alternative courses of action.   (Hayenhjelm and Wolff 2012)

Much of the economic and popular literature on the GFC with its focus on aggregate data reveals a consequentialist bias. Talk of unemployment rates, consumer debt levels etc. reflects a consequentialist perspective on what matters morally: That the aggregate sum of the costs imposed onto the victims of the GFC outweighs the benefits of its preceding credit expansion. Quite surprisingly, to the best of my knowledge, there is no strictly consequentialist philosophical literature on financial crises. In order to progress my argument, I assume here that a charitable consequentialist perspective on bank contributions to financial crises would state that such contributions are wrong if an alternative course of action was available that would have a minimal impact on SFR.[13] For illustration, consider the following example:

> Land Loan 3: Alongside other banks' efforts in contributing to a credit expansion, CB approves the loan to GTA Inc. The result of the credit expansion will likely be a financial crisis the costs of which by far outweigh the benefits of the credit expansion. Had sufficiently many banks not provided loans similar to the one approved by CB, the crisis would have had a far less severe impact on its victims.

The consequentialist will evaluate CB's action as wrong because it contributes to a collective action that generates significant harm for third parties—it leads to a worse outcome than could have been achieved. Thus, consequentialists need not appeal to a lack of virtues to explain why CB acted wrongly. Unfortunately, consequentialism is highly insensitive to the distribution of costs and benefits among those affected. To see this, consider the following case:

> Land Loan 4: If CB and sufficiently many banks approve their respective loans, the overwhelmingly likely outcome of this practice is a financial crisis in which a minority of individual third parties will suffer from extreme poverty (say half a million people), while the large majority will enjoy a long-term purchasing power increase of $1 per month (say 4 billion people). The aggregate increase in purchasing power slightly outweighs the aggregate suffering caused by extreme poverty. If CB does not approve the loan, it does not contribute to the collective action that brings about a financial crisis.

---

[13] I thus assume a contributory consequences account of consequentialism (Regan 1980, 13). For discussion, see Nefsky (2017) and Kagan (2011).

Improper bank lending in *Land Loan 4* thus generates minor benefits for a large part of the population but risks that a minority of the population ends up in extreme poverty. Notice that the example is not far-fetched: Many countries, including the USA, have experienced a stark rise in inequality after the GFC (Almeida 2015).

But because the aggregate benefit outweighs the aggregate costs, the consequentialist would argue that CB ought to approve the loan. Cases like *Land Loan 4* demonstrate that consequentialism does not consider bank contributions as wrong merely because they constitute a risk imposition. This is an important drawback of the consequentialist analysis: We might think that there is nothing wrong with imposing risks onto third parties insofar as they would benefit accordingly from risky practices. Consequentialism does not acknowledge this qualification. What matters is only the aggregate balance of costs and benefits. According to the consequentialist calculus, it is not wrong to expose a third party to a significant risk of harm and hand the potential benefits accompanying the risk to an entirely different party.[14] This excessive focus on aggregate effects is a principled problem in consequentialist reasoning that informed banking regulation and fiscal policy should demonstrate awareness of (Cochrane 2014). Scanlonian contractualism, which I discuss in the next section, is a response to precisely this problem.

6. Scanlonian Contractualism

Scanlonian contractualism (from here on: contractualism) has rarely been applied to financial crises, except for some notable exceptions such as James (2012) and Scharding (2019). In its standard formulation, contractualism states that:

> An action is wrong if its performance under the circumstances would be disallowed by any set of principles for the general regulation of behaviour that no one could reasonably reject.   (Scanlon 1998, 153)

The gist of contractualism is that whether an action is right or wrong is best determined via fair negotiations between those affected by the action's consequences.[15] Strictly speaking, the participants in these negotiations do not evaluate each action on its own, but rather approve or reject principles which would permit

---

[14] For the classic formulation of the so-called separateness of persons objection against consequentialism, see Rawls (1999, 164).

[15] It should be pointed out that contractualists often acknowledge that the wrongness of an action does not depend exclusively on its (expected) consequences. See for example Kumar (2015, 37). Because I am exclusively concerned with the contributions to harmful collective actions in this chapter, I bracket this debate here.

the action to be performed.[16] The negotiations are subject to two constraints: First, each participant can only approve or disapprove of a principle on her behalf. This "Individualist Restriction" rules out the kind of aggregation that is involved in consequentialism. Contractualism hence does not allow greater aggregate benefits for a majority to outweigh the costs imposed onto a minority. Second, participants cannot reject a principle if all alternative principles would impose even greater costs onto others. This is known as the "Greater Burden Principle." For illustration, consider a variation of *Land Loan 4*:

> *Land Loan 5*: CB again faces a choice between approving GTA Inc.'s loan or not. If CB and sufficiently many other banks approve similar loans, the outcome is identical to the one in *Land Loan 4*. Bert is one of the unlucky few who stand to suffer from extreme poverty if CB and other banks approve the loan. Ernie is one of those who would gain a $1 increase in purchasing power.

If CB approves the loan, Bert has a complaint against CB's approval corresponding in strength to whatever his risk of suffering extreme poverty amounts to. But there are others who have a complaint against CB not approving the loan, such as Ernie. Both Bert and Ernie can only object to CB's approval or denial of the loan on their behalf. But because Bert stands to lose much more than Ernie stands to gain if the loan is approved, Bert's complaint against CB's approval outweighs Ernie's. Thus, Bert's complaint determines that it would be wrong for CB to approve the loan. Contractualism hence states that CB's loan approval is wrong due to the fact that it avoidably imposes a much greater burden on individuals such as Bert than on individuals such as Ernie.

Notice that contractualism circumvents the problems of both virtue ethics and consequentialism. Virtue ethical approaches will trace the source of wrongness back to a lack of virtue, but not all bank contributions are an expression of a lack of virtue. We have reason to consider bank contributions wrong in general insofar as they causally contribute to SFR, regardless of whether they additionally express a lack of virtue. Consequentialist approaches will maintain that it is not wrong to impose risks onto third parties if these risks are offset by some sufficient aggregate benefit—but this benefit need not accrue to the victims. Contractualism, however, avoids both problems: It does not stipulate a lack of virtue to arrive at the conclusion that bank contributions are pro tanto wrong and, by the Individualist Restriction, it requires offsetting benefits to accrue to those who have been exposed to the risk of suffering harm due to a financial crisis.

However, the discussion of contractualism thus far has been subject to an important simplification: The outcomes in *Land Loan 4* and *5* are not certain.

---

[16] To simplify the discussion, I modify the contractualist framework such that persons reject actions directly, instead of objecting to principles which permit actions when suitable.

To account for this, we need to consider risk-sensitive versions of contractualism. Contractualists put forward two mutually exclusive risk-sensitive variants of their theory, Ex Post and Ex Ante contractualism. These two variants differ in how they calculate the weight of burdens. Ex Post contractualism insists that the relevant burden to be considered is the full burden were the risk to materialize. In *Land Loan 5*, Bert's burden thus amounts to suffering from extreme poverty with certainty. Ex Ante contractualism permits discounting this burden by its probability. Hence, Bert's burden amounts to suffering extreme poverty discounted by the probability with which he would face this outcome. Only Ex Post contractualism is capable of reliably delivering the result that it is wrong to expose third parties to severe risks without offsetting the risk. To see this, consider the following case:

> *Land Loan 6*: CB again faces a choice between approving or not approving GTA Inc.'s loan. If approved, all employees of GTA Inc. will receive their wages as planned. Otherwise, their wages will be waived for three months. However, a financial crisis again looms in the not-so-distant future. If the crisis occurs, all domestic residents face a one-in-a-million chance of falling below the poverty line.

According to Ex Ante contractualism, CB ought to approve the loan, even though falling below the poverty line is a much larger burden than missing out on one's wage for three months. Ex Ante contractualism permits the loan approval because it is the discounted burden that counts, not the full burden should the crisis materialize. Missing out on one's wage for three months with certainty is hence the comparatively weightier burden. Thus, Ex Ante contractualism states that it would not be wrong to approve the loan.[17]

Ex Post contractualists will argue that this result is unintuitive. According to their view, we ought not discount uncertain burdens, since "harm is just as bad when suffered 'by accident' as when it is inflicted" (Scanlon 1998, 209). If the domestic population is sufficiently larger than one million, irrespective of how small the risk is, we know with virtual certainty that some will fall below the poverty line if a crisis were to occur as a result of excessive credit expansion.[18] The problem Ex Ante contractualism faces is hence similar to the problem faced by consequentialism: Ex Ante contractualism is far too insensitive toward the distribution of benefits and burdens that result from risky practices. In opposition to this result, Ex Post Contractualism states that widespread credit expansion

---

[17] For a related discussion on Ex Ante Rules, see Frick (2015, 201).
[18] This problem with Ex Ante Contractualism is well-known in the literature. See for example Frick (2015), Holm (2018), and Rüger (2018).

can be reasonably rejected, because it imposes unjustifiably severe risks onto third parties.

In this final section of the chapter, let us go back once more to *Harmless Torturers*: In this case, no individual torturer imposes harm on the margin, yet all of them together torture the victim with no apparent justification. By focusing primarily on the burden of the victim, instead of a lack of virtue exhibited by the torturers or the aggregate balance of benefits and burdens, Ex Post contractualists can explain why this is wrong: Whatever each individual torturer gains from pushing their button cannot outweigh the severe pain that the victim is suffering. Throughout this chapter, I argued that we ought to consider cases of bank contributions to financial crises through a similar lens: Whatever individual banks stand to gain from contributing to SFR cannot (at least not as a matter of principle) outweigh the severe burden faced by the worst off should a financial crisis occur.

Ex Post contractualism thus enriches our understanding of what we need to do in order to address the pro tanto wrongfulness of credit expansions driven by bank contributions: We need to offset the burden that impacts those most affected by SFR if a risk materializes, irrespective of how miniscule the risk is to each of them individually.[19] In order to render risky practices justifiable to each, the resulting balance of benefits and burdens must be acceptable to all potentially affected by the respective risks. Banks need to consider carefully how they drive hedge economies toward instability and minimize risks for themselves and others wherever possible. But this will not be enough. Some risks will persist and need to be counterbalanced with benefits provided to those most at risk. Such benefits should include not only better access to banking services, such as depository services and readily available access to affordable credit, but also well-designed social welfare programs that cushion the losses of the worst-off when the next inevitable financial crisis occurs. To put the matter in a well-known slogan, when banks contribute to financial crises, it is unjustifiable that the collectively brought about resulting distribution of SFR amounts to "privatized gains and socialized losses." The risks inherently created by our financial system must be mitigated and offset to offer protection specifically to those who stand to lose the most.

7. Conclusion

Individual banks have a role in safeguarding financial stability. Because of its potentially destructive impact, the conduct of individual banks is a legitimate

---

[19] Due to space constraints, I am here unable to discuss the various points of criticism launched against Ex Post Contractualism. For examples, see Ashford (2003) and Frick (2015). For responses to these criticisms, see for example Rüger (2018) and Steuwer (2021).

target of moral evaluation. Insofar as regulation has the objective of reining in morally unjustifiable conduct, it matters what features of a particular kind of conduct we conceive of as morally wrong. If bankers are "greedy," we might be more inclined to look for policies which show promise in combatting greedy dispositions. If financial crises are the result of practices that just did not result in sufficient aggregate benefits, we might be more inclined to permit more, rather than less risky practices. Conversely, if our goal is to protect those who are affected the most by financial crises, we might consider constraining the most excessively risky methods by which financial firms can generate profits and provide economic support for those who stand to suffer the most.

With this in mind, I proposed in this chapter that any moral theory aiming at evaluating bank contributions to SFR should at least in principle be capable of acknowledging that we have a pro tanto reason to consider bank contributions to financial crises as morally wrong. More explicitly, I argued that while virtue ethical and consequentialist analyses of bank contributions deliver this result, they suffer from significant drawbacks. The virtue ethical analysis suffers from a limited scope focused only on bank contributions that result from a lack of virtue, while the consequentialist analysis is insensitive to distribution and thus permits small benefits to some to offset immense costs to others. In a last section, I argued that contractualism does not suffer from these drawbacks. More specifically, the (Ex Post) contractualist view yields the most defensible evaluation of bank contributions. Future research informed by a contractualist perspective could prove invaluable in providing insight into the types of fiscal policy and banking regulations that could render the systemic risks generated by banks justifiable to all.

Acknowledgements

For helpful comments on previous drafts of this chapter, I would like to thank Joakim Sandberg, Lisa Warenski and an anonymous reviewer, as well as the participants at the Practical Philosophy research seminar at the University of Gothenburg.

References

Acharya, Viral V., Lasse H. Pedersen, Thomas Philippon, and Matthew Richardson. 2012. Measuring Systemic Risk. CEPR Discussion Paper No. DP8824. https://ssrn.com/abstract=2013815

Adams, Robert M. 2006. *A Theory of Virtue: Excellence in Being for the Good*. Oxford: Oxford University Press.

Admati, Ana, Franklin Allen, Richard Brealey et al. 2010. Healthy Banking Is the Goal, Not Profitable Banks, *Financial Times*, November 9. https://www.ft.com/content/63fa6b9e-eb8e-11df-bbb5-00144feab49a

Admati, Anat and Martin Hellwig. 2013. *The Bankers' New Clothes: What's Wrong with Banking and What to Do about It.* Princeton, NJ: Princeton University Press.

Almeida, Vanda. 2015. *Inequality and Redistribution in the Aftermath of the 2007–2008 Crisis: The US Case.* http://www.bsi-economics.org/545-inequality-and-redistribution-in-the-aftermath-of-the-2007-2008-crisis-the-us-case

Ashford, Elizabeth. 2003. The Demandingness of Scanlon's Contractualism, *Ethics* 113(2): 273–302.

Besley, Tim and Peter Hennessy. 2009. The Global Financial Crisis: Why Didn't Anybody Take Notice?, *British Academy Review* 14, 8–10.

Bhattacharya, Sudipto, Charles A. E. Goodhart, Dimitrios P. Tsomocos, and Alexandros P. Vardoulakis. 2015. A Reconsideration of Minsky's Financial Instability Hypothesis, *Journal of Money, Credit and Banking* 47(5): 931–73.

Braham, Matthew and Martin van Hees. 2012. An Anatomy of Moral Responsibility, *Mind* 121 (483): 601–34.

Brunnermaier, M. and Martin Oehmke. 2012. Bubbles, Financial Crises and Systemic Risk. NBER Working Paper No. 18398. https://www.nber.org/papers/w18398

Cochrane, John H. 2014. Challenges for Cost–Benefit Analysis of Financial Regulation, *Journal of Legal Studies* 43(2): 63–105.

Das, Ramon. 2003. Virtue Ethics and Right Action, *Australasian Journal of Philosophy* 81 (3): 324–39.

de Bruin, Boudewijn. 2015. *Ethics and the Global Financial Crisis: Why Incompetence Is Worse than Greed.* Cambridge: Cambridge University Press.

Eggertsson, Gauti B. and Paul Krugman. 2012. Debt, Deleveraging, and the Liquidity Trap: A Fisher–Minsky–Koo Approach, *Quarterly Journal of Economics* 127(3): 1469–513.

European Central Bank. 2019. Economic Shocks and Contagion in the Euro Area Banking Sector: A New Micro-Structural Approach, *ECB Financial Stability Review* (May).

Financial Crisis Inquiry Commission [FCIC]. 2011. *The Financial Crisis Inquiry Report: Final Report of the National Commission on the Causes of the Financial and Economic Crisis in the United States.* https://www.govinfo.gov/content/pkg/GPO-FCIC/pdf/GPO-FCIC.pdf

French, Peter A. 1979. The Corporation as a Moral Person, *American Philosophical Quarterly* 16(3): 207–15.

Frick, Johann. 2015. Contractualism and Social Risk, *Philosophy and Public Affairs* 43(3): 175–223.

Gabor, Daniela, Yannis Dafermos, and Jo Mitchell. 2020. Institutional Supercycles: An Evolutionary Macro-Finance Approach, *Rebuilding Macroeconomics.* Working Paper Series No. 15. https://www.rebuildingmacroeconomics.ac.uk/managing-supercycles

Graafland, Johan J. and Bert W. van de Ven. 2011. The Credit Crisis and the Moral Responsibility of Professionals in Finance, *Journal of Business Ethics* 103(4): 605–19.

Hansson, Sven O. 2007. Philosophical Problems in Cost–Benefit Analysis, *Economics and Philosophy* 23(2): 163–83.

Hayenhjelm, Madeleine and Jonathan Wolff. 2012. The Moral Problem of Risk Impositions: A Survey of the Literature, *European Journal of Philosophy* 20(1): E25–E51.

Holm, Sune. 2018. The Luckless and the Doomed: Contractualism on Justified Risk-Imposition, *Ethical Theory and Moral Practice* 21(2): 231–44.

Hooker, Brad. 2002. The Collapse of Virtue Ethics, *Utilitas* 14(1): 22–40.

Hursthouse, Rosalind. 1999. *On Virtue Ethics*. Oxford: Oxford University Press.

International Labor Organization. 2009. *Global Employment Trends: May 2009 Update.* https://www.ilo.org/wcmsp5/groups/public/—ed_emp/—emp_elm/—trends/documents/publication/wcms_114102.pdf

James, Aaron. 2012. *Fairness in Practice: A Social Contract for a Global Economy.* Oxford: Oxford University Press.

Johnson, Robert. 2003. Virtue and Right, *Ethics* 113(4): 810–34.

Kagan, Shelly. 2011. Do I Make a Difference?, *Philosophy and Public Affairs* 39(2): 105–41.

Kindleberger, Charles and Robert Z. Aliber. [1978] 2005. *Manias, Panics and Crashes: A History of Financial Crises*, 5th ed. Hoboken, NJ: Wiley.

Kumar, Rahul. 2015. Risking and Wronging, *Philosophy and Public Affairs* 43(1): 27–51.

Kutz, Christopher. 2000. *Complicity: Ethics and Law for a Collective Age*, Cambridge: Cambridge University Press.

Maruthappu, Mahiben, Johnathan Watkins, Aisyah Mohd Noor et al. 2016. Economic Downturns, Universal Health Coverage, and Cancer Mortality in High-Income and Middle-Income Countries, 1990–2010: A Longitudinal Analysis, *Lancet* 388(10045): 684–95.

Meyer, Marco. 2018. The Right to Credit, *Journal of Political Philosophy* 26(3): 304–26.

Minsky, Hyman. 1982. The Financial-Instability Hypothesis: Capitalist Processes and the Behavior of the Economy. *Hyman Minsky Archive Paper 282.*

Minsky, Hyman. [1986] 2008. *Stabilizing an Unstable Economy.* New York: McGraw-Hill.

Moore, Geoff. 2012. The Virtue of Governance, the Governance of Virtue, *Business Ethics Quarterly* 22(2): 293–318.

Nefsky, Julia. 2017. How You Can Help, without Making a Difference, *Philosophical Studies* 174(11): 2743–67.

New York Times. 2014. *Text of Obama's Speech on Financial Reform*, September 14. https://www.nytimes.com/2009/09/15/business/15obamatext.html

Oberdiek, John. 2017. *Imposing Risk: A Normative Framework*. Oxford: Oxford University Press.

Parfit, Derek. 1986. *Reasons and Persons*. Oxford: Oxford University Press.

Pettifor, Ann. 2016. *The Production of Money*. London: Verso.

Rawls, John. 1999 [1971]. *A Theory of Justice*. Cambridge, MA: Harvard University Press.

Regan, Donald. 1980. *Utilitarianism and Co-operation*. Oxford: Oxford University Press.

Reinhart, Carmen M. and Kenneth S. Rogoff. 2009. *This Time Is Different: Eight Centuries of Financial Folly*. Princeton, NJ: Princeton University Press.

Rüger, Korbinian. 2018. On Ex Ante Contractualism, *Journal of Ethics and Social Philosophy* 13(3): 240–58.

Sandberg, Joakim. 2011. My Emissions Make No Difference, *Environmental Ethics* 33(3): 229–48.

Scanlon, Thomas M. 1998. *What We Owe to Each Other*. Cambridge, MA: Harvard University Press.

Scharding, Tobey. 2019. Structured Finance and the Social Contract: How Tranching Challenges Contractualist Approaches to Financial Risk, *Business Ethics Quarterly* 29(1): 1–24.

Shiller, Robert. 2012. *Finance and the Good Society*. Princeton, NJ: Princeton University Press.

Sinnott-Armstrong, Walter. 2005. It's not my Fault. In W. Sinnott-Armstrong and R. Howarth (eds.), *Perspectives on Climate Change. Science, Economics, Politics, Ethics*: 285–307. Amsterdam: Elsevier.

Sison, Alejo José G. and Ignacio Ferrero. 2019. Is Financialisation a Vice? Perspectives from Virtue Ethics and Catholic Social Teaching. In Christopher Cowton, James Dempsey, and Tom Sorell (eds.), *Business Ethics After the Global Financial Crisis: Lessons from the Crash*. London: Routledge.

Smaga, Pawel. 2014. The Concept of Systemic Risk, *SRC Special Paper No. 5*. http://eprints.lse.ac.uk/61214/1/sp-5.pdf

Spiekermann, Kai. 2014. Small Impacts and Imperceptible Effects: Causing Harm with Others, *Midwest Studies in Philosophy* 38(1): 75–90.

Steuwer, Bastian. 2021. Contractualism, Complaints, and Risk, *Journal of Ethics and Social Philosophy* 19 (2): 111–47.

Tooze, Adam. 2018. *Crashed: How a Decade of Financial Crises Changed the World*. New York: Viking.

van Zyn, Liezl. 2009. Accidental Rightness, *Philosophia* 37: 91–104.

World Bank. 2010. *World Economic Situation and Prospect 2010*. https://www.un.org/en/development/desa/policy/wesp/wesp_archive/2010wespdf

12

Money in the Social Contract

Aaron James

> Credit ... is a right to "satisfaction." This right depends on no statute,
> but on common or customary law. It is inherent in the very nature of
> credit throughout the world. It is credit.
>
> A. Mitchell Innes, 1913

What relationship, if any, does money bear to state legitimacy?

A standard answer is instrumentalism. Monetary incentives—in taxes, subsidies, or direct payments—are an easy way to get people to do things, with no need of outright force or coercion, in the service of the state's objectives, whatever they happen to be. But, in this picture, everything depends on the legitimacy of those objectives; state money, a mere tool, is neither legitimate nor illegitimate itself. The state may have a special role in supplying and managing a money as a public good for everyone's use as a means of exchange, store of value, unit of account, and so forth. But that role raises no special legitimacy issue of its own, at least no more so than any other tool for state action.

Yet if the state uses money to exert a powerful influence over people's lives, how could that *not* raise questions of legitimacy in its own right? To the social contract tradition of Hobbes, Locke, Rousseau, Kant, and, in our own day, Rawls and Scanlon, any exercise of state power must be morally legitimated, which is to say, justified as part of some principled terms of cooperation—a social contract—that we can reasonably expect people to abide by. Surely money is no exception.

Plausible as that may be, the social contract tradition is curiously inattentive to state monetary powers. Money was not important for Hobbes or Rousseau, except as an element of private property generally. Locke wrote a treatise on money, assuming a commodity theory, though his political philosophy relies only on money's store of value function (in order to bolster his argument for the legitimacy of unlimited appropriation of private property in money, which does not spoil). Kant ([1797] 2017: 76–7) plainly stated a state money, chartalist theory, but only in passing.[1] Perhaps money was less important in earlier eras. Yet even in the

---

[1] I thank Stuart Chapin for noting the Kant passage.

Aaron James, *Money in the Social Contract* In: *The Philosophy of Money and Finance*. Edited by: Joakim Sandberg and Lisa Warenski, Oxford University Press. © Oxford University Press 2024. DOI: 10.1093/oso/9780192898807.003.0013

twentieth century, well after the rise of central banking, Rawls (1971) makes only cursory mention of monetary policy institutions.[2]

So it's worth asking afresh how money might bear upon state legitimacy in a direct, non-instrumental fashion. This discussion explores one such possibility: state legitimacy is constrained by moral requirements built into the very nature of money as a cooperative credit–debt relationship. I'll assume a particular credit–debt theory of money, which I state momentarily. On that basis, I explain how the state can be seen as an active participant in a credit economy of its own making, subject to moral obligations of promissory fidelity that are part and parcel of any credit and monetary economy.

To see this, we'll need to consider the debt swap, which is to say, settlement of one debt with another. I'll defend a moral principle of redemption, what financier and diplomat A. Mitchell Innes called the "right to satisfaction" (in the passage quoted in the epigraph). While the principle applies beyond money—it applies to any swap of promissory debts—I'll suggest that its general acceptance is constitutive of the very existence of a money and credit economy, much as Innes (1913; 1914) claimed. Insofar as a state issues or recognizes a money as a means of ruling people's lives, then, it can be legitimate only by reliably honoring moral principles of redemption. As I'll explain, this has significant implications for state management of a modern economy, the centerpiece of a social compact.

1. Basic Picture

I begin with some assumptions. For starters, money is "that which pays," a promissory IOU one can spend, because it is widely enough accepted in tendering payment, i.e. settlement of a commercial or public debt.[3]

Money may thus take any number of forms depending on what credit–debt media is available (e.g. coins, paper notes or ledger entries). It differs from items such sundry as crypto-tokens, gift cards, store coupons, or vouchers, each of which may be more or less money-like, depending on how widely it's accepted among people—its domain—and what range of obligations it's accepted for—its degree of fungibility.

This view contrasts with both the commodity theory associated with Adam Smith ([1776] 1994: 24, ch. IV, bk. 1), on the one hand, and state or chartalist

---

[2] See van't Klooster (2018) and James (2023b).
[3] See Hockett and James (2020: ch. 1) on "basic money." Our view falls within the "endogenous money" tradition, which includes Steuart ([1767] 1966); Macleod (1855; 1856); Wicksell (1898); Innes (1913; 1914); Keynes (1914; 1930); Schumpeter (1933); and Minsky (1986).

theories associated with G. F. Knapp ([1905] 1973), or Immanuel Kant before him ([1797] 2017: 76–7), on the other.[4]

Following Smith, orthodox economists have often noted money's various functions as a store of value, unit of account, means of deferred payment, and so forth, only to treat them as secondary to its basic function as a means of exchange or transaction technology. Ludwig von Mises ([1912] 2013: 34–5) went so far as to claim that, among the "half dozen further 'functions' ... all of them can be deduced from the function of money as a common medium of exchange."[5] On the present view, Smith and the orthodox tradition erred in supposing that a money could be at bottom a mere medium of exchange, such as gold or silver, which is needed to avoid the inconveniences of barter. A mere means of exchange, however convenient, is not necessarily a money, as opposed to another barter object. It begins to approximate a money—perhaps as do coupons used within a certain chain of stores, or as do crypto tokens used in a specific digital enclave—only when used to settle *debts*, as a recognized credit in some unit of debt accounting.

The present account nonetheless agrees with the orthodox Smithian tradition, as against state or chartalist theories, in one key respect: money does not necessarily depend on government, or any other (e.g. religious or community) public authority. In principle, the requisite promissory IOUs can enjoy confidence in future redemption within the context of a decentralized credit cooperative, run on customary understandings and their informal social enforcement. When cigarettes circulate in certain prisons or concentration camps, for instance, they may serve as tokens of promissory IOUs, which are implicitly counted as credits in settling for debts owed for goods or services (a clean towel or a newspaper, perhaps). On the present account, they may well be good money in the prison community, with or without authorization by state or prison officials, even when state money creeps into the mix as a parallel currency.[6]

To be sure, especially in modern times, states tend to issue their own money (with exceptions such as a currency union or state recognition of a foreign state money). What governments are doing here, as a matter of legal and social

---

[4] Recent "Modern Monetary Theory" (Bell 2001; Bell and Nell 2003; Wray 2004; 2014), though part of the heterodox tradition noted earlier, often associates itself with the state money chartalism of Knapp and (on one reading) Keynes (1930). Innes (1913; 1914) is sometimes cited as well, but often not distinguished from chartalism, as I think appropriate (for reasons suggested below). See also Douglas 2016, esp. Part 3, for discussion of credit–debt and state money views.

[5] Italics mine. See also Menger (1892); Brunner and Meltzer (1971); Alchian (1977); Starr (2012) and Smit et al. (2014).

[6] This does not help orthodox economics with the "Hahn problem," viz, that money must simply be posited, since, seen as a mere means of exchange, it does not fit into general equilibrium models, at least not in ways that make a significant difference (see Peacock 2013 and Bridel 2014). Douglas (2016) ultimately favors a state theory over a pure credit theory for related reasons. I agree a state is usually necessary but take informal understandings and enforcement to suffice, at least in theory, as I suggest later.

dynamics, is running a credit–debt cooperative, this time with both "vertical" and "horizontal" dimensions. The state imposes vertical legal debts upon its subjects, in the form of fees, fines, and taxes, to be settled only in some chosen unit of account. And in issuing or recognizing a money, that very unit then serves as a credit that pays the imposed debts. But because the state threatens prison when debts owed to it are not settled in timely manner, its chosen money will normally gain currency horizontally between members of society as well. People will go to considerable trouble to secure their continued freedom, and since it is inconvenient to conduct business in a great many currencies, they'll tend to use the state's money in all manner of credit–debt relationships, including commercial exchange, borrowing and lending, employment and social networking, or even (alas) marriage.

Here governments are not simply providing a money, much as they might provide, supply, or facilitate any useful public good, such as national defense or public parks and beaches. In issuing or recognizing a money, they thereby make themselves another party to the very credit cooperatives they create. And, as I'll explain, as a creditor on and a debtor to other parties, they are themselves subject to the principles of redemption whose general acceptance is constitutive of the very existence and functioning of a monetary credit cooperative. Moreover, given the inordinate power states thereby exercise over peoples' lives, those principles amount to requirements for a state's very legitimacy. If a state does not conduct its administrative practice and monetary policy in order to foster appropriate credibility in redemption, it imperils its very moral legitimacy—as a creditor, debtor, and state.

To develop this picture, I consider how we generally settle one debt with another, focusing on three key debt swaps, which are as follows.

Promises: I make you a promise, incurring a promissory debt to you, an IOU. Later you make me a promise, incurring a comparable debt to me, your IOU to me. Instead of doing as promised, we "call it even."

Commerce: I'm buying your apples and owe you payment—i.e. a settlement of the commercial debt I owe if the apples are to become mine. I hand over a government IOU, such as a dollar or pound note. You accept this as payment, settling our private debt with a public debt.

Taxes: We owe a debt to society, in the form of legally imposed fees, fines, and taxes, and we settle with the government by tendering that same government's IOUs, i.e. public debt. Our debt to the public is settled with a public debt to us.

In section 2, I suggest that the same principle is at work in each of these cases, a moral right of redemption, with corresponding obligations of settlement, which I express as a "Redemption Principle." To also capture how debt swaps also vary across the case of promises, commerce, and taxes, I then consider "state of nature" cases (section 3), credit cooperatives without a state (section 4), and sovereign membership (section 5). I close explaining the upshot for money management and state legitimacy (section 6).

2. What We Owe Each Other

Consider further the debt swaps noted—in promises, commerce, and taxes.

Promissory debt swap. Suppose I promise to help you move your couch. I now owe you the help. You have my IOU to help you with the couch. As your debtor, you are thus my creditor: my outstanding debt to you just is your credit on me. Or, put another way, my liability in my obligation to you is your asset in your claim against me. (Credits and debts, assets and liabilities, always so travel together, necessarily and by definition.)

Now suppose you later promise to walk my dog. Let's stipulate that you do this for entirely independent reasons, with no thought of the couch help. Symmetrically, because you promised, you now owe a debt to me; I have your promissory IOU, which is a credit I have on you. You thereby have a liability in your obligation to walk the dog, and I have an asset in my claim that you do it.

Ordinarily, I might have every right to hold you to your promise, which, after all was a promise to walk the dog. If you showed signs of wavering, I might "demand" it or "lay claim" to it ("... and the dog?"). I might even refuse to release you from your obligation, if you asked. After all, you did promise.

While contemporary accounts of promissory obligation focus on this kind of case, a promissory debt swap is rather different: I can't insist upon what lawyers call "specific performance," at least not reasonably. For even if you haven't yet walked the dog, as specifically promised, given your credit on me for the couch help, you can come back to me expect a settlement without your performance. If you decide you're not so keen to walk a loud and territorial Pomeranian after all, and you're willing to forgo your own claim to help with the couch, you could just propose "let's call it even." Our respective debts and credits may or may not be of comparable value, or of similar importance, to be sure. But if it is evident to both of us that they are comparable, our asset–liability pairs in effect cancel, summing to zero. So when you do ask for—or indeed insist on or demand—a settlement of your debt, I can't simply refuse; you'd oblige me, presumptively, to agree to call it even. If I griped, protesting "But you promised!," you could rejoin: "yes, and you promised me as well; but now you're not helping with my couch, which I was also counting on. So, sorry, but we're even."[7]

---

[7] I believe I disagree here with Shiffrin (2007: 725), who notes that while "It may sometimes be permissible for the promisor to *ask* the promisee to shoulder [the] burden [of non-performance],"

Exchange. You have three apples. I have three oranges. We agree to swap fruits. The goods will change hands in a physical sense—albeit not quite as they do when I throw a cigarette at your head, which lands in your hand, after which you throw an eraser at my head, which lands in my hand. The physical transposition of goods is not necessarily an *exchange,* in the economic sense, which requires a change in normative status. What distinguishes the fruit swap is the swap of debts. When I take hold of your apples, it's in exchange for a *credit* on me, my debt to you, if I'm to acquire title. Before anything further happens, I owe you. Likewise, you take hold of my oranges giving me a credit on you, your debt to me, if you are to acquire title. If nothing else happens, you owe me. And if we agree these credits and debts are of comparable value, our respective asset–liability pairs cancel. As we apply the credits we each have on the other, our debts to each other are, as lawyers put it, "extinguished."

This is a bartered exchange. In a monetary exchange, a further kind of debt is relied on to settle accounts. If you're selling apples on the street for the offering price for $1.25 per apple, and I stroll by and take hold of one apple and ask "what do I owe ya?," I'm acknowledging that I owe a debt to you if I'm to acquire title. Your price offer is my debt (to the tune of $1.25), assuming we don't haggle. When I then lay my coins on the apple cart counter, or transfer bank credits with a card swipe, I give you credits in the amount of $1.25, which settles that debt to you (the asset cancelling my liability). Here the swap of debts is different from a bartered exchange, where we settled things in reciprocal private credits. In a case of dollar payment, I pay with a credit in someone else's debt—namely, a debt of the United States government, issued by the Federal Reserve Bank ("for all debts, public and private"), or a debt of a chartered bank acting in the US's name, which in each case are credits for us. You offered in a dollar price, and so we swap a private commercial debt (for the apple) for a public debt, i.e. dollars.

Rendering unto Caesar: Assuming we owe things to society, we settle our legal debt to it—in fees, fines, and taxes—with its government's chosen money. By selling apples or labor for dollars in the marketplace, we procure the government's debt in money, which is a credit for us, and then pay our debt to the government in those credits, its debt to us. Once presented as payment to tax officials, and duly noted in the public record, our public money credits offset or cancel our legal public debts, the assets reducing or zeroing out the outstanding liability amount. When a British pound bears the inscription, "I promise to pay the bearer on demand the sum of five [or ten or twenty . . .] pounds," or an American dollar note reads "Federal Reserve Note"—"Note" being legalese for "Promissory Note"— both make an express public promise to do just this sort of accounting. The

---

normally a promisor would lack standing to demand settlement: "it would usually be unacceptable for the promisor to insist were the promisee to refuse." She does admit that it can be wrong for a promisee "to refuse to mitigate" depending on the nature of the relationship and other factors.

promise assures us of a debt swap—freeing us from legal exposure for tax delinquency or evasion, for the year at least (or until death frees us).

In each of the foregoing cases, even routine payment is governed by our recognition of principles. We see this when things go wrong. Perhaps I promise to gladly pay you Tuesday for a hamburger today, but never return. Or perhaps I feign to care about what I owe you for sale of an apple and then abscond with it. Or maybe you ask to settle your promissory debt to me with my promissory debt to you, and I refuse.

When you think better of walking my Pomeranian, despite having promised to do so, you haven't necessarily broken your promise (yet) if you return to me and propose a settlement. (This is before the promised walk time.) What you're doing is redeeming a credit you hold on me (for my help with the couch). You're freeing me from my own debt obligation for the couch help, offering it as "payment." And, again, I can't simply refuse to "accept back" my own IOU in settlement, not reasonably.

I could of course cover my ears, holler, and walk away. I could also argue that the favor debts aren't comparable, and so that a clean swap would be unfair. But it seems I am nevertheless obliged, presumptively, to accept my returned IOU in settlement of the debt you owe me, if they are indeed of comparable value. In that case you have a presumptive right to "satisfaction" of your credit on me, a right to settle your debt to me with it, which is just to say: a right to have me count your credit on me in cancelling your debt to me and settle our accounts, calling us "even."

The case would be different if you were asking me to *waive* the debt, releasing you from your obligation. I may not be obliged to do that; it's up to me to forgive. In the present case you are paying your debt to me, fair and square, and that's what I'm unfree to refuse. The case would also be different if the promises were interdependent, such that our promissory obligations were each conditional upon the other performing as promised. Then you might come back to me to renegotiate, which is different from settling our independent promissory debts. Some debts may be so great (e.g. to one's parents) as to never be repaid. There is then no comparable debt, owed to you, one could swap in settlement. And even when debts are comparable, the right to a settlement surely isn't absolute. Though you demand I call us even, I might reasonably refuse you in the right circumstances. Even so, I do have a presumptive obligation to settle things.

The operative principle here might be expressed as follows:

The Redemption Principle: if (1) a party, A, has a debt—an IOU—to one or more other parties B, whereby B has a credit on A; and (2) B in turn incurs a debt or IOU of comparable value to A; after which (3) B presents A's debt—A's IOU to B—in proposed settlement of B's debt to A, then A is obliged, presumptively, to settle, i.e. to count B's credit on A as cancelling or offsetting B's debt to A, absent special justification.[8]

Arguably, no one can reasonably complain of this principle as a general rule of conduct.[9] As potential promissory creditors, we do have good reason to want people to be obliged to perform as they promise and owe us, unless we release them—if only for the sake of assurance.[10] At the same time, we also each have strong reason to be allowed to settle our debts to creditors with debts those or other creditors owe to us; to be denied that prerogative is to be denied an important kind of freedom. Did Shylock have an absolute right to his promised pound of flesh? Surely not, as Shakespeare's play suggests. One may need a certain level of assurance, but it would be unreasonable to reject any obligation whatsoever to renegotiate provided offsetting debts. One can't reasonably insist on an absolute right of refusal—even of a perfectly fair settlement—on the grounds that a person in fact made a valid promise. And since a debt swap can be perfectly fair to a creditor as a matter of debt accounting (when credits and debts cancel), no one can complain of unfair or arbitrary treatment.

Note this is not to say money should always settle a promissory debt. Contracts do typically work this way: one can either comply or pony up. But we also have good reasons to limit scope of monetary settlement, much as we ban the commercial purchase of babies, organs, and sex. We may be morally forbidden from paying money to buy our way out of a promissory debt—for special moral reasons, for its inconsistency with marriage or friendship, or, more generally, for reasons of fairness or of the meaning we attach to particular goods or relationships (Sandel 2012).

3. Natural Justice

The Redemption Principle is also a right against the state. Suppose you're trying to settle your debt to the public at the tax office and officials are not obliging. You've presented enough of the government's money, but due to his indigestion, or his lunch break, or his plan to pocket your cash, the guy behind the counter refuses to mark you down as having rendered payment. As long has your debt has not been settled in the official reckoning, you remain liable for tax evasion and could face a judge garnishing your wages or ordering your incarceration. When your demand

---

[8] See also Innes (1914).

[9] Here I assume Scanlon's contractualist moral theory (1998). The Redemption Principle is distinct from and consistent with the family of principles for expectation creation Scanlon discusses (1990; 1998, ch. 7).

[10] Scanlon (1990; 1998), especially "Principle F."

for settlement is refused, the Redemption Principle is violated in an act of administrative tyranny.

Or suppose officials are rolling out a plan to harass and intimidate a certain minority group. One stratagem is to deny them any payment option, if only as a convenient pretext ("Tax dodgers! Parasites!") for legal actions aimed to either round them up or scare them off to a foreign country. Much as when I refuse to settle your dog-walking debt to me, the Redemption Principle is violated—this time as an illegitimate exercise of the inordinate power the state has over all of us.

In a republic, when faced with the abuse of power, one can make demands for settlement by the standing afforded by the recognized rights of a citizen, say, to due process. In a country such as the USA, anyone who holds a dollar note has standing to demand redemption by the promise inscribed on a dollar note itself ("for all debts, public . . ."). Bill in hand, one could patiently explain the inscription ("Look here, 'Federal Reserve *Note*', meaning 'Promissory note'!"), which publicly commits the government and its officials to our right of "satisfaction." In waving the bill, you'd in effect laying claim to that claim-right, which is the officials' bookkeeping obligation.[11] Yet the inscription is but a formal commitment laid upon an underlying moral right, the one specified by the Redemption Principle, as extra an assurance against administrative tyranny.

The Redemption Principle is thus a matter of natural justice, in the olden sense of a moral requirement that does not depend on a sovereign's recognition of it. That's not quite to say we have moral rights in a "state of nature," depending on what scenario is imagined. The Redemption Principle does assume certain ongoing interactions: one party issues a debt, another party returns to claim redemption, tendering his or her credit in payment of his or her own debt, and so on. Perhaps Crusoe is joined by a second castaway, who borrows Crusoe's shovel on a promise to return it later. Crusoe later borrows coconuts on his own promise, after which the pair call it even. It would be wrong, presumptively, for either party to refuse settlement (if their debts are assumed to be of comparable value), whether or not the Redemption Principle is already recognized, whether by law, convention, or mutual understanding.

4. Credit Cooperatives

These limited debt swaps are not yet money, which exists only within a specific sort of ongoing social practice. One might doubt the Redemption Principle as natural justice (contrary to what I've suggested). But turning now to money, we in

---

[11] See Feinberg (1970) and Gilbert (2018) for the close general connection between "claim-rights" and "standing to demand."

any case need to assume that it—or something like it—is being taken for granted as the operative principle of a credit cooperative.

For starters, if an IOU is to gain currency as money, it must be transferable among different parties, perhaps an indefinite number of parties. And if people are to have reason to accept an IOU today in payment for goods or services rendered on the expectation of its future value, they'll require reasonable confidence in the prospect of its redemption with others in future debt swaps, whether private (horizontal commercial purchase of future goods or services), or public (vertical payment of future debts to a government). They'll have that confidence in future redemption only if they can expect enough parties to accept the IOUs in recognition of the Redemption Principle, if not by a good many private parties, then at very least by public officials. Otherwise, why bank on them? Accordingly, the very existence of a money, which we've assumed just *is* a kind of credit–debt relationship, depends constitutively on a general confidence in a generally recognized right of redemption.

According to the chartalists, for a money to become established, it suffices if a sovereign ruler or state issues it and imposes a legal liability to pay taxes in it, backed by the threat of prison (Kant [1797] 2017: 76–7); Knapp ([1905] 1973).[12] But where true, this works reliably only because payments rendered can indeed be generally expected to settle debts, by the taxman and perhaps the merchant as well. The Redemption Principle, it must be assumed, will be recognized and honored in good faith.

"Recognized" in what way? Enough people must implicitly *believe* in the principle's moral validity, or at very least accept it for practical purposes. They'll accept it, for instance, by honoring requests for redemption as a matter of course, or at least acquiescing to demands for settlement without too much argument.[13] In that sense a monetary practice can be said to reflect not only the threat of prison (though there's that) but also a group's common sense of fairness. A defense of the Redemption Principle by constructive interpretation could cite *both* the reasons for its moral validity and its wide acceptance (Dworkin 1986; James 2005; 2013). A "catholic" version (Postema 1987; James 2013) might draw less from substantive moral truth than from what's generally understood in commercial practice. After all, even greedy bankers, not to mention prudent merchants the world over, know full well that their livelihoods depend on their reputations for fidelity.

If "money is a creature of law" as Knapp says, a state would seem to be not only sufficient but also necessary for money—as Kant clearly maintained ([1797] 2017: 77). But that's too strong; custom can suffice. Perhaps money has nearly always been backed by some political authority—if only a religious authority or

---

[12] Keynes (1930: 6, note 1, ch. 1, sec. iv) also seems to agree, at least as a sufficient condition for money's gaining currency.

[13] I probe the minimal requirements of "acceptance" in James (2023a).

town or village council. Yet it matters, conceptually speaking, if money is possible with no centralized authority at all.[14] As I've already suggested in the prison cigarettes case, what's strictly necessary is only a credit cooperative run by the informal social enforcement of shared understandings and general if begrudging acceptance of the Redemption Principle.

To better appreciate this possibility, consider the error in Adam Smith's famous money from barter parable. Before the invention of money, how were two parties to trade when they happened not to have what the other wanted or want what the other had? They couldn't trade, Smith reasoned; they'd "have nothing to offer in exchange.... No change can in this case be made between them" ([1776] 1994: 24, ch. IV, bk. 1). They'd have to establish some intermediary "medium," such as silver or gold, which they could then trade.

Smith's parable was wrong about money in history, a point amply confirmed by sociology and anthropology (e.g. Humphrey 1985). What's worse, as Innes (1913) explained, it overlooked an obvious possibility, indeed the normal way of commercial exchange. If bartering a dead elk for a fine suit was inconvenient, two parties could just swap a good for a credit. To use Smith's own example, the baker has bread and wants meat. The butcher, who has meat, does not want bread. Even so, they can exchange: the baker can simply buy the meat on credit, paying today with an IOU, a trusted promise for later provision of some equivalent (see also Douglas 2016: chs. 18–20).

A single baker's promissory IOU to the butcher, by itself, wouldn't necessarily have currency in a community. But, Innes suggests, so long as such promissory IOUs were trusted well enough to circulate widely—perhaps at some point with a trusted scorekeeper tracking credits and debts on a common ledger—the credit cooperative would indeed suffice to enable commerce, the exchange of a commodity or service for a bank credit (Innes 1913; 1914). And that trust might be gained with only a few extra steps, none of which strictly require government.

Transfer. For starters, the parties in a community could come to understand that their IOUs can be transferred amongst them. Suppose the butcher wanted candlesticks, but the candlestick-maker was a vegetarian. Here he could buy candlesticks on credit from her, on the strength of his promise to deliver something of comparable value to her later. Better still, if she wants bread, and he has the baker's IOU, which is good for one bread delivery, then he could pay her today, settling his debt to her by giving her his IOU. If all are amenable, and the bread is delivered, all debts would be cleared or settled. If they kept up this shared understanding, their IOUs will have become a proto-money: a transferable

---

[14] Keynes (1930: 4) seems ambivalent on this point, mentioning "Law or Custom," "the State or the Community," repeatedly—suggesting that a full-fledged contemporary state is not necessary, because "custom" or "community" would suffice. Over decade earlier, Innes (1913) was reviewed by Keynes (1914) and helped persuade him to agree that money is a credit–debt relationship, which needn't require a state.

promissory IOU, which they could swap in settlement of their debt for certain goods or services.[15]

General acceptance. Are such IOUs promissory or even a promise, strictly speaking? If promises always generate presumptive obligations to do what was specifically promised (Shiffrin 2007: sec. II; 2008), it may seem unclear how a promise could be transferable from one party to another. But here we may think of a credit cooperative as founded on a kind of standing, perhaps tacit agreement, run on confidence. Within an ongoing practice, issuance or use of an IOU may be understood to signal an intention to comply with the expectations that make that issuance or use possible, a sort of a tacit personal, associational promise to settle accounts good faith in recognition of the Redemption Principle. Others would be entitled to rely on one as expected, in a sort of promissory reliance.

Of course, where the agreement is tacit, a merchant who suddenly decides not to accept her own IOUs back in settlement would not have broken an express promise she never made. Yet the violation would still have deeper significance, as an indication of what cannot happen too often. For if a circulating IOU is to have any real value, for her and for the cooperative, the promise of its eventual redemption will have to be credible, and it will only be credible because enough people like her who use it also honor it, accepting it in setting accounts. The sensible merchant will appreciate that failing to honor it would diminish her reputation in the community—in part perhaps for offending their or her own sense of fair play. Perhaps she'd fall short of her obligation of fair play, which requires one to participate in practices from which one benefits as a matter of fairness (Hart 1961; Rawls 1971). But the Redemption Principle itself, a specific term of cooperation, does more than proscribe financial free riding. For its general acceptance in a community is precisely what constitutes a credit and monetary practice as the kind of practice it is. But for its general acceptance, the IOUs would not be money.

Unit of account. While all this might work well enough among relative intimates who already trust one another, one can see why things might become complicated as the cooperative attracts ever larger numbers, including the doctor, the cobbler, and the metalsmith as well. As disputes break out over the relative value of different IOUs, the members might agree to value them in some common measure—whether lamas, or lama points, or indeed *any* arbitrary unit they could all use as a standard to compare their credits and debts. By someone's proposal or salient signal, they'd select and adopt a unit of account, which they'd use to keep track of what they owe each other.

Banking. If memory and raggedy slips marked "IOU three loaves" may have served well enough at first, the expanding circle of members would quickly find it

---

[15] See also the family economy in Hockett and James (2020: ch. 7).

helpful to keep their own paper books, marked in indelible ink, which they could point to in case of dispute. And as the need to clear up confusion heightens, even with the new unit adopted, they'd naturally clean up their bookkeeping practices. They might post a ledger in a common space, each noting a change in what was owed to them, or what they owed to others, for example. Better still, they'll entrust the ledger to one trustworthy party, a debt scorekeeper, much like a baseball game scorekeeper—which is to say, a banker.

As for how to compensate the trusted bankers for their bookkeeping labors, the bankers can in effect pay themselves: they might not only intermediate in the settlement of circulating IOUs, but issue IOUs in their own names—by issuing loans for a promise of repayment with interest. Then they aren't just neutral scorekeepers; they become another party to the credit cooperative, assuming and issuing IOUs in their own names. And with debt swapping as their meal ticket, they'd naturally be very concerned about their reputations, which would turn on their own perceived observance of the Redemption Principle.

5. Sovereign Membership

Today's public system of accounting is much the same as in the story just outlined: the banks, who manage the payments system, are our credit–debt scorekeepers, as well as participants in the economy of credit–debt. What's different since at least the last hundred or so years are the public central banks that overlay (nominally private) chartered private banks. They regulate private lending and modulate the overall supply of credit-money in the economy, ideally in a counter-cyclical manner (usually by adjusting interbank interest rates or by paying interest on central bank reserves). Such public centralization, atop private bank issuance of IOUs, can seem inevitable in retrospect. As populations grew and commerce broadened, it was difficult for private banks to maintain trust—especially given all the temptations of fractional reserve banking, which cursed economies with boom-to-bust cycles. And so state sovereigns gradually took over, appropriating local and once fully private banking cooperatives, or instituting them from scratch as public banks.

States took over by issuing their own IOUs, or simply authorizing private bank IOUs in their names. Just as credit cooperative IOUs were money because of an assured promise of future redemption amongst one another, if a government is to get involved, its own IOUs would be money only because people had firm confidence in their future redemption in payment of taxes or other debts. And much as with an IOU-issuing private bank, a state operating *as a* creditor and debtor thereby incurs an associative promissory obligation to accept back its own IOUs in payment of a tax debt to it, as according to the Redemption Principle.

For a state, that principle is equally a requirement for its basic legitimacy. Why? Because of power—the extraordinary power the state exercises over everyone in its domain, in part via its monetary powers. At the most basic level, if a ruler legally imposes any debt upon people, the imposing fellow and his minions surely must also provide for some means of settling that debt, lest potentially arbitrary commands ever further indebt them without recourse. A ruler's money is precisely what allows us to be free, debt-free, rather than being continually subject to that ruler's will, in effect enslaved. Establishment of a money, as a means of debt settlement, is thus a basic prerequisite of republican liberty. And liberty will be secure and enjoyed only if the money is accepted back, and known to be accepted, year after year in routine settlement by the sovereign's taxmen. To be legitimate, a sovereign must therefore hold our confidence, which is not simply a matter of money's buying power or the avoidance of excessive inflation and deflation, the sort of delicacies we now leave to central banks. It's the very foundation of money's promise and the state's legitimate rule over our lives.

6. Confidence and Legitimacy

For John Rawls (1993; 2001), political legitimacy is in part a test of confidence—of whether people who are prone to revolt or disaffection and alienation can, if reasonable, be brought to comply in good faith with some promising terms of cooperation over time. The test equally applies to money: if a state does not secure confidence in the promise in its money, it imperils its very legitimacy.

Read narrowly, the Redemption Principle is violated only when an IOU is presented for settlement and refused. That rarely happens in modern republics amidst the flood of daily payments, both commercial and public. But a state can also lack full legitimacy for failing to secure confidence that a right of redemption will indeed be generally observed. As I'll now suggest with examples, a state's legitimacy is secure only when its money is plentiful enough, well-enough distributed, and neither overvalued nor undervalued so to secure everyone's hopeful participation in an economy over time.[16]

In general, a government's money can come only from that very government or its authorized bank distributors. If people are to pay debts to a government in its money, that government must itself have first issued enough of it into circulation, through spending or authorized lending. (Where else would people get it? Counterfeiting is nearly always illegal and punished harshly.) In the simplest case of illegitimacy, then, if a government simply spends too little in frugal austerity (without compensatory lending), there may not be enough money to

---

[16] The remainder of this section overlaps with James (2022).

go around. Perhaps only a select few can in fact pay their public debts, while the rest are exposed without recourse in legal liability to arrest and incarceration.

Even when there is a great deal of money in the aggregate, much or nearly all of it may be held in very few private bank accounts. This is not simply inequitable, other things being equal, but delegitimating. Every last debtor is under threat of prison if they cannot themselves get ahold of the necessary money, and it won't help them if there is plenty of money in a few bank accounts but no way for them to procure it. In fact, most public money is created by chartered private banks as loans made for profit. But suppose the banks dispense money only to those with most credible promise of repayment, to the exclusion of large numbers of people. Perhaps banks require major prior possessions such as a home, which few own, as collateral. Or perhaps only those with a favored skin color can be assumed to have sound income prospects, as everyone else is deemed a credit risk. A state will lack legitimacy for allowing this, much as it would if it all money created were simply handed over in sweetheart deals to a small class of elites, who then order around everyone else, offering the carrot of money against the implicit threat of state incarceration for failure to pay taxes. Perhaps most people are forced to work at subsistence wages, at least those lucky enough to find work and eat. The rest will be hungry for revolt.

Likewise, a spell of hyperinflation often brings round condemnation of a government's having debased its currency, for allowing too much of it relative to goods and services available. The value of its money is undercut precisely because of collapsing expectations about its future redeemability, if not in payment of taxes (which may remain the same nominal "price"), then in payment for the basic goods of life. No less delegitimating are deflationary spells, for having too little money relative to goods or services available, such as those caused by the late nineteenth century gold standard. Unsurprisingly in hindsight, tying total money issuance to the amount of certain yellow rocks extracted from the ground over a solar year brought repeated economic crises, which in turn rightly upended politics.

So money and state legitimacy seem to go hand in hand. For a government to be legitimate, every last person in debt to it must have a reasonable opportunity to procure enough of its money via exchange, work, loans, grants, or some other method, in a legitimating set of cooperative expectations—a social contract—they can be asked to comply with.

That is of course the familiar thrust of the social contract tradition. But, as I've now explained, the issue is really a matter of money. What the tradition missed for its curious inattention to money is a, if not the, central way we account for what we owe each other, along with its distinctive promissory morality. Money isn't just another tool of the state, to be used for legitimate or illegitimate ends. Given a government's extraordinary ability to shape who has its money in monetary, property and labor law, court rulings and administrative practice, the design of its banking and credit-checking system, and especially fiscal and monetary policy, money is the central credit–debt relationship around which modern society is run. Along with our rightful demands of promissory fidelity, among other claims of justice, it is part and parcel of any grand social contract with our government and each other.

References

Alchian, A., 1977. "Why Money?" *Journal of Money, Credit and Banking* 9: 133–40.

Bell, Stephanie, 2001. "The Role of the State and the Hierarchy of Money." *Cambridge Journal of Economics* 25: 148–63.

Bell, Stephanie and Edward J. Nell, 2003. *The State, the Market, and the Euro: Chartalism versus Metalism in the Theory of Money.* Cheltenham: Edward Elgar.

Bridel, Pascal, 2014. "Why Is There Money? Or Yet a New Attempt to Solve the Hahn Problem." *Economics and Literature* 4(4): 623–35.

Brunner, K. and A. Meltzer, 1971. "The Uses of Money: Money in the Theory of an Exchange Economy." *American Economic Review* 61: 784–804.

Douglas, Alexander X., 2016. *The Philosophy of Debt.* New York: Routledge.

Dworkin, Ronald, 1986. *Law's Empire.* Cambridge, MA: Belknap/Harvard University Press.

Feinberg, Joel, 1970. "The Nature and Value of Rights." *Journal of Value Inquiry*, 4: 243–57.

Gilbert, Margaret, 2018. *Rights and Demands: A Foundational Inquiry.* Oxford: Oxford University Press.

Hart, H. L. A, 1961. *The Concept of Law.* Oxford: Oxford University Press.

Hockett, Robert and Aaron James, 2020. *Money from Nothing: Or Why We Should Stop Worrying about Debt and Learn to Love the Federal Reserve.* New York: Melville.

Humphrey, Caroline, 1985. "Barter and Economic Disintegration." *Man* 20.

Innes, A. Mitchell, 1913. "What Is Money?" *Banking Law Journal* 30: 377–408. https://www.community-exchange.org/docs/what%20is%20money.htm

Innes, A. Mitchell, 1914. "The Credit Theory of Money." *Banking Law Journal* 31: 151–68. https://modernmoneynetwork.org/sites/default/files/biblio/the_credit_theory_of_money.pdf

James, Aaron, 2005. "Constructing Justice for Existing Practice: Rawls and the Status Quo." *Philosophy & Public Affairs* 33(3): 281–316.

James, Aaron, 2013. "Why Practices?" *Raison Politiques* 51, Summer.

James, Aaron, 2022. "Money as a Currency of Justice," *Journal of Contemporary Issues*, 22(2): 207–34.

James, Aaron, 2023a. "Money, Recognition, and the Outer Limit of Obliviousness," *Synthese*, 202(2): 1–24.

James, Aaron, 2023b. "Rawls, Lerner, and the Tax-and-Spend Booby Trap: What Happened to Monetary Policy." In Paul Weithman (ed.), *A Theory of Justice at 50*. Cambridge: Cambridge University Press.

Kant, Immanuel ([1797] 2017). *The Metaphysics of Morals*. Ed. Lara Denis, trans. Mary Gregor. Cambridge: Cambridge University Press.

Keynes, J. M., 1914. "*What Is Money?* By A. Mitchell Innes," *Economic Journal* 24(95): 419–21.

Keynes, J. M., 1930. *A Treatise on Money*, vols. 1–2. London: Macmillan.

Knapp, G. F. [1905] 1973. *The State Theory of Money*. Clifton, NY: Augustus M. Kelley.

Macleod, Henry Dunning, 1855. *The Theory and Practice of Banking, Volume I*. London: Longman, Brown, Green & Longmans.

Macleod, Henry Dunning, 1856. *The Theory and Practice of Banking, Volume II*. London: Longman, Brown, Green & Longmans.

Menger, K. 1892. "On the Origin of Money." Trans. C. A. Foley. *Economic Journal* 2: 239–55.

Minsky, H. P. 1986. *Stabilizing an Unstable Economy*. New Haven, CT: Yale University Press.

Mises (von Mises), Ludwig, (1912) 2013. *The Theory of Money and Credit*, trans. H. E. Batson. New York: Skyhorse Publishing.

Peacock, Mark, 2013. *Introducing Money*. New York: Routledge.

Postema, Gerald, 1987. "'Protestant' Interpretation and Social Practices." *Law and Philosophy* 6(3): 283–319.

Rawls, John, 1971. *A Theory of Justice*. Cambridge, MA: Harvard University Press.

Rawls, John, 1993. *Political Liberalism*. New York: Columbia University Press.

Rawls, John, 2001. *Justice as Fairness: A Restatement*. Ed. Erin Kelly. Cambridge, MA: Harvard University Press.

Sandel, Michael, 2012. *What Money Can't Buy: The Moral Limits of Markets*. New York: Farrar, Straus and Giroux.

Scanlon, T. M., 1990. "Promises and Practices." *Philosophy and Public Affairs* 19(3): 199–226.

Scanlon, T. M., 1998. *What We Owe to Each Other*. Cambridge, MA: Harvard University Press.

Shiffrin, Seana, 2007. "The Divergence of Contract and Promise." 120 *Harvard Law Review* 708, 730–3.

Shiffrin, Seana, 2008. "Promising, Intimate Relationships and Conventionalism." *Philosophical Review* 117(4): 481–524.

Schumpeter, J. A., 1934. *The Theory of Economic Development: An Inquiry into Profits, Capital, Credit, Interest and the Business Cycle*. Cambridge, MA: Harvard University Press.

Smit, J. P., F. Buekens, and S. Du Plessis, 2014. "Cigarettes, Dollars and Bitcoins—An Essay on the Ontology of Money." *Journal of Institutional Economics* 12(2): 324–47.

Smith, Adam, [1776] 1994. *The Wealth of Nations*. Ed. Edwin Cannan. New York: Modern Library.

Starr, Ross M, 2012. *Why Is there Money? Walrasian General Equilibrium Foundations of Monetary Theory*. Cheltenham: Edward Elgar.

Steuart, Sir James, [1767] 1966. *An Inquiry into the Principles of Political Economy*. Scottish Economic Society. London: Oliver and Boyd.

van't Klooster, Jens, 2018. "Central Banking in Rawls's Property-Owning Democracy." *Political Theory* 47(5): 674–98.

Wicksell, Knut, 1898. *Geldzins und Güterpreise* (Jena).

Wray, L. Randall, 2004. *Credit and State Theories of Money*. Cheltenham: Edward Elgar.

Wray, L. Randall, 2014. "From the State Theory of Money to Modern Money Theory." Levy Institute Working Paper no. 792. http://www.levyinstitute.org/pubs/wp_792.pdf

PART IV
POLITICAL PHILOSOPHY

13

Credit and Distributive Justice

Marco Meyer

Does the credit system make society more just, or less? The French social reformer Barthélemy Enfantin (1796–1864) called credit a "weapon" in the "fight against the conservative social system founded on private property and birth privileges" (Zouache and Boureille, 2009: 73). In his view, bankers help workers in their struggle against the idle by making capital available for productive purposes.

More recently, Elisabeth Anderson has argued that modern credit has improved personal freedom and equality (Anderson, 2004: 350). Anderson's point is a comparative one: modern credit relations are seen as beneficial to borrowers as well as creditors and carry no moral opprobrium. She argues that this an improvement over feudal debt relations which made debtors subordinate to creditors.

The micro-credit movement has high hopes for the ability of credit to transform social conditions, too. Proponents see credit as the best way to make capital available for economic development, poverty reduction, and improvements in the welfare of people worldwide. Hence proponents have argued that there is a moral imperative to make credit accessible to all (Hudon, 2009; Hudon and Sandberg, 2013; Yunus, 1987).

For credit to have these beneficial effects, it needs to be available to the groups these authors have in mind at affordable rates. I have argued elsewhere for the right to credit, which is the right to access to credit for creditworthy purposes at reasonable rates (Meyer, 2018b). By creditworthy purposes I mean that there is a sufficiently high likelihood that borrowers will repay. By reasonable rates I mean that the interest charged is proportionate to the cost of making capital available and the remaining risk that the lender faces. In a nutshell, the reason that I think there is such a right is that private property is inherently exclusionary: it prohibits everyone else from controlling the things you own, and vice versa. Non-owners lack sufficient reason to respect others' property rights unless a right to credit mitigates the exclusionary character of private property. Hence, capitalist societies, which are based on private property, should recognize a right to credit.

Having our claims recognized is no doubt an important part of justice. But rights do not exhaust justice. Another important dimension concerns distributive justice: What are the effects of credit on the distribution of economic burdens and benefits? How does the credit system affect poverty and inequality?

Marco Meyer, *Credit and Distributive Justice* In: *The Philosophy of Money and Finance*. Edited by: Joakim Sandberg and Lisa Warenski, Oxford University Press. © Oxford University Press 2024. DOI: 10.1093/oso/9780192898807.003.0014

The tradition critical of credit has mostly focused on negative consequences of credit for distributive justice. The main concern with credit in the Christian tradition is with usury, extracting high payments from the poor (Mayer, 2013). Usury and interest payments have received special attention in Islamic banking, leading to alternative financial arrangements. Rather than taking out rigid loans, borrowers pay a service fee in proportion to the profits that accrue to them, sharing risks between borrowers and bank (Mansour et al., 2015).

Since the financial crisis in 2008/2009, philosophers have given renewed attention to the harmful effects of credit on distributive justice. Lisa Herzog has argued that private debt can be a mechanism for structural injustice (Herzog, 2017). She acknowledges the liberating potential of credit but emphasizes the risks if borrowers do not enter credit contracts freely, or on a spectrum between forced and free. This is an issue for already vulnerable people and the worst-off. As a result, credit can exacerbate injustices.[1]

These critical perspectives on credit remind us that the credit system can work against the poorest and the most vulnerable. It may also favor some birth cohorts over others, as times of cheap credit make mortgages more affordable, leading to an increase of property prices; consequently, subsequent cohorts, who may also be subject to higher interest rates, must pay more. How can we reconcile this insight with the hope that credit may help to alleviate poverty? In order to understand the real-world effects of the credit system on distributive justice, we need to investigate the mechanisms that determine the price of credit, and engage with the empirical literature on the effects of credit on inequality and poverty.

I will focus on retail credit and argue that cheap credit on commercial terms is only available to people in the upper half of the wealth distribution. By contrast, the forms of credit available more widely are too expensive to make taking out credit a realistic option to escape poverty for most. However, credit can play a positive role if (mostly wealthy) entrepreneurs borrow for purposes that create jobs, or states spend borrowed funds on programs that address poverty or inequality. For those reasons, access to credit turns out to be less important from the perspective of distributive justice than whether other institutions such as the tax system and labor laws support the spreading of wealth to the poor and the less well-off.

In section 1, I suggest we should think of distributive justice as assessing how economic institutions divide benefits and burdens. Access to credit is a special kind of economic benefit: it allows borrowers to push financial obligations into the future. I introduce two assessment criteria for the distribution of benefits and

---

[1] Christian Barry, Anahi Wiedenbrüg, and Gabriel Wollner have explored the harmful effects of sovereign credit, emphasizing that over-indebted states often enter debt arrangements in conditions that undermine their duty to service the debt (Barry, 2011; Wiedenbrüg, 2018; Wollner, 2018).

burdens: the impact of an institution on poverty, and its impact on the worst-off members of society.

In section 2, I give an overview of different types of credit and develop the distinction between secured and unsecured credit, which is at the heart of my argument for why cheap credit is mostly available to the comparatively wealthy. I explain why secured credit tends to be long-term credit at low interest rates, while unsecured credit is expensive and short-term.

Based on the distinction between secured and unsecured credit, I show in sections 3 and 4 why credit tends to exacerbate existing wealth inequalities, and thus weakens egalitarian justice. Section 3 focuses on secured credit and shows that it cannot be democratized without massive redistribution of wealth, as suggested by proponents of a property-owning democracy and stakeholder grants.

Section 4 shows that democratizing access to unsecured credit does little to eradicate poverty and has only a limited effect on the worst-off. Still, keeping income constant, gaining access to unsecured credit is generally beneficial. Yet we should not evaluate the credit system in isolation. In fact, in many advanced economies, credit expands as incomes shrink in real terms for the bottom half of the income distribution. Replacing income with access to credit makes people worse off, not better.

In section 5, I discuss the indirect effects of the broader credit system on poverty and inequality, which points to a reduction in inequality. I conclude by listing some features to look for when evaluating a credit system from the perspective of distributive justice.

1. Credit through the Lens of Distributive Justice

By "distributive justice," I mean the area of inquiry concerned with how economic benefits and burdens are distributed in society. Institutions and the way they are regulated are powerful determinants of distributive justice. The goal of distributive justice is to propose institutional arrangements that will lead to distributive consequences that are justifiable to everyone affected.

What criteria do we use when evaluating institutional arrangements? In my view, distributive justice is fundamentally about regulating institutions according to principles that cannot be reasonably rejected by any individual (Scanlon, 1998). The key here is to consider the impact on the individuals affected, rather than focusing on an aggregate metric such as social welfare. There is no consensus what it takes to make an institution justifiable to everyone affected. Nonetheless, we can make progress by focusing on distributive outcomes that are clearly unacceptable (Sen, 2011). I will focus on two considerations: poverty and negative impacts on the worst-off. The credit system has both been the object of great hopes for alleviating poverty and been suspected of perpetuating it. Hence one key question is what impact the credit system currently has on poverty, and what impact it can have potentially. Concerning the impact of institutions on the worst-off, John Rawls maintained that once basic rights are secured, additional inequalities are only justifiable to the extent that they necessarily benefit the worst-off (Rawls, 2001). As we will see, availability and cost of some types of credit is highly sensitive to whether you are rich or poor.

What makes the credit system special is that it distributes a particular kind of economic advantage: not money, like the tax system or the labor market, but access to credit. Credit enables you to push financial obligations into the future, for the price of interest payments. The economic benefit for creditors is simply the interest paid by borrowers. Yet what is in it for borrowers? During the term of the loan, borrowed money works like any other money. But borrowed money needs to be repaid; there's the rub.

One advantage is to "smooth out consumption." Cashed out in human terms, smoothing out consumption means being able to absorb an expense that you could not otherwise immediately afford—be that a new washing machine, a holiday, or urgent medical care. The other crucial advantage that credit bestows is to make investments you could not otherwise afford. If smoothing out consumption is about stretching out payment over time with no effect on your income, investment is about increasing your future income.

Investments can be big, like buying a house, starting a company, or paying for university. But investments can also be much smaller. Perhaps you cannot find a job close by. With credit, you can buy a small used car that you otherwise could not afford. With the car, you can get to workplaces further away. Thanks to the new job that car gives you access to, you can repay the loan and much besides.

2. Secured vs. Unsecured Credit

Credit is often distinguished by the borrowing entity, dividing credit into household, corporate, and sovereign credit. Yet there is another crucial distinction that cuts across these categories that is much more informative for our purposes. In this section, I will lay out the distinction between secured credit such as mortgages, and unsecured credit such as credit card debt. This distinction will play a major role understanding what credit can and cannot do to advance distributive justice.

Secured credit is the cheapest form of using other people's money, because it makes costly assessments of the willingness and ability of borrowers to repay unnecessary. Secured credit is cheap because of *rigid* repayment terms and *collateralization*. Credit terms are rigid if they are insensitive to changes in the circumstances of the borrower. As a result, creditors have a claim to the exact same repayments, regardless of how the financial situation of borrowers develops.

Credit is collateralized if creditors have an enforceable right to seize a sufficiently valuable asset to cover their loan from the borrower in case they default in repayment.

Mortgages are examples of secured credit, making up the vast majority—around 80 percent—of household credit in advanced economies (Burrows et al., 2015). Banks expects repayment as agreed regardless of how the value of the house or the income situation of the borrower develops. Moreover, if the borrower fails to make timely payments, the bank repossesses and sells the house, which serves as collateral.

Granted, banks do assess the creditworthiness of mortgage borrowers. That is partly for the purpose of consumer protection, as ordered by regulators. Partly it is because banks prefer borrowers to repay, as they are in the business of lending money and not of speculating in the property market. However, seen strictly economically, collateral makes an enormous difference in ensuring the bank that it can recoup a loan by enforcing their claim to the property applicant's collateral.

Why would borrowers agree to such an unforgiving arrangement? Would it not be more attractive to borrowers if the bank shared at least some of the risk with borrowers? Banks could do that by lending up to the full price of the house, or even more than that, as some indeed have before the financial crisis (Admati and Hellwig, 2013). Or banks could allow creditors to reduce repayments in times of financial difficulty, as is indeed widely practiced in such extraordinary global circumstances as the current global pandemic. To do so on regular and individual basis is suggested by Islamic banking (Islahi, 2018; Mansour et al., 2015).

The reason borrowers agree to the usual terms of mortgages is that rigidity and collateralization dramatically decrease the interest rates banks need to charge to account for the risk that borrowers won't repay (Holmstrom, 2015). The magic of secured credit is that it mitigates the need for assessing the likelihood that a borrower will repay. Collateral provides the lender with insurance against default. This keeps interest rates low compared to unsecured credit and enables repayment schedules that can span decades. If banks shared even some risk with borrowers, they would have to much more carefully gauge the willingness and ability of potential borrowers to repay.

Unsecured credit, by contrast, works according to a different logic. Unsecured credit is more widely accessible because it does not require collateral. Yet for that very reason, unsecured credit commands high interest rates and is often short-term. All in all, unsecured consumer credit accounts for about 10 percent of household credit in advanced economies (Burrows et al., 2015). Most of this unsecured credit is credit card debt and consumer loans. Payday loans have received public attention because of the excessive interest rates charged by lenders. In terms of the volume of loans, however, payday loans play only a minor role. For instance, the value of UK payday loans issued in 2015 has been estimated at £2.5 billion (Citizens Advice, 2016). Since payday loans are taken out for short durations only, their volume at any given point in time was less than £200 million—not even a ten thousandth of the volume of mortgage credit.

The differences in term length and interest rates between secured and unsecured credit are big. Unsecured credit typically is by one order of magnitude more expensive than secured credit, commanding interest rates in the double digits even in low interest rate environments. Whereas the term of secured credit can span decades, as in the case of mortgages, unsecured credit is typically granted for months or even weeks. High interest rates make taking out large sums of money for a long time too expensive. The short-term nature of unsecured credit limits the effectiveness of micro-credit, which is also a form of unsecured credit, since using capital for productive purposes typically needs a long-term planning horizon.

Student loans appear to be a counterexample to the rule that unsecured credit is expensive and short-term. Student loans are clearly unsecured. Yet in many countries, they have long terms of repayment. In the UK, for example, student loans are not rigid, because repayment typically depends on the future income of students. How is it possible that interest rates on student loans are in the single digits? The answer is that student loans are guaranteed by the government. As a result, student loans are cheap for students, but costly for government. The UK government expects to lose 40 pence on every pound borrowed through the national student loan scheme (Shen and Ziderman, 2009; Warrell, 2015).

3. Access to Long-Term Credit at Low Interest Rates Is Limited to the Wealthy

Armed with the distinction between secured and unsecured credit and some basic facts about the wealth distribution, we'll see in this section why Enfantin's vision is bound to fail. Cheap, long-term credit that is not subsidized by the state is not an instrument to empower the least well-off, because access is limited to people who are affluent already.

Secured credit is cheap and readily available, but only to those with the financial means to secure it. The interest rate banks charge on mortgages is inversely proportional to the size of the down payment that borrowers can provide. This mechanism is the main reason why the credit system amplifies existing wealth inequalities. The wealthier people are, the more money they can borrow at more favorable rates.

One complicating factor is that some young and less affluent households can rely on their parents for support with down payments on mortgages.[2] The ability

---

[2] I am grateful to Daniel Halliday for pointing this out to me.

and willingness of parents to lend or gift money to their children can make a difference to young adults' capacity to get mortgages. Lending markets may trigger intergenerational transfers sooner than they might otherwise occur, namely as bequests. This practice tends to reduce inequality, if measured at the household level, because parents tend to be wealthier than their kids. Of course, once inequality is assessed at the level of class rather than households, that same practice will appear to increase rather than reduce inequality (Halliday, 2020).

Which assets can be collateralized? As a rule, collateralizable assets need to be sufficiently liquid and a stable store of value. Cash in a stable currency is the most welcome collateral; yet, having cash available undermines the purpose of taking out credit in the first place. By contrast, Bitcoin is bad collateral, because its value fluctuates widely. Real estate is the most used collateral. Banks usually accept it with varying degrees of abatement to reflect its liquidity, that is the number of potential buyers; a log cabin in the woods may be rejected.

Mortgages are typically secured with the real estate people are looking to buy. Can then anyone obtain mortgage credit by virtue of the fact that the house they are buying can serve as collateral? As a rule, the amount a bank agrees to lend is lower than the price of the house. The reason is that the bank needs to ensure that, should the borrower default, it will be able to recoup the value of the credit even when there is a dip in the housing market. As a result, borrowers need to make a down payment, to make up for the difference between the price of the house and the amount of credit the bank is willing to grant against its collateral. While the bars set by banks and regulators vary between countries and over time, ever since the subprime crisis of 2007 households in capitalist societies typically need to contribute 15 to 30 percent of the price of the house.

Who owns collateralizable assets? The distribution of wealth varies between societies, but some stylized facts apply across the board. The main contribution of Piketty's *Capital in the Twenty-First Century* is to present historical data on long-term trends in the development of wealth inequality. Piketty finds that regardless of the economic system, in all known societies and at all times half the population own virtually nothing. The top decile of the population owns between 60 and 90 percent of wealth. The remainder of the population own from 5 to 35 percent of all wealth (Piketty, 2014: 336).

This implies that in societies as we know them, inexpensive, secured credit is generally not available to those in the bottom half of the wealth distribution. The richer you are, the lower your cost of borrowing. If you are rich enough to have collateralizable assets, you may be able to get a business loan that a less wealthy person would not be able to obtain. What is more, the logic of secured credit is insensitive to whether a less wealthy potential competitor has ten times your business acumen.

Hence, the direct redistributive effects of secured credit on the poor and the least well-off are insignificant, as these groups are excluded from access (Beck et al., 2008; Black et al., 1996). Rather, secured credit will help the 40 percent situated between the median and the top 10 percent. Secured debt is a way for people belonging to the upper half of the wealth distribution to build more wealth. As a result, credit can reduce the gap between the middleclass and the wealthy but will also pull the middleclass further away from the bottom 50 percent in the wealth distribution (Banerjee and Newman, 1993; Greenwood and Jovanovic, 1989).

In theory, the state could help by guaranteeing mortgages and thereby improving access. However, as the example of the UK student loan scheme shows, loan guarantees do not come for free. Loan guarantees are only needed when there is a chance that they need to be realized. The financial crisis of 2007/2010 demonstrates that even remote possibilities can eventually become actual. Prior to the crisis, the US government attempted to increase access to mortgages for citizens lacking sufficient assets to meet established lending standards. The intention was to assist citizens in getting credit. To this end the government-sponsored enterprises Fannie Mae and Freddie Mac were set up. These enterprises were committed to buying mortgages meeting certain criteria from banks and package them into so-called mortgage-backed securities. These mortgage-backed securities were then sold to large institutional investors on Wall Street. By the time the financial crisis hit, Fannie Mae and Freddie Mac required a bailout of $187 billion. The bailout of the wider financial system cost multiples of this staggering sum.

Despite the sobering example of Fannie Mae and Freddie Mac, we should not dismiss state-guaranteed lending. While guarantees for student loans cost taxpayers money, the system is preferable to one where only the wealthy can afford to go to university. But it is important to realize that such schemes combine aspects of credit with aspects of redistribution. No doubt, redistributive policies can diminish wealth inequality. But it would be a mistake to attribute this redistributive aspect to credit. Instead, redistribution is due to the subsidies baked into such schemes.

That the bottom half of just about any population does not own collateralizable assets is a striking empirical regularity, but not a law of nature. Political philosophers have proposed schemes to change just that by dispersing wealth throughout the population. Stakeholder grants, financed by inheritance taxes, would transfer basic capital to everyone who comes of age (Ackerman and Alstott, 1999). Property-owning democrats similarly envision transferring a certain amount of capital to every citizen (O'Neill and Williamson, 2012). According to property-owning democracy, capital should become widely dispersed in society, rather than owned by a small proportion of the population. Such schemes would make secured credit much more widely available, enhancing its distributive effects.

Absent such policies, however, secured household credit amplifies existing inequalities. In societies as we know them, all households in the bottom half of wealth distribution will miss out entirely. Benefits accrue to borrowers in proportion to the amount of assets they can collateralize. Enthusiasm for the potential of credit to advance distributive justice is due to the mistaken assumption that the attractive terms of secured credit can be made available to borrowers who lack collateral. Similarly, some moral indignation about high-interest personal loans is grounded in the mistaken assumption that lenders pocket high-interest payments as profits. Neither is warranted.

4. Unsecured Credit Is No Substitute for Income

If secured credit can do little to eradicate poverty or benefit the least well-off, can perhaps unsecured credit come to the rescue? Democratizing access to unsecured credit has just as little potential to advance distributive justice—and may actually undermine it. In fact, in many developing countries, unsecured credit expands as incomes shrink in real terms for the bottom half of the income distribution. Keeping income constant, gaining access to credit is generally beneficial. But replacing income with access to credit puts people at a disadvantage.

There is a rich literature investigating the effects of unsecured credit on poverty and entrepreneurial activity. Macro-level studies on the impact of the credit system on absolute poverty typically find no conclusive evidence that micro-credit diminishes absolute poverty (Mader, 2015; Sorell and Cabrera, 2015, ch. 2, sec. II). This is in line with what we would expect based on the distinction between secured and unsecured credit. Households taking out micro-credit do not have assets that they can collateralize—otherwise they could obtain credit at better conditions in the regular banking system. Even though micro-credit lenders often pursue a social mission, they still often charge high interest rates, sometimes up to 70 to 100 percent per year (Sandberg, 2012). Micro-credit lenders also typically insist on short lending terms. As a result, micro-credit can only be used for investment activity that pays off very quickly. There appear to be too few oppor-tunities of this sort to make a dent in poverty.

Where unsecured credit does seem to help overcoming poverty is by keeping children in school, and thereby improving their prospects of earning a higher income than their parents. The mechanism works by breaking the dependence of poor households on the labor of their children when they need to cover a lumpy expense or overcome a short period of lowered income. Rather than making up for temporarily lower income by relying on the additional labor of their children, poor households can "smooth out" income by taking out credit. This mechanism has been observed in Tanzania and Guatemala, as well as in a large panel study (Beegle et al., 2006; Guarcello et al., 2009).

Unsecured credit can be beneficial for the least well-off well beyond keeping their children in school. Most of the unsecured debt in advanced economies is credit card debt, whereas payday loans are mainly taken out by borrowers who cannot get a credit card. Access to unsecured credit can help people pay their rent or fuel their cars until the next paycheck arrives. Although expensive, taking out such credit is much preferable to losing your home or not being able to get to work. Empirical studies of payday loans show that despite the dark sides of high-interest credit, an outright ban is bad for the worst-off—though much can be done to regulate them better (Skiba, 2012). Overall, the empirical literature suggests that unsecured credit is beneficial for those who can get it relative to the status quo. Despite the devastating impacts that unsecured credit has on borrowers who end up in debt spirals, on balance the literature seems to suggest that even in circumstances that cannot be characterized as fully free, having access to unsecured credit is beneficial for most borrowers.

However, I want to stress that access to unsecured credit is valuable only as an *addition*, not as a replacement for shrinking wages and public benefits. The rise of unsecured credit is most concerning in countries that restrict social benefits and experience falling real wages in lower-income brackets. Consider the situation in the United Kingdom. Unsecured credit is on the rise while savings rates are at a historic low. This occurs while real incomes fall at the lower end of the income spectrum, and government cuts in the provision of public goods including education and healthcare (Pardoe et al., 2015). The benefits of access to unsecured credit pale in comparison to these developments. While low-income households can sometimes avoid the worst by taking out high-interest credit to afford necessities like healthcare, justice is better served by raising incomes or making healthcare more accessible.

Analyzing the credit system in isolation from these trends and obscuring the critical distinction between secured and unsecured credit has led authors to overestimate how much credit can do to promote social justice, including my own work (Meyer, 2018b). The right to credit requires that lenders may not discriminate between applicants other than for creditworthiness. I still believe that my argument for the right to credit is sound. But I now wonder whether it obscures as much as it elucidates.[3] By failing to draw a clear line between secured and unsecured credit, it can give the wrong impression that the credit system could make cheap and long-term credit available to the worst-off. As things stand, the rise in credit taken out by the lower half of households in the wealth distribution is unsecured credit. While discrimination in credit markets is an important problem that only gets trickier and more acute in times of algorithmic

---

[3] Thanks to Titus Stahl, who made a version of this point when I presented a section of what was then still an early draft of my PhD at a workshop at the University of Groningen. I have come to think that he is right: Failing to foreground the distinction between secured and unsecured credit and failing to look at the credit system in the context of other economic institutions risks obscuring really important distributive effects of credit.

credit scoring (Fourcade and Healy, 2013), cuts in public provision and falling wages have greater effects on the worst-off (Offer, 2017).

For a full assessment of the credit system from the perspective of distributive justice, it needs to be evaluated in light of trends on labor markets. When the worst-off earn a living wage, an expansion of unsecured lending may not be concerning. In fact, the majority of poor households might benefit from increased access to unsecured lending. Yet when real incomes are decreasing for the poorest deciles of the population, a rise in unsecured lending is a sign of an unsustainable replacement of income for credit.

5. The Main Benefit of Credit to the Worst-off Come from Indirect Effects of Corporate Credit and Sovereign Borrowing

I have so far focused on the direct effects of household credit, accruing primarily to borrowers. But credit has important indirect effects also, especially when it is put to productive use and creates jobs. As Elisabeth Anderson has remarked, credit is necessary for nearly every occupation in the transatlantic economy since the nineteenth century (Anderson, 2004: 349). Corporate credit and trade credit plays an important role in creating jobs. States can funnel money minted through sovereign borrowing to poorer households to help them cope with shocks like the Covid-19 pandemic, and to support the economy in getting back on track. This suggests that credit is a necessary enabler of growth, which has lifted billions of people out of poverty over the last two centuries.

Anderson points to the indirect effects of credit. Indirect benefits are benefits that accrue not to the borrowers or lenders, but to third parties. Consider household credit first. While the direct benefits of mortgages accrue to the mostly "middle-class" borrowers, they also stimulate the housing market. That leads to more jobs in the construction sector, benefitting the less well-off also.

The most sizable benefits to the poor and the least well-off, however, come from the indirect effects of corporate credit and sovereign borrowing. Most empirical studies converge on the result that a more developed credit system tends to decrease income inequality. As Demigurc-Kunt and Levine point out in their literature review: "The emerging bulk of empirical research points tentatively toward the conclusion that improvements in financial contracts, markets, and intermediaries [...] reduce persistent inequality and tighten the distribution of income" (Demirgüç-Kunt and Levine, 2009: 2). This result holds for different methodologies, including most large panel studies (Beck et al., 2007; Clarke et al., 2006; Li et al., 1998), calibrated general equilibrium models (Giné and Townsend, 2004), and studies of natural experiments. It is worth noting that most studies look at Gini coefficients, and thus includes impact on middle-class as well as the bottom 50 percent. There is also some contrary evidence, pointing to an increase of inequality (Denk and Cournède, 2015; Lin and Tomaskovic-Devey, 2013). Still, the empirical literature seems to point to an overall tightening of the income distribution. In developing countries, studies find that expanding the banking system diminishes poverty (Burgess and Pande, 2005; Karlan et al., 2014).

What explains this equalizing effect of credit? The economic models developed by Greenwood and Jovanovic as well as by Banerjee and Newman assume that the credit system only services the better-off (Banerjee and Newman, 1993; Greenwood and Jovanovic, 1989). This is in line with our observation that the bottom half of the wealth distribution have little access to secured credit. Since credit does not reach poor individuals, the model predicts that the direct effect of the credit system is an increase in inequality. But its overall impact depends on the effects of increased entrepreneurial activity on wages. How finance affects inequality is a function of the share of profits that go to labor or to capital.

In a detailed study of the expansion of the banking system in Thailand, Giné and Townsend find evidence for these theoretical models (Giné and Townsend, 2004). As predicted by the model, access to credit was mostly limited to the well-off in the period studied and benefitted only them directly. At first, this increased income inequality. Since much of the credit was used for entrepreneurial activity, however, new jobs were created, driving up wages. Thus, over time, the credit system decreased income inequality, even though only the well-off gained access to credit.

Another proposed mechanism is that more developed credit systems are more competitive, leading to better lending terms. Since less well-off customers are more price-sensitive, increased competition leads to better financial inclusion (Dietsch, 2010). Less well-off borrowers put loans to productive uses, thereby increasing their incomes. Beck et al. found evidence of this mechanism in their study of bank deregulation in the United States (Beck et al., 2010). Between 1970 and 1990, most states removed restrictions on intrastate branching, intensifying bank competition and bank performance. After deregulation, income inequality decreased relative to the previous status quo. Income inequality also decreased relative to other states that had not yet deregulated. Generally, income inequality was reduced by boosting the wages of workers earning below the median, rather than by hurting the rich.

A type of credit that often has positive distributive effects is sovereign debt. On the expenditure side, the distributive impact of sovereign debt depends on how the government spends it. Spending that goes to welfare programs will directly benefit the less well-off. Investment spending is likely to benefit the less well-off indirectly, in the same way corporate credit is. On the financial side, sovereign debt needs to be financed through future taxation. Hence the distributive effects of credit also depend on how progressive the tax system is.

We found in the previous section that keeping trends on the labor market in view is crucial for evaluating the effects of household credit from the perspective of distributive justice. This discussion of the indirect benefits of corporate and sovereign borrowing point to additional factors to watch out for. One important variable is the labor share of income. The labor share of income is the share of national income that employees earn as wages or salaries. What happens with the rest? That is disbursed to owners of capital in the form of capital income. Economists have assumed for a long time that the labor share of income is stable over time. But there is now overwhelming evidence that the labor share of income is falling, due to technology and labor market reforms (Autor et al., 2017). The lower the labor share of income, the less indirect benefits from corporate credit will accrue to employees in the form of labor income.

6. Conclusion

So, does the credit system make society more just, or less? All said, the answer is more. But crucially the bulk of these benefits do not stem from credit that households in the bottom half of the wealth distribution take out themselves. They have little access to secured credit to begin with. Unsecured credit has some real benefits but will only rarely enable households to materially improve their economic condition. As a result, the direct effect of credit is to increase the wealth gap between the "middle class" and the bottom half of households in the wealth distribution.

There is a silver lining. The benefits of credit to the least well-off stem mostly from the credit corporations, the government, and more affluent households take out. Credit can help to create jobs and stimulate economic activity, which can lead to higher incomes for those at the bottom of the payroll. While the direct effects of the credit system are to amplify inequality, there is a sizable indirect positive effect of the credit system on people in the bottom half of the income distribution. Hence access to credit for the less well-off turns out to be less important from the perspective of distributive justice than whether other institutions such as the tax system and labor laws support the spreading of wealth to the poor and the less well-off.

How much benefit the least well-off derive from the credit system depends on other parts of the economic system, such as the wealth distribution, regulation on the labor market, the tax system, and the borrowing strategy of the government.[4] Let me summarize some of the key factors to watch out for when evaluating a credit system from the perspective of distributive justice.

---

[4] For an excellent discussion of how to regulate credit from the perspective of distributive justice, see Linarelli (2020); see also Meyer (2018a).

The wealth distribution: Access to secured credit requires collateralizable assets. In societies as we know them, households in the bottom half of the wealth distribution will have little access to secured credit. But we could change that through redistribution, for instance based on higher inheritance taxes. In a more equal society, secured credit would be available more broadly.

Trends in wages and incomes: A particularly concerning trend is the rise of unsecured credit in societies with stagnant or declining real wages. Unsecured credit is no sustainable way of propping up incomes.

The labor share of income: The indirect effects of corporate credit depend on the share of income that accrues to employees. The key variable to watch is the labor share of income. Other things equal, the higher the labor share of income, the higher the indirect benefits of credit to the less-well off.

Corporate and capital taxation: If the capital share of income increases, the least well-off can still benefit if corporate profits and capital income are sufficiently taxed, and the government uses the tax income to redistribute income to the less well-off members of society.

Hence the balance of distributive effects of the credit system depends on other aspects of the economic system. Both unconditional endorsements and repudiations of the potential of credit to improve justice are misplaced. This creates opportunities for political philosophers to evaluate the impact of the credit system in context of other economic institutions. Moreover, proposals to reform other economic institutions should take the effects of the credit system into account.

Acknowledgements

I am grateful to Lisa Warenski, Joakim Sandberg, Daniel Halliday and two anonymous reviewers for excellent comments on earlier drafts of this chapter, as well as helpful feedback from audiences at the University of Hamburg, Wasada University, and the University of Gothenburg, as well as at an online workshop of the Debt and Distributive Justice Network.

References

Ackerman, B. and Alstott, A. (1999) *The Stakeholder Society.* Yale University Press.

Admati, A. R. and Hellwig, M. F. (2013) *The Bankers' New Clothes: What's Wrong with Banking and What to Do about It.* Princeton University Press.

Anderson, E. (2004) Ethical Assumptions in Economic Theory: Some Lessons from the History of Credit and Bankruptcy. *Ethical Theory and Moral Practice* 7(4): 347–60. DOI: 10.1007/s10677-004-2202-7.

Autor, D., Dorn, D., Katz, L. F. et al. (2017) Concentrating on the Fall of the Labor Share. *American Economic Review* 107(5): 180–5. DOI: 10.1257/aer.p.20171102.

Banerjee, A. V. and Newman, A. F. (1993) Occupational Choice and the Process of Development. *Journal of Political Economy* 101(2): 274–98.

Barry, C. (2011) Sovereign Debt, Human Rights, and Policy Conditionality. *Journal of Political Philosophy* 19(3): 282–305.

Beck, T., Büyükkarabacak, B., Rioja, F. et al. (2008) Who Gets the Credit? And Does It Matter? Household vs. Firm Lending across Countries. https://openknowledge. worldbank.com/handle/10986/6855 (accessed December 14, 2014).

Beck, T., Demirgüç-Kunt, A., and Levine, R. (2007) Finance, Inequality and the Poor. *Journal of Economic Growth* 12(1): 27–49. DOI: 10.1007/s10887-007-9010-6.

Beck, T., Levine, R., and Levkov, A. (2010) Big Bad Banks? The Winners and Losers from Bank Deregulation in the United States. *Journal of Finance* 65(5): 1637–67.

Beegle, K., Dehejia, R. H., and Gatti, R. (2006) Child Labor and Agricultural Shocks. *Journal of Development Economics* 81(1): 80–96. DOI: 10.1016/j. jdeveco.2005.05.003.

Black, J., de Meza, D., and Jeffreys, D. (1996) House Prices: The Supply of Collateral and the Enterprise Economy. *Economic Journal* 106(434): 60–75. DOI: 10.2307/2234931.

Burgess, R. and Pande, R. (2005) Do Rural Banks Matter? Evidence from the Indian Social Banking Experiment. *American Economic Review* 95(2): 780–95.

Burrows, O., Low, K., and Cumming, F. (2015) *Mapping the UK Financial System*. ID 2620599, SSRN Scholarly Paper, June, 18. Rochester, NY: Social Science Research Network. http://papers.ssrn.com/abstract=2620599 (accessed July 27, 2016).

Citizens Advice (2016) Payday Loans: An Improved Market? https://www.citizensadvice. org.uk/Global/CitizensAdvice/Debt%20and%20Money%20Publications/For%20pub lication%20-%20Part1-Overviewofthetrendsinthepaydaymarketreport.pdf (accessed July 27, 2016).

Clarke, G. R. G., Xu, L. C., and Zou, H. (2006) Finance and Income Inequality: What Do the Data Tell Us? *Southern Economic Journal* 72(3): 578–96. DOI: 10.2307/20111834.

Demirgüç-Kunt, A. and Levine, R. (2009) Finance and Inequality: Theory and Evidence. *Annual Review of Financial Economics* 1(1): 287–318. DOI: 10.1146/ annurev.financial.050808.114334.

Denk, O. and Cournède, B. (2015) *Finance and Income Inequality in OECD Countries*. OECD Economics Department Working Papers, June 17. Paris: Organisation for Economic Co-operation and Development. http://www.oecd-ilibrary.org/content/ workingpaper/5js04v5jm2hl-en (accessed October 26, 2016).

Dietsch, P. (2010) The Market, Competition, and Equality. *Politics, Philosophy & Economics* 9(2): 213–44. DOI: 10.1177/1470594X09359148.

Fourcade, M. and Healy, K. (2013) Classification Situations: Life-Chances in the Neoliberal Era. *Accounting, Organizations and Society* 38(8): 559–72. DOI: 10.1016/j.aos.2013.11.002.

Giné, X. and Townsend, R. M. (2004) Evaluation of Financial Liberalization: A General Equilibrium Model with Constrained Occupation Choice. *Journal of Development Economics* 74(2): 269–307. DOI: 10.1016/j.jdeveco.2003.03.005.

Greenwood, J. and Jovanovic, B. (1989) *Financial Development, Growth, and the Distribution of Income.* 3189, Working Paper, December. National Bureau of Economic Research. http://www.nber.org/papers/w3189 (accessed June 18, 2016).

Guarcello, L., Mealli, F., and Rosati, F. C. (2009) Household Vulnerability and Child Labor: The Effect of Shocks, Credit Rationing, and Insurance. *Journal of Population Economics* 23(1): 169–98. DOI: 10.1007/s00148-008-0233-4.

Halliday, D. (2020) On the Problem of Inherited Wealth in Political Philosophy: Replies to Macleod, Barry, Braun, Wolff and Fleischer. *Law, Ethics and Philosophy* 8(8): 107–23. DOI: 10.31009/LEAP.2020.V8.08.

Herzog, L. (2017) What Could Be Wrong with a Mortgage? Private Debt Markets from a Perspective of Structural Injustice. *Journal of Political Philosophy* 25(4): 411–34. DOI: 10.1111/jopp.12107.

Holmstrom, B. (2015) *Understanding the Role of Debt in the Financial System.* 479, BIS Working Paper, January 1. Social Science Research Network. https://papers.ssrn.com/abstract=2552018 (accessed February 5, 2020).

Hudon, M. (2009) Should Access to Credit Be a Right? *Journal of Business Ethics* 84(1): 17–28.

Hudon, M. and Sandberg, J. (2013) The Ethical Crisis in Microfinance: Issues, Findings, and Implications. *Business Ethics Quarterly* 23(4): 561–89. DOI: 10.5840/beq201323440.

Islahi, A. A. (2018) History of Islamic Banking and Finance. *Intellectual Discourse* 26: 403–29.

Karlan, D., Osei, R., Osei-Akoto, I. et al. (2014) Agricultural Decisions after Relaxing Credit and Risk Constraints. *Quarterly Journal of Economics* 129(2): 597–652. DOI: 10.1093/qje/qju002.

Li, H., Squire, L., and Zou, H. (1998) Explaining International and Intertemporal Variations in Income Inequality. *Economic Journal* 108(446): 26–43. DOI: 10.1111/1468-0297.00271.

Lin, K.-H. and Tomaskovic-Devey, D. (2013) Financialization and US Income Inequality, 1970–2008. *American Journal of Sociology* 118(5): 1284–329.

Linarelli, J. (2020) Debt in Just Societies: A General Framework for Regulating Credit. *Regulation & Governance* 14(3): 409–27. DOI: https://doi.org/10.1111/rego.12219.

Mader, P. (2015) *The Political Economy of Microfinance: Financializing Poverty.* Palgrave Macmillan UK. DOI: 10.1057/9781137364210.

Mansour, W., Jedidia, K. B., and Majdoub, J. (2015) How Ethical Is Islamic Banking in the Light of the Objectives of Islamic Law? *Journal of Religious Ethics* 43(1): 51–77. DOI: https://doi.org/10.1111/jore.12086.

Mayer, R. (2013) When and Why Usury Should Be Prohibited. *Journal of Business Ethics* 116(3): 513–27. DOI: https://doi.org/10.1007/s10551-012-1483-3.

Meyer, M. (2018a) The Ethics of Consumer Credit: Balancing Wrongful Inclusion and Wrongful Exclusion. *Midwest Studies in Philosophy* 42(1): 294–313. DOI: 10.1111/misp.12095.

Meyer, M. (2018b) The Right to Credit. *Journal of Political Philosophy* 26(3): 304–26. DOI: 10.1111/jopp.12138.

Offer, A. (2017) The Market Turn: From Social Democracy to Market Liberalism: The Market Turn. *Economic History Review* 70(4): 1051–71. DOI: 10.1111/ehr.12537.

O'Neill, M. and Williamson, T. (2012) *Property-Owning Democracy: Rawls and Beyond.* Wiley.

Pardoe, A., Lane, J., Lane, P. et al. (2015) *Unsecured and insecure?* Citizens Advice. https://www.citizensadvice.org.uk/Global/CitizensAdvice/Debt%20and%20Money%20Publications/UnsecuredorinsecureFinal.pdf.

Piketty, T. (2014) *Capital in the Twenty-First Century* (trans. A. Goldhammer). MP3 Una edition. Brilliance Audio.

Rawls, J. (2001) *Justice as Fairness: A Restatement.* Harvard University Press.

Sandberg, J. (2012) Mega-interest on Microcredit: Are Lenders Exploiting the Poor? *Journal of Applied Philosophy* 29(3): 169–85.

Scanlon, T. (1998) *What We Owe to Each Other.* Belknap Press of Harvard University Press.

Sen, A. (2011) *The Idea of Justice.* Harvard University Press.

Shen, H. and Ziderman, A. (2009) Student Loans Repayment and Recovery: International Comparisons. *Higher Education* 57(3): 315–33. DOI: 10.1007/s10734-008-9146-0.

Skiba, P. M. (2012) Regulation of Payday Loans: Misguided Regulation in the Fringe Economy Symposium. *Washington and Lee Law Review* 69(2): 1023–50.

Sorell, T. and Cabrera, L. (eds) (2015) *Microfinance, Rights and Global Justice.* Cambridge University Press. http://ebooks.cambridge.org/ref/id/CBO9781316275634 (accessed March 20, 2016).

Warrell, H. (2015) UK Ministers Grapple with Problem of Unpaid Student Loans. *Financial Times*, May 21. https://next.ft.com/content/13aefac0-fed4-11e4-84b2-00144feabdc0 (accessed July 27, 2016).

Wiedenbrüg, A. (2018) What Citizens Owe: Two Grounds for Challenging Debt Repayment. *Journal of Political Philosophy* 26(3): 368–87. DOI: https://doi.org/10.1111/jopp.12163.

Wollner, G. (2018) Morally Bankrupt: International Financial Governance and the Ethics of Sovereign Default. *Journal of Political Philosophy* 26(3): 344–67. DOI: 10.1111/jopp.12151.

Yunus, M. (1987) *Credit for Self-Employment: A Fundamental Human Right.* Grameen Bank.

Zouache, A. and Boureille, B. (2009) How to Coordinate Economic Activities in a Social Order: An Essay on the Sait-Simonian Economic Doctrine (1825–1832). *History of Economic Ideas* 17(2): 65–76.

14

Freedom and Financial Market Reform

Joshua Preiss

1. Introduction

My argument in this chapter is a relatively simple one, but with major implications for freedom and markets and the ends of financial market reform. It proceeds in two parts. First, drawing upon not only political philosophy but also economic and legal history, I argue that economic freedom depends on the accountability of the institutions that structure individual market choices. It cannot be reduced to either freedom of choice within markets or the range of goods and services available. This fact is frequently ignored in contemporary discourse on freedom in markets in general and debates over financial market regulation and reform in particular. Second, I demonstrate the ways in which this ignorance enables trends in finance and regulation that undermine accountability. Failing to recognize that economic freedom depends upon institutional accountability gives license to concentrations of political and economic power and exacerbates principal–agent problems, creating firms that are often too big to fail, and an industry whose regulation is often too complex to enforce. These trends virtually guarantee regulatory capture and the outsourcing of one of the central tasks of government in a free society: the creation and maintenance of institutions that structure markets. Freedom-minded financial market reform should be directed at a simpler and more narrow banking and regulatory system, one that mitigates the ways in which complexity, instability, power and information asymmetries, regulatory capture, and a general lack of accountability undermine freedom.

2. Economic Freedom as Less Government (or More Stuff)

"The battle over the global code of capital," Katharina Pistor writes, "is all about who should determine the contents and meaning of property rights: states or private parties; the democratic public or captains of industry" (Pistor 2019, p. 138).[1] In this

---

[1] As Pistor demonstrates in her recent book, law *codes* certain assets (often the code *is* the asset) endowing them with the capacity to protect and produce private wealth. She identifies a common denominator for different forms of private property: the legal coding that provides security, priority,

Joshua Preiss, *Freedom and Financial Market Reform* In: *The Philosophy of Money and Finance*. Edited by: Joakim Sandberg and Lisa Warenski, Oxford University Press. © Oxford University Press 2024. DOI: 10.1093/oso/9780192898807.003.0015

chapter, I argue that freedom in many ways depends upon who wins these battles. More precisely, it depends upon the public or political accountability of the laws and institutions that structure markets. My concern is that without a clear understanding of the normative stakes, and the sorts of weapons or tools crucial to victory, the democratic public is destined to lose.

Debates over financial market reform habitually ignore issues of freedom. Instead, they focus on stability, economic growth, and (occasionally) on the distributive impact of money and finance. When proponents of reform do discuss economic freedom, they characterize it as some combination of the upholding of private property, the absence of legal (governmental) coercion in individual freedom of choice in markets, and the depth and breadth of financial goods and services available to consumers. The standard, in short, is to understand freedom in terms that reflect "textbook" microeconomic economic models of complete and competitive markets. These models do not reflect sustained moral analysis or argument on the nature and importance of freedom as an individual or collective value. Instead, they proceed by stipulating a definition of freedom that promises aggregate gains to wealth and welfare. Such coercion limits the ability of individuals to select the option that best satisfies their preferences. In the process, it distorts the functioning of the price mechanism, produces unnecessary scarcity, and undermines market completion.

This instrumental understanding of the value of freedom is reflected in prominent measures of economic freedom, including those offered by "free market" think tanks such as the Cato Institute in the United States and the Fraser Institute in Canada. A particularly illustrative example is provided by the Heritage Foundation in the *2021 Index of Economic Freedom*. The *Index* scores financial freedom according to five broad factors:

- The extent of government regulation of financial services,
- The degree of state intervention in banks and other financial firms through direct and indirect ownership,
- The extent of financial and capital market development,
- Government influence of the allocation of credit, and
- Openness to foreign competition.[2]

Economic Freedom of the World[3] utilizes a similar standard, focusing on the "size of government" and the imposition of regulations that limit mutually advantageous exchange, including capital controls. While the introductory

---

durability, universality, and convertibility to property rights claims. Instead of thinking of capital as a physical input (one of two factors of production) it is far more useful to think of it as "the ability to capture and monetize expected returns" (Pistor 2019, p. 116).

[2] http://www.heritage.org/index/financial-freedom

[3] https://www.cato.org/search/category/economic-freedom-world

chapter to this report stipulates "economic freedom is based on the concept of self-ownership," the report understands economic freedom in a given country largely in terms of "how closely its institutions and policies compare with the idealized structure implied by standard textbook analysis of microeconomics" (ch. 1, pp. 2–3).[4] When discussing "government regulation," the "degree of intervention and public ownership" or "government influence," the indexes don't distinguish between freedom-enhancing and freedom threatening intervention, regulation, public ownership, or influence. When government agents do any of these things, the indexes by stipulation treat it as a lack of freedom. There is no discussion of political or institutional accountability or the relative power of different participants in markets. As proponents of the aforementioned indexes argue, in general countries that score the highest on the economic freedom index also tend to be among the wealthiest countries in the world.

This instrumental understanding of the content and value of economic freedom pervades decades of arguments for financial market liberalization.[5] When I write that financial markets "liberalized" in the decades leading up to the Great Financial Crisis, I don't mean that finance was now subject to *fewer* regulations in number. The volumes of regulation continued to grow.[6] Liberalization in this case involves the removal or weakening of central forms of regulation, including the lowering of reserve and equity requirements, the repeal of laws that separated commercial banking from investment banking, and the removal of barriers to capital mobility, interest rate caps, and other forms of macroprudential regulations. Financial market liberalization brought with it explosive financial market development, which prominent indices also treat as constitutive of freedom. Financial services companies introduced new forms of contractual balance-sheet maturity and transformation via increasingly complex financial instruments such as collateralized debt obligations (CDOs) credit default swaps (CDSs) and other derivatives, creating a deep market of securities of different capital and liability structures.[7] As a result, consumers had easier access to credit and a much larger

---

[4] The point, of course, is not that all contributors to Cato, the Fraser Institute, or any of the other 70 plus think tanks involved in the publication share the same understanding of freedom. Both between and within these organizations there is surely philosophical diversity. Nonetheless, this signature publication claims to offer a definitive and comprehensive (within the limitations of available data) statement on economic freedom in the world.

[5] Numerous excellent books and articles have been written about the liberalization of financial markets in the lead-up to the Great Financial Crisis and the political and ideological transformations that helped to shape important reforms. A far-from-comprehensive list includes Admati and Hellwig 2013, Kay 2015, Krippner 2011, Streek 2014, Tooze 2018, Turner 2012, 2016, Wolf 2015. Despite disagreements (and different points of emphasis) one common current in all these accounts is that proponents of reform paid little to no attention to the links between economic freedom, institutional accountability, and political and structural power.

[6] In some ways, this growth is a consequence of expanding ideas of what counts as private property. For a discussion of this issue with respect to market-based environmental policy, see Preiss 2022, Rose 2009.

[7] That is, outstanding contracts—legal claims for certain payments under certain scenarios.

menu of financial services to choose from. In these ways, according to the aforementioned indexes (and much of the discourse of this era of liberalization) reforms made financial markets far freer.

3. Freedom and Accountability

To illustrate the link between individual freedom and institutional accountability,[8] I ask readers to consider a simple economy where most individuals make their living as independent farmers (Preiss 2021b). Then, a small group of individuals gain control of the existing government, seize the land of farmers, and offer them work on their (now) large industrial farms. In such an economy, formerly independent farmers would have multiple offers of employment, be free to exit a particular firm when they choose, be able to negotiate wages with their employers, and so on. Such an economy, moreover, may in the aggregate be more productive, if also more unequal, than the previous one. Nonetheless, it is clear that the individual farmers are less free, as others are able to structure the economy in ways that are completely unaccountable to them, in ways that alter the means in which they must conduct their lives in order to live the sort of life that they want to live. In many cases, it affects what individuals must do to secure their basic interests.

This chapter builds on earlier work, where I make explicitly republican arguments about economic freedom (Preiss 2014, 2019, 2021a, 2021b). In contemporary academic philosophy, the republican tradition is most closely associated with Philip Pettit, Quentin Skinner, and Frank Lovett and other neo-republicans who contrast their understanding of *freedom as non-domination* with liberal accounts of *freedom as non-interference* (Pettit 2012, Lovett 2010, Pettit 1997, 2012, Skinner 1998, 2008). Citing cases like the slave who, through flattering and obsequiousness (or a generally tolerant master) is able to avoid interference at the hands of a master that dominates them (Skinner 2008, pp. 96–97) neo-republicans argue that the idea of freedom as non-interference is deeply counterintuitive. Liberals like Ian Carter, Matthew Kramer, and Charles Larmore, by contrast, argue that there is little to nothing that is distinctive in this "neo-Roman" republican tradition[9]

---

[8] This chapter relies on an intuitive notion of accountability that parallels use in relevant economic and legal history and analysis. It proceeds from the idea that powerlessness and opacity undermine accountability on a wide range of compelling accounts of the principle in theory and practice. For an overview of scholarship on accountability in a wide range of academic disciplines, see Bovens, Goodin, and Schillermans 2014. For recent work on accountability and legitimacy in central banking, see Dietsch et al. 2018, Dietsch 2020, Heldt and Herzog 2021, van't Klooster 2018.

[9] In this context, the term "Neo-Roman" refers to republicans who, though they recognize the importance of political participation and civic virtue as instruments for securing and preserving liberty, do not (*contra* "Neo-Greek" republicans) characterize them as essential components of human flourishing. Freedom as non-domination is an expressly negative conception of liberty.

(Carter 1999, 2007, 2008, Kramer 2003, 2008, Larmore 2001, Patten 1996). The liberal idea of freedom, they argue, can account for the freedom-restricting nature of domination. More than that, some argue that liberal freedom is normatively, conceptually, or epistemologically prior to freedom as non-domination.[10]

My goal in this section is not to fully rehearse, much less resolve, these intricate debates over the fundamental nature of freedom. For our present purposes, it is far more instructive to focus on what these republicans and liberals have in common: they recognize a deep empirical connection between political and economic domination[11] and individual freedom. Kramer writes:

> For anyone who desires to minimize the likelihood of the exercise of oppressive powers, the best route will typically be to minimize the accumulation of such powers in the first place. Once those powers have been amassed by some person or group of people, the chance of their being exerted is typically extremely high; almost always, then, the freedom constricting consequences of relationships of domination can most effectively be averted if the relationships themselves are nipped in the bud. A reliance on the sheer benevolence or indifference of people in a position of domination is a far, far less effective tack.
>
> (Kramer 2008, p. 46)[12]

For the liberal who gives complete priority to freedom as non-interference, or the pluralist who recognizes both senses of liberty (along with other values) it will not always be clear how to trade off policies which eliminate forms of interference in the status quo, but at the expense of greater concentrating power. What is clear, however, is that both liberals and republicans have reason to see concentrations of power or control as a threat to freedom.

It is important not to draw the wrong political or policy conclusion from this empirical overlap: to conclude that since concentrations of power are a significant threat to freedom, and government agencies represent some of the greatest concentrations of power, that whatever weakens the power or reach of government safeguards individual freedom. The lesson from my example is not that we should prefer markets over government, much less understand economic freedom as the absence of government. Instead, it shows how the accountability of agents who set the basic rules of markets—whether they nominally represent governments, non-governmental organizations, for-profit corporations, or merely themselves—is essential to securing and maintaining individual freedom within

---

[10] For an overview of these debates, see de Bruin 2009 and Lovett 2018.

[11] Most basically, domination is a kind of unconstrained or unaccountable imbalance of power that enables some agents to control other agents or the conditions of their actions, including the institutions that structure their economic choices.

[12] See also Carter 2008, pp. 70–1.

those markets.[13] When thinking about the institutions conducive to freedom, the relevant distinction is not public vs. private power per se, in the sense that the power of government limits freedom but "private" power does not.[14] Great concentrations of wealth and power pose a fundamental threat to individual liberty, even when (or precisely because) governments refrain from certain forms of market intervention.

My example is not fanciful. Consider the 1913 Native Land Act in South Africa, which forced Black landowners off of their lands in 87 percent of South Africa. The ends of this act were not only to reserve lands for the white minority, but also to generate millions of desperate (and therefore cheap) laborers for white-owned agricultural and mining industries. The Native Land Act of 1913 would not have been possible if the South African government was accountable to the Black majority. Nor would the "color bar" that banned Black South Africans from most skilled professions and other institutional changes that came to be known as apartheid (Acemoglu and Robinson 2019, ch. 14). Consider also the United States in the eighteenth and nineteenth centuries, where the philosophical concepts of *discovery* and *improvement* came to redefine the legal regime of individual property rights to land. Through a series of legal rulings, Native Americans, who played no role in coding these property rights, became squatters on the land they had long inhabited, extinguishing first in time claims to property and providing legal title to past capture and conquest (Pistor 2019, pp. 34–35). These cases illustrate the link between economic freedom and institutional accountability, regardless of whether we understand domination itself as a form unfreedom (*à la* republicans) or merely something that makes coercive interference far more likely (*à la* liberals).

Of course, it is not necessary to literally seize the land of others in order to change the relative power of different individuals, what they are able or unable to do, and whose permission they need to do it. Other institutional changes, including more subtle changes to our understanding of property rights, can have a similar impact. Few people at this point dispute the moral importance of property rights. Nonetheless, support for property rights in general does not resolve a number of essential normative questions, including: What sort of things do people have a right to? Whose claims take priority when competing rights claims come

---

[13] In part for reasons that lions of liberalism such as Adam Smith and Benjamin Constant recognized long ago. In his famous indictment of French revolutionaries, who foolishly focused on the *liberty of the ancients* in the modern world, Benjamin Constant urges us not to conflate individual liberty with political participation. Nonetheless, he warns citizens of modern commercial societies that they must not forget the great danger "that, absorbed in the enjoyment of our private independence, and in pursuit of our particular interests, we should surrender our right to share in political power too easily" (Constant 1988, p. 316). Constant is deeply worried that, in their enjoyment of private liberties, citizens will neglect and even subvert the political institutions that make these private liberties possible. For more on Smith's political economy, see Preiss 2021a, ch. 1, 7.

[14] What matters, as Daron Acemoglu and James Robinson argue, is "dominance, whatever its source" (Acemoglu and Robinson 2019, p. 7).

into conflict? Over what duration do those rights extend? In what ways does such a right entitle the rights holder to limit the freedom of others? Which regulations are property rights holders subject to? Which forms of property are subject to taxation (and how much)? And, most basically, who gets to decide these things? These questions are never settled once and for all—a set of fixed background rules of markets. Instead, they remain the subject of contestation, elaboration, and, in many cases, revolution and radical revision. What history teaches us—Acemoglu and Robinson discuss a myriad of examples, from the ancient Umayyad and Abbasid states to medieval Italian communes to Zululand under Shaka to the former Soviet Republics—is that when central institutions are not accountable to society as a whole, the rules of the game for markets will be written or rewritten to the benefit of dominant players in those markets. The likely result from this loss in freedom is that human creativity will often be directed toward more ingenious forms of rent-taking or wealth capture by those in control, rather than the sorts of innovations that lead to broad-based economic growth (Acemoglu and Robinson 2019).

4. Freedom and Financial Markets

Both my example and the history of acquisition (and legal coding) of capital make vivid a set of basic realities: actual economies function according to the institutions that structure them. Any change to these institutions—including changes to the nature of property rights—will impact the well-being of participants in these economies. The rules of the game of markets don't spontaneously develop according to neoclassical models of perfect competition. Since collectives need to make ongoing decisions about how to structure markets, the accountability of these decisions remains relevant to even the most diehard proponent of markets. Those concerned with freedom and markets, therefore, must address themselves not only to individual freedom of choice within markets, but also the accountability of the institutions that structure those market choices. Accountability is no less crucial as the economy shifts from physical land to less "tangible" forms of property such as digital networks, biological processes, pharmaceuticals, and (most centrally for our present concerns) financial assets. In this section I identify a number of threats to accountability from the evolution of financial markets and the role of finance in contemporary political economy. For clarity, I divide these threats into two categories: *powerlessness* and *opacity*.

One way in which financial market reforms undermine individual freedom is by generating or exacerbating great inequalities in political and economic power. In the United States, the financial sector's share of business more than doubled in the decades before the Great Financial Crisis, with parallel trends in Europe and Asia (Krippner 2011, Turner 2016). In the process, large financial firms translate their exploding profits into political influence through lobbying and campaign contributions. Political influence is notoriously difficult to quantify, and the interests of large financial firms are not uniform. More work can and should be done to conceptualize and quantify the influence of large banks on the political process. Nonetheless, there is a large and growing consensus across disciplines that this influence played an important role both in the lead-up to the crisis and in attempts to reform financial markets after the crash.[15] To quote one recent example of this literature, Macartney et al. argue that:

> Two central features of countries that experienced the worst banking crises in 2007–2008 are in large measure explained by the bank influence hypothesis: the fact that the largest US- and EU-headquartered banks achieved favorable terms prior to the financial crisis was not fortuitous, but the result of their manipulation of the political process; and the fact that these favorable conditions and the deferential approach of state managers helped to fuel—rather than reign in—the excessive behavior that culminated in financial instability.
>
> (Macartney et al. 2020, p. 5)

My point is not that there is a monolithic, transatlantic financial cabal pulling the strings of legislation, but that both direct, political influence and structural power enable representatives of large banks to structure market institutions to their particular benefit, undermining accountability in the process. The most obvious source of structural power is the role of credit in the modern economy and the "too big to fail" (TBTF) status of the dominant players in the financial markets. It is far from clear that post-crisis reforms succeed in countering the tendency (and incentive) for banks to become TBTF. In addition, despite significant changes to bailout structures and new resolution regimes, there is widespread skepticism that governments would be willing to risk further "shocking the system" by putting large banks, including "national champion banks," into resolution in times of economic crisis. The implicit guarantees of being TBTF both boosts share prices and lowers borrowing costs, giving larger banks a substantial competitive advantage (Admati and Hellwig 2013, Alessandri and Haldane 2009, Balasubramnian and Cyree 2011, Hau et al. 2013, O'Hara and Shaw 1990).

Banks used their market power to gain exemptions from local laws governing property. For example, "representatives of derivatives traders, the modern captains of finance," Pistor notes, "successfully lobbied the legislatures in more than fifty countries to amend their bankruptcy codes and create a 'safe harbor' for derivatives and repos, thereby exempting these financial assets from rules that are binding for everyone else" (Pistor 2019, pp. 144–145). In what way(s) are these

---

[15] Examples include Admati and Hellwig 2013, ch. 12, Bair 2012, Engelen et al. 2012, Helleiner et al. 2010, Helleiner 2014, Igan et al. 2011, Kay 2015, Wolf 2015, ch. 4.

harbors "safe?" The initial concern was that due to the relatively slow machinery of the bankruptcy process, the default of a single counterparty would spread through the sovereign debt market. Over time, however, through sustained lobbying by (most notably) the International Swaps and Derivatives Association (ISDA) this narrow exemption was expanded to a wide range of financial assets in the United States. After further lobbying, the European Commission, fearing that its member states would be excluded from the rapidly growing global derivatives market, issued a directive that made the whole of the EU a safe harbor as well. These harbors were particularly "safe" for derivatives traders. After all, they were able to rewrite the code of capital according to a "master agreement" that constrains the traditional role judges play under existing bankruptcy statues, sets aside the usual wait period for enforcing creditor claims, and ensures that their assets had priority over everyone else, including workers and suppliers, in the case of default (Morgan 2008).

These reforms reflect a more general concern that regulation leads to disinvestment. At times, the structural power of finance encourages both elected officials and central bankers to be deliberately obfuscating, even when (particularly when) their impact on the functioning of markets is greatest. Ewa Karwowski writes:

> But "market people"[16] have different interests than citizens. In fact, the need for policies and budgets to be market-conforming, which Merkel recognized in the midst of the Greek crisis in 2011, can seriously undermine democratic institutions which are meant to represent and work for citizens. The past decade of financial crises demonstrated this conflict-of-interest time and time again. Thus, at the height of the subprime mortgage crisis containment the Fed used all legal means at its disposal to prevent detailed information about international support measures, including swap lines, from being revealed.
>
> (Karwowski 2019, p. 1473)

In his account of the political sources of recent financial crises, Adam Tooze quotes[17] Eurogroup chair (of eurozone finance ministers) Jean-Claude Juncker, "I am for secret, dark debates ... I'm ready to be insulted as being insufficiently democratic, but I want to be serious ... When it becomes serious, you have to lie" (Tooze 2018, p. 382). This power engenders the oft-mentioned "revolving door" between financial firms and the government agencies that are charged with regulating them. Independent regulatory agencies such as the International Accounting Standards Board (IASB) in turn, may understand "public accountability" primarily in terms of investors and other participants in financial markets,

---

[16] Meaning financial investors, in Wolfgang Streek's terminology (Streek 2014).
[17] Also mentioned in Karwowski 2019.

rather than the citizens of wider society that are also impacted by accounting rules (Helleiner 2014, ch. 4).

Such a revolving door is a logical consequence of another trend that undermines public accountability in the creation and maintenance of institutions that structure markets: the rapidly growing complexity of finance. Liberalization raises the cost and scope of financial market regulation, as complex and intense[18] financial markets require more regulation even as fewer and fewer people possess the technical expertise to effectively serve as regulators. Faced with this challenge, it is not surprising that elected representatives "delegate" the central task of setting the rules of the game of markets to non-governmental agents or reply upon those agents as chief consultants. Most of them lack the highly specialized or insider knowledge that *appears* indispensable for the effective governance of modern economies. In part for this reason, elected officials played little to no role in the Third Basel Accord (Basel III), which set the global regulatory framework on capital adequacy, stress testing, and market liquidity risk assessment.

The result was a set of reforms that in many ways doubled-down on the complexity of Basel II. Like its predecessor, Basel III sets capital requirements via an elaborate system that attaches a risk weight to each asset, defining the denominator of the capital ratio as the sum of these risk-weighted assets. In addition, it allows for the use of internal bank models for determining the risk of these assets, each of which is assigned a grade according to the particular model adopted by the bank. The US's answer to the Great Financial Crisis, the 2010 Dodd–Frank Wall Street Reform and Consumer Protection Act, checked in at over 848 pages long, with more than 27,000 new regulations to adjudicate. My point is not that we should believe that the number of regulations is a problem because each individual regulation lessens freedom.[19] Instead, my concern is that due to information asymmetries, it is difficult to sustain such complex regulation over time. Both Basel III and Dodd–Frank raised capital requirements. They also provide significant opportunity for regulatory arbitrage.[20] The sheer size and complexity of these regimes, which rely upon massive information gathering and analysis on a firm-by-firm basis, makes regulatory capture and outsourcing an inevitability (Bair 2012, Lucca et al. 2014, White 2010). They also encourage the greater concentration of capital in the hands of large firms that can more easily traverse these complexities (Admati and Hellwig 2013, Behn et al. 2016, Haldane 2015, US Department of the Treasury 2018, Zuluaga 2018).

---

[18] Intensification here refers to the growth in scope, scale, and volume of financial activity.
[19] See also Taylor 1985.
[20] That is, it provides significant opportunity to restructure transactions so that they are governed by a more favorable regulatory framework.

5. Freedom-Minded Financial Market Reform

If the goal was to design a system whose complexity made accountability difficult to impossible, it is hard to imagine a better regime than the status quo. In addition to large banks being TBTF, existing legislation may provide the additional privilege of being *too complex to enforce* (TCTE) much less do so in a non-arbitrary way. While critics of recent financial market reforms tend to focus on the threats to stability and the ways in which unnecessary complexity causes all sorts of market distortions, it is crucial to recognize that the opacity of financial markets and the political and structural power of large financial firms generate a potent cocktail of democratic dysfunction precisely where freedom most depends on accountability: the institutions that structure our political and economic choices. Since civil society cannot play its fundamental role in "shackling the leviathan," to use Acemoglu and Robinson's terminology, we should expect growth from financial market development to be increasingly extractive rather than inclusive (Acemoglu and Robinson 2012, 2019).[21] This freedom-centered analysis complements a growing body of research that suggests that though financial development (and access to basic banking services) is essential to economic growth, beyond a certain threshold an "overgrown" financial sector may actually function as a drag on the rest of the economy.[22]

The phenomenon of political and regulatory capture demands greater clarity regarding the link between industry regulation and individual freedom. Much work on freedom, justice, and markets, and much popular commentary in the wake of the Great Financial Crisis, asks: "how much" or "how little" should governments be involved in the economy. The Great Financial Crisis itself, then, provided proverbial grist for the mill of those who saw the crisis as reflecting the folly of deregulation[23] or, from the perspective of public choice theory (Tullock 2002) a classic example of what happens when governments get involved in markets: that the mechanisms of government are inevitably captured by wealthy or concentrated private interests. Both of these analyses threaten to miss the moral of the story. The central question for freedom is not "how much do governments regulate markets?" But, instead, "do the regulations themselves mitigate or exacerbate information and power asymmetries within markets, and the ability of powerful market actors to control the institutions that shape our lives and choices?" If efforts to bring about "small government" effectively euthanize central

---

[21] While inclusive institutions help bring about widely shared participation and prosperity, extractive institutions, which concentrate control in relatively few hands, enable a small segment of the population to largely exclude much of the rest of the population from the fruits of economic growth.

[22] Including people at the IMF, an organization that long championed financial market deepening (Sahay et al. 2015).

[23] Indeed, even proponents of liberalization at times predicted financial crisis as the product of their efforts (Oren and Blyth 2019).

sources of accountability, then their ostensibly freedom-minded proponents fail to incorporate a central political lesson from regulatory capture. Absent account-ability, reforms often function to entrench the power and privileges of those who currently hold dominant positions in our political economy, regardless of whether or not they entail "bigger" or "smaller" government, or more or less regulation or "intervention."

The lack of freedom through lack of accountability plays a central role in determining who bears the costs of instability. With these power and information asymmetries, the predictable result of financial crisis is that large banks will be bailed out while individuals who default on their mortgages will not. To para-phrase Mervyn King, while these corporations live globally, they die nationally. Comparatively poor and powerless citizens pay for their funerals, or more often the costs of life-saving interventions, with cuts in public spending. As Mark Blyth argues in *Angrynomics*, "the bottom 80 percent were effectively paying for the mistakes of the top one percent . . . as the private sector liabilities of the banking system ended up being put on the public balance sheet of states as more public debt" (Blyth and Lonergan 2020, p. 85). Then, states were criticized for over-spending on social welfare programs, with devastating austerity to follow in parts of the eurozone. There is a clear, intuitive case that the relationship between powerful economic actors (who played a central role in reshaping the economy to their particular benefit) and that of ordinary citizens (who paid much of the costs of the former's mistakes) is one of domination. It should surprise no one that this state of affairs led to widespread anger, as well as the erosion of democratic norms and institutions that increasingly seemed like a sham. Except for members of a rather small privileged class, the result is a vicious cycle of unfreedom, with national leaders repeatedly claiming to lack the power to do anything differently in the face of the power and mobility of capital, and citizens increasingly reaching for authoritarian alternatives that promise (however incredibly) that they can (Blyth and Lonergan 2020, Preiss 2021a, Sandbu 2020).

Unless they are paired with reforms that target the size and complexity of financial markets, calls for greater "disclosure" or "transparency"—a constant refrain in the wake of the Great Financial Crisis (Helleiner 2014)—will ultimately fail to address this poverty of public accountability. Freedom, like stability, depends upon "strong institutional frameworks, supported by clear mandates, objectives, and instruments" (Haldane et al. 2018, p. 27). Simplicity makes public accountability far more feasible. It also addresses principal–agent problems within financial markets themselves, which enable insiders to take advantage of infor-mation asymmetries to collect rents on the productive activity of the rest of the economy (Preiss 2021b, Woolley 2010). Due to space constraints, and the fact that any reform proposal will need to consider both institutional path dependencies and possible tradeoffs between freedom and other values, I hesitate to provide a one-reform-fits-all contexts proposal here. Nonetheless, my analysis provides additional normative force behind efforts to make banking "boring," "simple," and "narrow" again, by raising capital or equity requirements, re-establishing short, direct links between savers and users of capital, reducing trading volumes to more modest levels that serve the real needs of the non-financial economy, and encouraging long-term investment over short-term financial arbitrage.[24] Such reforms may include a financial transaction tax, a modified version of Glass–Steagall that is sensitive to attempts to move speculative activity over to a shadow-banking sector,[25] higher equity requirements, and other capital flow management measures (CFMs).

Admati and Hellwig argue that financial market regulation should require banks to act like other healthy corporations, which regularly maintain high levels of equity even when tax codes favor debt (Admati and Hellwig 2013). Making sure banks have more equity "is the simplest and most cost-effective way" to ensure stability, while removing most of the distortionary effects of financial markets as constituted.[26] They continue:

> Higher equity requirements would therefore alleviate the problem of banks' being too big, too interconnected, or too political to fail. Not only would banks be less likely to fail; they would bear more of their own losses should they incur losses, and they would be less able to take advantage of the subsidized cheap borrowing that their status as too big to fail has incurred on them. Best of all, these many critical benefits of significantly higher equity requirements could be obtained at virtually no cost to society.   (Admati and Hellwig 2013, p. 221)

Finally, far from equating economic freedom with unrestricted capital flows, freedom-mined reformers need to consider the ways in which such flows (1) transfer power and control from comparatively accountable democratic legislatures to multinational corporations and non-governmental organizations (Rodrik 2011) (2) facilitate tax competition that significantly limits the scope of domestic policy (Dietsch 2015) and (3) generate or exacerbate inequalities within and between nations (Eichengreen et al. 2021, Furceri, Loungani, and Ostry 2019, Hyde 2020, Milanovic 2016).[27] To be sure, many freedom-centered reforms to existing regulation would include provisions that, from the perspective of freedom

---

[24] Examples include Admati and Hellwig 2011, 2013, Behn et al. 2016, Gai et al. 2011, Haldane et al. 2010, Haldane et al. 2018, Haldane and Madouros 2012, Hoenig 2013, Kay 2015.

[25] Shadow banking refers to financial activities that take place among non-bank institutions, outside the scope of existing regulations.

[26] In addition to stability, growing evidence suggests that greater bank capital can limit the costs of crisis, including the ability to lend during and after the crisis Carlson et al. 2013, Jordá et al. 2017, Kapan and Minoiu 2013.

[27] If my arguments here are compelling, we need not posit something like the inherent value of national sovereignty or self-determination, or directly link an individual's freedom with their membership in a particular state, to recognize how such flows can undermine freedom.

as non-interference, represent a source of unfreedom. Individuals could point to deals they might have made in a different institutional context. When we recognize the links between individual freedom, political and economic power, and institutional accountability, however, gains to freedom may far outweigh the losses.

6. Conclusion

Freedom should be added to the cost–benefit analysis of any set of reform proposals. The narrow focus on systemic risk (important though it is) misses much of what is at stake in financial market reform. The political and structural power of large financial firms, and concerns for short-term declines in growth, may make it hard to envision reforms on the scale proposed by Admati, Hellwig, and others. Nonetheless, we must recognize the price we pay in freedom, in addition to concerns about stability and efficiency. In addition, absent greater accountability, growth from financial market innovation will likely be extractive rather than inclusive. Not all growth is morally equivalent.[28] Though they may be harder to quantify, the moral and political implications of financial crises and a "financialized" global economy cannot be ignored. Confronted by these fundamental issues of contemporary political economy, the idea of economic freedom as "the absence of government intervention" seems increasingly incomplete, at best, and dangerously misguided at worst. Though more plausible, the idea that one is free to the extent that they have a wide range of goods and services from which they are free to choose is also limited.

A compelling account of economic freedom must move beyond individual freedom of choice within markets. With respect to the fundamental issue of who controls the laws and institutions that structure our economic life, including the legal coding of property rights, the relevant distinction is not "markets or the state" but "democracy or authoritarianism." Freedom-minded reform, therefore, must consider whether or not regulations themselves mitigate or exacerbate information and power asymmetries within markets, and the ability of powerful market actors to control the institutions that structure our shared social, political, and economic lives. History tells us that, absent such accountability, those decisions will likely be made to entrench the power and wealth of those who currently dominate markets, whether that means more or less regulation or intervention. My analysis directs us to reforms that make possible a simpler and more narrow banking and regulatory regime. While the devil of reform and regulation is in the details, such reforms offer great potential to counter the ways in which

---

[28] And measurements of growth are not morally neutral. See also Mazzucato 2018.

complexity, instability, power and information asymmetries, regulatory capture, and (most basically) a lack of institutional accountability make people less free.

Acknowledgements

I am grateful to Joakim Sandberg, Lisa Warenski, Peter Dietsch, Alan Thomas, and David Svolba for feedback on an earlier version of this chapter. Thanks also to Clément Fontan, Boudewijn de Bruin, and the other participants in a paper workshop hosted by the Financial Ethics Research Group at the University of Gothenburg. Finally, my thanks to two anonymous reviewers at Oxford University Press for their detailed comments.

References

Acemoglu, Daron, and James A. Robinson. 2012. *Why Nations Fail: The Origins of Power, Prosperity, and Poverty.* New York: Crown.

Acemoglu, Daron, and James A. Robinson. 2019. *The Narrow Corridor: States, Societies, and the Future of Liberty.* New York: Penguin Press.

Admati, Anat R., and Martin Hellwig. 2011. Good Banking Regulation Needs Clear Focus, Sensible Tools, and Political Will. *International Centre for Financial Regulation Research Paper.*

Admati, Anat R., and Martin F. Hellwig. 2013. *The Bankers' New Clothes: What's Wrong with Banking and What to Do About It?* Princeton: Princeton University Press.

Alessandri, Piergiorgio, and Andrew Haldane. 2009. Banking on the State. Federal Reserve Bank of Chicago Twelfth Annual International Banking Conference, "The International Financial Crisis: Have the Rules of Finance Changed?" Chicago, September 25, 2009. https://www.bis.org/review/r091111e.pdf.

Bair, Sheila. 2012. *Bull by the Horns: Fighting to Save Main Street from Wall Street and Wall Street from Itself.* New York: Free Press.

Balasubramnian, B., and K. B. Cyree. 2011. Market Discipline and Banks: Why Are Yield Spreads on Bank-Issued Subordinated Notes and Debentures Not Sensitive to Bank Risks? *Journal of Banking and Finance* 35: 21–35.

Behn, Markus, Rainer Haselmann, and Vikrant Vig. 2016. The Limits of Model-Based Regulation. *European Central Bank Working Paper. https://www.ecb.europa.eu/pub/pdf/scpwps/ecbwp1928.en.pdf*

Blyth, Mark, and Eric Lonergan. 2020. *Angrynomics.* New York: Agenda Publishing.

Bovens, Mark, Robert E. Goodin, and Thomas Schillemans (eds.). 2014. *The Oxford Handbook of Public Accountability.* Oxford: Oxford University Press.

Carlson, M., H. Shan, and M. Warusawitharana. 2013. Capital Ratios and Bank Lending: A Matched Bank Approach. *Journal of Financial Intermediation*, 22(4): 663–87.

Carter, Ian. 1999. *A Measure of Freedom*. Oxford: Oxford University Press.

Carter, Ian. 2007. Social Power and Negative Freedom. *Homo Economicus*, 24(1): 187–229.

Carter, Ian. 2008. How Are Power and Unfreedom Related? In Cecile Laborde and John Maynor (eds.), *Republicanism and Political Theory*. Malden, MA: Blackwell.

Constant, Benjamin. 1988. *Political Writings*. Edited by Biancamaria Fontana. Cambridge: Cambridge University Press.

De Bruin, Boudewijn. 2009. Liberal and Republican Freedom. *Journal of Political Philosophy* 17(4): 418–39.

Dietsch, Peter. 2015. *Catching Capital*. New York: Oxford University Press.

Dietsch, Peter. 2020. Independent Agencies, Distribution, and Legitimacy: The Case of Central Banks. *American Political Science Review* 114(2): 591–5.

Dietsch, Peter, François Claveau, and Clément Fontan. 2018. *Do Central Banks Serve the People*. New York: Polity.

Eichengreen, Barry, Balazs Csonto, Asmaa El-Ganainy, and Zsoka Koczan. 2021. Financial Globalization and Inequality: Capital Flows as a Two-Edged Sword. *IMF Working Paper*.

Engelen, E., I. Ertürk, J. Froud, S. Johal, A. Leaver, M. Moran, A. Nilsson, and K. Williams. 2012. *After the Great Complacence: Financial Crisis and the Politics of Reform*. Oxford: Oxford University Press.

Furceri, Davide, Prakash Loungaini, and Jonathan D. Ostry. 2019. The Aggregate and Distributional Effects of Financial Globalization: Evidence from Macro and Sectoral Data. *Journal of Money, Credit, and Banking* 5(1): 163–98.

Gai, Prasanna, Andrew Haldane, and Sujit Kapadia. 2011. Complexity, Concentration and Contagion. *Journal of Monetary Economics* 58(5): 453–70.

Haldane, Andrew. 2015. Multi-Polar Regulation. *International Journal of Central Banking* 11(3): 385–401.

Haldane, Andrew, David Aikman, Marc Hinterschweiger, and Sujit Kapadia. 2018. Rethinking Financial Stability. *Bank of England Working Paper 712*. https://www.bankofengland.co.uk/working-paper/2018/rethinking-financial-stability

Haldane, Andrew, Simon Brennan, and Vasileios Madouros. 2010. What Is the Contribution of the Financial Sector: Miracle or Mirage? In Andrew Haldane, Adair Turner, Paul Woolley (eds.) *The Future of Finance*. London: London School of Economics, 87–120.

Haldane, Andrew, and Vasileios Madouros. 2012. The Dog and the Frisbee. Paper for Federal Reserve Bank of Kansas City's 36th Economic Policy Symposium. http://www.bankofengland.co.uk/archive/Documents/historicpubs/news/2012/075.pdf

Hau, H., S. Langfield, and D. Marques-Ibanez. 2013. Bank Ratings: Who Determines Their Quality? *Economic Policy* 28(74): 289–333.

Heldt, Eugénia C., and Lisa Herzog. 2021. The Limits of Transparency: Expert Knowledge and Meaningful Accountability in Central Banking. *Government and Opposition* 57(2): 217–32.

Helleiner, Eric. 2014. *The Status Quo Crisis: Global Financial Governance After the 2008 Meltdown*. New York: Oxford University Press.

Helleiner, E., S. Pagliari, and H. Zimmerman (eds.). 2010. *Global Finance in Crisis: The Politics of International Regulatory Change*. London: Routledge.

Hoenig, Thomas. 2013. Basel III: A Well-Intentioned Illusion. Speech to Association of Deposit Insurers, April 9. https://www.fdic.gov/news/news/speeches/spapr0913.html

Hyde, Allen. 2020. "Left Behind?" Financialization and Income Inequality Between the Affluent, Middle Class, and the Poor. *Journal of Sociological Inquiry* 90(4): 891–919.

Igan, Deniz, Prachi Mishra, and Thierry Tressel. 2011. A Fistful of Dollars: Lobbying and the Financial Crisis. *NBER Macroeconomics Annual* 26(1): 195–230.

Jordà, Ò., B. Richter, M. Schularick, and A. M. Taylor. 2017. Bank Capital Redux: Solvency, Liquidity, and Crisis (No. w23287). *National Bureau of Economic Research*.

Kapan, M. T., and C. Minoiu. 2013. Balance Sheet Strength and Bank Lending during the Global Financial Crisis. *IMF Working Paper No. 13–102*.

Karwowski, Ewa. 2019. How Financialization Undermines Democracy. *Development and Change* 50(5): 1466–81.

Kay, John. 2015. *Other People's Money: The Real Business of Finance*. New York: Norton.

Kramer, Matthew. 2003. *The Quality of Freedom*. Oxford: Oxford University Press.

Kramer, Matthew. 2008. Liberty and Domination. In Cecile Laborde and John Maynor (eds.), *Republicanism and Political Theory*. Malden, MA: Blackwell.

Krippner, Greta R. 2011. *Capitalizing on Crisis: The Political Origins of the Rise of Finance*. Cambridge, MA: Harvard University Press.

Larmore, Charles. 2001. A Critique of Phillip Pettit's Republicanism. *Philosophical Issues* 11: 229–43.

Lovett, Frank. 2010. *A General Theory of Domination and Justice*. Oxford: Oxford University Press.

Lovett, Frank. 2018. Republicanism. *Stanford Encyclopedia of Philosophy*. https://plato.stanford.edu/entries/republicanism/

Lucca, David, Amit Seru, and Francesco Trebbi. 2014. The Revolving Door and Worker Flows in Banking Regulation. *Journal of Monetary Economics* 65: 17–32.

Macartney, Huw, David Horwath, and Scott James. 2020. Bank Power and Public Policy since the Financial Crisis. *Business and Politics* 22(1): 1–24.

Mazzucato, Mariana. 2018. *The Value of Everything: Making and Taking in the Global Economy*. New York: Public Affairs.

Milanovic, Branko. 2016. *Global Inequality: A New Approach for the Age of Globalization*. Cambridge, MA: Belknap Press of Harvard University Press.

Morgan, Glenn. 2008. Market Formation and Governance in International Financial Markets: The Case of OTC Derivatives. *Human Relations* 61(5): 637–60.

O'Hara, M., and W. Shaw. 1990. Deposit Insurance and Wealth Effects: The Value of Being "Too Big to Fail." *Journal of Finance* 45: 1587–600.

Oren, Tami, and Mark Blyth. 2019. From Big Bang to Big Crash: The Early Origins of the UK's Finance-led Growth and the Persistence of Bad Policy Ideas. *New Political Economy* 24(5): 605–22.

Patten, Alan. 1996. The Republican Critique of Liberalism. *British Journal of Political Science* 26: 25–44.

Pettit, Philip. 1997. *Republicanism: A Theory of Freedom and Government*. Oxford: Oxford University Press.

Pettit, Phillip. 2012 *On the People's Terms: A Republican Theory and Model of Democracy*. Oxford: Oxford University Press.

Pistor, Katharina. 2019. *Code of Capital: How the Law Creates Wealth and Inequality*. Princeton, NJ: Princeton University Press.

Preiss, Joshua. 2014. Global Labor Justice and the Limits of Economic Analysis. *Business Ethics Quarterly* 24(1): 55–83.

Preiss, Joshua. 2019. Freedom Autonomy and Harm in Global Supply Chains. *Journal of Business Ethics* 160: 881–91.

Preiss, Joshua. 2021a. *Just Work for All: The American Dream in the 21st Century*. New York: Routledge.

Preiss, Joshua. 2021b. Did We Trade Freedom for Credit? Finance, Domination, and the Political Economy of Freedom. *European Journal of Political Theory* 20(3): 486–509.

Preiss, Joshua. 2022. Command and Control. In Benjamin Hale, and Andrew Light (eds.), *Routledge Companion to Environmental Ethics*. New York: Routledge, 667–74.

Rodrik, Dani. 2011. *The Globalization Paradox: Democracy and the Future of the World Economy*. New York: Norton.

Rose, Carol M. 2009. Liberty, Property, and Environmentalism. *Social Philosophy and Policy* 10: 1–25.

Sahay, Ratna, Martin Čuhák, Papa N'Diaye, et al. 2015. Rethinking Financial Deepening: Stability and Growth in Emerging Markets. IMF Discussion Note. https://www.imf.org/external/pubs/ft/sdn/2015/sdn1508.pdf

Sandbu, Martin. 2020. *The Economics of Belonging: A Radical Plan to Win Back the Left Behind and Achieve Prosperity for All*. Princeton, NJ: Princeton University Press.

Skinner, Quentin. 1998. *Liberty before Liberalism*. Cambridge: Cambridge University Press.

Skinner, Quentin. 2008. Freedom as the Absence of Arbitrary Power. In Céceile Laborde and John Maynor (eds.), *Republicanism and Political Theory*. Oxford: Blackwell.

Streek, Wolfgang. 2014. *Buying Time: The Delayed Crisis of Democratic Capitalism*. London: Verso.

Taylor, Charles. 1985. What's Wrong with Negative Liberty. In *Philosophy and the Human Sciences: Philosophical Papers 2*. Cambridge: Cambridge University Press.

Tooze, Adam. 2018. *Crashed: How a Decade of Financial Crises Changed the World*. London: Penguin Random House.

Tullock, Gordon. 2002. People Are People: The Elements of Public Choice. In Gordon Tullock, Arthur Seldon, and Gordon L. Brady (eds.), *Government Failure: A Primer in Public Choice*. Washington, DC: Cato Institute, 3–16.

Turner. Adair. 2012. *Economics After the Crisis: Objectives and Means*. Cambridge, MA: MIT Press.

Turner, Adair. 2016. *Between Debt and the Devil: Money, Credit, and Fixing Global Finance*. Princeton, NJ: Princeton University Press.

US Department of the Treasury. 2018. A Financial System that Creates Economic Opportunities: Nonbank Financials, Fintech, and Innovation. https://home.treas ury.gov/sites/default/files/2018-07/A-Financial-System-that-Creates-Economic-Opportunities—Nonbank-Financi....pdf

van't Klooster, Jens. 2018. Democracy and the European Bank's Emergency Power. *Midwest Studies in Philosophy* 42(1): 270–93.

White, Lawrence J. 2010. The Credit Ratings Agencies. *Journal of Economic Perspectives* 24(2): 211–26.

Wolf, Martin. 2015. *The Shifts and the Shocks: What We've Learned—And Have Still to Learn—From the Financial Crisis*. New York: Penguin.

Woolley, Paul. 2010. Why are Financial Markets so Inefficient and Exploitative—And a Suggested Remedy. In Paul Woolley et al., *The Future of Finance*. London: London School of Economics.

Zuluaga, Diego. 2018. Dodd–Frank Is in Trouble—And for Good Reason. *Cato Institute*. March 26.

15

Green Central Banking

Peter Dietsch, Clément Fontan, Jérémie Dion,
and François Claveau

1. Introduction

In response to the global financial crisis, central banks grew into what experts have dubbed 'the only game in town' in macroeconomic policy (El-Erian 2017). The policy response to Covid-19 has cemented further the key role that monetary policy plays in our economies today. Moreover, calls have grown louder in recent years for central banks not only to do their traditional job of ensuring price stability and financial stability, but also to keep an eye on other policy objectives. Notably, there is growing public pressure for central bankers to support the transition to a low-carbon economy with their monetary policy tools. For example, in March 2021, Greenpeace activists paraglided onto the European Central Bank (ECB)'s roof to denounce the fact that its monetary policy helps to fund fossil fuel companies.[1]

Should central bankers support the transition to a low-carbon economy? The contribution of this chapter lies in formulating an answer to this question from the perspective of legitimacy. To wit, can independent central banks justify employing their monetary policy tools in the name of 'green central banking', and, if so, under what conditions?

Our argument proceeds in three steps. First, we explain what we mean both by green central banking and by the concept of legitimacy that we use as a normative benchmark. More specifically, we focus on monetary policy measures that not only incorporate climate change concerns when they pose a risk to the core central bank mandate of price stability, but also take seriously potential trade-offs with other policy objectives. Furthermore, we show that central banks face a dilemma between violating norms of either input legitimacy or output legitimacy when it comes to green central banking.

Second, we analyse where the monetary policy experts themselves stand on the issue thanks to a computer-assisted discourse analysis of 17,105 speeches from central bankers around the world. We show that there is a significant amount of

---

[1] Johanna Treeck, 'Greenpeace lands on ECB tower in climate finance protest', *Politico*, accessed on October 29, 2021, https://www.politico.eu/article/greenpeace-protest-european-central-bank-paraglider-climate-finance-carbon/

Peter Dietsch, Clément Fontan, Jérémie Dion, and François Claveau, *Green Central Banking* In: *The Philosophy of Money and Finance*. Edited by: Joakim Sandberg and Lisa Warenski, Oxford University Press. © Oxford University Press 2024.
DOI: 10.1093/oso/9780192898807.003.0016

disagreement among them about whether they should actively support the transition to a low-carbon economy. Interestingly, the positions we find in the central banking community today fail to overcome the dilemma identified in earlier parts of the chapter.

The final section of the chapter points to ways in which the dilemma could in fact be overcome. It spells out the conditions that need to be met for a central bank to legitimately deploy monetary policy tools that impact the transition to a low-carbon economy. In a nutshell, the most promising way for central banks to balance the demands of input and output legitimacy is to coordinate their policies with elected officials.

2. Green Central Banking: Monetary Policy and Political Legitimacy

2.1 Using Monetary Policy as a Greening Technology

Before addressing the issue of whether central banks should be sensitive to environmental concerns in their decision-making, and how doing or not doing so affects their legitimacy, we explore the various ways in which central banks can show such sensitivity. In other words, we provide the conceptual background against which the debate on the legitimacy of green central banking takes place.

Similar to central bankers' discourse (see next section), theoretical work on this issue has been evolving rapidly in recent years (e.g. Baer et al. 2021; Bolton et al. 2020; Campiglio et al. 2018; D'Orazio and Popoyan 2020; Barmes and Livingstone 2021; Monnin 2018; Dikau and Ryan-Collins 2017; Volz 2017).[2] For our purposes, we rely on the classification developed by Baer et al. (2021), which characterizes central bank actions along three dimensions.

First, Baer and co-authors distinguish between prudential and promotional motives central banks might have to intervene (Baer 2021: 2–3). Whereas prudential motives refer to the mitigation of risks within the traditional mandate of central banks—e.g. the risks climate change poses to financial or price stability—when a central bank acts with policy objectives outside its traditional mandate in mind—in the present case, supporting the transition towards a low-carbon economy[3]—it acts for promotional motives. Our chapter focuses on the latter. According to many researchers, the enormous potential of using the social technology of money creation to promote the green transition is obvious (cf. Ingham 2020; Hockett and

---

[2] More than half of the 60-odd articles on Scopus mentioning both 'central banks' and 'climate change' have appeared since 2020.

[3] Similar arguments could be developed for other aspects of environmental policy such as, for instance, the protection of biodiversity. For reasons of space, we focus on the transition towards a low-carbon economy here.

James 2020). However, acting on such promotional motives is where the primary challenge to the legitimacy of independent central banks lies.[4]

Second, Baer and co-authors list three types of measures that central banks can take to pursue their prudential or promotional policy objectives, including the transition to a low-carbon economy: they can ensure the availability of information on markets, for instance, by requiring commercial banks to disclose the climate-related risks on their books; they can incentivize commercial banks to adopt certain kinds of behaviour, for example 'by including [climate-related risks] in the evaluation of asset eligibility as part of collateral frameworks or asset purchase programs' (Baer et al. 2021: 3); finally, they can impose quotas on certain financial flows through sectoral credit targets and the like. For our chapter, the distinction between these three types is secondary. While more coercive measures, such as quotas, perhaps tend to raise more forceful challenges to legitimacy, the fact that they do so ultimately stems from their promotional character.

Third, Baer and co-authors emphasize that the actions of delegated agencies such as central banks have to be assessed in conjunction with the actions of political agencies. In other words, a comprehensive look at the actions of the agent—the central bank—also requires an eye on the actions of the principal—the governments and parliaments that formulate the central bank's mandate (Elgie 2002).

In the present context, this distinction between delegated and political agencies has an important consequence for legitimacy. From a normative perspective, actual mandates are secondary. What matters is what *should* be in the mandate or, more generally, how the division of labour between governments and central banks should be structured. Put differently, an evaluation of the legitimacy of central banks based on current mandates and practices would be shortsighted. Instead, this evaluation can be done only as part of an evaluation of the overall institutional structure that central banks form a part of, and of the social objectives pursued by the latter. We shall come back to this issue in section 4.

2.2 The *Legitimacy* of Green Central Banking

What is the criterion to assess the legitimacy of a public institution?[5] Legitimacy hinges on the capacity to provide a justification for the coercive political power exercised over citizens (cf. Peter 2017; see also Buchanan 2002; Peter 2009). In societies that aim at some form of collective self-determination, such justifications

---

[4] Note, however, that legitimacy challenges can also arise from unintentional consequences that central bank actions on goals contained in their mandate—e.g. price stability—might have on policy objectives outside their mandate—e.g. inequality or climate change. We have focused on these unintentional consequences in previous work (e.g. Fontan et al. 2016).

[5] The section is in part informed by Dietsch (2020).

typically take two basic forms (Scharpf 1997). First, political decisions should be derived, directly or not, from the preferences of citizens. Second, political decisions should be effective at 'achieving the goals, and avoiding the dangers, that citizens collectively care about' (Scharpf 1997, 19) In the political science literature, 'input legitimacy' and 'output legitimacy,' respectively, have been used to label these two kinds of justification (Scharpf 1997, Steffek 2019).

A dominant view today is that some institutional configurations are more effective at delivering what citizens want by partially removing the influence of elected representatives on political decisions. The creation of more and more independent agencies that make policy at arm's length from parliament is a symptom of this increasing emphasis on output legitimacy (Majone 1996; OECD 2002).[6] The operational independence of central banks is one paradigmatic example for such independent agencies. According to the Central Bank Independence (CBI) template, which was widely implemented in the 1990s, central banks should be granted operational independence while operating within a narrow mandate (see also Dietsch et al. 2018, ch. 1).[7] Nominations and some accountability procedures, such as parliamentary hearings, are in place to ensure that central banks do not stray too far from the preferences of citizens, but this infusion of input legitimacy happens only sporadically.

According to the same dominant view, some decisions, namely those with distributive consequences, should be made by elected representatives (e.g. Tucker 2018). Citizens are likely to disagree on who should gain and lose from these political decisions. It is thus considered more input-legitimate to leave them to policymakers who have a direct democratic mandate, even if that might mean less effectiveness. This explains why the idea of distributive neutrality is tightly associated with contemporary central banks and other macroeconomic regulatory institutions. According to central bankers themselves, their high level of independence does not allow them to favour one economic player or sector over another (Issing et al. 2001). This is why the CBI template prescribes a strict division of labour between central bankers and government. The former should aim only at price stability, while the latter should take monetary policy as a given and adjust its budgetary and fiscal policies to address potential distributive concerns.

When a public institution either acquires new competencies or, by virtue of adjusting the policy tools used to fulfill its traditional role, finds itself in a situation where its policies create trade-offs with other important societal goals, its

---

[6] At the theoretical level, an example of this emphasis on output legitimacy is the instrumentalist case for democracy, which assesses democracy through a consequentialist lens while not according weight to the procedural values of democracy (e.g. Arneson 2003; Brennan 2016; for a critical discussion, see Viehoff 2023).

[7] Such narrow mandates do not necessarily imply an exclusive focus on price stability in all cases. The most well-known exception is the US Federal Reserve and its dual mandate of price stability and the promotion of employment.

legitimacy needs to be reassessed.[8] Central banks find themselves in this situation today. The prospect of green central banking confronts them with a dilemma that can be expressed as a tension between input versus output legitimacy.

On the one hand, citizens clearly want to avoid extreme climate change. As such, they demand that political institutions deliver on international climate pledges. Hence, even though environmental goals are usually not part of central bank mandates today, pursuing policies that might undermine such goals is deemed unacceptable in an era dominated by climate change as the single most important threat to humanity. If central bank actions lack sensitivity to climate change, this undermines their output legitimacy. In fact, climate-insensitive central banks could be perceived as part of the problem by the public at large or by elected officials who could score political points by threatening to remove central bankers.[9]

On the other hand, environmental policies come with strong distributional consequences. Climate policies generate winners and losers, and there is no consensus on who should bear the burden. Citizens should thus have relatively direct control on the political institutions fighting climate change. Hence, from the perspective of input legitimacy, independent central banks should not make climate decisions.

3. Green Central Banking: A Discourse Analysis

In this section, we examine how central bankers themselves view the effect that adopting green policies of various types might have on their legitimacy. For reasons of space, both the discourse analysis in this section and the evaluation of legitimacy in section 4 will focus on monetary policy as opposed to some of the other regulatory roles played by central banks, such as financial supervision. For instance, we will focus on promotional monetary policy tools such as green asset purchase programmes and collateral frameworks rather than supervisory policies such as green capital requirements.

The computer-assisted discourse analysis is based on 17,105 speeches from central bankers around the world. Our method allows us to retrieve the few relevant segments in this large corpus, which are then interpreted manually. The methodological details of our analysis as well as our corpus are available in a web appendix.[10]

---

[8] For the case that regular reassessment should be a constitutive part of any delegation to an independent agency in a democracy to begin with, see Downey (2021).

[9] See, e.g. US Democrats using this strategy (Thomas, August 31, 2021, https://www.bbc.com/news/business-58400767). Polls conducted by the NGFS (2019) showed that reputational concerns were the first motivation for the integration of Socially Responsible Investment guidelines within central banks.

[10] The web appendix on Zenodo: https://zenodo.org/record/5998034. These speeches are also available on the website of the Bank for International Settlements: https://www.bis.org/cbspeeches/ (last accessed: 2021-10-24). References to the speeches from our corpus are given in footnotes rather than as in-text references. The discourse analysis ends in November 2021.

We show that central bankers in South East Asia were the first to discuss and implement green monetary policy, without much controversy since it was in line with their focus on economic development. By contrast, we shall see that Western independent central banks were slower to agree on a consensual set of theoretical principles. We end our discursive analysis by outlining a number of disagreements among European central bankers on whether they can legitimately implement measures to promote the transition to a low-carbon economy. These disagreements nicely illustrate the dilemma identified in section 2 that central banks face when it comes to green central banking.

3.1 It Started in South East Asia: The Road to Climate Awareness

Central bankers have developed an interest in climate issues only recently (see Figure 1), when they realized that climate change could negatively affect their policy objectives such as price or financial stability. The consensual position used to be that the best way for them to contribute to societal efforts to implement a low-carbon economy was to remain focused on their narrow price stability objective. Jean-Claude Trichet, the ECB chairperson from 2003 to 2011, expressed this consensus in 2008:

> The [price stability] task is complicated by interaction with the other factors—for example, by the impact of global resource constraints or the growing concerns about climate change—but monetary policy stays firmly focused on delivering price stability, which is important for the efficient working of the market system and the optimal allocation of resources.[11]

However, this position started to evolve in South East Asia in the aftermath of the global financial crisis. In the majority of countries in that region, central banks have long been either playing a developmental role, in which they implement their monetary and prudential tools to target economic sectors and objectives prioritized by their governments, or working in close collaboration with governmental agencies (Volz 2017). From this perspective, adding new green objectives to the central bank purview is in line with their regular mode of operations and does not create new legitimacy dilemmas, because the decisions in question are validated by officials benefiting from some form of input legitimacy.

For example, Boediono, the governor of Bank Indonesia between 2008 and 2009, stated that during the 2007 UN Climate Change Conference in Bali '187 nations [. . .] acknowledged the unequivocal evidence of global warming and risks

---

[11] Trichet, June 3, 2008.

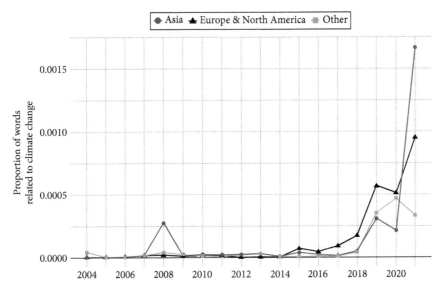

Figure 1 The global evolution of central banks' discourse on climate change
Source: https://www.bis.org/cbspeeches/

of severe climate change impacts'.[12] In connection with these observations, the governor underlined that 'to properly define our role, [...] we need to spell out as precisely as we can the ramification of the macroeconomic impact of global climate change.'[13] Bank Indonesia was at the vanguard of adopting promotional policy objectives with informational tools. In turn, other central banks, such as the Bank of Bangladesh and the People's Bank of China (PBOC), implemented similar measures and went even further, as they were the first to implement credit refinancing lines at favourable terms for green activities as well as quotas for lending to carbon-intensive sectors (Dikau and Ryan-Collins 2017). In other words, they added incentives and quotas to the arsenal of promotional tools employed by central banks in South East Asia.

3.2 The Consensus View in the Western World

In the Western world, awareness of the links between climate change and central banking has been slower to materialize. A 2015 speech by the then governor of the Bank of England, Mark Carney, on 'breaking the tragedy of the horizon' is usually considered the starting point of the 'green turn' among Western central bankers. In this speech, Carney outlined two risks faced by central banks: physical risks

---

[12] Boediono, August 1–2, 2008.   [13] Boediono, August 1–2, 2008.

(i.e. the material damages related to climate change on economic systems) and transition risks (i.e. the impact of the race towards net zero objectives on firms with a heavy carbon footprint). While Carney warned about the urgency to act on these risks, the responsibilities he saw as lying with delegated agencies were minimal:

> Financial policymakers will not drive the transition to a low-carbon economy [. . .] But the risks that I have outlined mean financial policymakers do, however, have a clear interest in ensuring the financial system is resilient to any transition [. . .] [O]ur role can be in developing the frameworks that help the market itself to adjust efficiently.[14]

This speech was influential for other independent central bankers to define a minimal consensus view on green central banking, which sets both lower and upper bounds to central bank involvement in the transition.

Regarding the lower bounds of the consensus, even central bankers who are staunch defenders of the narrow CBI template recognize the links between climate risks and their policy objectives. For instance, Jens Weidmann, who was at the helm of the German central bank from 2011 to 2021, grants that '[c]limate change, in particular, is one of the most pressing challenges of our times. All public and private institutions should therefore take action within their respective mandate to tackle them'.[15] Representatives from the Federal Reserve and the Bank of Canada, both laggards in the implementation of green measures, accept that it is important for them to 'study the implications of climate change for the economy and the financial system and to adapt our work accordingly'.[16] In short, today, the debate on whether central banks should consider climate change for prudential motives with informational tools is settled. Even the most reluctant central bankers agree with this minimal commitment.

Turning to the upper bounds of the consensus, central bankers who are advocates of green central banking, such as Isabel Schnabel or Frank Elderson, at the time of writing the two newest members of the board of the ECB, recognize two kinds of limits to their commitment. First, Schnabel grants that monetary policy follows an inherently cyclical logic, which is ill-suited to the structural challenge of climate change.[17] On this point, Schnabel echoes the analysis of Weidmann, who otherwise holds opposite views on the desirability of green central banking: 'Ultimately, monetary policy is not a structural policy instrument: it is cyclical in nature'.[18] Second, in line with the first point and with Carney's speech, central bankers highlight that they should eschew policy trade-offs with their regular policy objectives, notably with price stability.[19] Moreover, they emphasize that they

---

[14] Carney, September 29, 2015.   [15] Weidmann, February 3, 2020.
[16] Brainard, November 8, 2019. See also Lane, March 2, 2017.   [17] Schnabel, March 3, 2021.
[18] Weidmann, July 1, 2021.   [19] Cœuré, November 8, 2018.

should also respect their mandates. In the case of the ECB, the mandate includes 'the principles of proportionality and an "open market economy"'.[20]

The policy upshot of these limits is that central banks should only play a subordinated role to governments when it comes to climate change. For example, even though the Bank of England has implemented many green measures since Carney's speech in 2015,[21] its current governor repeats Carney's arguments about the division of labour between delegated and political agencies: 'We are not here to "solve" climate change or drive the transition. Those with the mandate and the tools to lead this fight sit elsewhere'.[22] Other Western central bankers who claim that they are committed to fight climate change, such as the Finnish central bank, rehearse the same argument: 'Central banks should not be the primary actors in mitigating climate change and reducing biodiversity loss'.[23]

These consensual views take direct cues from the CBI template and can be interpreted in terms of the balance between input and output legitimacy (cf. section 2). Central banks have the toolbox and the mandate to care primarily about price stability, where they consider their output legitimacy to lie.[24] By contrast, governments have the toolbox and the input legitimacy to be the primary drivers of the transition to a low-carbon economy, for which many decisions will have distributive consequences that are too important to be left to an independent public institution. Incidentally, note that central bankers rely on a parallel argument when it comes to defending their massive asset purchases in recent years against the charge that they have an unintended exacerbating effect on inequality (Fontan et al. 2016; Dietsch et al. 2018).

3.3 Divergent Interpretations of the Mandate and the Menu of Policy Options

Contrary to issues pertaining to economic inequalities, the gloss of consensus among central bankers on green central banking—adopt prudential measures, leave the driver seat to elected decision makers, and avoid measures that entail trade-offs with price and financial stability—quickly fades away when it comes to concrete policy implications. Today, central bankers support different green policy options, depending on how they interpret their mandate and the balance of threats to their input and output legitimacies. In this section, we rely on the case

---

[20] Schnabel, March 3, 2021.
[21] See the dedicated page on the Bank's website: https://www.bankofengland.co.uk/climate-change (last accessed: 2021–11–01).
[22] Bailey, June 1, 2021.   [23] Nykänen, May 21, 2021.
[24] As mentioned in section 2, this narrow construal of their output legitimacy is problematic, as the output legitimacy of public institutions needs to be evaluated *as a whole*. We shall come back to this point in section 4.

of the Eurosystem[25] to show that, even when central bankers have the same mandate, they can interpret it in different ways and, accordingly, advocate for a more or less active role in fighting climate change.

On the one hand, the Eurosystem members who would like to return to a narrow model of central banking emphasize that they do not have the mandate and the input legitimacy to go beyond policies backed by prudential motives.

> We can use our expertise to conduct research and analysis to deepen our understanding of how climate change will affect both the financial system and economies. However, it is clear that central banks do not have a mandate to address the causes of climate change or the transition to a low-carbon economy itself.[26]

These central bankers put forward three justifications for the interpretation of their mandate and legitimacy. First, they underline that playing an active greening role would push them onto the field of distributive politics:

> Climate change poses the risk of considerable social costs and economic disruption. The challenges of climate change are social issues. The analysis and choice of possible solutions, including suitable instruments and their financing, require rigorous political debate. And no matter which path a society takes, the potential changes can have serious effects on sectors, regions, the distribution of income and wealth, and generations over time. Economically, there will be relative winners and losers. It is therefore the responsibility of elected representatives to decide on the best solutions.[27]

Second, they argue that some potential greening measures, such as removing securities of fossil fuel companies from the ECB asset purchase, programmes would undermine the principle of market neutrality: 'We have to make sure that we are not creating market distortions, of course—we have to remain market-neutral'.[28]

Third, they insist that, even if their lack of input legitimacy was mitigated by an official delegation of new policy objectives, these new objectives could lead to efficiency losses, mission creep, and, ultimately, the loss of independence:

> A monetary policy which pursues explicitly environmental policy objectives is at risk of being overburdened. And in the long run, the central bank's independence might be called into question.[29]

---

[25] On the different stances and alliances within the Eurosystem, see Ferrara 2019.

[26] Donnery, January 31, 2020. See also Mersch, November 27, 2018.

[27] Mersch, November 27, 2018. See also: Weidmann, October 29, 2019; Weidmann, July 1, 2021.

[28] Lautenschläger, October 30, 2019. See also Mersch, November 27, 2018.

[29] Weidmann, October 29, 2019. See also Maechler and Moser, November 14, 2019; Mersch, November 27, 2018; Weidmann, July 1, 2021.

On the other hand, Eurosystem central bankers who support a wider model of central banking tend to interpret the ECB mandate in a more flexible way and as supporting both incentive-based and quota-based promotional policy measures. For example, Isabel Schnabel[30] and Frank Elderson[31] argue that the ECB's primary mandate requires it to consider climate change, while its secondary mandate, which asks the ECB to support general EU economic objectives, provides an additional justification since EU States explicitly make the protection of the environment a priority. They also add that this secondary mandate could be a tiebreaker between different policies: 'If faced with a choice between two monetary policy measures that have the same impact on price stability, the ECB would have to choose the one that is more in line with EU policies'.[32]

To defend their interpretation, these central bankers directly confront the arguments put forward by the advocates of the narrow mandate model, who are portrayed as 'conservatives' because they 'are concerned only about central banks' action against inflation'.[33] By contrast, their opponents present fighting climate change as 'an imperative that we must pursue in the very name of our current mandate and to ensure the smooth implementation of monetary policy'.[34]

Moreover, Schnabel[35] has played a key role in the criticism of the market neutrality concept. She argues that central banks must recognize the existence of 'market failures' in pricing risks related to the environmental catastrophe ('environmental externalities'). In view of these failures, she maintains that the 'market neutrality' principle must be replaced with the 'market efficiency' principle. Under the latter, central banks would recognize the suboptimality of a 'neutral market allocation' in the presence of market failures and implement 'tilting strategies," thus deviating from market neutrality, for example by incrementally removing fossil fuel companies from their asset purchase programmes.[36]

Finally, both Schnabel[37] and Elderson[38] argue that concerns over mission creep are misplaced for two reasons. First, 'the risk of doing too little too late is significantly larger than the risk of central banks and supervisors overstepping their mandate'.[39] Second, central banks should, within their mandate, dynamically interpret their objectives in line with citizens' concerns and contemporary challenges:

---

[30] Schnabel, May 27, 2021.

[31] See Elderson's argument published on the ECB blog: https://www.ecb.europa.eu/press/blog/date/2021/html/ecb.blog210213~7e26af8606.en.html

[32] Schnabel, March 3, 2021.   [33] Villeroy de Galhau, February 11, 2021.

[34] Villeroy de Galhau, February 11, 2021.   [35] Schnabel, June 14, 2021.

[36] Importantly, the argument by Schnabel discussed in this paragraph debunks the idea held by conservative central bankers that adopting market neutrality is not a political choice and, therefore, does not require input legitimacy. In fact, asset purchases are political choices whether they are market neutral or not (Van 't Klooster & Fontan, 2020). As we shall see in section 4, the logical next step that Schnabel fails to take is ask how the input legitimacy of central banks could be bolstered.

[37] Schnabel, May 27, 2021.   [38] Elderson, June 3, 2021.   [39] Elderson, June 3, 2021.

The challenges central banks are facing today are fundamentally different from the ones that were relevant when they gained broad political independence. Inflation is less of a concern to many people, in large part reflecting the achievements of central banks over time. As a result, expectations towards central banks have changed.[40]

In sum, our discursive analysis of central bankers' speeches on the role they should play to transition to a low-carbon economy shows a contrasted landscape. On the one hand, central bankers in the Western world agree on a thin consensus view: they should pay attention to climate change when doing so helps to fulfil their mandate (prudential motives). They also agree that their room for manoeuvre is formally constrained by their mandate (including the prioritization of their price stability objective). On the other hand, central bankers' views, especially in the Eurosystem, differ radically on the substantive interpretation of their mandate when it comes to acting on climate change and, in addition, on whether their monetary policy should be informed only by prudential motives (the 'conservative' view) or also by promotional motives (the 'progressive' view).

4. Ways for Central Banks to Meet the Legitimacy Challenge

Central bankers have divergent interpretations of the extent to which they can act decisively against climate change while preserving an appropriate level of input and output legitimacy. The discourse analysis in the previous section highlights important aspects of this divergence. Strikingly, their disagreement is focused on a topic that is not at the core of the expertise of central bankers. Rather than relating to the numerous technical questions underlying monetary policy and financial supervision, the disagreement hinges on the normative question of how the mission of central banks should respond to our historically unique circumstances. On this issue, we have no reason to defer to the epistemic authority of central bankers, even if they were unanimous. Their contributions to the discussion should rather be taken as informed points of view and be combined with other perspectives in an effort to select reasonable options in a context characterized by fundamental uncertainty and high stakes.

We have to grant certain premises to both sides of the disagreement among central bankers. Given the climate urgency, those who maintain that central banks should *promote* the transition have a strong point. The threat is immense, and solutions will necessarily involve departing from the status quo in many institutional settings. Yet, conservative central bankers are right that independent central

---

[40] Schnabel, May 27, 2021. In the inflationary context of 2022 and early 2023, this kind of argument rests on shaky foundations.

banks hardly have the input legitimacy today to promote the transition. From a democratic perspective, even though decisions speeding up the transition to a low-carbon economy benefit from strong output legitimacy, it is unpalatable to let unelected technocrats stretch the interpretation of their mandates to deliberately pick which economic sectors should thrive or shrink. Once these two premises are accepted, the next step is to think about ways for central banks to have sufficient input legitimacy to engage in more active climate policies.

As we saw in section 3, central bankers themselves thus far remain silent on how to overcome their lack of input legitimacy. For example, the 2021 ECB announcement on its next climate strategy[41] does not tackle the issue of legitimacy and coordination with other institutions. In this section, we discuss two strategies to address the legitimacy dilemma of green central banking: broadening mandates and increasing coordination. While the first tends to dominate debates on how to institutionally embed green central banking, we argue that the second strategy is actually the more promising one (see also de Boer and Van 't Klooster 2020).

A first line of reform consists in adding additional environmental objectives to central bank mandates while preserving their operational independence. For example, in March 2021, the UK government asked the Bank of England to 'take into account the Government's legally binding commitment to transition to a net zero economy by 2050'[42] and updated its mandate accordingly. The thought is that explicitly including this goal in the central bank's mandate can overcome the dilemma of legitimacy, because the institution formulating the mandate—government—provides the input legitimacy the central bank lacks. However, on closer inspection, this is clearly not sufficient.

To take a concrete example, if central banks had a formal mandate to tilt their asset purchases in favour of green assets (incentive-based policy for promotional motives; see section 2), their discretionary decisions made on these grounds would have obvious distributive consequences and thus still run afoul of input legitimacy. One apparent solution would be to specify precisely what central banks ought to do and what they are forbidden to do in their mandates, but this option is not a feasible one. For good reasons, central bank mandates are left deliberately vague and provide little guidance on the permissibility of specific monetary operations or on specific targets that must be reached (Van 't Klooster 2020).[43] This is why democratic oversight of central bank activities is performed through accountability procedures rather than by reducing their operational discretion. In turn,

---

[41] The press release is accessible at https://www.ecb.europa.eu/press/pr/date/2021/html/ecb. pr210708_1~f104919225.en.html

[42] See the announcement at https://www.gov.uk/government/news/climate-considerations-now-fully-embedded-across-uk-principal-financial-regulators

[43] This vagueness is motivated by the so-called Goodhart's law: when central banks are asked to reach specific targets, financial operators try to anticipate central banks' monetary policy and alter its outcome (Goodhart 1984).

accountability considerations explain why central banks tasked with multiple objectives usually benefit from a lower level of independence than single-objective central banks: political authorities need more oversight of central bank activities to weigh in on the trade-offs related to the attainment of their multiple objectives (Goodhart and Meade 2004). Consequently, delegating new tasks to central banks without adjusting the mechanisms of checks and balances creates democratic risks (Elgie 2002; Héritier and Lehmkuhl 2011).

Furthermore, mandate revision faces formidable feasibility constraints in the case of some central banks. For example, the ECB is often considered the most independent central bank in the world precisely because political fragmentation and legal dispositions preclude mandate change: All 27 EU member states would need to agree on Treaty changes through referendums or preliminary approval (Quaglia 2008). In sum, changing the mandate is not a strategy to reach a sufficient level of input legitimacy. Nor is it a feasible strategy in some cases.

A second strategy consists in building new channels of coordination between elected officials, central bankers and other actors in order to inject input legitimacy to green central banking. Such coordination was common in Western Europe during the Bretton Woods era and is still present in developing economies today (cf. section 2). For example, in post-WWII France, mixed committees including central bankers, government representatives and private economic agents steered credit towards strategic economic sectors (Lemoine 2016; Monnet 2018). In China, central bankers have been working with financial regulators and government officials on the definition of green credit guidelines since 2007. In the context of Western independent central banks, these new channels of coordination could challenge the CBI status quo to varying degrees. For example, a mild reform to CBI consists in 'comply or explain' procedures whereby central bankers would take the input of elected officials to decide which 'dirty' assets should be removed from asset purchase programmes. Alternatively, central bankers could be asked to systematically let their monetary policy decisions be informed by green public taxonomies, that is, classifications of economic activities into various shades of green that are produced and updated by experts and elected representatives (Alessi et al. 2021).[44] In the same vein, central banks could offer more liquidity at favourable terms to public investment banks, which would then be responsible for channeling this liquidity towards low-carbon economic sectors. Finally, they might play a role in facilitating the issuance of long-term climate bonds designed to share the burden of the transition to a low-carbon economy

---

[44] One caveat here is that such taxonomies only define the criteria that economic sectors must meet to be classified as green, but they do not assess which financial assets are green or not. Hence, when central banks operationalize green monetary policy, they would have to keep an important level of discretion. As a result, fears regarding input legitimacy would persist.

between generations and to weaken the feasibility constraints on climate action (Broome and Foley 2016).[45]

Considering a more radical rupture from CBI, new mixed committees with representatives from the central bank and elected officials could be created to make decisions on credit allocation to low-carbon economic sectors. While boosting the input legitimacy of green central banking, these committees could have an additional benefit. By bringing more diverse perspectives to the policy-making process, the resulting higher level of epistemic diversity would make it more likely that effective error-correction mechanisms are in place when making decisions on difficult policy trade-offs that have significant distributive consequences (see Dietsch et al. 2018: ch. 4).

Increased coordination does not imply that central bankers lose their independence from political authorities completely. History shows that central bank independence is not a binary issue but rather comes in degrees (Singleton 2010). In the case of green central banking, losing a certain degree of operational independence might be a small price to pay to secure the necessary input legitimacy.[46]

Increased coordination also comes with potential drawbacks that must be acknowledged. If the vested interests and worldviews of participants to mixed committees are too diverse, the decision-making process might be mired in political deadlock or the search for the lowest common denominator. More generally, any well-intentioned reform can backfire and lead central banks to be less effective at what they do and, consequently, less output-legitimate. Ultimately, much hinges on whether we consider that the climate crisis calls for bold actions. Given that the institutional status quo leads us to a dreadful destination, reform is worth pursuing even if its outcomes are far from certain. Better to adjust our course on the way than to keep running straight towards the precipice.

5. Conclusion

Our argument is that central banks are faced with a dilemma in relation to green central banking. On the one hand, they risk being accused of lacking the necessary input legitimacy if they support the initiative, while on the other hand, disregarding climate concerns would weaken their output legitimacy.

---

[45] Note that these moderate reforms can be implemented without changing the mandate.

[46] This holds even if it turned out that it required a sacrifice in terms of output legitimacy, because, for instance, attaining price stability for some reason became harder under that institutional arrangement. This is a logical consequence of accepting the tension between the two kinds of legitimacy. Note that this undermines the position of some central bankers that we should not pursue certain avenues merely because they make attaining price stability harder. All that said, it is not obvious, theoretically or empirically, that boosting input legitimacy in the ways presented here actually would entail costs in terms of output legitimacy.

Our analysis of central bankers' discourse has shown two things. First, representatives of the same central bank who operate under the same mandate disagree on whether certain aspects of green central banking are a good idea. Perhaps more worrisome, this disagreement seems grounded not so much in their expertise on monetary policy, but in issues at the periphery of their competencies. Second, neither the conservative nor the progressive central bankers defend positions that have the potential to overcome the legitimacy dilemma we have formulated.

To do so, changing a central bank's mandate is not enough. Instead, this requires coordination of various kinds between central bankers and elected officials. Be it through political input into the kind of assets they purchase, via the creation of joint committees of central bankers and members of parliament, to the collaboration with a green investment bank, the only way for central banks to overcome their lack of input legitimacy regarding policies with distributive consequences is to coordinate with those who have it. Clearly, this entails giving up some of the operational independence most Western central banks have grown used to.

References

Alessi, L., Ossola, E., & Panzica, R. (2021). "What greenium matters in the stock market? The role of greenhouse gas emissions and environmental disclosures," *Journal of Financial Stability*, 54. DOI: 10.1016/j.jfs.2021.100869

Arneson, R. J. (2003). "Defending the purely instrumental account of democratic legitimacy," *Journal of Political Philosophy*, 11/1: 122–32. DOI: 10.1111/1467–9760.00170

Baer, M., Campiglio, E., & Deyris, J. (2021). "It takes two to dance: Institutional dynamics and climate-related financial policies," *Ecological Economics*, 190: 107210. DOI: 10.1016/j.ecolecon.2021.107210

Barmes, D., & Livingstone, Z. (2021). *The Green Central Banking Scorecard: How Green Are G20 Central Banks And Financial Supervisors?* Positive Money. Retrieved October 28, 2021, from <http://positivemoney.org/wp-content/uploads/2021/05/Positive-Money-Strategy-2021-Single-final.pdf>

Boer, N. de, & Van 't Klooster, J. (2020). "The ECB, the courts and the issue of democratic legitimacy after Weiss," *Common Market Law Review*, 57/6: 1689–724.

Bolton, P., Despres, M., Da Silva, L. A. P., Samama, F., & Svartzman, R. (2020). "The green swan," *BIS Books*. Bank for International Settlements.

Brennan, J. (2016). *Against Democracy*. Princeton: Princeton University Press. DOI: 10.1515/9781400882939

Broome, J., & Foley, D. K. (2016). "A World Climate Bank." In Gonzalez-Ricoy, I. & Gosseries, A. (eds.), *Institutions for Future Generations*. Oxford: Oxford University Press, pp. 156–69.

Buchanan, A. (2002). "Political legitimacy and democracy," *Ethics*, 112/4: 689–719. DOI: 10.1086/340313

Campiglio, E., Dafermos, Y., Monnin, P., Ryan-Collins, J., Schotten, G., & Tanaka, M. (2018). "Climate change challenges for central banks and financial regulators," *Nature Climate Change*, 8/6: 462.

Dietsch, P., (2020). "Independent Agencies, Distribution, and Legitimacy: The Case of Central Banks," *American Political Science Review*, letter, 114/2: 591-95.

Dietsch, P., Claveau, F., & Fontan, C. (2018). *Do Central Banks Serve the People?* Cambridge: Polity.

Dikau, S., & Ryan-Collins, J. (2017). "Green central banking in emerging market in developing country economies." New Economics Foundation. Retrieved from <https://neweconomics.org/uploads/files/Green-Central-Banking.pdf>

D'Orazio, P., & Popoyan, L. (2020). "Taking up the climate change challenge: A new perspective on central banking" (No. 2020/19). *LEM Papers Series*, LEM Papers Series. Pisa, Italy: Laboratory of Economics and Management (LEM), Sant'Anna School of Advanced Studies. Retrieved October 28, 2021, from <https://ideas.repec.org/p/ssa/lemwps/2020-19.html>

Downey, L. (2021). "Delegation in democracy: A temporal analysis," *Journal of Political Philosophy* 29/3: 305–29.

El-Erian, M. A. (2017). *The Only Game in Town: Central Banks, Instability, and Avoiding the Next Collapse.* New York: Random House.

Elgie, R. (2002). "The politics of the European Central Bank: principal–agent theory and the democratic deficit," *Journal of European Public Policy*, 9/2: 186–200. DOI: 10.1080/13501760110120219

Ferrara, F. M. (2019). "The battle of ideas on the euro crisis: Evidence from ECB inter-meeting speeches," *Journal of European Public Policy*, 27/10: 1463–86. DOI: 10.1080/13501763.2019.1670231

Fontan, C., Claveau, F., & Dietsch, P. (2016). "Central banking and inequalities: Taking off the blinders," *Politics, Philosophy & Economics*, 15/4: 319–57.

Goodhart, C. A. E. (1984). "Problems of Monetary Management: The UK Experience". *Monetary Theory and Practice*, pp. 91–121. Palgrave: London. DOI: 10.1007/978-1-349-17295-5_4

Goodhart, C., & Meade, E. (2004). "Central banks and supreme courts," *Moneda y Crédito*, 218: 11–42.

Héritier, A., & Lehmkuhl, D. (2011). "New modes of governance and democratic accountability," *Government and Opposition*, 46/1: 126–44.

Hockett, R., & James, A. (2020). *Money from Nothing: Or, Why We Should Learn to Stop Worrying about Debt and Love the Federal Reserve.* Brooklyn, NY: Melville House.

Ingham, G. K. (2020). *Money: What Is Political Economy?* Medford, MA: Polity.

Issing, O., Gaspar, V., Angeloni, I., & Tristani, O. (2001). *Monetary Policy in the Euro Area: Strategy and Decision-Making at the European Central Bank.* Cambridge: Cambridge University Press.

Lemoine, B. (2016). *L'ordre de la dette: Enquête sur les infortunes de l'État et la prospérité du marché.* Paris: La Découverte.

Majone, G. (Ed.). (1996). *Regulating Europe.* New York: Routledge.

Monnet, E. (2018). *Controlling Credit: Central Banking and the Planned Economy in Postwar France, 1948-1973.* Cambridge: Cambridge University Press.

Monnin, P. (2018). "Central banks should reflect climate risks in monetary policy operations" (SUERF Policy Note No. No 41)., p. 9. European Money and Finance Forum.

NGFS Secretariat/Banque de France. (2019). "A sustainable and responsible investment guide for central banks' portfolio management" (NGFS Technical document), p. 41. Network for Greening the Financial System.

OECD. (2002). *Distributed Public Governance: Agencies, Authorities and other Government Bodies.* Paris: Organisation for Economic Co-operation and Development.

Peter, F. (2009). *Democratic Legitimacy.* New York: Routledge.

Peter, F. (2017). "Political legitimacy." In: E. N. Zalta, (ed.), *Stanford Encyclopedia of Philosophy.*

Quaglia, L. (2008). *Central Banking Governance in the European Union: A Comparative Analysis.* London: Routledge.

Scharpf, F. W. (1997). "Economic integration, democracy and the welfare state," *Journal of European Public Policy,* 4/1: 18–36.

Singleton, J. (2010). *Central Banking in the Twentieth Century.* Cambridge: Cambridge University Press.

Steffek, J. (2019). "The limits of proceduralism: Critical remarks on the rise of 'throughput legitimacy.'" *Public Administration,* 97/4: 784–96.

Tucker, P. (2018). *Unelected Power: The Quest for Legitimacy in Central Banking and the Regulatory State.* Princeton: Princeton University Press.

Van 't Klooster, J. (2020). "The ethics of delegating monetary policy," *Journal of Politics,* 82/2: 587–99.

Van 't Klooster, J., & Fontan, C. (2020). "The myth of market neutrality: A comparative study of the European Central Bank's and the Swiss National Bank's corporate security purchases," *New Political Economy,* 25/6: 865–79.

Viehoff, D. (2023). "Challenging democratic commitments: On liberal arguments for instrumentalism about democracy". In Sobel, D. & Wall, S. (eds.), *Oxford Studies in Political Philosophy,* vol. 9. Oxford: Oxford University Press, pp. 183-212.

Volz, U. (2017). "On the role of central banks in enhancing green finance". UN environment inquiry working paper 17/01.

Appendix: Cited Documents from Our Corpus

Bailey, Andrew (Bank of England), June 1, 2021, "Tackling climate for real—The role of central banks," at Reuters Events Responsible Business. https://www.bis.org/review/r210602a.htm

Boediono (Bank of Indonesia), August 1–2, 2008, "Macroeconomic impact of climate change—Opportunities and challenges (Keynote speech)," at Bank Indonesia's Annual International Seminar on "Macroeconomic impact of climate change—opportunities and challenges," Nusa Dua, Bali. https://www.bis.org/review/r080901c.htm

Brainard, Lael (Federal Reserve System), November 8, 2019, "The economics of climate change," a research conference sponsored by the Federal Reserve Bank of San Francisco, San Francisco, California. https://www.bis.org/review/r191111a.htm

Carney, Mark (Bank of England), September 29, 2015, "Breaking the tragedy of the horizon—Climate change and financial stability," Lloyd's of London, London, United Kingdom. https://www.bis.org/review/r151009a.htm

Cœuré, Benoît (European Central Bank), November 8, 2018, "Monetary policy and climate change," at a conference on "Scaling up Green Finance: The Role of Central Banks," organized by the Network for Greening the Financial System, the Deutsche Bundesbank and the Council on Economic Policies, Berlin. https://www.bis.org/review/r181109f.htm

Donnery, Sharon (Bank of Ireland), January 31, 2020, "Central banks and public policy—stability in an interconnected world," at the Warwick Economics Summit, Warwick. https://www.bis.org/review/r200203i.htm

Elderson, Frank (European Central Bank), June 3, 2021, "The embrace of the horizon—forcefully moving with the changing tide for climate action in financial sector policies," at the Green Swan 2021 Global Virtual Conference. https://www.bis.org/review/r210604c.htm

Lane, Timothy (Bank of Canada), March 2, 2017, "Thermometer rising—climate change and Canada's economic future," at the Finance and Sustainability Initiative, Montréal, Québec. https://www.bis.org/review/r170405b.htm

Lautenschläger, Sabine (European Central Bank), October 30, 2019, "A call for Europe," at lecture series "Mein Europa," Heinrich-Heine University, Düsseldorf. https://www.bis.org/review/r191031b.htm

Maechler, Andréa M. (Swiss National Bank) and Thomas Moser (Swiss National Bank), November 14, 2019, "Climate risks and central banks—An SNB perspective," at the Money Market Event, Geneva. https://www.bis.org/review/r191115a.htm

Mersch, Yves (European Central Bank), November 27, 2018. "Climate change and central banking," at the Workshop discussion "Sustainability is becoming mainstream," Frankfurt am Main, Germany. https://www.bis.org/review/r181128b.htm

Nykänen, Marja (Bank of Finland), May 21, 2021, "Maintaining the EU as global leader in sustainable finance," at the European SSM Round Table, digital conference. https://www.bis.org/review/r210521b.htm

Schnabel, Isabel (European Central Bank), June 14, 2021, "From market neutrality to market efficiency," at the ECB DG-Research Symposium "Climate change, financial markets and green growth," Frankfurt am Main. https://www.bis.org/review/r210614a.htm

Schnabel, Isabel (European Central Bank), May 27, 2021, "Societal responsibility and central bank independence," at the "VIII. New Paradigm Workshop," organized by the Forum New Economy, Frankfurt am Main. https://www.bis.org/review/r210528e.htm

Schnabel, Isabel (European Central Bank), March 3, 2021, "From green neglect to green dominance?," at the "Greening Monetary Policy—Central Banking and Climate Change" online seminar, organized as part of the "Cleveland Fed Conversations on Central Banking," Frankfurt am Main. https://www.bis.org/review/r210304c.htm

Trichet, Jean-Claude (European Central Bank), June 3, 2008, "Monetary policy in challenging times," Barcelona, Spain. https://www.ecb.europa.eu/press/key/date/2008/html/sp080603.en.html

Villeroy de Galhau, François (Bank of France), February 11, 2021, "The role of central banks in the greening of the economy," at the 5th edition of the Rencontres on "Climate Change and Sustainable Finance," organized jointly with Option Finance. Paris. https://www.bis.org/review/r210211g.htm

Weidmann, Jens (Deutsche Bundesbank), July 1, 2021, "Monetary policy and the role of central banks—An outlook," to the Freundeskreis of the Ludwig-Erhard-Stiftung, virtual speech. https://www.bis.org/review/r210809b.htm

Weidmann, Jens (Deutsche Bundesbank), October 29, 2019, "Climate change and central banks," at the Deutsche Bundesbank's second financial market conference, Frankfurt am Main. https://www.bis.org/review/r191029a.htm

Weidmann, Jens (Deutsche Bundesbank), February 3, 2020, "Change and continuity," at Deutsche Börse's New Year's reception, Eschborn. https://www.bis.org/review/r200204b.htm

16

Bitcoins Left and Right

A Normative Assessment of a Digital Currency

Joakim Sandberg and Lars Lindblom

1. Introduction

Suddenly, Bitcoin was everywhere. It was a new kind of money increasing in circulation each day. Some heralded it as the currency of the future: an electronic and private money better fit for a digitalized world. But others argued that it was only a fad. Yet again others warned of its dangers, for example its connection to "hacktivism" and criminality (for overviews, see Ammous, 2021; Birch, 2020; Vigna & Casey, 2016). It seems fair to say that Bitcoin is a dividing phenomenon in contemporary society. Countries such as Iceland and Bolivia have banned it altogether, mainly due to concerns with money laundering. In the USA, there is no general regulation of Bitcoin but a patchwork of rules on both federal and state levels that seek to address various concerns. The discussion within the EU is yet to be resolved.

We will not try to speculate about the future of Bitcoin here, as this seems almost impossible to determine. However, this chapter is among the first to discuss the justification of digital or virtual currencies from the perspective of political philosophy. Our central concern is whether there is a normative case for Bitcoin—that is, is it a superior (or inferior) form of money from a moral or political–philosophical point of view? It is important to qualify this question further since contemporary debates about Bitcoin concern a range of related yet disparate issues. For example, some are discussing the appropriate response from individual consumers and businesses; whether we as individuals should be supportive of its development (cf. Angel & McCabe, 2015). Others are discussing the appropriate political response; whether Bitcoin should be banned, allowed, or promoted as a (national) currency (cf. Lambrecht & Larue, 2018; Scharding, 2019). Our focus will be on a realistic version of the latter question. That is, we will discuss whether there is a normative case for (politically) allowing or promoting Bitcoin as a major currency in society. By "major" we mean that it is used in a significant portion of economic transactions, either alongside or even instead of other (national) currencies. We take this question to be both practically

Joakim Sandberg and Lars Lindblom, *Bitcoins Left and Right: A Normative Assessment of a Digital Currency* In: *The Philosophy of Money and Finance*. Edited by: Joakim Sandberg and Lisa Warenski, Oxford University Press.
© Oxford University Press 2024. DOI: 10.1093/oso/9780192898807.003.0017

and theoretically salient, and thus it provides a fair test of the normative standing of digital money.

Our discussion is focused on Bitcoin, but the intention is to be relevant also for other examples of "cryptocurrency" or digital money.[1] There are several contemporary examples with striking resemblances to Bitcoin, such as Litecoin, Dogecoin, Ethereum, and Cardano. However, given the enormous speed of innovation in the area, we cannot guarantee that all aspects of our discussion will be relevant to all variations. In any case, we have chosen to focus on Bitcoin since (i) it was the first major digital currency, (ii) it is still the most popular such currency, and (iii) it seems that its normative underpinnings have been made most clear by its supporters. Examining Bitcoin thus seems like the natural first step in normatively assessing the phenomenon of digital money.

The chapter proceeds as follows: section 2 gives some further background on the history and basics of Bitcoin. Thereafter we proceed to the normative analysis, which focuses on two central theories of moral and political philosophy: section 3 discusses libertarianism (which is often associated with "right-wing" politics) and whether it can provide a justification for Bitcoin; and section 4 discusses egalitarianism (which is often associated with "left-wing" politics) in the same regard. In the concluding section, we summarize a few findings as they relate to the more general question of what kind of money there ought to be.

2. What Is Bitcoin?

The concept of Bitcoin was first introduced in 2008, in a paper by Satoshi Nakamoto posted to an online cryptography mailing list (Nakamoto, 2008). It is controversial whether this Nakamoto is a real person, a pseudonym, or perhaps the name of a larger group of people (Davis, 2011; McGrath Goodman, 2014). In any case, the paper described the design of an electronic payment system using cryptography and peer-to-peer networking to ensure the security of transactions. This design would displace the need for financial intermediaries such as banks to ensure security. As Nakamoto put it, it was a payment system "based on crypto-graphic proof instead of trust" (Nakamoto, 2008: 1).

That the system is electronic or digital means that bitcoins (the individual units of Bitcoin) do not exist as physical coins or bills but only as information on a computer network. When a transaction is made, a digital message is sent through

---

[1] The terminology is somewhat unclear in the area and new currencies can be referred to as cryptocurrencies, digital currencies, virtual currencies, or online currencies. The term "cryptocurrency" highlights the connection to cryptography, while both "digital" and "virtual" highlight the connection to online rather than physical existence and use. We have chosen to use "digital currency" as the general term. We realize that also traditional money often is digital in the sense of existing only on a bank's servers, but this is not our concern here.

the network to transfer the ownership of coins. The technique here is known as the "blockchain" and may ultimately prove useful in a variety of contexts. It is a crucial element of Bitcoin that the transaction is recorded in a ledger on a wider network, rather than on a central server. This means that transactions are "public" and beyond control by individual users. Furthermore, it means that the transactions are non-revocable; that is, that the bitcoins "change hands" in a final way (Ammous, 2021). In this respect Bitcoin is similar to bank notes, but dissimilar to credit card payments that can be cancelled at a later time. While the transactions are public, the identities of the transactors and owners of bitcoins remain anonymous. Privacy is secured through a strong public-key encryption which restricts access to individual electronic accounts (known as "wallets"). Thus, the introduction of Bitcoin means that we can transact "anonymously and untraceably" on the internet.[2]

One might ask: Where do bitcoins come from? The somewhat surprising answer is that, just like gold, they are mined. However, the mining process is electronic. In order to get a hold of new bitcoins one must set one's computer to help maintain and expand the Bitcoin cryptographic ledger, which basically involves solving very difficult mathematical puzzles. Success in this is presently rewarded with 6.25 bitcoins per "block." In order to have an orderly introduction of coins into circulation, the rewards per block will decrease over time. Moreover, there is only a limited amount of coins that can ever be put into circulation. There can never be more than 21 million bitcoins (Nakamoto, 2008). That might sound like very little money, but each coin is divisible to the eighth decimal which should ensure that there is enough coinage for most transactions.

The limited supply of bitcoins will likely mean that their value will rise over time, especially in our scenario where Bitcoin is allowed or promoted as a major currency in society. In this way, one could say that deflation is built into the design of the currency (ECB, 2012; Franco, 2014). As the value of Bitcoin grows, namely, the prices of goods and services quoted in Bitcoin will decrease (which is the opposite of inflation). Moreover, since the supply of coins is fully determined by the algorithm and the miners, there is no room for governments or central banks to adjust the growth of the money supply. This means that the supply and value of Bitcoin is beyond the reach of governments and public authorities.

The first Bitcoin client was released in January 2009, allowing the first mining of bitcoins and transactions between users. During the first year or so, users were mainly a small group of cryptography fans. However, attention slowly started to grow and the value of bitcoins started to rise. In 2011, sites such as WikiLeaks

---

[2] Since partial information on the transactions are public (amounts, dates, and so on), some argue that this is not true anonymity (Brito & Castillo, 2013). Indeed, researchers have shown that sophisticated statistical or network analyses of transaction patterns can reveal the likely identities of many Bitcoin users (Reid & Harrigan, 2013).

started to accept donations in Bitcoin and, by 2012, thousands of internet merchants had started to accept payments in the currency. The value of a bitcoin has famously gone up and down like a roller coaster since then (see Chart 1). It is largely understood that most of these movements are due to financial speculation rather than the use of Bitcoin for purchasing goods and services (cf. Dwyer 2015). With rising attention also came rising concerns. In 2013, the US FBI shut down the "Silk Road" online black market (charged for selling drugs and other illegal goods) and seized bitcoins worth US$28.5 million (Vigna & Casey, 2016). Another major scandal was when the online exchange "Mt.Gox"—which handled around 70 percent of all transactions at the time—went bankrupt after large amounts of bitcoins were reported missing or stolen.

In order to put the above into context, it is interesting to ask whether Bitcoin really is, or can ever be, money. The standard position in economics is that money is anything that serves three main functions: it is (i) a medium of exchange, (ii) a store of value, and (iii) a unit of account (Mankiw, 2009). It seems clear that Bitcoin can serve as medium of exchange; at least to a limited extent it already does. Due to its clever design and low transaction costs, it could even be a superior medium of exchange for online transactions (Brito & Castillo, 2013). But the prospects seem much bleaker when it comes to being a store of value and a unit of account. As we have seen, the value of bitcoins in relation to other currencies has fluctuated immensely during its history, and repeated heists and scandals have raised concerns about its security. The fact that the supply is capped at 21 million bitcoins is a further problem in the context, which we will discuss below. For these

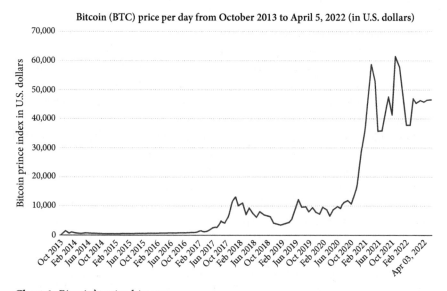

Chart 1 Bitcoin's price history

Source: CoinGecko (www.coingecko.com) through Statista (www.statista.com)

reasons, even the merchants that accept Bitcoin tend to use other currencies as their principal accounting unit, and they still pay their employees in dollars or euros. This suggests that Bitcoin lacks the public trust needed to be classified as money in the theoretical sense, at least at the present time (cf. Bjerg, 2016; Lo & Wang, 2014). But it seems impossible to predict what the future has in store in this regard.

For the purposes of this chapter, we need not take sides in the debate about whether Bitcoin is money or not, but we note that a central factor determining its success in general is the public's trust in the currency (cf. Dodd, 2018). If people are to be persuaded to use bitcoins rather than dollars and euros, and thus if Bitcoin shall work as a major currency, they need to be confident in its function as a store of value and a unit of account. We think that the centrality of public trust makes a normative assessment of Bitcoin all the more important. Let us now turn to such an assessment.

3. The Libertarian Case for Bitcoin

Libertarianism is a moral and political philosophy which emphasizes the primacy of individual liberty and autonomy (Boaz, 1997; Nozick, 1974). It should be up to each individual how he or she wishes to live his or her life, and this includes choice of religion, sexual partner, and pattern of consumption and trade. Safeguarding these liberties are strong moral rights which put limits on what others can legitimately do to people without their consent. In this way, one could say that libertarianism is designed to protect a moral personal sphere. The central rights are so-called negative rights, i.e. rights *not* to be treated in various ways without one's consent, rather than positive rights, i.e. rights to physical or economic support from others. In line with this, libertarians are typically known for defending the free market as the only economic system consistent with strong individual rights, including strong property rights. The main role of the state should be to protect people's rights and it has no business in steering people's lives beyond this. Only a night-watchman state can, hence, be fully compatible with libertarianism.

It should be obvious from the previous section that that the Bitcoin movement to a large extent has been driven by libertarian ambitions (see also Golumbia, 2015; Lambrecht & Larue, 2018; Tourianski, 2014). The goal has been to create a decentralized and private currency, a means of transaction without government interference or oversight whose value would be determined entirely by its users (i.e. the free market). As further evidence of this, some of the concrete algorithms used by Nakamoto (2008) were drawn from the so-called cypherpunk community, which is a name for anarcho-libertarian programmers supporting the use of cryptography to defend privacy and anonymity on the internet. Interestingly, the ECB seems to have much higher regard of Nakamoto when suggesting that "[t]he theoretical roots of Bitcoin can be found in the Austrian school of economics and its criticism of the current fiat system" (ECB, 2012: 23). The Austrian school is a tradition of economic thought that shares many tenets with libertarianism, such as emphasis on individual liberty, the free market and a minimal state.[3]

It is perhaps less obvious how far one should take the libertarian ambition in this context. As previously noted, contemporary debates about Bitcoin are ambiguous and contain a range of viewpoints. Some merely argue against a ban on Bitcoin, implying that there may be a plethora of different currencies for each individual to choose from. Others argue that Bitcoin is so advantageous that it should be the standard currency of any modern society. We will try to avoid the extremes here and therefore focus on a semi-strong version of the argument. Taking queue from a similar line of reasoning that can be found in the Austrian school of economics (cf. Hülsmann, 2008; Schlichter, 2014), we take the libertarian case for Bitcoin to have the following form: (1) individuals have a right to choose whatever currency they want including Bitcoin; (2) many people would (rationally) choose to transact in Bitcoin rather than state money if they had the choice; therefore (3) Bitcoin should be allowed or promoted as a major currency in society.

It is possible to debate both premises of this argument. For example, premise (2) seems empirically dubious at the present stage since Bitcoin is still a fringe currency. Moreover, what we said above about its extreme volatility and security problems seems to cast doubts on whether people have rational grounds to prefer it over state money. However, we will grant this premise for the sake of argument. That is, we will assume that Bitcoin will tend to spread "naturally" if it is not regulated. Our focus will instead be on the plausibility of premise (1). More precisely, we will make a series of attempts at understanding the right that this premise appeals to. What is the moral basis for a right to choose Bitcoin, and how does such a right relate to other libertarian rights?

3.1 Right to Oneself

The strongest moral right there is, according to libertarianism, is people's right to themselves. This right protects a basic personal sphere in which people can exercise their autonomy, i.e. their ability to be their own masters. The right to oneself is often taken to subsume a number of more specific rights such as right to life, right to one's body, and right to one's talents (cf. Cohen, 1995). Right to life in the libertarian sense means that all individuals have supreme moral authority over their own life and may, for example, choose to terminate it in a manner and at a time of their choosing. Right to one's body means that individuals have sole

---

[3] Strictly speaking, Austrian economists would prefer going back to the gold standard, and have expressly criticized Bitcoin for lacking intrinsic value in this way (Matonis, 2011; Schlichter, 2014).

authority over the use of their body and that others may not touch, use or harm it without their consent. Similarly with the right to one's talents.

The strongest libertarian justification of Bitcoin would arguably be an appeal to this right to self-ownership. If people have a right to do what they wish with themselves, and they wish to use Bitcoin, then perhaps they have a right to do so. Moreover, if the preference for Bitcoin has a "natural" tendency to spread, as we have assumed, then it is only right that it becomes a major currency in society.

But does this argument really work? We think that it does not, and it is important in this context to note the reason. Unlike in the original examples, the choice of currency is not a deeply and primarily personal matter; that is, it is not a choice that concerns the very foundation of people's autonomy and only indirectly affects others. Instead it is an essentially social choice, that is, it concerns forms of interaction with others in a larger society or economy. It is in this sense more similar to, for example, choice of school or business partner; choices whose availability and realization to a large degree depend on the willingness of others. The point is that a right that extends only to the individual, like the right to oneself, does not have sufficient reach to protect choices that essentially concern social relationships. For this reason, the choice of Bitcoin is not protected by the right to oneself *simpliciter*.

3.2 Freedom of Contract

A second kind of right, which does concern social relationships and which many libertarians take to be central to economic interaction, is the freedom of contract. This right allows individuals to expand their personal sphere to include material goods and services by way of voluntary exchanges with others.[4] The basic rule is that individuals should be free to enter into whatever contracts or exchanges they choose as long as they respect the rights, and thereby the autonomy, of others. By protecting free exchanges on free markets, libertarians argue that they give people the opportunity to exercise their autonomy also in their economic life.

It may seem straightforward that a choice of Bitcoin is protected by the freedom of contract. However, matters are more complicated than that. As just noted, there are limits to the freedom of contract—one is not allowed to enter into contracts that infringe upon the rights or autonomy of others. In order to determine the limits, then, we need an understanding of the consequences of choosing Bitcoin on other members of society. Since the choice of currency is an essentially social choice, as we have argued, our main concern here is with the social consequences of allowing Bitcoin to grow into a major currency in society. Our discussion will first take a broad view of

---

[4] Of course, there is also a further way of acquiring things: the just acquisition of previously unowned goods. It is a fascinating question whether freshly mined bitcoins should be considered as traded or previously unowned goods. However, since nothing in our argument seems to turn on this, we will not pursue the question further here.

the types of consequences that seem morally relevant; thereafter we will inquire whether they are also relevant for libertarians.

A central aspect of Bitcoin is that it challenges the power of the state, which typically is the guarantor of individual rights. Most straightforwardly, it challenges the state's ability to use monetary policy; that is, to control the type and amount of money used in the economy. Some proponents see this as positive. For example, Wallace (2011) argues that Bitcoin's predetermined supply cap means that it is "immune to printing-press-happy central bankers and Weimar Republic-style hyperinflation." The thought here seems to be that individuals face a reduced risk of having their fortunes shrink due to deliberate inflation from central banks (cf. Lambrecht & Larue, 2018). This argument expresses a high level of distrust in central bankers which we think is premature, at least without further evidence and debate (which we cannot delve into here).

The starting point should rather be to inquire what monetary policy is used for. According to most economists, monetary policy is an absolutely necessary tool for stabilizing prices, mitigating shocks and promoting economic growth. Let us focus on the dramatic case of economic depressions. When people are hesitant to engage in economic interaction due to a depression, monetary policy can be very helpful through reducing the price of money and thereby increasing its demand (Blanchard, 2009; O'Sullivan et al., 2008). What happens is basically that the central bank lowers its interest rate which makes it cheaper for companies to take out loans and make new investments, which in turn increases their economic activity and helps to move the economy out of its depressed state. But it seems that the possibility of using this mechanism for economic policy decreases in direct proportion to the growth of Bitcoin into a major currency in society, since the supply of Bitcoin is set and the price therefore is wholly determined by the market. Furthermore, the built-in deflationary mechanism of Bitcoin will only serve to drive up the price of money over time. The result is that the use of Bitcoin as a major currency is likely to lead to prolonged economic depressions (Ali et al., 2014; Scharding, 2019). In human terms, this means prolonged periods of unemployment and insecurity for large groups of people.

Perhaps some free-market economists could reply that a privatized currency reduces the risk for depressions to occur. This argument starts from the assumption that it is state interference in the free market that causes the imbalances that overturn the economy (cf. Rothbard, 2007). While we cannot discuss this argument here, we contend that it seems inconsistent with historical evidence.[5] And in any case, just because bad monetary policy can cause major problems, we cannot conclude that we should abandon one of the best solutions we have to economic disturbances.

---

[5] For example, it seems that both the Great Depression and the financial crisis of 2008 were brought about through excessive speculation and the lack of regulation, to name just two problems, rather than the mere existence of fiat money (cf. Stiglitz, 2010).

The potential effects of Bitcoin on economic depressions are concerning, and we will note further negative effects below that speak against its suitability as a major currency in society. However, let us now turn to the question of whether libertarians care about these effects. As noted above, the freedom of contract entails that individuals should be free to enter into whatever exchanges they choose as long as they respect the rights and autonomy of others. From a libertarian point of view, then, the only relevant consequences are those that concern other people's rights and autonomy (cf. Brennan & Tomasi, 2012; Steiner, 1994; Vallentyne & van der Vossen, 2014). So what do the effects above entail in such terms?

We think that an argument can be made for resisting Bitcoin on libertarianism's own grounds, although we admit that this argument is speculative. The central idea is that the effects above are also negative in terms of rights and autonomy. Consider the case of unemployment due to economic depressions. Empirical studies confirm that employment is a central source of individual autonomy through its connection to income, social relationships, and the use of our faculties (Goldsmith et al., 1996). This aspect is sometimes invoked in favor of a right to work. When people lose their jobs, then, their autonomy is seriously diminished. So the widespread adoption of Bitcoin potentially restricts individual autonomy. In contrast, a state monopoly on money does not seem to restrict individual autonomy as such. Whereas the form of economic interaction is predetermined, no individual economic transactions are blocked—that is, you can still buy an apple, a car, or the collected works of James Joyce with state money. This suggests that the amount of autonomy gained by having a right to choose Bitcoin is, at best, miniscule (at least in most countries).

We think that the argument above should be persuasive to most readers. However, there may be some hardcore libertarians that it fails to convince. One complication here is the distinction between negative and positive rights. If the right to work is considered a positive right (which it most often is), then some libertarians may choose to disregard it entirely. Moreover, Nozick (1974: 8–30) argues that libertarianism should not be viewed as a form of "utilitarianism of rights," i.e. as an appeal to the maximization of autonomy. This point may be used against our argument about the relatively small gain but massive loss of autonomy in a society with Bitcoin. However, we must admit that we find these objections strange. It is hard to see how libertarians can ground their whole philosophy in an appeal to autonomy, yet at the same time give no weight at all to the very negative effects on autonomy noted above.[6] Moreover, our argument concerns the justification of specific rights. It does not question the notion that rights should be thought of as side-constraints, and it does not say that libertarians should take a

---

[6] For similar reasons, Nozick's view has been described as a "libertarianism without foundations" (Nagel, 1981; see also Vallentyne & van der Vossen, 2014).

consequentialist approach to rights-violations. This shows that the argument does not rest on a view of libertarianism as a utilitarianism of rights.

We conclude from the above that the argument for a right to choose Bitcoin based on the freedom of contract is unconvincing. Once again, a central problem is the essentially social nature of choices of currency, which entails that such choices have consequences on broader society.

3.3   Right to Privacy

Let us finally consider whether a choice of Bitcoin can be protected by the libertarian right to privacy. This right is fairly straightforwardly aimed to protect the individual's personal sphere from the curiosity and view of others, including from public authorities. In this way it is obvious how it can be grounded in an appeal to individual liberty and autonomy. The right to privacy is typically taken to cover both an inner sphere—such as thoughts, feelings, and secrets—as well as an outer sphere—such as one's body, home, and property. But perhaps its reach is even greater than that: There has been much debate in recent years about whether the right to privacy covers, for example, one's internet behavior, peer-to-peer filesharing, and other personal activities in public spaces (cf. Nissenbaum, 2009).

It is easy to see how an argument for Bitcoin could appeal to the right to privacy since, as we have seen, it makes it possible to transact anonymously and untraceably on the internet (cf. Lambrecht & Larue, 2018). If the right to privacy includes a right to make one's economic transactions anonymously, then this would be a fairly strong justification of Bitcoin. However, there are good reasons to believe that such a justification is not forthcoming. Economic transactions are essentially social activities, as we have said, and therefore clearly fall outside of people's most basic personal sphere. Furthermore, we may now note the possibly devastating effects of introducing a currency for general use that rules out all public oversight over transactions. This would not only mean that governments lost access to monetary policy, but they may also lose access to fiscal policy. That is, it would be much more difficult for states to collect taxes, such as VAT and income tax, if many transactions were anonymous and untraceable (Stewart & Johnston, 2012).[7]

This would have devastating effects on society insofar as states would have difficulties in, for example, funding public education, infrastructure, and various welfare programs, as well as in safeguarding the security of both markets and social life. It is clear that all of this involves serious negative effects on people's autonomy as well as infringements of their rights. Importantly, note that both

---

[7] We say "more difficult" but not impossible. There may of course be alternative ways in which states could collect taxes; for example, through voluntary taxation schemes, property taxes. But none of these measures can get close to the kind of reliability and effectiveness of, for example, the VAT and income tax.

positive and negative rights are in jeopardy. This is since even the night-watchman state, irrespective of how small it is, arguably must be supported by some form of taxation scheme to work. Alternatively, maybe some hardcore libertarians will also bite this bullet and hope for enough voluntary contributions to support the night-watchman state (cf. Rothbard, 1973), but this group now seems exceedingly small. Thus it seems that even most libertarians have reason to conclude that the right to privacy should not be extended to cover the choice of Bitcoin.

We conclude from the considerations above that the libertarian case for Bitcoin does not succeed, since it fails to offer a plausible justification of a moral right to choose whatever currency one wants. This does not mean that we have shown that Bitcoin should be forbidden or that people who make transactions in Bitcoin are guilty of moral wrongdoing. What the argument shows is that libertarianism fails to provide a convincing argument for why Bitcoin should be allowed or promoted as a major currency in society.

4. The Egalitarian Case for Bitcoin

What we have called the libertarian case is a philosophical reconstruction of one group of popular arguments for Bitcoin. In this section, we will look at a different group of arguments and our goal is to develop them into a tentative egalitarian case for Bitcoin. The starting point for these arguments is the thought that Bitcoin not only has the potential to disrupt the power of the state, but it also challenges the political and economic power of banks and the current financial establishment.

While the state is the ultimate guarantor of fiat money, it should be noted that our current system gives much power and leeway over both the value and supply of money to banks and other financial institutions (cf. King, 2014; Ryan-Collins et al., 2011). For example, banks have the power to create new money through extending credit and to determine the value of money through engaging in currency specula-tion. Many commentators put the Bitcoin movement in the context of the financial crisis of 2008, and the ensuing massive bailouts of Wall Street. As Wallace (2011) notes, "Bitcoin required no faith in the politicians or financiers who had wrecked the economy—just in Nakamoto's elegant algorithms." In a similar regard, Bitcoin is sometimes connected to the Occupy Wall Street movement and its more general critique of the financial system (Jeffries, 2013; King, 2014).

We suggest that two more distinct arguments can be distilled from the above connections. One has to do with *power and democracy*. It seems a central concern of both Occupy protesters and Bitcoin proponents that the financial establishment wields an unjustified power over the economy and ultimately over people's lives. The Occupy movement expresses this in their slogan "we are the 99%"; the idea is that the financial system fails to serve the majority of average-income people. Since Bitcoin removes some of the power over financial matters from states and banks and gives it to the people, i.e. to internet users, it may be seen to increase a form of financial democracy. (Of course, not all power is given to users since the Bitcoin technology itself also has a central role.) As one proponent expresses it, "Bitcoin is [an] embodiment of the idea that we now have the technology to democratize money" (Jeffries, 2013). We take this point to be similar to the libertarian appeal to autonomy above, but broader in that it emphasizes the positive aspect of empowerment.

The other argument concerns *welfare and distribution*. The "1%" targeted by the Occupy movement are people of extreme wealth whose errands the financial system is said to run. Similarly, Bitcoin proponents have been vocal about unjustified bank fees that are said to serve rich bankers (cf. Ammous, 2021). A prime example here is the fee that commercial banks charge on credit card transactions which, taken together with their support of a "cash free world," comes close to being a private taxation scheme: for every dollar one spends on goods or services, a few cents go to the financial establishment. But this is not the case with Bitcoin.[8] In this way, it can be said to counteract the increasingly unequal distribution of resources in society (Brito & Castillo, 2013).

Even though the arguments above often are put forward under the guise of libertarian ideas, we suggest that they should be most attractive to egalitarians. Their main thrust is namely the need for a more equal distribution of both power and resources. Egalitarianism is a moral and political philosophy which emphasizes the primacy of equality. There are different views on exactly what should be distributed equally; for example, resources, power, opportunities, or something else. There are also different views on what kind of policies are best for making society more equal (cf. Kymlicka, 2002). But we may put these discussions to the side here. Our impression is that many people with egalitarian convictions have been wary of Bitcoin. But is there good reason for this skepticism? In what follows, we argue that the answer must ultimately depend on the political and economic context—that is, there are societies where there is good reason to implement Bitcoin, but there are also others where it probably should not be supported.

4.1 A Promising Case

Let us first look at a quite promising case. Recent reports suggest that Bitcoin is making much headway in developing economies throughout Africa and Asia (Mellor, 2021). An especially interesting example is Kenya where several money-like financial technologies are in use. The most popular of these is M-Pesa (roughly

---

[8] This should not be taken to mean that Bitcoin is incompatible with contemporary banking services. It seems entirely possible that similar banking behavior would arise in an economy based largely on Bitcoin. Moreover, there might of course be other ways of avoiding high transaction costs besides Bitcoin.

"mobile money") which was introduced by the mobile operator Safaricom in 2007. It is basically a form of credits stored on mobile phones which allows users to make transfers with each other. In 2019, it was estimated that around 20 million Kenyans, or 79 percent of the adult population, used M-Pesa for their daily economic transactions (Finacess, 2019). The great success of M-Pesa is likely due to the rural majority's lack of access to formal banking services, and the more general failure of traditional banks to make positive investments in Kenyan society (Cawrey, 2013; Ndung'u, 2018). Since 2012, Safaricom also offers M-Shwari which is a microfinance service attached to M-Pesa that allows users to open savings accounts and obtain microloans at favorable rates.

Bitcoin may be seen as a competitor to M-Pesa, but initiatives have been launched to integrate them into a common payment system. Bitcoin is probably a safer system in that it uses stronger cryptography and allows for online rather than mobile wallets.[9] More importantly, Bitcoin facilitates international transactions such as remittances. It has been argued that mainstream remittance companies often are failing the very poorest populations; people that live in remote areas, that are drastically affected by high fees, and whose transfers sometimes are arbitrarily blocked (Ndung'u, 2018). These problems would be less likely with Bitcoin, although there are also other possible remedies.

From the standpoint of our two egalitarian arguments above, there seem to be clear benefits to the use of Bitcoin in societies like Kenya. First, with regards to welfare and distribution, the low presence of mainstream banks in rural areas, and their high entry fees, is a problem that digital currencies can help to alleviate. Such currencies may not only increase people's access to money as such, but also their access to microfinance services that cater to the needs of poor populations. Second, with regards to power and democracy, Bitcoin moves some of the power over financial matters from states and banks to the general population. This seems especially justified in frail economies where governments are failing to do their job, such as in situations of hyperinflation (Brito & Castillo, 2013), or when corrupt and despotic leaders actually rig the system in order to grab the money for themselves (Scharding, 2019).

Now, these benefits should of course be weighed against the drawbacks of Bitcoin noted above, i.e. the diminished possibility of states to use monetary and fiscal policy. But it seems that, in at least some cases, the benefits are likely to outweigh the drawbacks. This is so since when the states are incompetent or corrupt, of course, such diminished possibilities are actually a further benefit. Thus, given the unavailability of other solutions that may prove to be even better (such as, perhaps, a stronger UN mandate to deal with corrupt regimes), we have seemingly found a case where Bitcoin should indeed be allowed or promoted as a major currency.

---

[9] A complication is of course that rural Kenyans may lack access to secure online services.

4.2 A Well-ordered Society

But do these conclusions generalize? Now compare with what we may call, with terminology borrowed from Rawls (1971), a perfectly well-ordered society. It has a strong and benevolent state that uses monetary policy to improve the rate of employment (while controlling for inflation) and fiscal policy to improve the situation of the worst-off citizens. Financial agents such as banks are regulated, inspected, and taxed in an efficient manner. Moreover, the banks accept some degree of social responsibility and work with the authorities to reach previously excluded client groups. We may assume that there is much leeway in this society for citizens to make anonymous transactions as long as they do not interfere with the previously stated functions. It seems quite clear, judging from our egalitarian arguments above, that Bitcoin should not be promoted as a major currency in this type of society. In contrast to our previous example, it would no longer have any benefits in terms of financial democracy or distributive equality; it would only have the effect of undermining the positive activities in both of these areas by both the state and the banks.

Actual societies may of course be more or less well-ordered in this sense, and it is not as easy to determine the best route forward in real-life cases.[10] However, our conjecture is that there is weak justification for Bitcoin to grow into a larger currency in reasonably well-ordered societies such as those in Western Europe and North America. While there are clear problems of equality in these societies, those are probably better addressed by other means such as public policies, corporate social responsibility, or civil society initiatives. At least in societies with well-functioning systems for monetary and fiscal policy, the burden of proof is very heavy on those that think that Bitcoin could be an improvement in terms of equality of power or resources. The situation is quite different in societies that have severe problems in these areas, which is why the case for Bitcoin in developing countries is much stronger (cf. Scharding, 2019).

To sum up, the difference between the libertarian and egalitarian cases for Bitcoin is that one is absolute whereas the other is not. The libertarian argument purports to show that the power of states and banks always should be undermined in favor of individual autonomy, but we have seen that such a stance has drastic effects on the possibilities of both individual and collective aspirations in society. In contrast, our egalitarian arguments imply that the power of states and banks sometimes should be undermined—especially when they are corrupt or only cater to the interests of a small elite. This provides good reason to support the growth of Bitcoin in societies like Kenya. However, it should probably not be supported in well-ordered societies where both states and banks take active responsibility for developing democracy and distributive justice.

---

[10] Our reasoning here has affinities with the contemporary debate about ideal versus non-ideal theory in political philosophy, cf. Thompson 2020.

5. Concluding Remarks

Our results in this chapter have mostly been negative. We have argued that the libertarian case for Bitcoin is not convincing, but that there is some potential in egalitarian arguments for it. However, we have ultimately judged that Bitcoin should not be promoted as a major currency in reasonably well-ordered societies, since it has more drawbacks than benefits. We understand, of course, that our argumentation here will not mean the end of cryptocurrencies. Although it seems almost impossible to determine the future of Bitcoin as such, it seems likely that new forms of digital money will continue to appear. As concluding remarks, we will therefore offer some more positive notes on what kind of money there should be, based on the considerations uncovered in our analysis. This will not amount to a full normative theory of money, but simply a list of four important desiderata for normatively successful monetary design.

We may start with the most attractive aspect of Bitcoin: It is preferable that money is designed so that it *protects economic freedom and privacy*. Nobody in this discussion has doubted the basic soundness of a market-based system which ultimately rests on the ability of individuals to make free and private choices. The more of our economic lives that are spent on the internet, the greater the challenge becomes to make adequate room for this, especially for economic privacy. But it is also important to recognize that there are other values at stake that may come into conflict with freedom and privacy. We have in particular discussed one such aspect that is problematic for Bitcoin: that money *must be taxable*. If money is designed so that it becomes virtually impossible for outside parties to trace it, tax collection will become very difficult. That in turn will make it much harder to fund social goods such as education, infrastructure and security. It will also make it difficult to redistribute wealth for the sake of social equality.

The trade-off above is a central challenge of money design, but there are also other considerations to take into account. One of those concerns the *possibility to conduct monetary policy* in an appropriate manner. We have warned that the growth of Bitcoin may lead to prolonged economic depressions since it becomes more difficult to decrease the price of money to jumpstart the economy. The reader may think that this consideration is the final nail in the coffin for private currencies, since monetary policy only can be conducted with state-controlled money. However, it is not inconceivable that there could be a private cryptocurrency that makes monetary policy possible. For instance, Freicoin is designed to insure that people do not hoard money by imposing a kind of negative interest rate, or a demurrage fee, on money in users' accounts (Bradbury, 2013). One way of conducting monetary policy could be through varying this demurrage fee.

We end with the most important point, namely that money *requires trust*. If people will not trust something to be money, then it simply cannot work as money. This is especially so for fiat money, but arguably also for money that is convertible to some commodity, and even more so for digital money. Contrary to what Nakamoto (2008) says, "cryptographic proof" is no substitute for trust. It seems that a background explanation of the rise of Bitcoin is that some people do not trust the state, and therefore they do not trust state money. However, it seems equally clear that many people do not trust private issuers of money which may explain why so few people have put their life savings in Bitcoin. This chapter has rested on the idea that how a currency fares on moral grounds may ultimately be central to its ability to command the public's trust.

References

Ali, R., Barrdear, J., Clews, R., and Southgate, J. (2014). "The Economics of Digital Currencies." *Quarterly Bulletin of Bank of England*, Q3, 1–11.

Ammous, S. (2021). *The Bitcoin Standard: The Decentralized Alternative to Central Banking*. Wiley, Hoboken, NJ.

Angel, J. J. and McCabe, D. (2015). "The Ethics of Payments: Paper, Plastic, or Bitcoin?" *Journal of Business Ethics* 132(3), 603–11.

Birch, D. (2020). *The Currency Cold War*. London Publishing Partnership, London.

Bjerg, O. (2016). "How Is Bitcoin Money?" *Theory, Culture & Society* 33(1), 53–72.

Blanchard, O. (2009). *Macroeconomics*, 5th ed. Prentice Hall, London.

Boaz, D. (1997). *Libertarianism—A Primer*. Free Press, New York.

Bradbury, D. (2013). "Freicoin's Attempt to Free the Economy." *CoinDesk*, June 11.

Brennan, J. and Tomasi, J. (2012). "Classical Liberalism." In D. Estlund (ed.), *Oxford Handbook of Political Philosophy*. Oxford University Press, New York, 115–32.

Brito, J. and Castillo, A. (2013). *Bitcoin: A Primer for Policymakers*. Mercatus Center, Arlington.

Cawrey, D. (2013). "Bitcoin and M-Pesa: Why Money in Kenya Has Gone Digital." *CoinDesk*, July 10.

Cohen, G.A. (1995). *Self-Ownership, Freedom, and Equality*. Cambridge University Press, Cambridge.

Davis, J. (2011). "The Crypto-Currency: Bitcoin and Its Mysterious Inventor." *New Yorker*, October 10.

Dodd, N. (2018). "The Social Life of Bitcoin." *Theory, Culture & Society*, 35(3), 35–56.

Dwyer, G. P. (2015). "The Economics of Bitcoin and Similar Private Digital Currencies." *Journal of Financial Stability* 17: 81–91.

European Central Bank. (2012). *Virtual Currency Schemes*. ECB, Frankfurt am Main.

Finacess (2019). 2019 FinAcess Household Survey, available online at https://www.fsdkenya.org/blogs-publications/publications/the-2019-finaccess-household-survey/

Franco, P. (2014). *Understanding Bitcoin: Cryptography, Engineering and Economics.* Wiley, Hoboken, NJ.

Goldsmith, A. H., Veum, J. R., and Darity, W. (1996). "The Psychological Impact of Unemployment and Joblessness." *Journal of Socio-Economics* 25(3), 333–58.

Golumbia, D. (2015). "Bitcoin as Politics: Distributed Right-Wing Extremism." In G. Lovink, N. Tkacz, and P. de Vries (eds.), *MoneyLab Reader: An Intervention in Digital Economy.* Institute of Network Cultures, Amsterdam, 117–31.

Hülsmann, J. G. (2008). *The Ethics of Money Production.* Ludwig von Mises Institute, Auburn.

Jeffries, A. (2013). "Why Won't Bitcoin Die?" *The Verge*, May 21.

King, B. (2014). *Breaking Banks: The Innovators, Rogues, and Strategists Rebooting Banking.* Wiley, Hoboken, NJ.

Kymlicka, W. (2002). *Contemporary Political Philosophy—An Introduction*, 2nd ed. Oxford University Press, Oxford.

Lambrecht, M. and Larue, L. (2018). "After the (virtual) Gold Rush: Is Bitcoin More Than a Speculative Bubble?," *Internet Policy Review* 7(4): 1–22.

Lo, S. and Wang, J. C. (2014). "Bitcoin as Money?," *Current Policy Perspectives* 14–4, Federal Reserve Bank of Boston.

McGrath Goodman, L. (2014). "The Face behind Bitcoin." *Newsweek*, March 6.

Mankiw, N. G. (2009). *Macroeconomics*, 7th ed. Worth Publishers, New York.

Matonis, J. (2011). "Why Are Libertarians Against Bitcoin?" *The Monetary Future*, June 16.

Mellor, S. (2021). "From Mining to Spending, Emerging Markets Are Leading the Way on Cryptocurrencies," *Fortune*, June 14.

Nagel, T. (1981). "Libertarianism without Foundations." In J. Paul (ed.), *Reading Nozick*. Rowman and Littlefield, Ottowa, 191–205.

Nakamoto, S. (2008). "Bitcoin: A Peer-to-Peer Electronic Cash System." Unpublished paper.

Ndung'u, N. (2018). "The M-Pesa Technological Revolution for Financial Services in Kenya: A Platform for Financial Inclusion." In D. Lee, K. Chuen, and R. Deng (eds.), *Handbook of Blockchain, Digital Finance, and Inclusion* (vol. 1), Academic Press, Cambridge, MA, 37–56.

Nissenbaum, H. (2009). *Privacy in Context: Technology, Policy, and the Integrity of Social Life.* Stanford University Press, Stanford.

Nozick, R. (1974). *Anarchy, State, and Utopia.* Basic Books, New York.

O'Sullivan, A., Scheffrin, S., and Perez, S. (2008). *Macroeconomics: Principles, Applications, and Tools*, 5th ed. Prentice Hall, Upper Saddle River.

Rawls, J. (1971). *A Theory of Justice.* Harvard University Press, Cambridge, MA.

Reid, F. and Harrigan, M. (2013). "An Analysis of Anonymity in the Bitcoin System." In Y. Altshuler, Y. Elovici, A. B. Cremers, N. Aharony, and A. Pentland (eds.), *Security and Privacy in Social Networks.* Springer, New York, 197–223.

Rothbard, M. (1973). *For a New Liberty*. Macmillan, New York.

Rothbard, M. (2007). *Economic Depressions: Their Cause and Cure*. Ludwig von Mises Institute, Auburn.

Ryan-Collins, J., Greenham, T., Werner, R., and Jackson, A. (2011). *Where Does Money Come from?* New Economics Foundation, London.

Scharding, T. (2019). "National Currency, World Currency, Cryptocurrency: A Fichtean Approach to the Ethics of Bitcoin." *Business and Society Review* 124, 219–38.

Schlichter, D. S. (2014). *Paper Money Collapse: The Folly of Elastic Money*, 2nd ed. Wiley, Hoboken, NJ.

Steiner, H. (1994). *An Essay on Rights*. Blackwell, Cambridge.

Stewart, D. D. and Johnston, S. S. (2012). "Digital Currency: A New Worry for Tax Administrators?" *TaxAnalysts*, November 7.

Stiglitz, J. (2010). *Freefall*. Penguin, London.

Thompson, C. (2020). "Ideal and Nonideal Theory in Political Philosophy," *Oxford Research Encyclopedia of Politics*, 27 August.

Tourianski, J. (2014). "The Declaration of Bitcoin's Independence," *Bitcoin Magazine*, May 14.

Vallentyne, P. and van der Vossen, B. (2014). "Libertarianism." In E. N. Zalta (ed.), *The Stanford Encyclopedia of Philosophy*, Fall 2014 Edition.

Vigna, P. and Casey, M. J. (2016). *The Age of Cryptocurrency*. Picador, London.

Wallace, B. (2011). "The Rise and Fall of Bitcoin." *Wired Magazine*, November 23.

Index